NIV

BIBLE STUDY
COMMENTARY

NEW INTERNATIONAL VERSION

NIV

BIBLE STUDY
COMMENTARY

JOHN H. SAILHAMER

Abridged by David A. Frees

ZONDERVAN

NIV Bible Study Commentary
Copyright © 2011 by John H. Sailhamer

This title is also available as a Zondervan ebook.

Requests for information should be addressed to:

Zondervan, 3900 Sparks Dr. SE, Grand Rapids, Michigan 49546

Library of Congress Cataloging-in-Publication Data

Sailhamer, John H.
    NIV Bible study commentary / John H. Sailhamer; abridged by David A. Frees.
      p. cm.
    ISBN 978-0-310-33119-3 (softcover)
    1. Bible—Commentaries. I. Frees, David A. II. Sailhamer, John. NIV compact
Bible commentary. III. Title.
BS491.3.S25 2010
    220.7—dc22
                                            2010049409

Interior design and composition: Ben Fetterley, Greg Johnson/Textbook Perfect

Printed in the United States of America

HB 10.29.2021

CONTENTS

ABBREVIATIONS

Books of the Bible

Ge	Genesis	**Jer**	Jeremiah
Ex	Exodus	**La**	Lamentations
Lev	Leviticus	**Eze**	Ezekiel
Nu	Numbers	**Da**	Daniel
Dt	Deuteronomy	**Hos**	Hosea
Jos	Joshua	**Joel**	Joel
Jdg	Judges	**Am**	Amos
Ru	Ruth	**Ob**	Obadiah
1Sa	1 Samuel	**Jnh**	Jonah
2Sa	2 Samuel	**Mic**	Micah
1Ki	1 Kings	**Na**	Nahum
2Ki	2 Kings	**Hab**	Habakkuk
1Ch	1 Chronicles	**Zep**	Zephaniah
2Ch	2 Chronicles	**Hag**	Haggai
Ezr	Ezra	**Zec**	Zechariah
Ne	Nehemiah	**Mal**	Malachi
Est	Esther	**Mt**	Matthew
Job	Job	**Mk**	Mark
Ps	Psalms	**Lk**	Luke
Pr	Proverbs	**Jn**	John
Ecc	Ecclesiastes	**Ac**	Acts
SS	Song of Songs	**Ro**	Romans
Isa	Isaiah	**1Co**	1 Corinthians

2Co	2 Corinthians
Gal	Galatians
Eph	Ephesians
Php	Philippians
Col	Colossians
1Th	1 Thessalonians
2Th	2 Thessalonians
1Ti	1 Timothy
2Ti	2 Timothy
Tit	Titus
Phm	Philemon
Heb	Hebrews
Jas	James
1Pe	1 Peter
2Pe	2 Peter
1Jn	1 John
2Jn	2 John
3Jn	3 John
Jude	Jude
Rev	Revelation

Other Abbreviations

c.	about
cf.	compare
ch(s).	chapter(s)
e.g.	for example
etc.	and so on
i.e.	that is
NT	New Testament
OT	Old Testament
v(v)	verse(s)
ff.	following verses

PREFACE

There are many different kinds of commentaries on the Bible — just as there are many reasons why one would want to use a commentary. Technical commentaries are essential for a detailed, close study of a biblical passage. Devotional commentaries help you as the reader see the application of a biblical passage to your life. Bible survey commentaries give the reader an overview of the contents of each book of the Bible. The *NIV Bible Study Commentary* does not fit exactly into any of those categories. It is not a technical commentary, even though it is based on a thorough technical reading of the Bible in both Hebrew and Greek. It is not a devotional commentary, in that its focus is on the meaning of the text rather than on life application. Nor is it a Bible survey, though in reading it one will certainly get a survey of the entire Bible.

This commentary is an abridgment of my *NIV Compact Bible Commentary*. Its purpose is to aid you in reading the Bible on your own. There is no substitute for reading the Bible, God's Word. This commentary will provide you with brief help in understanding the Bible while you are reading it. What is often lacking in reading the Bible is a sense of the whole Bible. We can easily get lost in the details, which only make sense if we have a view of the whole. We hope this commentary will give you a sense of the entire Bible and how that impacts the meaning of a particular passage.

There are great themes in the Bible. This commentary develops those themes throughout the Bible and shows how those themes and the images that depict them come into play in each passage.

I am thankful to David Frees for abridging the *NIV Compact Bible Commentary* and to Verlyn D. Verbrugge, senior editor at large at Zondervan, for seeing it through to completion.

INTRODUCTION

The Bible is a book made up of many books, written over many centuries by authors with vastly different backgrounds and cultures. Many are well-known: Moses, David, Solomon, Ezra, John, Paul. Such men are not only the leading characters in the Bible, they are also its leading producers. A surprisingly large number of the biblical authors, however, are nameless. Who wrote the books of Kings, for example? Who wrote the book of Hebrews?

Fortunately, the answers to such questions are not of major consequence in understanding the Bible. We know the Bible by reading these books. Some kinds of books, of course (e.g., a diary), require some information about its author before it can be properly understood. Other books, like works of literature and history, are written so that we do not have to know the author to understand and appreciate the work. The Bible is that way. It is written simply to be read.

The Bible is a unique book. It is the Word of God. That means basically two things: (1) The Bible is divine revelation; (2) the Bible is divinely inspired.

The Bible teaches that God has left signs of his existence and power in his work of creation. From the world around us and from within ourselves, we can see evidences of God's glory. From the world we can see that he is a powerful and wonderful God. From within our own conscience we can know that he is a personal and holy God. But there is a limit to what can be known about God in that way. For example, apart from the Bible we cannot know God's will or his love for us. We may know that we need God's grace and mercy, but without God himself speaking to us we cannot know how to receive it. The Bible tells us so.

God has revealed his will for us in a book written by God himself. The Bible is a written text. If we can read, we can understand it. This sounds elementary, but it is important nonetheless. Some suggest that the Bible is nothing more than human thoughts and aspirations about God. The Christian idea of revelation is much more than that. The Bible may be human words, but those words express the very words God wants us to know.

How is it possible for human words to express God's will? In answer we must speak of the notion of *inspiration*. The books of the Bible were written by human beings who were "carried along" in their writing by the Holy Spirit (2Pe 1:21). But the Bible is not any more specific than that. It does not tell us how the Holy Spirit moved these writers so that they expressed God's will. There are thus some unanswered questions. Given that fact, we should not attempt to explain it in any more detail. As far as we know, God did not dictate the words of the Bible to the writers, but neither did he merely give them suggestions on what to write, leaving the choice of words to them.

There is really no description of the process by which God inspired certain persons to write Scripture. What we do have, however, is a clear statement that the written words, as we now have them in the Bible, are "God-breathed" (2Ti 3:16). What the human writers wrote, God intended to say to us. We can thus know God's will if we study and reflect on Scripture.

But just exactly what Bible are we talking about? Isn't there some disagreement on what books are in the Bible? The answer, of course, is yes, but there is not as much disagreement as one might think. The standard for what books are in the Bible and what books are not is called "the canon." The word *canon* itself means "standard, rule" in Greek.

For the first part of the Bible, the Old Testament, the standard was determined long before the birth of Jesus. We have little direct knowledge of the process, but we can say with certainty that the Old Testament that we have today is the same as the one Jesus knew. It was the accepted standard of the Jews in the first century.

In some parts of the Christian church, before the time of printing, additional books were put alongside the canon of the Old Testament in some manuscripts. These were popular works used in worship and devotion. Some of these works were later considered part of the canon of the Bible by the Roman Catholic Church and the Eastern Orthodox churches, though not having exactly the same authority as the Bible. These books, called the Apocrypha, are thus included in their Bibles.

There is no dispute about the canon of the New Testament. At an early stage in the history of the church, the New Testament canon was closed. No additional books have been added.

For both Testaments, the criterion for including a book in the canon was twofold: (1) universal acceptance among God's people — Israel for the Old Testament and the church for the New Testament; (2) internal witness of the Holy Spirit. The Spirit of God bore witness to the early readers of Scripture that these books and no others were the inspired Word of God.

How do we know the early church accepted the right books and genuinely witnessed the Spirit's confirmation? This is the most important question. For the Old Testament we have the additional confirmation of Jesus. Throughout his ministry, Jesus quoted and used the Scriptures as God's Word. To accept the authority of Jesus is to accept the authority of the Old Testament. For the New Testament we have the confirmation of the apostles. Thus the additional basis for the acceptance of the New Testament books is apostolic authority. The apostles had received direct instruction from Jesus during his earthly ministry. It is their acceptance and confirmation of the canon of the New Testament that assures us of its authority in our lives today.

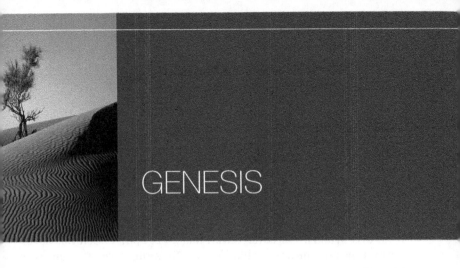

GENESIS

Introduction

Genesis is a part of the Pentateuch (the first five books of the Bible), which Jewish tradition and the NT have ascribed to Moses (cf. Jn 1:17; 5:46). Nowhere in the work itself does the author identify himself, but throughout the narratives Moses is the person most closely associated with writing the material contained in them (Ex 17:14; 20:1; cf. also Jos 8:31 – 32).

Genesis records two types of events: those that happened on a global or cosmic scale (e.g., creation, the flood) and those that happened in a relatively isolated, localized way (e.g., Noah's drunkenness, Abraham's visions). By far most events in Genesis happened in a limited sphere of time and location and can best be described as "family matters."

The purpose of Genesis is intricately bound up with the purpose of the Pentateuch as a whole, which looks to the future as the time when God's faithful promises would be fulfilled.

I. Introduction to the Patriarchs and the Sinai Covenant (1:1 – 11:26)

Chapters 1 – 11 introduce both Genesis and the entire Pentateuch. They set the stage for the narratives of the patriarchs (Ge 12 – 50) as well as provide the appropriate background for understanding the central topic of the Pentateuch: the covenant God made with Israel at Mount Sinai (Ex 1 – Dt 34).

A. The Land and the Blessing (1:1 – 2:25)

1. The God of creation (1:1)

The Creator is identified as "God," the God of the fathers and of the covenant at Sinai. This distinguishes the God of Israel from the idol gods of the nations. This verse also explains that God alone is eternal and that everything owes its origin and existence to him.

2. Preparation of the land (1:2 – 2:3)

Verse 2 describes the condition of the land just before God prepared it for the human race (cf. Isa 45:18): it was "formless and empty" with "darkness" over it, and it was covered with water. The Spirit of God was hovering over the unformed world like an eagle "hovering" over its young with great concern (cf. Dt 32:11).

The sun, moon, and stars must be included in the usual meaning of the phrase "the heavens and the earth." Verse 3 thus describes the appearance of the sun through the darkness. The division between "day" and "night" leaves little room for an interpretation of "light" in v.3 as other than that of the sun.

On the second day God made the "vault" — a term that refers not only to the place of the sun, moon, and stars (v.14) but also to where the birds fly (v.20).

There are two distinct acts of God, both of which are called good, on the third day: the preparation of the dry land and the seas, and the furnishing of the dry land with vegetation.

On the fourth day the lights God had created on the first day are given a *purpose*, namely, "to separate the day from the night" and "to mark sacred times, and days and years." Behind this narrative is also the writer's concern to emphasize that God alone is to be given the glory and honor due only to him.

On the fifth day God created the sea and the sky creatures, and on the sixth day he created the land creatures — including man and woman. The word for "created" is used only seven times in the creation account (1:1, 21, 27 [3x]; 2:3, 4); elsewhere the word "to make" is used to describe God's actions.

The beginning of the creation of the human race is marked by the usual "Then God said." However, this time God said, "Let us make" ("us" hints at the Trinity). Moreover, man and woman were made "in our [God's] image." The creation of humankind is specifically noted as a creation of "male and female," stressing that God created "mankind" as "male and female."

God neither spoke nor worked on the seventh day. Rather, he "blessed" the day and "made it holy." The reader is left with a somber reminder that God did not work on the seventh day; human beings, created in his image, must do likewise (cf. Ex 20:8–11; Ps 95:11; Heb 3:11).

3. The gift of the land (2:4–24)

The description of the creation of the first man in 2:7 differs significantly from that of ch. 1. Though made in God's image, the first man did not begin as a "heavenly creature"; he was made of the "dust of the ground." This anticipates his destiny in the fall, when he will again return to the "dust" (3:19).

Much attention is given to the description of the "garden," where the Lord God "put" the man. God planted this garden "in the east, in Eden." The word "Eden" appears to be a specific place; it means "delight" and evokes a picture of idyllic delight and rest. "In the east" is striking, because elsewhere in Genesis, eastward is associated with judgment and separation from God (e.g., 3:24; 11:2; 13:11).

In the garden were beautiful, lush trees, including the elusive "tree of life" and "the tree of the knowledge of good and evil"; there was also a river with four "headwaters." The lands were rich in gold and precious jewels, and their location was closely aligned with the land later promised to Abraham and his descendants.

Beginning in v.15, the author gives two purposes God had in putting the man in the garden. (1) He was placed in the garden to rest, be safe, and have fellowship with God (3:8). (2) He was put there to worship God and obey him. (3) He was put in the garden "to work it and take care of it."

When God sees the man alone, he says, "It is not good for the man to be alone." At the close of ch. 2, the author puts the final touch on his account of what it means for human beings to be in God's "image" and "likeness." This entails a partnership of the man with his wife.

B. The Land and the Exile (2:25–3:24)

1. Disobedience (2:25–3:7)

The disobedience of our first parents is not so much an act of great wickedness as it is an act of great folly. Ultimately, the wisdom that the serpent promised led to the curse (v.14).

The snake speaks only twice, but that is enough to offset the balance of trust and obedience between the man and the woman and their Creator. The snake implied that God was keeping this knowledge *from* the man and the woman, while the sense of chs. 1–2 has been that God was working his knowledge *for* the man and the woman (e.g., 1:4, 10, 12).

Just before the fall, the woman "saw that the ... tree was good." Thus the temptation is not presented as a general rebellion from God's authority but rather a quest for wisdom and "the good" apart from God's provision.

2. Judgment (3:8 – 20)

The judgment scene opens with the "sound" of the Lord's coming. In response, Adam and his wife flee to the trees. God's only words to the rebellious pair come as questions (cf. 4:9 – 10; 18:21). Skillfully, by repeating "naked," the author allows the man to be convicted with his own words. The man counters by casting blame on the woman and on God. As a measure of the extent of the fall, he now sees God's good gift as the source of his trouble.

In v.15 the fates of the snake and the woman embody the fates of their seed — "enmity" between the snake and the woman and between their respective "offspring." The "offspring" of the woman ("he") will crush the head of the snake. This verse contains a puzzling yet important ambiguity: Who is the "offspring" of the woman? Its purpose is not to answer that question but rather to raise it.

The judgment against the woman (v.16) relates first to her children and then to her husband. She will bear children in increased pain or toil, and her husband will "rule over" her. What the woman once was to do as a blessing had become tainted by the curse.

As the result of human rebellion, the description of the land is reversed. This opens the way for "a new heaven and a new earth" (Rev 21:1; cf. Isa 65:17; Ro 8:22 – 24). Similarly, v.19 shows the reversal of the man's condition. Before the fall he was taken from the ground and given the "breath of life" (2:7). Now he must return to the dust from which he was taken.

3. Protection (3:21)

The mention of the type of clothing that God made — "garments of skins," i.e., tunics — perhaps recalls the state of the man and the woman before the fall: "naked" and "not ashamed" (2:25). The author may also be anticipating the notion of sacrifice in the animals slain for the making of the skin garments (cf. Ex 28:42).

4. Exile (3:22 – 24)

The verdict of death consisted of being cast out of the garden and barred from the tree of life (cf. 3:22 – 23; 4:14). Ironically, when the human race, created *like* God (cf. 1:26), sought to "be like God" (3:5 – 7), they found themselves after the fall no longer *with* God. As such, happiness does not consist of being *like* God as much as it does being *with* God (cf. Ps 16:11).

The depiction of the garden and the tree of life guarded by cherubim after the fall anticipates God's plan to restore blessing and life to the human race in the covenant at Sinai and in the law (Ex 25:10-22).

C. Life in Exile (4:1 – 26)

1. Worship (4:1 – 8)

Eve's first words after the fall are likely a form of a boast: just as the Lord had created a man, so now she has created a man, expressing her confidence in her own ability to fulfill the promise of 3:15. Note the contrast between Eve's words here at the beginning, *"I have gotten a man"* with her closing acknowledgment, *"God has appointed for me another offspring"* (v.25).

The narrative of Cain and Abel teaches a lesson on the kind of worship that pleases God — that which springs from a pure heart. Whatever the specific cause of God's rejection of Cain's offering, the narrative ultimately focuses our attention on Cain's twofold attitude of anger: (1) anger against God (v.5b) and (2) anger against Abel (v.8).

2. Repentance (4:9 – 15a)

The sense of "bear" in v.13 and the Lord's response to Cain in v.15 suggest that his words must not be understood as a complaint about his punishment but rather an expression of remorse and repentance over the extent of his iniquity. In v.14 Cain acknowledged that God's punishment (v.12) could result in his own death since he would not have the protection of an established community.

3. Protection (4:15b – 24)

The purpose of the "mark" "put on" Cain was to provide him with protection from vengeance. Though the sign is not explicitly identified, the narrative continues with an account of Cain's departure to the land of Nod, "east of Eden," where he built a city. In that city, culture developed. The primary components of city life were animal husbandry (Jabal, v.20), arts (Jubal, v.21), craftsmanship (Tubal-Cain, v.22), and, apparently, law (Lamech, vv.23-24). Lamech's words to his two wives are not a boasting arrogance, but appear as an appeal to a system of legal justice.

4. Blessing (4:25 – 26)

Though Cain's sons prospered and became the founders of the new world after the fall, the focus turns to the new son born "in place of Abel." The promised seed would come through the one whom God chooses. Cain is not a part of the line of the "offspring" (cf. Japheth, 10:2 – 5; Ham, 10:6 – 20; Nahor, 11:29; 22:20 – 24; Ishmael, 17:20; Lot, 19:19 – 38; Esau, ch. 36).

D. The Story of Noah (5:1 – 10:32)

A major break occurs at the beginning of ch. 5: "This is the book of the generations of Adam." This section, which concludes at 9:29, is built around a list of ten descendants of Adam, concluding with Noah. After Noah's death (9:29), a new list of his sons begins, ending with the Abram (11:26). The interweaving of narrative and genealogical lists occurs throughout Genesis.

1. Prologue (5:1 – 3)

This prologue (1) redirects the reader's attention back to the course of events in ch. 1 concerning the "likeness" of God, (2) ties ch. 5 together with 4:25 – 26 by continuing the pattern of "birth" and "naming," and (3) relates God's "blessing" to humankind back to the fall, insofar as God's original blessing will be restored through the seed of the woman.

2. The sons of Adam (5:4 – 32)

The genealogical list in ch. 5 is nearly identical in form to that of 11:10 – 26, the genealogy of Shem. The only difference is the inclusion of the clause "and he died" (ch. 5). The death of each patriarch highlights the exceptional case of Enoch, who "walked faithfully with God" and did not die. The pronouncement of death, in other words, is not the last word; a door is left open for a return to the tree of life. Enoch found that door by "walking faithfully with God."

Noah, the last one mentioned, stresses two points. (1) He will bring comfort from the labor and painful toil of the curse (v.29). Likely that comfort was the salvation of humankind in the ark and the reinstitution of the sacrifice after the flood (cf. 8:21). (2) Noah's rescue from death in the flood receives the same explanation for Enoch's rescue from death ("he walked faithfully with God"). When Noah did die, it came only after the story of his sin of drunkenness (9:18 – 29).

3. Epilogue (6:1 – 4)

This summarizes the state of affairs of Adam's descendants (cf. 10:31 – 32; 11:27 – 32; Ex 1:7) — namely, that they greatly increased in number, married, and continued to have children. In v.3 God speaks again about "man." The ages of people in those intervening verses stand in stark contrast to the "one hundred and twenty years" mentioned in this verse. The inference is that God's Spirit dwelling with these men gave them their long lives.

4. The flood (6:5 – 9:17)

Genesis 6:5-12 introduces the flood story. Its main purpose is not to show why God sent a flood but rather why God saved Noah. Noah's life becomes a model of the kind of life that finds grace in the sight of God.

The list of specifications for the ark (6:14-16) is not so much for us to see what the ark looked like but rather to appreciate the meticulous care Noah exercised as he obeyed God's will. The exact nature of the material the ark was made from is unknown. It had three stories, each with separate compartments, and it had an opening for light and a door in its side.

In 7:1-5 God commands Noah to enter the ark prior to the coming rains. Thereupon with great detail the procession of those entering the ark passes by the reader (7:6-24). When the rains stopped, those in the ark had to wait before God sent deliverance (ch. 8). Noah immediately began to look for signs of his impending deliverance. He sent out a raven and a dove, but no signs of dry land appeared. By the time Noah knew there was dry land, he had waited exactly one year (cf. 7:6, 11; 8:13-14). Those in the ark did not leave, however, until God commanded them (8:15-17).

By Noah's building an altar and offering sacrifices, the whole of the state of humankind before the flood is reestablished. The human race is still fallen (9:21), but through an offering on the altar they may yet find God's blessing.

5. Noah's drunkenness (9:18 – 29)

What we should not overlook in the episode of Noah's drunkenness the identification of Canaan as one of the sons of Ham. This is crucial to what follows (cf. vv.22, 25).

Just as in the creation God planted a garden for people to enjoy, so now Noah plants a vineyard. The outcomes are similar. Noah ate of the fruit of his vineyard and became naked (cf. 2:25; 3:7). That is, even after salvation from the flood, the enjoyment of God's good gifts by the human race could not be sustained. Noah, like Adam, sinned, and the effects were felt in the sons and daughters that followed.

Ham looked on his father's nakedness. Shem and Japheth instead covered it without looking on him. This contrast becomes the basis for the curse and the blessing that follow.

6. The line of Noah (10:1 – 32)

The list begins with "the sons of Japheth" (10:2-5), "the maritime peoples" (v.5). Later, when the focus is on the establishment of God's universal kingdom, these nations again come into view to show that God's plan includes all peoples (Ps 72:8, 10).

The list of the sons of Ham (vv.6–12) begins as did the list of the sons of Japheth, with the simple naming of Ham's four sons. Then the grandsons of the first listed (Cush) are given. But before going on to the next son (Egypt), the great-grandsons (sons of Raamah) are listed. The end result is a list of "seven sons"—a complete list. Immediately following this are the exploits of Nimrod and his cities, introducing the city of Babylon, the subject of 11:1–9. The genealogy continues with a list of the sons of Egypt, again seven names.

The list of descendants of Shem is also highly selective, focusing on Eber's son Joktan. Significantly, a second genealogy of Shem is given after the account of the building of Babylon (11:1–9), and there the line is continued to Abram through Eber's first, Peleg (11:10–26).

E. The City of Babylon (11:1–9)

The word "name" plays a central role here. The builders of the city wanted "to make a name" for themselves. The conclusion of the story returns to the "name" of the city, ironically associating it (Babylon/Babel) with the confusion of their language. "Scattered" is another key word. The purpose of the city was so that its inhabitants would not "be scattered over the face of the whole earth." Ironically, at the conclusion of the story, the Lord "scattered" the builders from the city "over the face of the whole earth."

F. The Line of Shem (11:10–26)

This list of ten descendants of Shem, like that of Adam in ch. 5, draws the line of the "faithful" (Noah to Abram) and bypasses the "unfaithful" (10:26–30). God's promise concerning the offspring of the woman cannot be thwarted by the confusion and scattering of the nations at Babylon.

II. Abraham (11:27 – 25:11)

A. The Line of Abraham (11:27 – 32)

The preceding genealogy provides the necessary background for understanding the events in Abram's life. Here we read that Terah and his family, including Abram and Lot, had left Ur of the Chaldeans and traveled as far as Harran. There is no mention of the call of God until 12:1, presumably after the death of Terah (v.32b). It appears, then, that Abram was called to leave his homeland while in Harran—after his father's death and not while in Ur.

A second look, however, suggests that the author intended us to understand the narrative differently. How so? Verses 27–32 show that Abram's birth took place in Ur of the Chaldeans, not Harran. Thus the command given to Abram to leave the place of his birth could only have been given at Ur. Putting the call of Abram within the setting of Ur aligns this narrative with themes in the later prophetic literature and connects his call (12:1 – 3) with the dispersion of the city of Babylon (11:1 – 9).

B. The Call of Abram (12:1 – 9)

Abram, like Noah, marks a new beginning as well as a return to God's original plan of blessing "all peoples on earth" (cf. 1:28). Abram is represented as a new Adam and his seed as a second Adam. Those who "bless" him, God will bless; those who "curse" him, God will curse. The way of *life and blessing*, which was once marked by the "tree of the knowledge of good and evil" (2:17) and by the ark (7:23b), is now marked by identification with Abram and his seed. The identity of the seed of Abraham is one of the chief themes of the following narratives.

C. Abram in Egypt (12:10 – 13:4)

A famine forced Abram to seek refuge in Egypt. But God remains faithful to his word and safeguards the promise. Abram's sojourn in Egypt parallels in many respects the account of God's deliverance of Israel from Egypt (Ge 41 – Ex 12). Abram's stay in Egypt prefigures Israel's later stay in Egypt (both initiated by a famine). Behind the situations stands a faithful, loving God. What he did with Abram, he will do for his people today and tomorrow.

D. The Lot Narratives (13:5 – 19:38)

1. Abram and Lot (13:5 – 18)

Abram's separation from Lot carries the theme of the promise into jeopardy. Ironically, Abram is on the verge of giving the Promised Land to Lot, who later became the father of the Ammonites and the Moabites (19:37 – 38).

The land Lot chose was "like the garden of the LORD" and "like the land of Egypt," a positive description within the context of Genesis. But there is a subtle foreshadowing of the fatal results of Lot's choice in the geographic marker "toward Zoar," where Lot fled for safety from Sodom and Gomorrah (19:22).

2. Abram and the nations (14:1 – 24)

The location now moves from Hebron (13:18) to an international arena and the wars of four kings. Lot is the link between the two accounts.

Immediately following the report of his capture (14:8–12), the narrative returns to Hebron (v.13b). "The LORD," the God whom Abram worshiped at Hebron, delivers the four kings of the east into Abram's hands. Abram asks nothing from the kings of this world (vv.22–23), and he is the only one who proves able to live peacefully in the land. As 12:3 has forecast, those who join with him (v.13b) enjoy his blessing (v.24b); those who separate from him, as Lot had done (13:12), will suffer the same fate as Sodom and Gomorrah (14:11–12).

After defeating the four kings, Abram is met by Melchizedek, who brings "bread and wine" as a priestly act and acknowledges that it is the "God Most High, Creator of heaven and earth" who has delivered the adversaries into Abram's hand. This king appears suddenly as if out of nowhere and just as quickly is gone (cf. Heb 7).

3. Abram and the covenant (15:1 – 21)

Abram's fear in v.1 relates back to the final outcome of God's promise to make his "offspring like the dust of the earth" (13:16; cf. 15:2). He feels little reason to hope that God will remain faithful to his word. God is about to enter a "covenant" (v.18) with Abram that will be the basis of all God's future dealings with him and his offspring (vv.7–21).

Verses 7–16 recount the establishment of a covenant between the Lord and Abram. In v.17, the act of dividing the animals and walking through the parts was apparently an ancient form of contractual agreement (cf. Jer 34:18). The sudden and solitary image of the birds of prey that Abram must drive away (v.11) gives a fleeting glimpse of the impending doom that awaits Abraham's seed, but it also points to the protective care of God's promises (cf. Mt 24:28).

In vv.18–21 the author again draws the promise of the land back into the narrative by concluding with a description of the geographical boundaries of the covenant land. The borders of the Promised Land appear to coincide with the border of the garden of Eden (cf. 2:10–14).

4. Hagar (16:1 – 16)

Twice we read that Hagar, *the Egyptian*, "despised" Sarai. As a consequence, Hagar was forced into the "desert" (v.7), where she was to stay until she submitted herself again to Sarai (cf. 12:3). Only then did the Lord offer Hagar a blessing (v.10; cf. 17:2, 20).

To deal with her barrenness, Sarai's plan of offering her maid to her husband so that she could bear him an heir was apparently acceptable within the social custom of the day. That plan, however, was one more example of the futility of human effort to achieve God's blessing. Although successful, the plan did not meet with divine approval (cf. 17:15–19).

5. Abram, Sarah, and Ishmael (17:1–27)

God is immediately identified as the "LORD," the God of the covenant at Sinai (Ex 3:15). Abram "fell facedown" (v.3), a sign of deep respect. His part in the covenant consisted of obedience, particularly that "every male among you ... must be circumcised." His wife's part in the covenant was to be the mother of nations, and "kings of peoples will come from her." As with Abraham, her new name—Sarah—was a sign of her part in the covenant.

Although Ishmael is excluded from the covenant with Abraham, he and his descendants are still to live under the blessing of God. In fact, in his blessing of Ishmael, God reiterated both his original blessing of all humanity in 1:28 and his blessing of Abraham in 12:2. Just as the "offspring" of Isaac would form a great nation of twelve tribes (49:1–27), so the "offspring" of Ishmael, under God's blessing, would form a great nation of twelve rulers (cf. 25:13–15).

Abraham obeyed the covenant (v.23); he circumcised all the male members of his household "as God told him." Such obedience reflects the injunction given in v.1: "Walk before me faithfully and be blameless" (cf. Enoch in 5:22, 24; Noah in 6:9).

6. Three visitors (18:1–33)

Three men visit Abraham, and he serves them a meal. They in turn promise that a son will be born to him and Sarah in about a year. Abraham and particularly Sarah were too old to have children. Throughout this story, the main obstacle to the fulfillment of the promise was Sarah's age (cf. 25:1–4). Therefore, Sarah laughed at the idea. The eventual name of this child (Isaac) means "he laughs" (21:1–7).

As the three men arose (v.16) and looked toward Sodom, Abraham accompanied them to send them off. The Lord then mused to himself about whether he should reveal his plans for Sodom to Abraham. Beginning in v.20, the Lord addressed Abraham. His words answer the question in v.17, revealing at this point that he would investigate the wickedness of Sodom and Gomorrah.

In v.22, the men (presumably all three) left to go to Sodom. But if three men leave Abraham, why do only "two messengers" (19:1) arrive in Sodom? What happens to the other "man"? The most common explanation is that the remaining "man" is a "christophany," i.e., an appearance of the second person of the Trinity in human form, before the incarnation. When the text says that "the men turned away and went toward Sodom" and that "Abraham remained standing before the LORD," one of the men must have stayed behind with Abraham. Thus this man may have been the preincarnate Christ, accompanied by two "angels."

The central issue in vv.23–33 is expressed in Abraham's question at the end of v.25. The Lord's answer is a resounding yes; the Lord will do right. Abraham then starts with a question about fifty righteous people in a city and concludes with the question of ten righteous ones. In ch. 13 Abram had intervened for Lot; here he intervenes for Lot again through intercession, which effects Lot's deliverance. The picture of Abram that emerges here is the same as in 20:7: "He is a prophet, and he will pray for you and you will live."

7. Lot and Sodom (19:1–38)

The men visiting Lot represent a visitation of the Lord (v.18). They came to carry out the Lord's retribution against the wickedness of the city (v.13b); but in response to Abraham's prayer for the righteous (18:23–32), they also came to rescue Lot (19:29).

The depiction of the events at Lot's house on the eve of the destruction of Sodom and Gomorrah justified God's judgment on the two cities. Even Lot, the righteous one who was ultimately rescued, was tainted by his association with Sodom. His suggestion that the men of the city take his own daughters and do with them as they pleased was not as a sign of his good character. In an ironic turn of events, Lot himself carried out his own horrible proposal (vv.30–38).

The men took Lot and his family by the hand and led out of the city to safety (vv.15ff.). This rescue was in response to the prayer of Abraham, for the angels' words explicitly recalled the words Abraham used (cf. 18:23; 19:15, 17; see esp. v.29, which reminds us that in Abraham and his offspring "all peoples on earth will be blessed," 12:3).

At the conclusion of Lot's rescue, he requested shelter in the nearby city of Zoar. Thus, the Lord saved that city from destruction. In other words, Lot's rescue is a result of two prayers — Abraham's and his own.

Lot's wife (v.26) and Abraham (v.28) both "looked" at the destruction of the cities, but with differing consequences. Lot's wife became a "pillar of salt" because she "looked back," thus disobeying the words of the rescuers (v.17). Abraham looked from a vantage point consistent with the men's words in v.17.

Lot was the father of the Moabites and the Ammonites (see Dt 2:9, 19). Both these people continued to play an important role in later biblical history.

E. Abraham and Abimelek (20:1 – 18)

Chapters 20 and 21 focus on the relationship between Abraham and the nations. Abraham's role as a prophetic intercessor led him to pray for the Philistines (20:7), and God healed them (v.17). In the narrative Abimelek played the role of a "righteous Gentile" with whom Abraham lived in peace and blessing. Abraham accepted the gifts from the Philistines and offered a prayer on their behalf in return (v.17). Only at this point do we discover the nature of God's words to Abimelek in v.7. The Lord had "kept all the women in Abimelek's household from conceiving."

F. Abraham and Isaac (21:1 – 25:11)

1. The birth of Isaac (21:1 – 7)

Verse 1 picks up the narrative from 18:10. Isaac's birth came about "as [the LORD] had said," stressed three times in vv.1 – 2. God is faithful to his word.

The importance of the announcement of Isaac's birth is seen in the statement that "the LORD was gracious" (v.1), which focuses on God's attentive care and concern. Also important is the reminder that Isaac was the "son ... in [Abraham's] old age" and that he was born "at the very time God had promised him." The narrative goes on to emphasize Abraham's obedience (v.4; cf. 17:12) and specific age (v.5; cf. 17:1, 24).

2. Hagar and Ishmael (21:8 – 21)

The celebration of Isaac's coming of age led to the expulsion of Ishmael (cf. ch. 16). Once again, the author has foreshadowed later events in earlier ones, in order to draw connections between important narratives. In this case the Lord's promise to Hagar (16:11 – 12) was recounted in a strikingly similar fashion to that of the fulfillment of the promise (vv.18 – 21).

3. Abraham and Abimelek (21:22 – 34)

The reappearance of Abimelek shows that Abraham was still living with the Philistines (cf. v.34). That is, he did not live out all his days in the Promised Land but spent many days in exile. Even Isaac, the son of the promise, was not born in Canaan but in exile and had to sojourn there with his father, who "wandered from nation to nation, from one kingdom to another" (Ps 105:13; cf. Heb 11:8 – 13). Abraham in exile typifies God's care of the righteous, who must suffer while waiting to enter the land.

4. The binding of Isaac (22:1 – 14)

God now "tested" Abraham, which reveals his real purpose in this incident.

There is no thought of an actual sacrifice of Isaac in the narrative, though in the mind of Abraham within the narrative that was the only thought that was entertained. No one says anything until Isaac finally broke the silence. When Abraham finally spoke, his reply to Isaac's question anticipated precisely the final outcome of the story: "The LORD will provide."

Few narratives can equal the dramatic tension of the last moments before God interrupted Abraham's action and called the test to a halt. At the last dramatic moment the Lord intervened and, as Abraham had already anticipated, provided a substitute. Abraham therefore named the altar he had built "The LORD will provide."

5. The angel of the Lord (22:15 – 19)

At the end of the narrative is a "second" encounter between Abraham and the angel, which shows that God's original promises to Abraham were not based on Abraham's specific actions in carrying out the test but rather on his faith and obedience. The reference to Abraham's act of obedience as the basis of the promise recalls 18:19.

6. The relatives of Abraham (22:20 – 24)

Immediately after the reiteration of the promise of a great multitude of descendants comes a notice regarding the increase of the family that Abraham and Sarah had left behind in Harran. The twelve names suggest an intentional comparison with the twelve sons of Jacob or the twelve sons of Ishmael in 25:12 – 15. The central purpose of the list is to introduce the future bride of Isaac, Rebekah, and to show that she was of the lineage of Milkah and not of Reumah.

7. Machpelah and Sarah's death (23:1 – 20)

Sarah died in Hebron, and Abraham apparently came there from Beersheba (cf. 22:19) to mourn her death. The point of ch. 23 is to show how Abraham first came into legal possession of a parcel of land in Canaan. Abraham bought not only a cave for the burial of his wife but also a large field with many trees. This became an important burial site for the patriarchs and their wives (cf. 49:30 – 32; 50:13). Just as Abraham would not accept a gift from the king of Sodom (14:23), so here he refused to accept the parcel of land as a gift. His purchase of land embodied his hope in God's promise that one day all the land would belong to him and his descendants (cf. Jer 32:6 – 15).

8. A bride for Isaac (24:1 – 67)

Here again, in the questions raised by Abraham's servant, his faith stands out. Abraham's reply proves to be both prophetic and thematic — it provides the central motive of the narrative, that God would go before the servant to prepare his way.

Once in Nahor, the servant spelled out specifically the nature of the sign he sought from the Lord (vv.12–14). God did prepare the way, bringing the young girl in question on the scene even before the servant finished speaking. Such divine preparation must be accompanied by the kind of appreciation seen in the servant in vv.26–27. The servant emphasizes that God's angel has made his "journey a success" (v.40) by gaining a wife for Isaac from his own family.

Laban and Bethuel acknowledged that the Lord had prepared the way for the servant to meet Rebekah. Thus several witnesses testified that these events were the work of God. The final witness was Rebekah herself, who agreed to return with the servant to Isaac. The simplicity of her response (v.58) reveals the nature of her trust in the God of Abraham (cf. Ru 1:16).

9. Abraham's death (25:1 – 11)

After Sarah's death, Abraham took another wife, Keturah. Abraham was a rejuvenated old man and continued to be rewarded with the blessing of many offspring. Surprisingly little attention is given to the details of Abraham's death "at a good old age" (cf. 15:15). His final resting place was in that portion of the Promised Land he rightfully owned—the field purchased from Ephron the Hittite.

III. The Account of Ishmael (25:12 – 18)

The Isaac stories open (cf. v.11) with a final statement regarding the line of Ishmael, consisting of a genealogy of the twelve leaders of Ishmael's clan, a report of the length of his life, and a report of his death. The number twelve appears again to be a deliberate attempt to set these individuals off as founders of a new and separate people (see comment on 22:20–24). The descendants of Ishmael continue to play a part in Genesis (28:9; 36:3; 37:27–28; 39:1).

IV. The Account of Isaac (25:19 – 35:29)

A. The Birth of Jacob and Esau (25:19 – 28)

The "account of the family line of Abraham's son Isaac" (v.19) almost immediately turns out to be about the sons of Isaac rather than Isaac himself. Because Rebekah, his wife, was barren, Isaac prayed for her (cf. 20:17); the Lord answered, and she bore two sons.

The struggle between the brothers began in Rebekah's womb. The point is not that the struggles were necessary to accomplish God's will; rather, God's will was accomplished in spite of the conflict. Another important motif is that "the older will serve the younger."

B. Selling the Birthright (25:29 – 34)

This story of Esau's rejecting his birthright shows that God's choice of Jacob over Esau did not run contrary to the wishes of either. Esau, though he had the right of the firstborn, "despised" his birthright, while Jacob went to great lengths to gain it.

C. Isaac and Abimelek (26:1 – 35)

As in the days of Abraham (12:10–20; cf. 20:1–18), famine struck during the life of Isaac. Verse 1 says that Isaac went down to Gerar to Abimelek; but in the warning Isaac received in the vision of v.2, we are informed he was on his way to Egypt. The Lord's warning became the occasion for a formal restatement of the blessing. In the face of the impending famine, the Lord promised to be with Isaac, to bless him, to make his seed great, to give him the land, and to bless all the nations of the land in him (cf. 12:2–3, 7).

There are several similarities between Isaac here and Abraham in ch. 20; these can hardly be coincidental. The final picture of Isaac is the discovery of a new well on the same day that Isaac had made peace with his neighbors. Consequently the writer associates the name of the city, "Beersheba" (lit., "well of the seven/oath"; cf. 21:31), with the "oath."

Initially the notice of the marriage of Esau (vv.34–35), who had despised his birthright (25:29–34), to two Hittite women seems insignificant. But this forms the background to the central event in ch. 27, the blessing of Jacob. Esau was not fit to inherit the blessing.

D. The Stolen Blessing (27:1 – 40)

Several elements heighten the suspense and highlight the deception of Jacob; thus Jacob's name, which means "the deceiver" (cf. v.36), has been appropriately chosen. Isaac is too old and too blind to distinguish between his two sons. This makes the story more believable and more suspenseful. Isaac's insistence on "tasty food" before the blessing recalls Esau's own trading of the birthright for a pot of stew and thus casts Isaac and Esau in similar roles. The suspense of the story is carried to the end, when Jacob left just as Esau returned from the hunt (cf. v.30).

The goal of Jacob's strategy was to wrest the blessing from Isaac for himself. Although Isaac did not appear completely convinced that he was speaking to Esau, in the end he blessed Jacob. This theme of "blessing" points out the relationship of this narrative both to the narratives that precede and those that follow. The promise to Abraham (12:2–3) is alluded to in the final words of Isaac's blessing (v.29). Similarly, his blessing foreshadows Jacob's later prophecy concerning the kingship of the house of Judah (cf. 49:8).

The reverse side of the blessing of Jacob is Esau's disappointment and anger. He is a tragic figure, a victim of his more resourceful and daring brother. Within the narrative, Isaac recounted the main points of the blessing given to Jacob a second time, underscoring the fact that he had blessed Jacob rather than Esau. Finally, with Esau in tears, Isaac answered his pleas for a blessing with a third reiteration of the central point of Jacob's blessing: "You will serve your brother." The blessing was irretrievably lost to Esau and would certainly be fulfilled in Jacob.

E. Jacob's Flight from Beersheba (27:41 – 28:5)

Jacob's scheme not only resulted in his obtaining the blessing from Isaac, but it also became the occasion for Jacob's journey to the house of Laban. Esau, a bitter and spiteful brother, made plans to kill Jacob and regain by force his birthright and blessing. Again Rebekah thwarted the plans, having Isaac send Jacob back to her homeland to find a wife. As often in Genesis, Isaac's words of blessing to the departing Jacob anticipate the eventual outcome of the ensuing story: Jacob visited Laban "for a while" (27:44), Esau's anger subsided (see ch. 33), and Jacob found a wife and returned as a great assembly of people. Within Isaac's farewell blessing is a final reiteration of the central theme of the preceding narrative: the promised blessings of Abraham and of Isaac were now the promised blessings of Jacob.

F. Esau's Bitterness (28:6 – 9)

Esau was a bitter son who now sought to spite his parents through deliberate disobedience. The marriage of Esau to the daughter of Ishmael reminds us that the promised offspring of Abraham was determined, not by the will of human beings, but by the will of God. The families of the two "older" sons (Ishmael and Esau) were united in the marriage, but neither received the blessing promised to Abraham.

G. Jacob at Bethel (28:10 – 22)

Jacob, like Abraham (ch. 15), received a confirmation of the promised blessing in "a dream." In both instances a divine confirmation was given about the establishment of the same covenant of promise.

The Lord's words in v.15 became the guiding principle that governed the course of Jacob's life. When he returned from Laban's house after many years, he went back to the same place, Bethel; there God again blessed him, promised to give him the land he had already promised to Abraham (35:12), and reaffirmed his decision to make Jacob's descendants into a great nation (35:11).

H. Jacob and Rachel (29:I – 14a)

Jacob's journey to find a wife is similar to that of Abraham's servant who sought a wife for Isaac (ch. 24). Here, however, Jacob was relatively silent. He did not reflect on God's guidance or on the Lord's promise to be with him wherever he went (28:15). It was his actions, not his words, that tell the story of God's help and guidance.

As with the servant in ch. 24, God directed Jacob to go to the well where Rachel was watering her flocks. Then, in a great show of emotion, Jacob kissed her and cried with a loud voice. Clearly Jacob saw in these circumstances the guiding hand of God (cf. 24:27).

I. Jacob's Marriages (29:14b – 30)

For the first time Jacob himself became the object of deception. In the case of the blessing (ch. 27), Jacob had exchanged the younger for the older; here Laban exchanged the older for the younger. The seven extra years that Jacob had to serve Laban appear as a repayment for his treatment of Esau. His past had caught up with him, and he had to accept the results and serve Laban seven more years.

J. The Birth of Jacob's Sons (29:31 – 30:24)

Interestingly, the Lord opened Leah's womb, "but Rachel remained childless." God apparently intended Jacob to have Leah as wife. Jacob sought to build a family through Rachel, but God opened Leah's womb. Jacob's schemes, therefore, were crumbling further. Human schemes can never carry out the plans of God.

In the end the Lord did hearken to Rachel, and Joseph was born (30:22). Nevertheless, Jacob's words to Rachel underscore that God had withheld sons from Rachel (30:2). All the ensuing conflict and tension between Joseph and his brothers — and particularly Joseph and Judah — are anticipated and foreshadowed here.

K. Jacob and Laban's Sheep (30:25 – 43)

After the account of the birth of Jacob's sons, we have the first mention of his planned departure from Harran. Laban, seeking the Lord's blessing on behalf of Jacob, wanted to settle his account for the work Jacob had done for him over the years. So he asked Jacob to name his wages. Laban's offer apparently contained a request that Jacob stay on with him and continue to watch over his herds. Jacob struck a bargain with Laban that resulted in great blessing and wealth for Jacob. The blessing did not come, however, from Laban; rather it was a gift from God (cf. Abraham's wealth in 14:21).

L. Jacob's Flight from Laban (31:1 – 55)

Just as Isaac's wealth had made the Philistines jealous (26:14), so Jacob learned that Laban was now angry and jealous of his wealth. At this time the Lord directed Jacob to return to the land of his fathers (v.3; cf. 28:15); thus Jacob's life again pointed toward Bethel, the place of the original promise.

Jacob's wives were willing to leave their own family and go with him to Canaan (cf. 24:58; Ru 1:16). More important, they were ready to put their trust in God and seek his blessing. An ominous note, however, is sounded about Rachel's stealing of Laban's "household gods" (v.19), gods that would presumably procure the headship of her father's goods. This event bears both a similarity and a contrast to Jacob's stealing his father's blessing (ch. 27).

The dispute over these gods allows the writer to restate his central theme (v.42): Jacob's wealth had not come through his association with Laban but through God's gracious care during Jacob's difficult sojourn. Jacob and Laban made covenant together.

M. Encounter with Esau (32:1 – 33:20)

The events of ch. 32 are couched between two encounters of Jacob with angels (vv.1, 25; the "man" at Peniel was probably an angel). Thus it recalls the early chapters of Genesis, when the Promised Land was guarded on its eastern borders by angels (3:24).

Like Jacob, we are not sure what Esau intended with four hundred men to meet Jacob. Jacob's fear of Esau seems well founded. Thus, his prayer for safety and his appeal to the covenant promises of God play a crucial role in reversing the state of affairs. True to form, Jacob schemes elaborate plans to save himself and his family in the face of Esau's potential threat. He provided his servants with abundant gifts for Esau and instructed them carefully on how to approach Esau when they met.

Jacob's wrestling with "a man" (likely an angel) epitomizes his whole life. He had struggled with his brother (chs. 25, 27), his father (ch. 27), and his father-in-law (chs. 29–31); now he struggled with God (ch. 32). His own words express the substance of these narratives about him: "I will not let you go unless you bless me." Significantly, Jacob emerged victorious in his struggle, for the angel "blessed him." The name "Peniel" is an important name because it identified the one with whom Jacob was wrestling as God.

When Jacob saw Esau and the four hundred men approaching, he divided his entourage again (cf. 32:7–8). He showed his preference for Rachel and Joseph by putting them last. Esau's greeting was totally unexpected. Jacob had expected revenge from Esau, or at least heavy bargaining and appeasement. Ironically, the four hundred men accompanying Esau turned out to be for safeguarding the final stage of Jacob's journey. Once again Jacob was one who had gone to great lengths to secure his own well-being, but his efforts proved pointless.

N. Jacob at Shechem (33:18 – 34:31)

Jacob returned to Bethel in ch. 35 and built an altar there, but no mention is made of his giving a "tenth" to the Lord (cf. 28:22). Perhaps the altar in 33:20 and in 35:7 and the offerings, or perhaps the "hundred pieces of silver" (33:19), represented that "tenth." The portion of land purchased by Jacob plays an important role in the later biblical narratives, for on this land the Israelites buried the bones of Joseph (Jos 24:32); thus they represented their hope in God's ultimate fulfillment of his promise of the land.

Dinah's birth was recorded without much comment in 30:21. But once Jacob and his descendants settled in the vicinity of Shechem (33:18–20), Dinah became the center of the conflict between Jacob and the inhabitants of Canaan. Though Shechem genuinely loved Dinah, he had laid with her, apparently against her will, and thus humiliated her. Simeon and Levi's final words express clearly how they viewed the situation: "Should he have treated our sister like a prostitute?" (v.31). Their motive in their actions was not plunder but the honor of their sister.

O. Jacobs Return to Bethel (35:1 – 15)

As Jacob had once fled to Bethel to escape the anger of his brother Esau (28:10–15), so now the Lord told Jacob to return to Bethel and live there because of the trouble that Simeon and Levi had stirred up. When Jacob obeyed, the Lord delivered him from the anger of the Canaanites who dwelt nearby. Significantly, Jacob called God the one "who answered me in the day of my distress and who has been with me wherever I have gone" (v.3). That summarizes the God who had been active throughout the Jacob narratives. God remained faithful to his promises and delivered Jacob from every distress.

P. Benjamin's Birth and Rachel's Death (35:16 – 20)

Rachel, Joseph's mother and Jacob's favorite wife, died giving birth to her second son, Benjamin. That account reflects back on 29:32 – 30:24. There the last son to have been born was Rachel's first son, Joseph, at which time Rachel had said, "May the LORD add to me another son" (30:24). Looking back to that request, Rachel's midwife said, "Don't despair, for you have another son."

The site of Rachel's burial, Ephrath, was clearly identified with the city of Bethlehem, an important place in biblical history (cf. 1Sa 17:12; Mic 5:2). This passage continued to play an important role in later biblical texts (cf. 48:7; Jer 31:15; Mic 5:2; Mt 2:18).

Q. The Sons of Jacob (35:21 – 26)

Reuben engaged in misconduct and forfeited his claim to be the favored son. Thus, Jacob's three oldest sons have fallen from favor (see ch. 34 for the violence of Simeon and Levi). The next brother in line was Judah, a son of Leah.

A major turning point is about to occur in Jacob's story. Two lines that have thus far run parallel are about to converge. Just as Abraham had two sons and only one was the son of promise, and just as Isaac had two sons and only one was the son of the blessing, so now Jacob, though he has twelve sons, had two wives (Leah and Rachel), and each had a son (Judah and Joseph) who could rightfully contend for the blessing.

V. The Death of Isaac (35:27 – 29)

The Jacob narratives end with the death of his father, Isaac. This notice shows the complete fulfillment of God's promise to Jacob (28:21). Jacob had asked God to watch over him and return him safely to "my father's household." Thus the conclusion of the Jacob narrative marks the fulfillment of these words.

VI. The Account of Esau (36:1 – 43)

Here the writer shows the progress and well-being of the line of Esau. He carefully notes that Esau is, in fact, "Edom." The repeated identification of Esau as Edom throughout the chapter prepares us for the future importance of Edom during Israel's later history. The unusually long genealogy of Esau ends with a list of Edomite kings (vv.31 – 39), introduced by the heading, "These were the kings who reigned in Edom before any Israelite king reigned." This anticipates an eventual kingship in Israel.

VII. The Account of Jacob (37:1 – 49:33)

A. Jacob in the Land (37:1)

Jacob is back in the Promised Land but is still living there like a sojourner, as his father and grandfather did (cf. Heb 11:13). He too is awaiting the fulfillment of God's promises. Verse 1 is a fitting transition to the narratives that trace the course of events by which his sons eventually leave that land and enter the land of Egypt.

B. Joseph's Dreams (37:2 – 11)

Jacob's special love for Rachel (29:30) carried over to that of her son Joseph. This story is filled with wordplays and reversals; thus, the reference to the "bad report" likely foreshadows the brothers' intended "harm" noted in 50:20.

The "ornate robe" Jacob made for Joseph illustrates the father's pref-erential love for Joseph. That preferred status was the central problem that angered his brothers and turned them against him. Moreover, Joseph recounted two dreams, both of which end with the image of his broth-ers "bowing down" to him. Why two dreams? See Joseph's explanation to Pharaoh that his two dreams indicate that the matter has been firmly decided by God (41:32).

C. Joseph's Journey to Egypt (37:12 – 36)

On a mission from his father, Joseph found his brothers in Dothan. When Joseph's brothers "saw him" approaching, they "plotted to kill him." Behind those plans lie Joseph's two dreams, which foreshadowed the divine plan. Little did they suspect that the very plan they were scheming would lead to the fulfillment of those dreams.

An important turn of events occurred with the arrival of the "Ishma-elites." They became the occasion for Judah to enter the story with the suggestion that the brothers could "sell [Joseph] to the Ishmaelites." The brothers did so, and the Ishmaelites (also called "Midianites" here) took Joseph to Egypt with them.

The brothers now must fall back on their original plan of telling their father that a "ferocious" (lit., "evil") animal had killed Joseph. The symbol of the brothers' hatred for Joseph becomes the means of the father's recognition of his loss. In the end the blood-stained coat is all that remains of Joseph; Jacob tore off his own coat and exchanged it for sackcloth.

D. Judah and Tamar (38:1 – 30)

Judah did nothing to further his own household. It took the "righteousness" of the woman Tamar (v.26) to preserve the seed of Judah. Judah's wife was a Canaanite, the daughter of Shua (v.2). Thus, the promise made to Abraham was in jeopardy, confirming the worst fears of Abraham (24:3) and Isaac (28:1). Through Tamar's clever plan, however, the seed of Abraham was preserved by not being allowed to continue through the sons of the Canaanite. Instead, it was continued through Judah and Tamar (who was probably not a Canaanite). The genealogy at the close of the narrative underscores this point.

The Judah narratives reach a fitting summary in the brief account of the birth of Perez and Zerah (vv.27 – 30). As the Jacob narrative began with an account of the struggle of twins (25:22), so now this story is marked by a similar struggle. In both cases the struggle resulted in a reversal of the right of the firstborn and the right of the blessing; the younger (Perez) gained the upper hand over the elder (Zerah); in Nu 26:20, Perez is regarded as the firstborn.

E. Joseph in the House of Potiphar (39:1 – 23)

The text resumes the account of Joseph. Verse 2 establishes the overall theme, while vv.3 – 6 relate the theme to the specific events that follow: Joseph's blessing from the Lord was recognized by his Egyptian master, and Joseph was put in charge of his household. Joseph's sojourn in Egypt, like that of his father, Jacob (30:27), resulted in an initial fulfillment of the Abrahamic promise that "all peoples on earth will be blessed through you" (12:3).

The epilogue (vv.21 – 23) emphasizes that God turned an intended evil against Joseph into a good. God was with Joseph and prospered his way. Lying behind these events is the lesson of the Joseph narratives: "You intended to harm me, but God intended it for good" (50:20).

F. Joseph in Jail (40:1 – 23)

Chapter 40 represents an intermediary stage in the development of the plot of the Joseph story. Joseph had been cast into jail and had risen to a position of prominence there. Two incarcerated royal officials each had a dream that Joseph correctly interpreted. When Pharaoh later had a dream, the butler remembered the events of this chapter and told the king about Joseph. Joseph, like Daniel, can interpret dreams and mysteries.

G. Joseph's Interpretation of Pharaoh's Dreams (41:1 – 36)

In Pharaoh's two dreams, seven good cows and seven good heads of grain represented seven good years; seven ugly cows and seven blighted heads of grain represented seven bad years to follow. Joseph not only was able to interpret the dreams, but, more importantly, he advised Pharaoh how to prepare for what was to come. Through the memory of the butler, this episode emphasizes both the wisdom of Joseph and the sovereign workings of God.

H. Joseph's Exaltation over Egypt (41:37 – 57)

At many points in the story, Joseph appears as the ideal of a truly wise and faithful man. By his obedience, he accomplished all that Adam failed to do. This story reflects what might have been had Adam remained obedient to God and trusted him for the "good." At the same time it anticipates what might yet be, if only God's people would, like Joseph, live in complete obedience and trust in God. Therefore the story of Joseph looks forward to one who was yet to come, the one from the house of Judah to whom the kingdom belongs (cf. 49:10). Thus the tension between the houses of Joseph and Judah is resolved by making the life of Joseph into a picture of the one who is to reign from the house of Judah.

I. Joseph's Brothers in Egypt (42:1 – 28)

The twelve sons of Jacob are divided into two groups throughout the story: the ten brothers of Joseph's (v.3) and the two sons of Jacob by Rachel—Joseph and Benjamin. These two sons are contrasted specifically with two sons of Leah—Reuben and Judah.

When his brothers approached Joseph to buy grain, he "pretended to be a stranger" (v.7) and spoke harshly, accusing them of being spies. Joseph's schemes and plans against his brothers were motivated by the dreams of the earlier narratives and not by revenge for what his brothers had done to him (v.9).

In response to Joseph's accusation that they were spies, the brothers defended their integrity by saying, "Your servants were twelve brothers"; but lest their integrity be found wanting, they added: "and one is no more." Joseph's schemes have provoked the first hint that the evil deed accomplished long past may yet rise up against them.

Joseph devised two plans to test his brothers. (1) "One" of the brothers should return for the youngest and the rest remain in prison. (2) After three days the second plan was announced: "one" of the brothers was to remain behind and the others were to return to get the youngest. The focus is on the "one" brother who rescues the others.

J. Joseph's Brothers Return for Benjamin (42:29–38)

The events of ch. 42 are now retold in an abbreviated form by the brothers, focusing on the plan of Joseph for bringing the youngest son to Egypt. Jacob's response in v.36 rings truer than he would ever have suspected. The brothers had deprived him of Joseph, and it was because of them that Simeon was not now with them and that Benjamin was to be taken away. Thus the brothers receive another reminder of the guilt that lingered over their treatment of Joseph.

K. Joseph's Identity (43:1–45:28)

1. The second trip to Egypt (43:1–34)

The famine was still severe, and the grain purchased earlier was gone; so the father sent his sons back for more. This time Judah insisted on taking Benjamin with them. In persuading his father, Judah offered to take full responsibility for Benjamin.

Jacob gave in. Just as Judah's plan ultimately saved the life of Joseph (37:26–27), so now his plan saved the life of Simeon and, in the end, of Benjamin. Jacob's farewell words in v.14 (note esp. the word "mercy") provide the narrative key to what follows. When Joseph saw Benjamin (v.29), we are told that "his mercy" was kindled toward his brother. Joseph, still unrecognized, was conspicuously careful to ask about the well-being of the brothers' father.

2. The silver cup (44:1–34)

Once more Joseph tricked his brothers by having his cup and Benjamin's money returned in Benjamin's sack of grain. The question the steward asked them carries on the central issue of the Joseph narratives: the contrast between the "evil" done by the brothers and the "good" intended and accomplished by God (cf. 50:20).

Joseph's plan worked as expected. Not knowing that the cup and money were in Benjamin's sack, the brothers made a rash vow, putting the life of Benjamin and their own freedom in jeopardy. When the cup was discovered, their response was one of complete hopelessness. "They tore their clothes" (44:13) and returned to the city — a response that mirrored their father's response when he heard their earlier report about Joseph (37:34).

Judah's retelling of the Joseph story reveals the brothers' perception of the events as well as the hopelessness of their situation. The overall sense of Judah's version is that the brothers had been mistreated, suggesting that if anyone was to blame, it was Joseph. Judah's words, however, also reveal that the ultimate fault did not lie with Joseph but with the "evil" intention of the brothers toward Joseph.

3. Joseph's revelation (45:1 – 28)

Joseph had taken no personal enjoyment in deceiving his brothers. When he could hold back no longer, he revealed his true identity. Joseph returned once again to the central theme of the narrative: though the brothers had intended evil, God was ultimately behind it all, accomplishing a "great deliverance" (v.7). In the second part of his speech (vv.9 – 20), Joseph made plans to bring his father to Egypt.

At first, when Jacob heard the news that Joseph was alive, he "was stunned" (v.26) and "did not believe." But when he heard everything that Joseph had said and saw all that he had sent to take him back to Egypt, "the spirit ... of Jacob revived," and he set out to go to him. A new dimension occurred in Jacob's faith.

L. Jacob's Journey to Egypt (46:1 – 7)

Before Jacob went to Egypt, he traveled to Beersheba, built an altar there, and offered sacrifices to the God of his father, Isaac. Special attention is given to the journey of Jacob and his household into Egypt. Just as Abraham had left Ur and then Harran and journeyed to Canaan (11:31; 12:4 – 5), so now Jacob left Canaan and journeyed to Egypt.

M. Jacob's Sons in Egypt (46:8 – 27)

This list of names appears to have been selected so that the total numbers "seventy" (v.27). It can hardly be coincidental that the number of nations in Ge 10 is also "seventy." Just as the "seventy nations" represent all the descendants of Adam, so now the "seventy sons" represent all the descendants of Abraham, Isaac, and Jacob. Note Dt 32:8, that God apportioned the boundaries of the nations (Ge 10) according to the number of the sons of Israel.

N. Settling in Goshen (46:28 – 47:12)

Curiously, it was Judah, not Joseph, who pointed out the way for the sons of Israel into the land of Goshen. Once again Judah is singled out for special attention over against Joseph. Such a special focus on Judah highlights his crucial role in God's plan to bring about Israel's deliverance (see 49:8–12).

Chapter 46 ends with Joseph's plan to secure the land of Goshen as a dwelling place for the sons of Israel. The plan was simply to tell the pharaoh that they were shepherds. Since the Egyptians hated shepherds, this would allow the Israelites to live by themselves in Goshen. That plan succeeded. In fact, Pharaoh's response in ch. 47 was even more generous than the previous narrative would have suggested. Pharaoh also put them in charge of his own livestock.

In 47:7–10 Jacob "blessed Pharaoh" when he was brought before him. Jacob's words to reflect the later promise that those who honor father and mother would "live long and that it may go well with you in the land" (Dt 5:16).

O. Joseph's Rule in Egypt (47:13–27)

The narrative returns to the story line of 41:57 with an account of the affairs of Joseph in Egypt and his work on behalf of the pharaoh. His dealings with the Egyptian people mirror the story about Jacob and his family. The Egyptians sought to buy grain from Joseph (cf. 42:2). Then they returned to Joseph "the following year," in which they expressed the desire "that we may live and not die" (cf. 43:8; 45:5).

The story of Joseph and his brothers began with Joseph being sold (37:28) into slavery (39:17) for twenty pieces of silver (37:28). Now, Joseph was selling the whole of the land of Egypt into slavery and taking their "money" (v.18), while the offspring of Abraham became "fruitful," "increased greatly in number" (v.27), and were living safely and prosperously in Goshen (cf. 1:28).

P. Jacob's Deathbed (47:28–49:33)

1. Jacob's burial instructions (47:28–31)

Seventeen years later, the time had come for Jacob to die (47:28–29). Jacob did not want to be buried in Egypt. A central element of the covenant with Abraham was the promise of the land. The request of the patriarchs to be buried in the land "with their fathers" emphasizes their trust in the faithfulness of God to his word.

2. Ephraim and Manasseh blessed (48:1–22)

As in the earlier patriarchal narratives, the blessing of the father is passed along to the next generation. Two features stand out here. (1) It was the younger son, Ephraim, who received the blessing of the firstborn rather than the older, Manasseh (v.19). Thus, once again, receiving the blessing offered by God does not rest with one's natural status in the world but is based solely on God's grace. (2) The blessing recorded here is largely subordinated to and superseded by the blessing for Judah in ch. 49.

In his words, Jacob recalled God's promise to him at Bethel (35:9–13) by repeating the Lord's words almost verbatim. The first blessing (vv.15–16) appears to be of Joseph rather than the two sons, but in the blessing itself, he referred to "these boys" (v.16), and that blessing ultimately focused on them. They were to be called by Jacob's "name" and the "names" of Abraham and Isaac; they were to "increase greatly," just as God had promised Abraham in 12:2.

3. Jacob's sons blessed (49:1 – 28)

At the close of Jacob's discourse (v.28), the writer draws a line connecting Jacob's words in this chapter to this theme of "the blessing" (repeated three times in Hebrew). As Jacob's last words looked to the future, he drew on the past — God's blessing of all humanity. The order of the sons follows roughly the order of the record of their birth (chs. 29–30).

There is no major blessing for Reuben (vv.3–4) or Simeon and Levi (vv. 5–7): Reuben because he violated the honor of his father (cf. 35:22); Simeon and Levi because they instigated the bloodshed against the city of Shechem (34:25). The latter two would not have their own portion in the inheritance of the land. As fulfillment, the tribe of Simeon virtually disappears from the biblical narratives after the conquest, and the tribe of Levi becomes the priestly tribe and receives no inheritance in the apportioning of the land.

Jacob's prediction for the tribe of Judah (vv.8–12) pictures him as the preeminent son. He is described as a victorious warrior who returns home from battle and is greeted by the shouts of praise from his brothers. This image is extended with the picture of Judah as a "lion's cub." In v.10 he is the one who holds the "scepter" and the "ruler's staff." Judah will hold that status among the tribes of Israel until one comes "to whom it belongs."

The most startling aspect of this description comes next: "and the obedience of the nations is his." The use of the plural word "nations" suggests that Jacob had in view a kingship that extends beyond the boundaries of the sons of Israel to include other nations as well.

Jacob's words regarding the remaining sons, with the exception of Joseph, are noticeable not only for their brevity, but also for their cryptic allusions to epic events that at the time lay yet in the future. Regarding Joseph (vv.22–26), Jacob's statements repeat much of what was said about the other brothers after Judah. The difference, however, is the repetition of the word "blessing."

In v.28, the writer sums up Jacob's words to his sons in terms of the theme of the blessing. This theme has been evident in all the sons after Judah, both in defeating enemies and in experiencing great prosperity and abundance.

4. Jacob's burial instructions repeated (49:29 – 33)

Jacob once more (cf. 47:29 – 30) requested his sons to bury him in the Promised Land with his fathers, specifically at "Machpelah," the cave purchased by Abraham in ch. 23 where he, Sarah, Isaac, Rebekah, and Leah were buried. This request renews our awareness of the promise of the land — that Jacob's seed would live in peace in the land promised to Abraham and Isaac. Jacob's faith in God's promises remained firm to the end.

Q. Jacob's Death and Burial (50:1 – 14)

Joseph himself mourned his father's death, as did the Egyptians. The pharaoh granted a special request to bury Jacob in his homeland, and a large entourage was provided as a burial procession to carry his body back to Canaan.

VIII. The Final Joseph Narrative (50:15 – 26)

The narrative turns one final time to Joseph and his brothers and to the central theme of the Joseph narratives: "You intended to harm [lit., evil] me, but God intended it for good ... [to] the saving of many lives" (v.20 cf. 45:5 – 7). Behind the entire Joseph story lies the unchanging plan of God — the same plan introduced at the beginning of the book, when God saw that what he had created was "good" (1:4 – 31). Through his dealings with the patriarchs and Joseph, God in his faithfulness had continued to bring about his good plan.

The final statement of Joseph to his brothers (vv. 22 – 26) gives the clearest expression of the kind of hope taught in these narratives: that God would bring them back (v.25). Genesis ends with the Israelites "in Egypt."

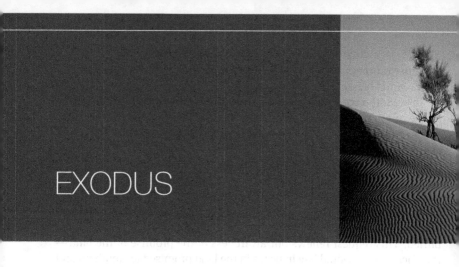

EXODUS

I. The Oppression of the Israelites (1:1 – 22)

The story of Exodus continues without interruption from Genesis by recounting the genealogical list of Jacob's sons who came down to Egypt (1:1 – 5; cf. Ge 46:3). The total number of persons given here is seventy (see comments on Ge 46:8 – 27).

Verse 6, which recounts the passing of the old generation, marks an important starting point for the next series of events. Verse 7 is transitional, passing most of the four hundred years Israel was in Egypt (cf. 12:40), and v.9 reports how the children of Israel have greatly increased (cf. Ge 12:2). Egypt now has "a new king [dynasty]," who saw the Israelites as a threat and began to oppress them.

II. The Preparation of a Deliverer — Moses (2:1 – 25)

One family protected their newborn son from the cruel decree of the pharaoh. His mother hid him for three months. Then she constructed a reed basket (an "ark"), sealed it, and placed the baby "among the reeds along the bank of the Nile" (v.3) — ironically, just as the king of Egypt had decreed (1:22). Furthermore, this child was saved by the pharaoh's own daughter. God was at work in the affairs of the world and would bring about his purposes.

This baby, Moses, grew up in the palace, but had to flee for his life into the wilderness, where he spent the next forty years. In v.24 the writer gives us the all-important clues to the meaning of the events about to be recounted. When the Israelites cried out to the Lord for help, God not only heard their cry, he also "remembered his covenant" with Abraham, Isaac, and Jacob (cf. Lev 26:42).

III. The Call of Moses (3:1 – 4:31)

A. God Calls Moses (3:1 – 10)

God identified himself to Moses as the "God of your father, the God of Abraham, the God of Isaac and the God of Jacob" (v.6), and proceeded to tell Moses of his plan: he was to deliver the Israelites from bondage in Egypt and bring them into the land promised to their ancestors (vv.7 – 10) and form them into a nation with the worship of God as its center.

B. Moses' Response to God's Call (3:11 – 4:31)

Moses, realizing the responsibility of his task, replied to God, "Who am I?" God responded not by building up Moses' confidence in himself, but by reassuring him that he would be with Moses in carrying out his task.

When Moses asked about the "name" of God, he was asking more than just the identity of God. He was asking about the very nature of God. The actual name of God, *Yahweh* (translated as "Lord" in English Bibles), is used. Its association with the expression "I am who I am" suggests that the Hebrew name *Yahweh* is meant to convey the sense of "he who is present with his people."

Moses continued to resist God's call by asking: "What if they do not believe me ... and say, 'The Lord did not appear to you'?" In answer, God gave Moses three "signs": (1) his staff became a snake (vv.2 – 5); (2) his hand became leprous (vv.6 – 7); (3) the water from the Nile River became blood when poured out (v.9).

Moses raised one final objection — "I have never been eloquent." Again, the Lord's response appealed to his creative power: "Who gave human beings their mouths? Who makes them deaf or mute? ... Is it not I, the Lord?" Then the Lord repeated his promise: "I ... will teach you what to say" (4:12). As Moses prepared to return to Egypt to deliver God's people, the Lord warned him, "I will harden [Pharaoh's] heart so that he will not let the people go" (4:21).

IV. The Deliverance from Egypt (5:1 – 15:21)

A. Oppression Worsens; Promises Renewed (5:1 – 6:30)

1. The pharaoh's refusal to free God's people (5:1 – 3)

Moses and Aaron went in to the pharaoh to request permission to leave Egypt for three days. The pharaoh's negative response ("Who is the Lord, that I should obey him[?] ... I do not know the LORD," 5:2) provides the setting for the following narratives. These words form the "motivation" for those events — events designed to demonstrate who the Lord is (cf. 7:5).

2. Israel's oppression increased (5:4 – 18)

Pharaoh's response also sets the stage for the events that follow. He increased the Israelites' arduous labor by cutting the supply of straw for making bricks. Earlier, the people cried out in their distress (cf. 2:23; 5:15), and their cry went up before God. By contrast here in 5:15, the cry of the people is before the pharaoh. In other words, the pharaoh was standing in God's way; this provides another motivation for the plagues that follow.

3. The Lord's plan announced (5:19 – 6:1)

The Israelite leaders were powerless before the pharaoh. But these verses show the key to the effective work of Moses: "Then the LORD said to Moses, 'Now you will see what I will do to Pharaoh'" (6:1). The work of Moses was the work of God. Thus Moses is not a miracle worker. Rather, he is the Lord's servant.

4. God, Moses, and the Patriarchs (6:2 – 8)

There are several issues here central to the message of the Pentateuch. (1) God made a covenant with the patriarchs to give them the land of Canaan (6:4). (2) He remembered his covenant when he heard the cry of the Israelites in Egyptian bondage (v.5). (3) He was now going to deliver Israel from their bondage and take them to himself as a people and be their God (v.6). (4) He would bring them into the land that he swore to give to their ancestors (v.8).

In the last analysis, the exodus was a work of God; even Moses and Aaron had to be commanded to bring the people out. God's initial call for faith and trust was met with doubt and fear. God then responded with a simple call for obedience.

5. Summary (6:14 – 30)

After a list of names, the writer summarizes the earlier narrative. We are taken back to Moses' objection, "Since I speak with faltering lips, why would Pharaoh listen to me?" (v.30). What was earlier given as a simple command by God to go before the pharaoh (6:13) is now expanded into the instructions for carrying out the "signs," or plagues, against the Egyptians.

B. The Plagues (Signs) (7:1 – 12:36)

1. The purpose of the plagues (7:1 – 7)

The "plagues" (signs) were to demonstrate God's power to the Egyptians (v.5) as well as to the Israelites (9:16). God was not out to destroy the Egyptians. Rather, he was unmasking the pharaoh's claims to deity and his claim to rule the universe.

2. Signs (7:8 – 12)

As Moses and Aaron approached the pharaoh, they perform a sign before the king in order to demonstrate the validity of their mission. Aaron threw down his staff, and it became a snake (or perhaps a crocodile, v.10). This was wholly a divine sign, not some magic Aaron did. In contrast, the pharaoh's magicians were able to repeat the sign using their "secret arts" (v.11). Though the Egyptian magicians were able to reproduce the sign, God was working through Moses to accomplish his own plan.

3. The first plague: The Nile becomes blood (7:14 – 25)

The waters of the Nile became blood. Curiously, the Egyptian magicians were able to duplicate the sign (v.22), suggesting that not "all of the water" of Egypt had been affected. After the Egyptian magicians carried through with their duplication of the signs, however, there was no fresh water available to drink (v.24).

4. The second plague: The frogs (8:1 – 15)

The frog, along with most creatures in the natural world, was worshiped by the ancient Egyptians. It was considered the giver of the breath of life, and thus it became a symbol of life. At the word of Moses' God, all the frogs in the land died. Pharaoh shows signs of giving in to Moses' request (8:8), but when the plague subsided, he had a change of heart.

5. The third plague: Gnats (8:16 – 19)

The Egyptians were unable to reproduce this miracle. When they could not succeed, the magicians concluded that "this is the finger of God"; it was not a trick like their own (8:19).

6. The fourth plague: Swarms of flies (8:20 – 32)

The Israelites were set apart from the swarms of flies, and only the Egyptians were affected (v.22). In the Hebrew text this is called a "deliverance" for the people of Israel (cf. Isa 50:2). Again the pharaoh appeared ready to give in to the request to let the people go to worship God. He set a limit, however, by not letting them leave the land (v.25). When Moses appealed to him, he gave in further but was vague on what limits he intended for them (v.28).

7. The fifth plague: Pestilence on the livestock (9:1–7)

Moses' words proved true. All the livestock of the Egyptians died of disease and yet not one of the livestock of the Israelites was affected. Still, the pharaoh's heart hardened and he did not let the people go.

8. The sixth plague: Boils on the Egyptians (9:8–12)

As before, the Israelites were not affected by the boils. This plague provides a graphic picture of the ultimate failure of the magicians to oppose the work of Moses and Aaron.

9. The seventh plague: Hailstorms (9:13–35)

The hail "struck down everything in the fields—both people and animals." Again, the Israelites were safe in Goshen. The Lord's words to the pharaoh in this plague expand to include that "you may know that there is no one like me in all the earth" (9:14).

10. The eighth plague: Locusts (10:1–20)

The eighth plague introduces a new element into the purpose of the plagues: so that Israel "may tell your children and grandchildren how I dealt harshly with the Egyptians ... that you may know that I am the Lord" (v.2).

The pharaoh appears fickle here. He first appeared to consent to the Israelites' request to leave the land with all their families and possessions (vv.8–10). But it quickly becomes clear that he intended to hold back their families and send only the men (v.11). With this Moses and Aaron were driven out of the kings' presence, and the plague was called down on the Egyptians.

11. The ninth plague: Darkness (10:21–29)

There is a marked finality to the ninth plague. (1) The pharaoh was down to his last ruse. The women and children could go but not the livestock. This was unacceptable to Moses because the livestock were needed for offerings. (2) The darkness of the plagues signaled their end. (3) Moses and Aaron were warned by the pharaoh never to return to him again. The pharaoh was resisting the request of Moses beyond all reasonable limits. Even his own servants seemed to scold him, "Do you not yet realize that Egypt is ruined?" (10:7). But the pharaoh continued to hold out because the Lord had hardened his heart.

12. The last plague: Death of the firstborn and Passover (11:1–12:30)

Before the tenth and last plague, Moses instructed the people to put the blood of a lamb on their doorposts (12:21–23). This was the only way the "destroyer," sent through the land to strike down the firstborn in Egypt, would *pass over* their house. In the overall argument of the Pentateuch, obedience to the word of the Lord in this instance gave evidence of the Israelites' faith and trust in him (see Heb 11:28).

The purpose of the Passover was to remind God's people of his gracious act of deliverance. When the children saw the feast, they were to ask, "What does this ceremony mean?" The parents could then tell them of God's grace and love.

The text has a certain symmetry between Egypt's treatment of Israel in the early chapters of Exodus and God's treatment of Egypt here. As Egypt had killed all the Israelite sons (1:22) and had oppressed God's firstborn, Israel (4:22–23), so now their firstborn were taken, and they were avenged for the mistreatment they had done.

13. Plunder from the Egyptians (12:31–36)

The author draws a connection between the wealth of the Egyptians given to the Israelites and God's promise of wealth and blessing to the patriarchs. Thus the promise to Abraham was fulfilled—"They will come out with great possessions" (Ge 15:14).

C. The Exodus (12:37–13:16)

1. Travel from Egypt (12:37–41)

Israel's travel would have taken them over dry and dusty flatlands, incapable of supporting even a small number of settlers. They could not have survived without the miraculous provisions of water, food, and clothing (Dt 8:2–5).

A great many non-Israelites went out with them (v.38). These were "proselytes" who had abandoned their pagan gods to follow the God of Israel.

Having left Egypt in haste the night before, the Israelites now must prepare their food with unleavened bread (v.39), which explains the Feast of Unleavened Bread.

The time of Israel's sojourn in Egypt is calculated "to the very day," that is, 430 years (vv.40–41). In Ge 15:13 the time is given in the round number of 400 years.

2. Instructions for future observance (12:42–51)

These additional instructions for the Passover Feast look to the time when Israel would dwell in their own land, living in their own cities and towns and in close contact with the world about them. Thus the basic question is whether "foreigners" could also eat the Passover meal. The answer is no; only permanent members of the community of God's people could partake.

3. Firstborn of Israel set apart (13:1–2)

The firstborn were set apart for the Lord because he had "passed over" them in the destruction of the firstborn of Egypt. They thus belonged to him and, as later was seen with the Levites, they were to serve him in worship (cf. 13:11–16; also Nu 3:13, 41).

4. Instructions for commemoration of the Feast of Unleavened Bread (13:3–10)

In contrast to 12:14–20, these instructions give more prominence to the Feast of Unleavened Bread in commemorating the night of the Passover and the exodus from Egypt. In times when there was no possibility of celebrating the Passover Feast, the Feast of Unleavened Bread could still function as the time of remembrance of what God had done for Israel.

5. Redemption of the firstborn (13:11–16)

Because God had redeemed the firstborn of Israel on the night of the exodus, the people were to devote every firstborn male to the service of worship. The firstborn of the clean animals were to be devoted to the Lord as offerings. The firstborn of the unclean animals (e.g., donkeys) and of human beings were to be redeemed by substitution (cf. Nu 18:15) —a sheep in the case of unclean animals and money in the case of the firstborn male child (Nu 18:16).

D. The Crossing of the Red Sea (13:17–15:21)

1. Travel from Egypt (13:17–20)

The shortest route to the land of Canaan was the well-guarded route that led directly up the coastline and was the main artery of Egypt's defenses against their northern neighbors. God knew his people were not ready for battle and that at the sight of war they would flee back to Egypt. He thus led them another way—a way that turned out to be no more successful for this generation of his people and had its own temptations to return to Egypt (e.g., 14:12; Nu 14:1–4).

2. Pillar of cloud and fire (13:21–22)

The pillar of cloud was to guide the Israelites through the desert. It thus went before the people, and they followed it. A second pillar, the pillar of fire, was to give them light at night. The Lord went with the people in the cloud and the fire.

3. Crossing the Red Sea (14:1 – 31)

The Lord intended to have Israel cross the sea in order to reveal once again his superiority over the power of the Egyptians and to show that he alone was to be honored as Lord (v.4). To accomplish this purpose, the Lord first instructed Israel to fall back into Egyptian territory (v.2), which led them to believe that the Israelites were wandering aimlessly in the land, afraid to go out into the desert. The pharaoh's heart was again hardened (vv.4, 8, 17), and he set out to regain control of the Israelites (vv.6 – 7).

The Israelites were frightened when they saw the Egyptians. Moses, however, stood out as a faithful leader, admonishing the people to be courageous and to "stand firm and you will see the deliverance the LORD will bring you today" (v.13). When the people saw the Lord fight for them and the defeated Egyptians lying along the shore, they "feared the LORD and put their trust in him and in Moses his servant" (v.31).

The number of adult males crossing the sea was at least 600,000 (12:37), so there would have been over two million people, plus their livestock, in the whole of the assembly. For so many people to pass through the sea in one night, the width of the parting of the sea would have been at least several miles.

4. The song of Moses (15:1 – 21)

God's defeat of the Egyptians and deliverance of Israel in the crossing of the sea provide the occasion for a hymn of praise sung by Moses and the Israelites. The scope of the song itself, however, goes far beyond the event of the crossing of the sea to include the conquest of Canaan (vv.13 – 16) and the establishment of the city of Jerusalem as the location of the temple (vv.17 – 18). Moses' words are prophetic. The poetic imagery that dominates the song is that of the Lord as a mighty warrior (v.3).

V. The Wilderness Wanderings (15:22 – 18:27)

A. God's Provision for Israel in the Desert (15:22 – 27)

After the destruction of the pharaoh's army, the Israelites continued their journey eastward into the Desert of Shur, a large semidesert region east of the Egyptian border frontier.

After three days without finding water, they arrived at Marah. Since the waters here were bitter, the people complained. So Moses called out to the Lord. He answered Moses by instructing on how to make the water sweet. Having learned the lesson of dependence on God and listening to his voice, the people moved on to Elim, where they found abundant water and nourishment (15:27).

B. The Manna and the Quail (16:1 – 36; Nu 11:4 – 35)

Though the Israelites often had other sources of food, by gathering manna and quail the Bible tells us the people witnessed daily miracles (Dt 8:3). God was directly involved in providing for his people. They were to take only what they could eat for the day and not keep it for the next day. Some, however, stored food for the next day (v.20). Their disobedient efforts were to no avail because "maggots" rose up in the manna and it putrefied by morning.

C. Water and War in the Desert (17:1 – 16)

Once again the Israelites were without water. Moses followed the Lord's instructions precisely here (cf. in Nu 20, where Moses failed to do that).

When the people raised the question, "Is the LORD among us or not?" (v.7), they put God's promise to Moses in 3:12 to the test, where the Lord had said, "And this will be the sign to you that it is I who have sent you: When you have brought the people out of Egypt, you will worship God on this mountain." Now, "at Horeb," the people found themselves "at Sinai." God's promise had been fulfilled, but they still questioned his presence.

The Amalekites (descendants of Amalek, the grandson of Esau, Ge 36:16) lived in southern Canaan (Nu 13:29) and were known as the "first among the nations" to wage war against God's people (Nu 24:20). The narrative here focuses on the means of their defeat. As long as Moses held up his hands, the battle favored the Israelites led by Joshua. Even when Moses' arms were tired and had to be propped up by Aaron and Hur (v.12), the battle continued in Israel's favor. The significance of Moses' raised hands is given at the close of the chapter, where Moses built an altar and called it "The LORD is my Banner": "Because hands were lifted up against the throne of the LORD."

D. Jethro, Moses' Father-in-law (18:1 – 27)

The father-in-law of Moses seems to go by several names: Reuel in 2:16 – 22; Jethro in 3:1; 4:18; and Hobab in Nu 10:29. Moses had lived with his father-in-law as a shepherd (3:1). Although 4:19 – 20 reports that Moses took his wife and two sons with him when he returned to Egypt, we learn here that Moses had returned them to his father-in-law before going to Egypt.

VI. The Covenant at Sinai (19:1 – 24:18)

A. God Meets with Moses (19:1 – 25)

1. Arrival and encampment at Sinai (19:1 – 2)

The Israelites arrived at the Desert of Sinai the third day of the third month, forty-eight days after Israel left Egypt. The next day they set up a new camp at the mountain (v.2b). The next morning, the fiftieth day (i.e., Pentecost), Moses went up to the mountain and received the covenant (see Dt 16:9 – 11). The Israelites remained here for nearly one year (see Nu 10:11).

2. The covenant announced (19:3 – 15)

On Mount Sinai, God made a covenant with Israel, with Moses as a mediator between God and Israel. This covenant called for obedience (v.5), and its purpose was to set Israel apart as a special people, a kingdom of priests and a holy nation (vv.5b – 6). This covenant was intended as a fulfillment of the promises to Abraham, Isaac, and Jacob (2:24); later in Exodus (ch. 32) it becomes clear that Israel could not obey this covenant, even while at Mount Sinai.

3. The Lord came down to Sinai (19:16 – 25)

The description of the setting of the giving of the Ten Commandments is vague. (1) On the one hand, it appears as if God first spoke the Ten Commandments to Moses (v.19) and then Moses gave these commandments to the people (v.25). The people were afraid to go near and hear God speak, so they asked Moses to go for them (20:19). (2) On the other hand, 19:25 can be understood that the Lord first spoke the Ten Commandments to both Moses *and all the people* from the mountain. The people, after hearing God speak, requested that God speak only to Moses and that Moses then speak to them (20:18 – 19; cf. also Dt 4:10 – 13; 10:4).

B. The Decalogue (20:1 – 17)

The Bible refers to God's commands simply by the expression "these words" (v.1). Later they are called the "Ten Commandments" (34:28; Dt 4:13; 10:4) or "his covenant ... which he commanded" Israel (Dt 4:13). They express God's will for his covenant people. These words were etched on both sides of two small stone documents (Ex 24:12), which were small enough for Moses to carry "in his hands" (32:15; Dt 9:15, 17).

1. Prologue (20:1 – 2)

The basis of the call to obedience in the covenant was God's act of salvation in the exodus. Thus the Lord identifies himself first not only as the only God but also as the God who delivered Israel from bondage.

2. The Ten Commandments (20:3 – 17)

(1) You shall have no other gods before me (vv.3–6). God is a jealous God and a personal God. As such, he will not be satisfied with anything less than a personal relationship with men and women created in his image. To worship an image of God (an "idol") rather than God himself violates God's purpose for the creation of man and woman in his image (Ge 1:26).

(2) You shall not misuse the name of the LORD *your God (v.7).* God had revealed to Israel his name ("Yahweh") and given to them the corresponding privilege of calling on that name in worship and in time of need. Along with this privilege came the responsibility of honor and respect. Israel was not to call on God's name for no good purpose. The instructions regarding Israel's worship and the building of the tabernacle (chs. 25–31) were intended to teach Israel the proper way to call on God's name.

(3) Remember the Sabbath day (vv.8–11). Under the covenant at Sinai, Israel was to set apart each seventh day of the week and keep it holy. In so doing they were following God's own pattern in creation (Ge 2:2–4). The Sabbath's purpose was to give rest from one's labor (Ex 23:12; Dt 5:14) and to serve as a day of "sacred assembly" for the nation (Lev 23:3).

(4) Honor your father and your mother (v.12). An important part of this commandment is the promise, "that you may live long in the land." This commandment is addressed primarily to adults who are not dependent on their father and mother. They must treat their parents with respect not only as long as *the parents* live, but also as long as *they themselves* live in the land the Lord God is giving them.

(5) You shall not murder (v.13). The basis of prohibiting murder and manslaughter was laid down in Genesis. The human race was created in God's image; thus, "Whoever sheds human blood, by humans shall their blood be shed; for in the image of God has God made mankind" (Ge 9:6). This commandment does not preclude capital punishment (see, e.g., 21:12; cf. Ge 9:5).

(6) You shall not commit adultery (v.14). Sexual intercourse outside of marriage is prohibited. God expressed his purpose for marriage in Ge 2:24.

(7) You shall not steal (v.15). Stealing includes not only the act of taking what does not belong to one but also the deception involved in that act.

(8) You shall not give false testimony (v.16). Honesty and accuracy in the administration of justice and in everyday affairs are essential.

(9) You shall not covet your neighbor's house (v.17a). The two statements in v.17 are intended to be read as distinct, which is suggested by the repeti-

tion of the verb "covet" in v.17a and v.17b. If we allow Dt 5:21 to govern our understanding of the Exodus text, what is prohibitied here is lusting after a neighbor's spouse.

(10) You shall not covet … anything that belongs to your neighbor (v.17b). This last commandment is a general prohibition of every other kind of coveting.

C. Worship and Idolatry (20:18 – 26)

The statement of the "Ten Commandments" (20:1 – 17) and the collection of "laws" (21:1 – 23:13) are joined with a short narrative link (20:18 – 21). The fear of the people is repeated, as well as the reason for the display of divine power at Sinai (see also Dt 5:22 – 33). As a result, the people made Moses the mediator of the covenant.

In vv.22 – 23, virtually the entire nature of the religion of the covenant is summarized, beginning with the warning against idolatry. Moses was to remind the Israelites that God had spoken to them directly and thus to warn them not to stray from God through worship of idols.

The description of true worship in vv.24 – 26 portrays the essence of the Sinai covenant in terms that are virtually identical to that of the religion of the patriarchs.

D. Laws (21:1 – 23:12)

This selection provides a basis for teaching the nature of divine justice. By studying specific cases of the application of God's will in concrete situations, the reader of the Pentateuch can learn the basic principles undergirding the covenant relationship. Whereas the Ten Commandments provided general principles of justice, these examples demonstrated how those principles, or ideals, were to be applied to real-life situations.

E. Prohibition of Idolatry (23:13)

The end of this section takes up again the first commandment, i.e., the warning against idolatry sounded at the beginning (20:3 – 6, 22 – 23). The continual return to the theme of idolatry throughout this section prepares for an understanding of the incident of the golden calf (ch. 32).

F. Proper Forms of Worship: Feasts (23:14 – 19)

The ceremonial year is divided into three feasts. The Feast of Unleavened Bread has been described in 12:14 – 20; 13:3 – 9. The Feasts of Harvest (23:16a) and Ingathering (23:16b) are mentioned here for the first time (see also Lev 23:5ff.; Nu 28:26; Dt 16:9–12). At these three annual feasts, all the men of the community were to appear before the Lord (v.17).

A central regulation is given for each of the three feasts. (1) For the Feast of Unleavened Bread nothing containing yeast was to accompany the sacrificial blood, and none of the Passover lamb (cf. 34:25b) was to be left over until morning (23:18). (2) For the Feast of Harvest, Israel was to bring the "best" of the firstfruits to the Lord's house (23:19). (3) For the Feast of Ingathering, only animals at least seven days old were to be brought as offerings (cf. 22:29; Lev 22:27). A young goat "in its mother's milk" is one that still suckles from its mother.

G. Plans for Taking the Land (23:20–33)

God's care and guidance of the Israelites are linked to his protection of the patriarchs. By means of explicit allusions to key passages in Genesis, the writer shows that what happened to the Israelites was the fulfillment of the promises God had made with the patriarchs.

H. Establishment of the Covenant (24:1–18)

Once again we read that Moses went down and spoke God's words and judgments to the people (cf. 19:25). When they heard Moses, they agreed together to obey the covenant (24:3b), which was then ratified in the ceremony at the foot of Sinai (vv.4–8).

Thereupon, Moses and Aaron "went up" (v.9) to feast with Nadab and Abihu and the seventy elders (vv.10–11). The location of this feast is not certain. The elders were apparently not the same group as the priests since the priests were to remain with the people (19:24). The elders with Moses, Aaron, Nadab, and Abihu "saw the God of Israel" (v.11) — presumably in a vision.

VII. The Tabernacle (25:1–31:18)

The fact that the tabernacle was to be built according to the "plan" or "pattern" that God had shown Moses on the mountain (Ex 25:9, 40; cf. 1Ch 28:11–12,18–19) gives rise to three important points. (1) The tabernacle was intended as a model or facsimile of God's heavenly abode. (2) It had a symbolic value as well as a practical purpose. (3) Its parts are explained in the text itself. Thus we, the readers, are invited to ponder over the description of the tabernacle with the expectation that they exhibit the pattern of the heavenly temple.

A. Offerings for the Tabernacle (25:1 – 9)

Materials to be used in the construction of the tabernacle are enumerated first (see vv.3 – 7). These materials were considered most precious and valuable to the Israelites, so no further explanation is needed (see a more complete list in 35:4 – 29).

After the list of building materials, the purpose of the tabernacle is explained — to be a sanctuary for God, his dwelling place among the people (v.8). In constructing the tabernacle, Israel was to follow the plan or "pattern" that God had shown Moses on the mountain (v.9).

B. The Ark (25:10 – 22; 37:1 – 9)

The ark was to be made of acacia wood (v.10a). Its size was three and a half feet in length, two and a half feet wide and high (v.10b). It was overlaid with gold, inside and out (v.11 a) and was to have a gold border (v.11b). Four gold rings were attached to its sides for the acacia poles used to carry the ark (vv.12 – 15).

The "testimony" (i.e., the stone tablets on which were written the Ten Commandments, Dt 10:2 – 3; cf. Dt 31:26) was to be put inside the ark (vv.16, 21b).

A gold "atonement cover" was put over the ark. Two gold cherubim were to be placed at either end of the "atonement cover" with outstretched wings covering the cover (vv.18 – 20).

The purpose of the ark is so that "above the cover between the two cherubim," God would meet with his people and give them his commands. This promise was fulfilled after the dedication of the altar in Nu 7:89.

C. The Table (25:23 – 30; 37:10 – 16)

The table was to be made of acacia wood (v.23a), overlaid with pure gold and with golden borders (v.24). There were four gold rings, one by each leg (v.26). The utensils for the table were also made of gold (v.29). Its purpose was to hold "the bread of the Presence" (v.30).

D. The Lampstand (25:31 – 40; 37:17 – 24; Nu 8:1 – 4)

The lampstand, made of hammered gold (v.31a), had three shafts on either side of a central shaft (v.32). Each shaft extending from the central shaft was to have three almond-blossom cups, a knob, and a bud (v.33). Seven lamps were to be put on each shaft (v.37).

E. The Tabernacle (26:1 – 37)

The tabernacle itself consisted of curtains attached to wooden boards. It had three distinct structures. (1) The tabernacle proper consisted of the boards and a first layer of curtains surrounded by a large courtyard. Each curtain was to be forty-two feet long and six feet wide. On the edge of each large section were fifty loops. The two sections were to be joined together. Woven into the fabric of the curtains were images of cherubim, which recalled the theme of "paradise lost" by alluding to the cherubim that guarded the "tree of life" in Ge 3:24.

(2) The second structure was a second layer of curtains made of goat hair (vv.7 – 14). There were eleven such curtains, made into two large sections.

(3) A third structure consisted merely of a layer of ram skins dyed red that covered the tent, as well as an additional "covering of other durable leather," an uncertain term indicating a material sometimes rendered "badgers' skins" or "porpoise skins."

The tabernacle was supported by upright boards of acacia wood, each about fifteen feet long and set into a pair of silver bases (vv.15 – 25). Along the length of the tabernacle were twenty frames. At the far end were eight frames overlaid with gold (v.29a).

A curtain was to be set up within the tabernacle to separate the Holy Place from the Most Holy Place (vv.31 – 35). The ark and its atonement cover were to be placed behind the curtain in the Most Holy Place, and the table and lampstand were to be placed in front of the curtain.

F. The Altar of Burnt Offering (27:1 – 8; 38:1 – 7)

An altar seven and a half feet square and four and a half feet high was to be constructed of acacia wood and overlaid with bronze. It was for "burnt offerings" (see 38:1). The corners of the altar were made with raised tips, called "horns." The utensils used at the altar were also made of bronze. The whole of the altar was carried with bronze rings and poles.

G. The Courtyard of the Tabernacle (27:9 – 19; 38:9 – 20)

A courtyard enclosed by curtains surrounded the tabernacle. Its opening faced east. It was about 150 feet long and 75 feet wide. The height of the curtains was seven and a half feet.

H. The Oil for the Lampstands (27:20 – 21)

The people were to supply clear, pressed olive oil for burning in the lamps.

I. The Priestly Garments (28:1 – 43; 39:1 – 31)

Aaron and his sons were set apart from the rest of the Israelites as priests (vv.1 – 5). They were to wear special garments to give them "dignity and honor" and for Aaron's "consecration."

The ephod (vv.6 – 14) had two shoulder pieces studded with onyx stones. The breastpiece (vv.15 – 30) was a small (nine inches by nine inches) pouch worn on the breast of the priest and attached by golden chains to the shoulder pieces. Inside it were the Urim and Thummim, implements for deciding God's will.

A blue tunic was worn over the shoulders of the high priest whenever he went into the Most Holy Place (vv.31 – 35). Gold bells were attached to the hem and could be heard while he was in the Holy Place. The purpose of the bells on the high priest's garments was that he might be heard going in and coming out of the Holy Place, "so that he will not die" (v.35).

A gold plate or plaque was to be worn on the priest's turban (vv.36 – 38), engraved with the words "HOLY TO THE LORD." The basic garment of the priests was a tunic, woven of fine linen, as were the turban and sash (vv.39 – 41). The undergarments were plain linen (vv.42 – 43).

J. The Consecration of the Priests (29:1 – 46)

A bull and two rams were required to consecrate Aaron and the priests (vv.10 – 28). These animals were to be ritually slaughtered "at the entrance to the tent of meeting." These offerings were "sin" offerings (see vv.35 – 37). The whole ceremony was to be repeated for seven days.

Instructions were given for the daily sacrifice to be carried out for all generations (vv.38 – 46). Two yearling lambs were to be offered, one at morning and the other at twilight.

K. The Altar of Incense (30:1 – 10; 37:25 – 29)

An altar for burning incense was to be made of acacia wood, one and a half feet square and three feet high. It was to have raised "horns" like the sacrificial altar (cf. 27:1 – 8) and was to be overlaid with gold. The altar of incense was to be put just in front of the curtain that separated the Most Holy Place from the remainder of the Holy Place. This altar was to provide a continual burning of incense before the presence of the Lord.

L. The Atonement Money (30:11 – 16; 38:21 – 31)

The expense of the tabernacle service was to be shared equally among all Israelites, whether rich or poor. A census was taken, and from that, a donation of one half-shekel of silver per individual Israelite was required.

M. The Basin for Washing (30:17 – 21; 38:8)

A bronze basin was to be constructed for the priests' preparation for service at the altar. Before their work at the altar, they were to wash their hands and feet in the basin.

N. The Anointing Oil and Incense (30:22 – 38)

Special oil was to be mixed and used for anointing the various parts of the tabernacle, including the priests. The purpose of this was to sanctify these persons and objects. It was strictly forbidden to use the same oil for profane purposes. Likewise, special incense was to be mixed for the incense altar in front of the curtain of the Most Holy Place. Its purpose was to set the Tent of Meeting off as a special holy place.

O. Bezalel and Oholiab (31:1 – 11)

God's work was to be done by means of his Spirit. Two skilled craftsmen were chosen by God — Bezalel from the tribe of Judah and Oholiab from the tribe of Dan.

P. The Sabbath (31:12 – 17)

God did his work in six days and rested on the seventh day; now Israel is to do likewise. Like God's work, building the tabernacle was to be holy work and was to be carried out by observing the holy times.

Q. Conclusion (31:18)

This last verse returns our attention to the flow of narrative from ch. 24. God has been talking to Moses at the top of Mount Sinai. When he finishes, Moses receives the two stone tablets on which are written the Ten Commandments, and he is ready to descend.

VIII. The Golden Calf (32:1 – 35)

A. The Making of the Calf (32:1 – 6)

The narrative returns to what was happening in the Israelite camp while Moses was receiving the covenant with the Ten Commandments on Mount

Sinai. Ironically, at this very time Israel was in the process of breaking the first of those commandments.

B. Moses on the Mountain (32:7 – 14)

As God recounts to Moses the news of the golden calf, the reader receives three aspects of the divine perspective on Israel's sin. (1) Though warned by God repeatedly not to make or worship and idol, Israel had made such an idol and was worshiping it (v.8). (2) Israel seemed incapable of obeying the covenant. God expressed a desire to destroy the people and start over by making a new nation with Moses (v.10). (3) Through Moses' intercession and appeal to the promises to the patriarchs, God had compassion on the people (v.14).

C. God's Judgment on Israel's Sin (32:15 – 35)

God expressed his wrath in vv.9 – 12, and it is carried out by Moses and the Levites (v.28). Moses, who had appealed for clemency for the people, now led the vanguard of divine judgment.

At the close of this narrative we are reminded that as a result of the incident of the idolatrous golden calf, the people were "running wild" (v.25). Exodus 32 clearly shows that the laws given to Israel at Sinai were not mere arbitrary restrictions but necessary controls on an otherwise desperate and helpless situation.

IX. The Restoration of Israel (33:1 – 34:35)

Moses returned to Mount Sinai and there, again, God spoke with him. Israel's relationship with God had been fundamentally affected by their "great sin" of worshiping the golden calf. There was now a growing distance between God and Israel. Each of the following sections specifically demonstrates the changes that have occurred in God's relationship to Israel.

A. The Angel (33:1 – 6)

Israel is once again waiting at the foot of Mount Sinai, and Moses is waiting to receive God's instruction on the mountain. The first instructions seem the same as before: Israel was to leave Sinai and enter the land promised to the patriarchs (33:1 – 3a), and God would send his angel before them (33:2). But the reason for God's sending his angel to go before them has changed: "I will send an angel before you.... But I will not go with you, because you are a stiff-necked people and I might destroy you on the way" (vv.2 – 3).

Whereas before God sent his angel to destroy *Israel's enemies* (23:23), now he would send his angel lest he destroy *Israel* (33:5).

B. The Tent of Meeting (33:7 – 11)

This "tent" was not the same as the tabernacle (which had not yet been built). It was a meeting place with God set up "outside the camp some distance away" (33:7). The Tent of Meeting was only for Moses and Joshua.

C. Moses and the Glory of the Lord (33:12 – 23)

After the incident with the golden calf, the revelation of God's glory had a different purpose. When Moses asked to see God's glory, the Lord answered, "I will cause all my goodness to pass in front of you.... I will have mercy on whom I will have mercy, and I will have compassion on whom I will have compassion" (33:19). Surprisingly, what Moses learned about God's glory after the "great sin" (32:30) of the golden calf was not further fear of God but rather that he was a gracious God, full of much compassion.

D. The Stone Tablets (34:1 – 28)

Moses was told to prepare two stone tablets (vv.1 – 10); God would write the Ten Commandments on them, just as with the first tablets. Moses carried out God's command (v.4a) and took the two tablets with him back up the mountain (v.4b). Once on the mountain, however, God told Moses to write the "words" (v.27). The text is clear that it was the Ten Commandments that were written (v.28b).

E. The Glory on the Face of Moses (34:29 – 35)

Again as with the preceding narratives there is a significant reversal in Israel's relationship with God noted in the events of this narrative. As Moses returned from the mountain with the two tablets in his hands, instead of Moses' amazement at what he saw in the camp, those in the camp were amazed at what they saw in Moses—his radiant face—"and they were afraid."

What had now happened to Moses was the beginning of the fulfillment of what God had earlier promised him on the mountain (see v.10). Henceforth, the covenant that God made with Israel would focus on the role of the mediator. Through him God would display his glory.

X. The Construction of the Tabernacle (35:1 – 40:38)

A. The Sabbath (35:1 – 3)

After the narrative of Israel's great sin of the golden calf and before the description of the work on the tabernacle, there is again a reminder of the necessity of the Sabbath rest (31:12 – 17).

B. Materials for the Tabernacle (35:4 – 29)

The emphasis here focuses on the role of women in Israel's worship (cf. 38:8); they were to bring yarn and fine linen for the construction of the tabernacle (v.25).

C. The Workmen: Bezalel and Oholiab (35:30 – 36:1)

God's preparation and choice of the skilled workers is repeated from 31:2 – 6, though mention is also made of many other skilled workers. These other workers were taught by the craftsmen whom God gifted with his Spirit. Even their ability to teach others was a divine gift.

D. The Response of the People (36:2 – 7)

This brief narrative depicts the zeal of the people for the work of the tabernacle. When the workmen were brought together to begin the project, the people not only brought what they needed, but they also continued "to bring freewill offerings morning after morning." In fact, the people eventually had to be restrained from bringing any more.

E. The Construction of the Tabernacle (36:8 – 39:31)

The description of the building of the tabernacle follows closely that which was given earlier in the instructions. The purpose of such redundancy in the narrative is to show that the workmen carried out God's instructions *just as he had commanded.*

F. Moses Inspects the Tabernacle (39:32 – 43)

In a way that recalls God's own inspection of his work in creation (Ge 1:31), "Moses inspected the work and saw that they had done it just as the LORD had commanded" (v.43). And as in God's work of creation, when a blessing followed the completion of the work (Ge 1:28), so also when the tabernacle was completed, Moses "blessed them" (39:43).

G. Setting Up the Tabernacle (40:1 – 38)

The Lord told Moses to set up the tabernacle on the first day of the first month of the second year (v.17). First the ark was put in place and then covered with the curtains. Next came the table, the lampstand, the golden altar of incense, and the curtain covering the doorway to the tabernacle. The altar of burnt offering was then put before the doorway of the tabernacle, and the basin was put between the altar and the tent. The curtains making the courtyard were then put up all around, with a curtain providing a gateway to the courtyard. When all was in place, it was anointed with oil and the priests were brought in, dressed, and anointed.

The Lord approved the work of building the tabernacle by sending the cloud of his glory over the Tent of Meeting, i.e., the tabernacle. This was a visual reminder of the purpose of the tabernacle expressed in 25:8.

LEVITICUS

Introduction

The book of Leviticus is a continuation of Exodus. The author focuses on the requirements of the covenant that relate to the "priests," who were from the tribe of Levi. Its central theme is holiness and shows how Israel was to fulfill its covenant responsibility to be "a kingdom of priests and a holy nation" (Ex 19:6; Deut 26:18–19).

I. The Offerings and Sacrifices (1:1 – 17:16)

These chapters briefly describe the various offerings and sacrifices used in the consecration of the priests and the people. They provide background for the dedication of the tabernacle and the priesthood in chs. 8–9 as well as for the rest of the Pentateuch.

A. The Laws of Sacrifice (1:1 – 7:38)

1. Introduction (1:1 – 2)

The instructions in chs. 1–7 do not introduce the practice of offerings (cf. Ge 4:3–4; 8:20; 46:1; Ex 18:12); rather, they provide regulations for the existing sacrifices and offerings among the Israelites in light of the newly established worship of God at the tabernacle.

2. The burnt offering (1:3 – 17)

Three types of burnt offerings could be brought to the tabernacle: animals (1) from the herd (vv.3–9), (2) from the flock (vv.10–13), and (3) from the birds (vv.14 – 17). The offering was presented at the entrance of the Tent of Meeting, the tabernacle, where the offerer would lay his hand on the head of the offering; if it was accepted, it would "make atonement" for him (v.4b).

3. The grain offering (2:1 – 16)

A grain offering was an offering of flour prepared in any number of ways: fresh, baked, prepared on a griddle, or cooked in a pan. The offering was brought to the priest, who took a small portion of it to burn on the altar.

4. The fellowship offering (3:1 – 17)

In the fellowship offering only the "fat portions" and the blood were burned. The rest of the animal was prepared and eaten by the priests and the offerer.

5. The sin offering (4:1 – 5:13)

The purpose of the sin offering was to atone for unintentionally breaking one of God's commandments (4:20, 26, 31, 35). Like the burnt offering, one brought the appropriate offering to the tabernacle, laid his hands on the animal, and slaughtered it. The priest took the blood and sprinkled it on the altar. As with the fellowship offering, the "fat portions" were burned on the altar. If a priest was involved in the sin, the remainder of the sacrificial animal was carried outside the camp and burned on the ash heap (4:12, 21; 6:30). If not, the meat was given to him to eat (6:26, 29; 7:7).

6. The guilt offering (5:14 – 6:7)

The guilt offering provided for the restitution of a wrong (5:16a; 6:5) along with atonement for the wrong itself (5:16b, 18; 6:7). When restitution was made, the proper value was determined and a fifth (5:16; 6:5) of that was added to the repayment. The atonement in each case was the offering of a ram (5:15; 6:6).

7. Sacrificial instructions pertaining to priests (6:8 – 7:38)

This section addresses the various laws regarding how the priests of Israel were to offer the various offerings presented to the Lord by the people. The offerings mentioned include the burnt offering (see 1:3 – 17), grain offering (see 2:1 – 16), sin offering (see 4:1 – 5:13), guilt offering (5:14 – 6:7), and the fellowship offering (3:1 – 17).

B. The Consecration of the Priests (8:1 – 9:24)

The writer carefully labels the various offerings according to the types of sacrifices described in the first part of the book. He underscores the priests' careful attention to detail by reminding us that all was done "as the LORD commanded Moses" (8:17, 21, 29).

After the seven days of consecration for the priests, Moses gathered Aaron, his sons, and the elders of Israel and instructed them to prepare for the appearance of the glory of the Lord at the tabernacle. At the conclusion, Moses and Aaron went into the Tent of Meeting (the tabernacle). The response of the people echoes God's acceptance of them: "when all the people saw it, they shouted for joy and fell facedown" (9:24).

C. The Death of Nadab and Abihu (10:1 – 20)

Following the death of Nadab and Abihu, Mishael and Elzaphan, the sons of Aaron's uncle Uzziel, were summoned to carry the bodies out of the tabernacle so that Aaron and his other sons would not become defiled.

It is important to note that Moses himself interpreted the severe judgment of Nadab and Abihu by laying down the principle, "Among those who approach me [God] I will be proved holy ... I will be honored" (v.3). The purpose of the instructions for sacrifices was to provide a means of treating God as holy and honoring him before all the people. Nadab and Abihu had refused to come before him "as he had commanded."

The overall lesson of this narrative plays an important role in delineating the ongoing responsibility of Aaron's priesthood, i.e., discerning between the holy and the profane, the clean and the unclean (vv.10–11; cf. Hag 2:11–12). In the chapters that follow, Moses will go into great detail in listing just these kinds of distinctions between the holy and the common, the unclean and the clean (11:47).

D. The Laws of Purity and Impurity (11:1 – 15:33)

1. Regulations concerning animals (11:1 – 47)

This chapter contains a selected list of creatures, dividing each type into various classes of purity. It has regulations about four major groups of animals: land animals, birds, water animals, and small creeping things. The determining category was whether a class of animals was unclean or clean (v.47). The goal was to determine whether or not an animal could be eaten. Violating any of these regulations rendered one unclean and thus unable to enter into community worship (12:4b). Ultimately, the purpose of the chapter is to tie the concept of holiness to God's own example of holiness (11:45b).

2. Purification relating to childbirth (12:1 – 8)

This short chapter concerns the case of purification related to a woman in childbirth. As long as the woman was unclean, "she must not touch anything sacred or go to the sanctuary" (v.4). The sense of impurity is thus defined with respect to the goal of the covenant and the goal of creation, i.e., the worship of God.

3. Regulations dealing with skin diseases (13:1 – 14:57)

The contents of this chapter are described as "the regulations for any defiling skin disease, for a sore, for defiling molds in fabric or in a house" (14:54 – 55). Its purpose was "to determine when something is clean or unclean" (v.57). Various tests for skin disease are enumerated first, and then the cleansing procedures are described.

When a skin disease was detected, there was no provision for healing the disease. Rather, the diseased person was required to "wear torn clothes, let their hair be unkempt, cover the lower part of their face and cry out, 'Unclean! Unclean!'" (13:45). Such a person was to live alone "outside the camp" (v.46). When clothing was infected, it was either washed and reexamined (v.54) or destroyed (vv.52, 57).

Chapter 14 deals with provisions for cleansing from the diseases enumerated in the preceding passage. This "cleansing" was a procedure for pronouncing that one had been healed. First, the provisions for cleansing diseases on the flesh are given (vv.1 – 32) and then those for cleansing diseases from the house (vv.33 – 53).

4. Discharges Causing Uncleanness (15:1 – 33)

There are two major sections in this chapter: (1) regulations for a man with a discharge (vv.3 – 18); (2) regulations for a woman with a discharge (vv.19 – 30). Instructions for cleansing are the same for both men and women. They were to wait seven days after the discharge had ceased. Then they were to wash their clothes and themselves with fresh water. On the eighth day, they were to offer two doves or pigeons at the Tent of Meeting — one a sin offering and the other a burnt offering. The chapter ends with an important reminder of the purpose of the purity laws.

E. The Day of Atonement (16:1 – 34)

As a prelude to the instructions for the Day of Atonement, the author recalls the tragic fate of Aaron's two sons, Nadab and Abihu (16:1). The fire that had consumed them served as a vivid reminder that God must be approached with utmost reverence and holiness.

On the Day of Atonement the high priest was first consecrated (vv.3 – 4) through the sacrifice of a young bull and ram for himself, and two male goats and a ram for the Israelite community. One of the goats was marked by lot as belonging to the Lord and other as a "scapegoat." The goat belonging to the Lord was offered as a sin offering for the people, and its blood was taken "behind the curtain" and sprinkled on the atonement cover (v.15). The second goat made atonement by being sent into the desert, bearing the sins of the nation. The high priest laid his hands on the goat, confessed all of Israel's sins, and sent the goat away.

The high priest then changed into his regular priestly garments and sacrificed the second ram for a burnt offering for himself and the community's ram for a burnt offering for them. The bull and goat used for the sin offering were taken outside the camp and completely burned.

F. Warnings against Improper Actions (17:1 – 16)

Verses 1 – 9 show that God's people at large had begun to sacrifice to "goat idols," a form of false worship that led them away from the worship of God prescribed in the Sinai covenant. What was needed, therefore, were more laws for the everyday life of the people to ensure that they remained holy and faithful to God. The rest of ch. 17 contains such laws.

II. Holiness in the Life of the People (18:1 – 27:34)

This section contains material concerned with the description and necessary instructions on how Israel was to become a holy nation — a nation set apart to God.

A. The Conduct of God's People (18:1 – 20:27)

Several features of this passage parallel Ge 9:20 – 27, where Noah's son Ham looked upon his father's nakedness; consequently the Canaanites, descendants of Ham, were cursed.

1. Introduction (18:1 – 5)

These laws were God's "decrees," and Israel was to "keep" them by obeying them (v.4). The result of keeping them was life (v.5).

2. The defilements of the Canaanites (18:6 – 30)

These laws were to distinguish the Israelites from the inhabitants of the land that they were to possess (v.24). Sexual relations are prohibited: (1) among family members (vv.6 – 18); (2) during the monthly period (v.19); (3) with a neighbor's wife (v.20); (4) in idolatry to Molek (v.21); (5) in homosexual relations (v.22); and (6) in bestiality (v.23).

3. Statutes and Judgments (19:1 – 37)

This section is introduced with the admonition, "Be holy because I, the LORD your God, am holy." The first section (vv.1 – 18) consists of a list of twenty-one laws. The second section (vv.19 – 37), also with twenty-one laws, is introduced with the admonition, "Keep my decrees" (v.19a) and concludes with a similar admonition (v.37a) and the statement, "I am the LORD" (v.37b; cf. vv.25, 28, 30, 31, 32, 34, 36).

4. Holiness laws (20:1 – 27)

This section consists of fourteen (2 x 7) laws, concluded by an extended appeal for holiness on the part of the nation when they possess the land of Canaan (vv.22 – 26). After the conclusion, the prohibition of mediums and spiritists (v.6) is restated (v.27).

B. The Condition of Priests within the Community (21:1 – 22:33)

1. Regulations for priests: First list (21:1 – 15)

The list has a brief introduction (v.1) and ends with the introduction to the next list (v.16). There are fourteen (2 x 7) laws in the list.

2. Regulations for priests: Second list (21:16 – 24)

This list is introduced by the expression "The LORD said to Moses, 'Say to Aaron ...'" (vv.16 – 17) and is concluded by the expression, "So Moses told this to Aaron ..." (v.24). There are fourteen (2 x 7) laws in the list.

3. Regulations for priests: Third list (22:1 – 33)

The first nine verses discuss things that profane a priest. Between a short introduction (vv.1 – 2) and concluding statement (v.9), seven laws are given.

Verses 10 – 15 give regulations on persons not authorized to eat the sacred offering. The basic principle was, "No one outside a priest's family may eat the sacred offering" (v.10). Then follow seven laws on priestly offerings (vv.17 – 25), which "will not be accepted on your behalf, because they are deformed and have defects" (v.25b).

The chapter closes with seven laws on time intervals of sacrifices (vv.26 – 33).

C. The Calendar of the Religious Seasons (23:1 – 24:23)

1. Seasonal Events (23:1 – 44)

Seven special seasons of the year are enumerated: the Sabbath, the Passover and Unleavened Bread, the Firstfruits, the Feast of Weeks, the Feast of Trumpets, the Day of Atonement, and the Feast of Tabernacles.

2. Continual offerings (24:1 – 9)

Two continual offerings are enumerated — the burning of oil in the golden lampstand (vv.1 – 4) and the preparation of the twelve loaves of bread on the golden table (vv.5 – 9). The bread was a regular part of the share of Aaron and his sons.

3. A blasphemer stoned and lex talionis (24:10 – 23)

Embedded in the narrative about the stoning of a blasphemer is a reminder of the penalty for murder. Note that the "entire assembly" was responsible for stoning the blasphemer (v.14). Thus, an important distinction is made between capital punishment and murder. Capital punishment was an act of the whole community, whereas murder was an individual act.

D. The Sabbath and Jubilee Years (25:1 – 55)

The central theme of this last set of instructions is that of restoration. Israel's life was to be governed by a pattern of seven-year periods, called sabbath years. After seven periods of seven years, the year of Jubilee promoted total restoration for God's people.

1. The sabbath year (25:1 – 7)

The sabbath year was to replicate God's provisions for the human race in the garden of Eden. Also, humanity was to share equally in all the good of God's provision (v.6). Here, as on many other occasions, the writer of the Pentateuch has envisioned Israel's possession of the good land promised to them as a return to Eden.

2. The Jubilee year (25:8 – 55)

Every seven sabbath years, Israel was to proclaim a special Sabbath year, a Jubilee year. This fiftieth year was set apart as a holy year in which to make total restoration of land, property, and debts. On the first day of that year, a ram's horn was to be sounded and the Jubilee year proclaimed (v.9). The term "Jubilee" is a word play on the Hebrew term for "ram's horn" (*yobel*).

In this year, all property bought or sold reverted to its original owner. Thus the land could not be sold permanently (v.23). This restriction was because all the land belonged to God and the people of Israel were considered tenants on God's land.

E. Final Conditions of the Covenant (26:1 – 46)

1. Introduction (26:1 – 2)

These verses summarize the conditions for the covenant reestablished after the incident of the golden calf. Thus, as has been the form throughout God's address to Israel on Mount Sinai, the statement of the conditions of the covenant is prefaced by a reminder of two central laws: the prohibition of idolatry (v.1) and the call to observe the Sabbath (v.2).

2. General statement of the purpose of the covenant (26:3 – 13)

If Israel obeyed God's decrees and commands, they would live with great blessing in the Promised Land. The description of life in the land is reminiscent of God's original blessing in the garden of Eden (see Ge 1:26, 28 – 29; 2:8; 3:8).

3. Warning of results of disobedience (26:14 – 39)

If Israel rejected God's decrees and commands, they would experience divine punishment (vv.14 – 31), their land would be destroyed (v.32), and they would be sent into exile (vv.33 – 39).

4. Hope for the future (26:40 – 46)

If Israel repented and humbled themselves, God would remember his covenant with Abraham, Isaac, and Jacob, and his promise of the land, and he would not break his covenant with them. He had remembered them in Egypt, and he would do so again.

F. Vows and Tithes (27:1 – 34)

Just as God's giving of the law at Sinai began with Ten Commandments, so it now ends with a list of ten laws. These laws deal with the process of payment of vows and tithes made to the Lord. Some vows allowed for payment with a substitute (sometimes with the one-fifth more value added); some did not. A heightened form of vow was called a "devotion" *(cherem;* see NIV note on v.28). In this vow the person or thing devoted was given without reservation to the Lord. Such a vow could not be reversed. Finally, a tenth of the livestock was given to the Lord (vv.32 – 33). The institution of the tithe had already been established (cf. Ge 28:20 – 22; 14:20). Here the tithe is said to belong to the Lord (see also Nu 18:8 – 32).

NUMBERS

Introduction

The English title "Numbers" is based on the "numbering," or census, of the people in chs. 1 and 26. The events recorded fall into the time of the last days at Sinai and the period of Israel's sojourn in the desert. There are two main divisions to the book, chs. 1–14 and chs. 15–36, which fall on either side of the account of Israel's failure to trust in God (ch. 14). In ch. 20 Moses and Aaron also failed to trust God. Both failures resulted in failure to receive God's blessing of the land.

I. The Census and the Organization of the People (1:1 – 2:34)

After the tabernacle had been set up, a census was taken in each of the tribes to determine who would serve in the military. The author gives an accurate picture of the scale of operations and necessary preparations for Israel's return to Canaan.

A. The Census (1:1 – 54)

Moses and Aaron were instructed to count all men in the camp twenty years old and up who were able to serve in the army. Twelve men, one from each tribe, were appointed to help with the count (see 1:5–15). The total from each tribe is listed in vv.16–46, giving a number of 603,550. The Levites (those of the tribe of Levi, including Moses and Aaron) were not included in the census. Their task was separate from the rest of the Israelites, and thus they conducted their own census in 3:15 and 4:34ff.

B. The Arrangement of the Tribal Camps (2:1 – 34)

The arrangement of the tribes around the tabernacle served to highlight the importance and centrality of the tribe of Judah, which had already gained the ascendancy over the other tribes (cf. Ge 49:1 – 27). It was from this tribe that the royal son would be born who would bring redemption to God's people.

II. The Levites (3:1 – 4:49)

The duties of the Levites were as follows:

(1) The Gershonites (camped west of the tabernacle) were to care for the tabernacle, its coverings, the curtain at the entrance to the Tent of Meeting, the curtains of the courtyard, the curtain at the entrance to the courtyard, and the ropes (3:21 – 26).

(2) The Kohathites (camped south of the tabernacle) were to care for the sanctuary — the ark, the table, the lampstand, the altars, the articles of the sanctuary, and the curtain (3:27 – 32).

(3) When the tabernacle was moved, the priests (sons of Aaron), under the guidance of Eleazar (4:16), were to go into the sanctuary to prepare it to be moved. The various holy articles were wrapped in cloth and skins and readied for carrying. When all had been prepared, the Kohathites were brought in to carry the various articles.

(4) The Merarites (camped north of the tabernacle) were to care for the frames of the tabernacle, the crossbars, posts, bases, tent pegs, and ropes (3:33 – 37).

III. Holiness among the People (5:1 – 6:27)

The writer now focuses on the individual Israelites. They also were to be a part of the holy nation (Ex 19:5). The writer demonstrates the importance of the total commitment of all the people to the requirements of God's covenant.

A. The Purity of the Camp (5:1 – 4)

In Lev 13 – 15 Moses had instructed the priests how to examine and identify diseases. As the camp became progressively purer, we notice that these commands were being carried out. This theme will not continue long, however, for the people quickly turned from God's way and failed to continue to trust in him.

B. Treachery against Others and God (5:5 – 10)

This narrative recalls the law given in Lev 5:14 – 6:7 in order to demonstrate the wrongfulness of acting treacherously against one's neighbor. One committing such an offense was "unfaithful to the LORD." The point is clear — wrongs committed among God's people were wrongs committed against God himself.

C. The Law of Jealousy (5:11 – 31)

The case of the jealous husband is a curious law that raises many questions about the nature of social relationships in ancient Israel. There is, however, not enough information given here to allow even a sketchy reconstruction of the details of this ritual.

D. The Nazirite (6:1 – 21)

Little is known about the origin and practice of the Nazirite vow in ancient Israel. God instructed Moses how to regulate that practice, not to establish it. Note how God made provisions not just for the priest but for all God's people to commit themselves to holiness before God.

The Nazirite vow entailed abstention from three things for a specified length of time: drinking wine or fermented drink (vv.3 – 4), cutting one's hair (v.5), and contacting a dead body (vv.6 – 7). At the conclusion of the vow, certain offerings were required (vv.13 – 20). An important provision was made for the Nazirite who, because of an emergency situation, had broken the vow (vv.9 – 12). In other words, some things in life superseded the requirements of the vow. After the emergency had passed, there were provisions for completing the vow (vv.9ff.).

E. The Priestly Blessing (6:22 – 27)

At the close of this section we find the priestly blessing; a central task of the priests was to be a source of blessing for God's people. Conversely, the people were to find their blessing only in the priesthood, not apart from it. The holiness and blessing of the people was dependent on their recognition of the divine sanction of the priesthood.

IV. The Dedication of the Tabernacle (7:1 – 9:23)

A. The Dedication of the Altar (7:1 – 89)

As God's people had been generous in giving to the construction of the tabernacle (Ex 35:4 – 29), now they showed the same generosity in its dedication. The whole of the nation gave sacrificially to God's work. The writer has delayed any mention of the fulfillment of God's promise to speak to the people from between the cherubim until the completion of the dedication of the altar.

B. The Lighting of the Golden Lampstand (8:1 – 4)

At the construction of the golden lampstand (cf. Ex 25:32 – 40; 37:17 – 24), no mention was made of its lighting. The writer has waited until now to tell us that, as part of the dedication of the tabernacle, the lamps were lit.

C. The Dedication of the Levites (8:5 – 26)

God had instructed Moses on how the Levites were to be consecrated (vv.5 – 19); now those instructions were faithfully carried out (8:20 – 26).

D. The Passover (9:1 – 14)

The Passover was celebrated on the fourteenth day of the first month of the second year as commanded by Moses (Ex 12). But an unanticipated problem arose. Some were unable to partake of the celebration because they were unclean. Moses' response to this new situation demonstrates how many of the laws in ancient Israel were carried out.

E. God's Leading in the Wilderness (9:15 – 23)

As God had led the Israelites to Sinai by the pillar of cloud and fire (Ex 13:21 – 22), so now he began to lead them to the Promised Land. At this point in their walk with the Lord, Israel was obedient and followed his guidance. Seven times this narrative says they obeyed the Lord's command and traveled when the cloud lifted from the tabernacle (9:18, 20, 23; cf. Ex 17:1).

V. The Departure from Sinai (10:1 – 12:16)

A. The Silver Trumpets (10:1 – 10)

As the people prepared to leave Sinai, a series of bugle calls sounded for the sons of Aaron to help lead the people on their march through the desert. As the people followed the cloud that led them through the wilderness, the blasts of the bugle kept the order in their ranks. The tribe of Judah moved out at the first blast. The rest of the tribes followed in order at each successive call of the bugle.

B. Departure from Sinai (10:11 – 36)

There was an orderly and obedient departure from Sinai, a far cry from the scene that Moses saw when he first returned from the mountain and found the nation celebrating before the golden calf by "running wild" (Ex 32:25). But as the narrative continues, it becomes apparent that the law had not resulted in any fundamental change in the ways of the people.

Moses asked his father-in-law (Hobab or Jethro) to remain with Israel because he knew this desert well and could help find suitable campsites (v.29), but he does not appear to have acceded to Moses' request. The Kohathites carried the ark ahead of the people "for three days" (10:33), and the people followed as God (Dt 1:32 – 33) led them through the desert by means of the cloud (Nu 9:15 – 23).

C. Fire from the Lord (11:1 – 3)

At the beginning of large narrative segments that deal with Israel's departure to the Promised Land, Israel comes face to face with God and the threat of his sudden wrath. This occasion is due to the people's complaining about their misfortunes.

D. Manna and the Spirit of God (11:4 – 35)

The people complained about manna in the desert and yearned to return to Egypt (vv.4 – 9). Moses discussed this complaint with God, and God responded by promising to send his Spirit on the select seventy elders (vv.10 – 17). Then God sent the people food in the form of quail, but as they were gathering the quail, this blessing suddenly became a kind of ironic punishment for those who had complained (vv.31 – 34).

The central purpose of this section appears to be to show the failure of Moses' office as mediator for the people. The kind of leadership exhibited by Moses is placed alongside the role of the Spirit of God.

E. Miriam and Aaron Oppose Moses (12:1 – 16)

Miriam and Aaron's opposition to Moses' leadership is brief and leaves many details unexplained. Its meaning, however, is clear from its relation to the previous chapter. Moses himself insinuated the superiority of this new form of leadership in saying, "I wish that all the LORD's people were prophets" (11:29). In this way, the narrative raises important questions about the role of a leader like Moses. This chapter vindicates Moses' divinely given leadership and brushes aside any further suggestion that the type of leadership epitomized in Moses was no longer valid.

VI. The Defeat of the First Generation (13:1 – 14:45)

This section introduces the theme of God's faithfulness in keeping the covenant and the unfaithfulness of human beings in trusting him. This is particularly notable in the account of sending the spies. The same theme is reintroduced in the account of Moses' giving water to the people from the rock (20:1 – 13).

A. Spying Out the Land of Canaan (13:1 – 25)

God instructed Moses to send spies from each of the tribes into the land. He sent twelve spies into the Negev and hill country to "see what the land is like and whether the people who live there are strong or weak, few or many" (v.18). The spies spent forty days in the land and returned to Moses at Kadesh with fruit they had gathered from the land (cf. also Dt 1:22 – 23).

B. The Report of the Spies (13:26 – 33)

The twelve spies reported that the land was filled with "milk and honey" and that there were strong fortified cities occupied by the descendants of Anak (v.28). However, they also gave a "bad report" saying, "We cannot attack those people; they are stronger than we are" (v.31). Only Joshua and Caleb trusted in God to help them take the land (v.30; 14:6 – 7).

C. The Unbelief of the People (14:1 – 12)

In the midst of the crying of the people, the Lord spoke to Moses in the Tent of Meeting, "How long will these people treat me with contempt … in spite of all the miraculous signs I have performed among them?" (vv.11 – 12). The Lord calls their fearful response to the spies' report an act of unbelief. They failed to trust in God. God was prepared to judge them with pestilence and to dispossess them for their lack of faith.

D. Moses' Intercession (14:13 – 19)

But as has happened before (e.g., Ex 32:11ff.), Moses interceded for Israel and replied to the Lord that his rejection of this people in the wilderness would have a lasting effect on the nations around them.

E. The People Are Judged (14:20–38)

Israel had broken their covenant with the Lord, and he could have right-fully cast them off. But the Lord was gracious to them, "slow to anger, abounding in love" (v.18; cf. Ex 33:19). He heard Moses' plea on behalf of the people. Though Israel proved unfaithful, God remained faithful and gracious.

The end result of Israel's lack of faith was nevertheless severe. With the exception of Joshua and Caleb, that whole generation who did not believe died in the desert (v.29) over the next forty years (v.33).

F. The Presumption of the People (14:39–45)

The people then decided to take the land without the Lord's help. This is the reverse side of their unbelief. Not only did they fail to trust God to give them the land, but in desperation and in unbelief they attempted to take it on their own. Without God's help, they failed.

VII. Laws Given during and at the Close of the Thirty-Eight Years (15:1–19:22)

A. Seven Laws (15:1–36)

Here are seven selected laws, the last of which is the penalty for "anyone who sins defiantly." Then follows an example of a defiant sin, namely, the willful disregard of God's Sabbath. After this example of the neglect of God's law, the law regarding the wearing of tassels was placed because the tassels were to serve as reminders to keep the law.

The laws here regarding grain offerings are not those of Lev 2, which were offered separately as a gift, but are introduced here for the first time and are to be offered along with either a burnt offering or fellowship offering.

In the case of the man caught gathering wood on the Sabbath (vv.32–36), it should be noted that Moses did not immediately put the offender to death, as stipulated in Ex 31:14 and 35:2. Rather, he put him away "because it was not clear what was to be done to him" (Nu 15:34).

B. Tassels (15:37–41)

The account of the command to make tassels for their garments demon-strates the underlying purpose of many of the laws given to Israel—so that

Israel might be reminded of the necessity of trusting God and obeying his commands.

C. Rebellion and Reaffirmation (16:1 – 18:32)

In 16:1–40, the Levites instigated an organized opposition to the authority of Aaron and the priests. They contended that in claiming the unique right and responsibility to represent the people before God, Moses and Aaron had "gone too far" (v.3). That Moses was aware of this fact surfaces in his response to the Levites: "You ... have gone too far!" (v.9, lit. trans.).

To show that the rebellion of the Levites represented the mood of the whole community, the writer places immediately after this narrative an account of the opposition of the "whole Israelite community" (vv.41 – 50). Rather than having felt contrition and repentance, the people grumbled at the Lord's punishment of the rebellious Levites.

Ironically, as the narrative concludes, it is the intercession of Aaron and his priesthood that ultimately saves the lives of the people in the ensuing plague. He "stood between the living and the dead, and the plague stopped" (v.48), and he "made atonement for them" (v.47).

As a continual reminder of the special office of priest and the importance of the house of Aaron, God gave Israel another "sign"—Aaron's budding staff (17:10)—to remind the people of the death of those who had tried to usurp the place of Aaron and his family and to go near to God in the tabernacle on their own.

Much of the material covered in ch. 18 has already been given in chs. 2–3 and in Lev 6. What is unique in the repetition of the material here is the fact that Moses is not mentioned in the instructions to the priests. Whereas earlier the Lord had spoken about the priests' duties to Moses as well as Aaron, here he speaks only to Aaron and his sons.

After a restatement of the distinct roles of the priests and Levites (18:1–7), the provisions for the priests (vv.8–20) and the Levites (vv.21–32) follow. The Levites were to be supported by the payment of a tithe (v.21). They in turn were to support the priests by paying a tithe of what was given to them (v.28).

D. Water of Cleansing (19:1 – 22)

Chapter 19 is about preparation of the "water of cleansing" (vv.1–10). Then follow two examples of the use of this water: purification from contact with a dead body (vv.11–13), and purification after being in the same tent with a dead body (vv.14–22).

To prepare the water required a "red heifer" without any blemish. The description of the red heifer ritual (vv.1 – 10) is then explained by the two examples of its use in vv.11 – 22. The two central features of the ritual are the "ashes" (vv.9 – 10) of the heifer and the "water of cleansing" (v.9) over which they are sprinkled.

VIII. Travel from Kadesh to the Border of Canaan (20:1 – 21:35)

A. Water from the Rock (20:1 – 13)

It was now the first month of their last year in the desert. The Israelites had been wandering in the Desert of Paran (13:3; 14:32 – 33) forty years (see 14:39 – 45; Dt 1:46), and they were now encamped at Kadesh (20:1). By 22:1, Israel reached the final destination in their travels in the Pentateuch, the "plains of Moab" (cf. 33:49).

The writer includes a brief notice of the death of Miriam in 20:1b in the fortieth year of their stay in the desert. Her death serves as a reminder that she did not enter the Promised Land with the new generation. Not even Aaron, the high priest, was allowed to enter into the Promised Land (see also 33:38). The central concern of ch. 20, however, is that Moses himself was not allowed to enter Canaan. What had happened to the people because of their unbelief in ch. 14 was now being repeated in Israel's leadership — Miriam, Aaron, and Moses were to die in the wilderness, not able to enjoy the blessings of the Sinai covenant, the gift of God's good land.

The writer was not so much interested that we know the details of this incident. Rather, the emphasis is that Moses and Aaron could not enter the land because they did not believe. Just as the people had failed to believe God and trust in him in ch. 14, so also Moses and Aaron have come up short in the area of faith.

B. Edom Denies Israel Passage (20:14 – 21)

A coherent sequence in the events of 20:14 – 21:4 is difficult to obtain from this narrative. Perhaps they are not listed in chronological order. Both the story of Israel's rebellion in ch. 14 and that of Moses in the previous episode are followed by reversals in warfare: Israel's defeat by the Amalekites (14:40 – 45) and Edom's refusal to let Israel pass through their land (20:14 – 21).

C. The Death of Aaron (20:22 – 29)

Surprisingly little is written of the death of Aaron. His death foreshadowed the death of Moses, perhaps because they were both guilty of the same sin, failure to trust the Lord (20:12), although here their sin is called "rebellion" (20:24; cf. Dt 32:48–50). Just as Moses would be commanded by the Lord to go to the top of a mountain and die (27:12–14; Dt 32:48–50; 34:5), so here Aaron was told to go up to Mount Hor and die.

D. Arad Destroyed (21:1–3)

In Ex 17, just after Moses brought forth water from the rock, the Amalekites were defeated while Moses held up his hands (in prayer). Now, after Israel's murmuring and of gaining water from the rock (Nu 20:1–13), Israel was attacked by the Canaanites but miraculously went on to defeat them because of Israel's prayer (21:1–3).

E. The Bronze Serpent (21:4–9)

Is it unusual that God would command Moses to make an image of a snake as a sign of Israel's faith since earlier God had forbidden them to make a likeness "of anything in heaven above or on the earth beneath" (Ex 20:4)? No, for this image was not intended as an idol for worship (though later it became that, see 2Ki 18:4). God honored this object when it was put up before the people, and they looked to it in faith. The bronze serpent is similar to Gideon's gold ephod, which later generations worshiped (see Jdg 8:27).

F. The Journey to Moab (21:10–20)

The Israelites moved around Edom and into the territory of Moab. The writer has also included a selection from "the Book of the Wars of the LORD." This book is not known apart from this one reference. The selection is apparently given to verify that the Arnon River was the border of Moab. The land of Moab is the central focus of the next several chapters of Numbers.

G. The Defeat of Sihon (21:21–32; cf. Dt 2:24–37)

Only the bare facts of the battle and its causes are noted here. Fortunately, the poetic sayings in vv.27ff. include further details. These sayings focus on the previous military conquests of Sihon when he defeated Moab and captured their territory (v.26). Such historical notes justify Israel's conquest of this area. The land once occupied by Moab was at this time in the hands of the Amorites. According to God's instructions, the territory belonging to the Moabites was not to be disturbed by the conquering Israelites because they were the descendants of Lot (Dt 2:9).

H. The Defeat of Og (21:33 – 35; Dt 3:1 – 11)

What God had done for Israel with their defeat of Sihon, he would continue to do with victories over the rest of Israel's enemies (see 21:34). This provides an interpretive context for the events in the more detailed story in chs. 22 – 24. As ch. 21 ends, we see Israel as a threat to Moab. Their king, Balak, resorted to magic and incantations to defeat God's people, but such means are futile against the plans of a sovereign God.

IX. Balaam (22:1 – 24:25)

The Balaam narratives have long puzzled readers of the Bible. The primary enigma centers on Balaam himself. As a historical character, he fits quite well among other ancient Near Eastern religious men. As a biblical character, however, Balaam appears to be neither fish nor fowl. He was not an Israelite (22:5), yet he appeared to know God (22:8), and God spoke through him (24:2 – 4, 15 – 16). He practiced magic and incantations (24:1) and eventually led Israel into apostasy (31:16). In the end he was killed by the Israelites in their destruction of the Midianites (31:8).

The narrative opens with an account of Balak's dread of the great numbers of Israel. Balak, the king of Moab, hired Balaam to curse the seed of Abraham, but as the story unfolds, God only permitted him to bless them. In spite of the nations' attempts to curse God's people, all that could ultimately happen is their blessing. Through Balaam the seed of Abraham is blessed and the seed of Moab is cursed (24:17; cf. Ge 12:3).

X. The Establishment of the New Leadership in Israel: The Priests and the Prophets (25:1 – 27:23)

A. The Failure of the Old Leaders: Moab Seduces Israel (25:1 – 18)

As is often the case in the Bible, God's act of salvation is immediately followed by the apostasy of the people. In this case, "the men began to indulge in sexual immorality with Moabite women" (v.1); this led to their following after their gods.

Amid this time of apostasy, the writer illustrates not only the horrible conditions among the Israelites but also the need for new forms of leadership. When Kozbi (v.15) was taken into the tent of an Israelite man before the eyes of Moses and the whole congregation, there was much distress but little action. Moses himself was remarkably ineffective in the face of a blatant transgression (v.6). The day was saved, however, by the decisive action of someone from the next generation of priests, Phinehas, the grandson of Aaron. Through his zeal for the Lord, he stayed God's judgment, and the house of Phinehas was rewarded with "a covenant of lasting priesthood" (v.13).

B. The Second Census (26:1 – 65)

This census took place in the plains of Moab (v.3), where the Israelites had camped just before the incident with Balak and Balaam (22:1). The author's purpose is to stress that none of the earlier generation had survived except for Joshua and Caleb (vv.64 – 65; cf. 14:22 – 24). What God had said has been fulfilled. In other words, God's word is sure and certain. What he has promised, he will do. The writer is thus building a case about God: he is faithful in both judgment and salvation (cf. Ge 41:32).

Instructions for the parceling out of the land by lot are given in vv.52 – 56.

C. Zelophehad's Daughters (27:1 – 11)

This narrative about the daughters of Zelophehad intentionally addresses this question: How can one preserve a lineage in the absence of sons? According to v.8, the property rights and family name were to go to the daughters if there were no sons in the family. If there were no daughters, the rights were to go to one of the brothers; and if no brothers, then the family rights were to go to the uncle or nearest of kin.

D. Joshua Appointed Successor to Moses (27:12 – 23)

The succession of Moses and Joshua is cast as a succession of the prophetic office guided by the Spirit of God. It is appropriate here that Moses refers to God in this passage as "the God who gives breath to all living things" (v.16).

Verse 21 describes the relationship between the two offices of priest and (prophetic) leader. The priest, Eleazar, was to enquire of the Lord by means of the Urim. The (prophetic) leader, Joshua, was to follow his advice.

XI. Regular Celebrations (28:1 – 29:40)

Instructions for the regular celebrations in Israel's worship calendar have been mentioned at various points in the Pentateuch, but there was still need of gathering these together into a summary statement and of specifying the nature of their additional offerings.

A. Daily Offerings (28:1 – 8)

These provisions, given in Ex 29:38 – 42, are repeated here for complete-ness, apparently because they had not been mentioned in Lev 23.

B. Sabbath Offerings (28:9 – 10)

Observance of the Sabbath rest was grounded in creation when God him-self "rested" from all his work (Ge 2:2 – 3). It was prescribed as part of the Decalogue in Ex 20:8 – 11 and was included as part of the regular celebra-tions in Lev 23:3. But Lev 23 made no mention about specific offerings on this day; it is mentioned here for the first time (cf. Eze 46:1ff.).

C. Monthly Offerings (28:11 – 15)

In the instructions for regular worship in Lev 23, setting apart the first of the month (the new moon) as a special day is not mentioned. In Nu 10:10, however, there is mention of the "first of the month" as a time set apart for celebration by the blowing of trumpets. In other words, this list is intended to be complete.

D. Yearly Celebrations (28:16 – 29:40)

1. The Passover and Unleavened Bread (28:16 – 25)

The Passover as described in Lev 23:5 – 8 recounts that a "food offering" was to be presented to the Lord for each of the seven days of the Feast of Unleavened Bread. In the present passage, the nature of this "food offer-ing" is described (28:19 – 22).

2. The Feast of Weeks (28:26 – 31; Dt 16:9 – 12)

Fifty days after the time of the "firstfruits" the Feast of Weeks was cel-ebrated. In Lev 23:18, this feast already called for the offering of seven lambs, a bull, and two rams. As this passage is traditionally interpreted, the offerings described here (two bulls, a ram, and seven lambs) were to be given in addition to those noted in Lev 23.

3. The Feast of Trumpets (29:1 – 6)

The Feast of Trumpets, celebrated on the first day of the seventh month, is mentioned in Lev 23:23 – 25 as a time of special remembrance. The offer-ings for that day are listed here. (Eventually this day was known as Rosh Hashanah, a New Year's Day feast.)

4. The Day of Atonement (29:7 – 11)

Instructions for the celebration of the Day of Atonement on the tenth day of the seventh month are recorded in Lev 23:27 – 32; the "atonement" offerings are described in Lev 16. Here the writer lists only those offerings prescribed in addition to those of Lev 16. The Day of Atonement was to have its own sin offering of a male goat (v.11).

5. The Feast of Tabernacles (29:12 – 40)

The Feast of Tabernacles is described in Lev 23:33 – 43. It was to mark the time of the "ingathering," or harvest, of crops and thus corresponds roughly to our Thanksgiving Day. The present chapter is devoted only to the special offerings for the eight days of its celebration. The sheer volume of the required offerings and sacrifices suggests that this was considered the grandest of the early feast days. On each successive day of the feast, one less bull was offered.

XII. Vows for Men and Women (30:1 – 16)

The mention of vows in 29:39 calls for an arrangement and placement of vows. This chapter focuses on the relationship between husbands and wives as well as fathers and daughters (see also Lev 27; Nu 6:1 – 21).

The section begins with a general statement of obligation in making vows: When a man made a vow, he was bound by it (v.2). A man was also responsible for vows made by women in his household. If he heard his daughter or his wife make a vow, a man could nullify the vow by speaking out. If he did not, the vow was left to stand. In the case of a widow or a divorced woman (i.e., where there was no father or husband), the word of the woman alone sufficed (v.9).

XIII. Battle with the Midianites (31:1 – 54)

The narrative now returns to the sin of the people at Baal Peor (ch. 25). Just as Phinehas was responsible for putting an end to the people's apostasy in ch. 25, so here he was called upon to carry out the revenge on the Midianites. In the ensuing battle, the 12,000 Israelite soldiers, under the command of Phinehas, killed "every man," including the five kings of Midian and Balaam, son of Beor.

By saving the women and children of Midian, the Israelite officers renewed the old threat of mixing with Canaanite women and thus forsaking the Lord. Hence they inadvertently returned to the dangerous conditions of ch. 25.

XIV. The Transjordan Tribes (32:1 – 42)

The half tribe of Manasseh is not mentioned along with Reuben and Gad at the beginning of the narrative. To clarify their also being allotted a portion of the area of the Transjordan, the writer concludes with an account of the conquests of the descendants of Manasseh in this region (vv.39–42).

The tribe of Manasseh was allotted Gilead (v.40), a parcel of land requested by Reuben and Gad (v.1). This implies that the initial request of Reuben and Gad included the allotment of Manasseh. Thus it appears that Gilead was given both to Reuben (v.1) and Manasseh (v.40). This difficulty is later explained, in that half of Gilead went to the tribe of Reuben and half to Manasseh (Dt 3:12–13; cf. Jos 13:24–31).

XV. Israel's Camps in the Desert (33:1 – 49)

The list of encampments in the desert begins with the Israelites' departure from Rameses in Egypt on the fifteenth day of the first month and concludes with their encampment on the "plains of Moab" (see 22:1). Between these two are forty camps, perhaps reflecting the forty years spent in the desert. But the list is selective, since some sites recorded earlier are not included (e.g., Shur, Taberah, and Hormah).

Within the list of encampments are two short narratives that center on the work of Moses (vv.2–3) and Aaron (vv.38–39). In these two segments are found the only dates for Israel's journeys (vv.3, 38b), marking the beginning and end of the forty-year period in the desert.

XVI. Preparation for Possession of the Promised Land (33:50 – 36:13)

A. The Division of the Land (33:50 – 34:29)

1. Instructions to drive out all the Canaanites (33:50 – 56)

Israel's possession of the land was an act of obedience to God's will. God was Lord of the land. He had created it "in the beginning" (Ge 1:1). He still owned it, and he gave it to whomever he pleased (cf. Jer 27:5). Thus, the

Israelites were not taking the land for their own gain but were acting as God's agents in punishing the idolatrous Canaanites. Thus they were to destroy all Canaanite idols and places of worship when they entered the land, and they were not to allow the Canaanites to remain among them. If Israel failed to obey God (which, in fact, proved to be the case), they too would become the objects of God's punishment. There is an ominous tone in the Lord's last words, "Then I will do to you what I plan to do to them" (v.56).

2. Description of the borders of the land (34:1 – 15)

Besides the obvious geographical markers such as the Mediterranean Sea, many of the sites noted in this chapter are not identifiable today. We can obtain a general outline of the area, however, by following the natural boundaries of the land itself. These boundaries were never fully realized during Israel's history. Thus, this list is a set of outside perimeters within which Israel was free to occupy territory. The writer's purpose is to show the work of God in allotting the land to his people.

3. List of leaders responsible for dividing the land (34:16 – 29)

The first three names in this list are well-known from the previous narratives — Joshua, Eleazar, and Caleb. The rest of the names are new. These men represent the new generation that was to take possession of the land. Each one is a tribal representative. The tribes of Reuben and Gad are omitted since the focus is only on the region west of the Jordan.

B. Cities for the Levites, Including Cities of Refuge (35:1 – 34)

Forty-eight cities were to be given to the tribe of Levi. Each lot was approximately 207 acres and consisted of a town and pasture. Six of these sites were to be cities of refuge. These instructions were carried out under Joshua's allotment of the land. In Jos 21 a list of these cities is given (see also 2Ch 31:15; Ezr 2:70).

After enumerating the provision for the cities of refuge, the writer inserts a complete description of the laws governing their use. The cities were to provide a shelter for anyone who committed a homicide. The natural assumption was that a close relative of a homicide victim would seek to avenge his death; thus provision was made to prevent this. Once the innocent manslayer had found a safe haven, a trial was to ensue. If it could be determined that he had intentionally slain the victim, it would be ruled a capital offense and he was to be put to death. If the death was ruled accidental, he was to remain under the protection of the city of refuge "until the death of the high priest" (v.25).

CITIES OF REFUGE

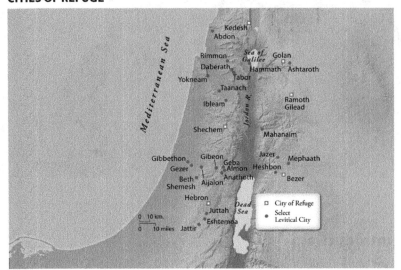

C. Inheritance of Zelophehad's Daughters (36:1 – 13)

An additional stipulation is given here to the decision about female inheritance in ch. 27. The women of any tribe who have inherited property cannot marry into another tribe. Such a rule ensures that a tribe's inheritance would not be taken into the inheritance of another tribe.

DEUTERONOMY

Introduction

The name Deuteronomy comes from the Greek rendering of Dt 17:18, where the phrase "copy of this law" was read as "a second law" *(deuteronomion)*. Though this was a misreading of the verse, the book continued to be called Deuteronomy. Much of its material has already been recorded in the earlier sections of the Pentateuch (cf. Ex 20 and Dt 5). But Deuteronomy is essentially an explanation of the law, not merely a repetition of it. The key to understanding this repetition is Moses' statement of the purpose of the book in 1:5: "to expound this law." It is like a commentary on earlier passages of the Pentateuch. At the same time, it is an integral part of the Pentateuch.

I. Introduction (1:1 – 5)

The opening section gives the setting of this part of the Pentateuch and its purpose: a collection of public addresses given by Moses to "all Israel." These addresses are his last words to the people as they were preparing to enter into the Promised Land, spoken across the Jordan, where the people were gathered after their forty years in the desert.

II. Historical Review of the Earlier Narratives (1:6 – 3:29)

Moses begins his explanation of the law with a historical review of God's gracious acts. The account begins with the historical account of Israel's departure from Sinai (cf. Nu 10:11–12). It does not go back to the events of the exodus, though in 1:30 Moses mentions the events in Egypt.

The reason why Moses' speech focuses here only on the most recent events is that they concern the new generation that is to take possession of the Promised Land. In telling the earlier events, Moses wants to cast light on the situation of his own listeners (and that of the readers).

A. Departure from Sinai (1:6–8; cf. Nu 10–20)

Moses begins by giving the basis of God's dealings with Israel, i.e., the promise of the land that God made to Abraham, Isaac, and Jacob. The boundaries of the land are those of the original promise in Ge 15:18–21.

B. The Appointment of Leaders (1:9–18)

Here Moses refers to Ex 18:13–26 (cf. Nu 11:16, 24), where on the advice of his father-in-law, he appointed experienced officials to help in the administration of the nation. One of the central purposes of that narrative was to show that the need for additional leaders in Israel stemmed from God's faithfulness in blessing the nation (cf. Ge 12:2; 15:5; Ex 1:7; Nu 23:10).

C. The Spies and Israel's Rebellion (1:19–46; cf. Nu 13–14)

The Israelites were en route to the "hill country of the Amorites" (v.19). They camped at the desert of Paran or Kadesh (Nu 12:16; 13:26). The differences between this rendition and Nu 13–14 can be harmonized. When challenged by Moses to take the land (Dt 1:20–21), the people, because of their lack of faith, requested that spies be sent first (v.22). Moses, who approved their plan (v.23a), took their request to the Lord (of which there is no mention in the text). The Lord also approved their plan and commanded Moses to appoint the spies (Nu 13:1ff.).

D. Passing through the Transjordan Desert (2:1–23)

The events of Israel's thirty-eight years in the desert are repeated by reminding the Israelites why the Edomite, Moabite, and Ammonite territories were not taken. It is also stressed in this section that the whole of the previous generation died during this time (vv.15–16).

E. Conquest of the Transjordan (2:24–3:11)

1. Defeat of Sihon (2:24–37)

As Moses retells the story of the conquest of the land of King Sihon, he makes several significant additions. He first shows that Israel's request to pass through Sihon's land was made on the best of terms (cf. Nu 21:21 – 22). It was an offering of peace to the king (Dt 2:26), not an act of war. He adds that Israel had originally offered to buy supplies from Sihon (Dt 2:28). Moreover, Israel's intention was not to take Sihon's land as their possession, but rather only to pass through his land on their way to the Promised Land (v.29; see comments on Nu 21:21 – 32).

But God had other intentions. He hardened Sihon's heart so that he resisted Israel. This was God's first act in delivering the land over into Israel's hands (vv.30 – 31). This stress on God's work helps account for the severity of Israel's actions in taking this land (v.34).

2. Defeat of Og (3:1 – 11)

Moses repeats the account of the defeat of Og from Nu 21:33 – 35 with one significant addition; it was the Lord's hand at work (v.3).

Verses 6 – 11 go beyond the earlier account of this battle in Nu 21:33 – 35, stressing the obedience and success of Israel in taking the Transjordan as well as the kingdom of Og. As was with the kingdom of Sihon, the whole of the kingdom of Og was destroyed.

F. Transjordan Given to Reuben and Gad (3:12 – 20)

Recalling events from Nu 32, Moses reiterates the division of the land among Reuben, Gad, and Manasseh. He adds a note about the conquest of part of this land by Jair (see Nu 32:41). The text adds specifically that Jair's conquest was in Bashan and thus was a part of the land given to the tribe of Manasseh (Dt 3:13).

G. Joshua Replaces Moses (3:21 – 29)

Moses adds two important details. He reminds the people of the encouragement he had given to Joshua, "Do not be afraid of them; the LORD your God himself will fight for you" (v.22). Next is Moses' prayer for clemency and permission to go into the Promised Land (vv.23 – 25). Though it was denied, Moses was allowed to see the land from the top of Mount Pisgah.

III. Moses' Speech: Call to Obedience (4:1 – 40)

Moses is now about to part ways with the people and to allow Joshua to take them into the land. Since he will not enter the land and guide the people in God's law, he gives them his explanation of the law. His goal is to draw out the chief ideas of the Sinai narratives (Ex 19 – 33).

A. The Torah Is Wisdom (4:1 – 14)

As frequently happens in Deuteronomy, Moses focuses on only a few central ideas taken from the previous narratives. His purpose is to give a general summary. First he turns to the issue of obedience to the will of God. This he explains within the context of "wisdom." What other nations sought in attempting to gain wisdom, Israel had found in the revelation of God's will at Sinai. Moses reminds the Israelites that the great display of God's power in the giving of the law at Sinai (cf. Ex 20:18 – 19) was to underscore the foundation of their wisdom — the fear of the Lord (cf. Ex 20:20).

B. Warning against Idolatry (4:15 – 24)

The second central idea of Moses is the warning against idolatry. Just as Israel had easily slipped into idolatry, even while at Mount Sinai (Ex 32), so Moses is careful to warn them of the constant danger of further apostasy. Moses is reiterating a lesson found in earlier narratives: even though Israel has had godly leadership, if the people fail to trust God, it will be to no avail. Thus he warns them, "Be careful not to forget the covenant of the LORD your God" (v.23).

C. The Exile (4:25 – 31)

In the same breath as he warns the people of the impending exile, Moses encourages the people by reminding them of God's great mercy. In no uncertain terms, he warns the Israelites that if they persist in idolatry, they will be taken off the land and scattered among all the nations (vv.25 – 28). Then Moses turns his attention to Israel's return from exile. When they return to the Lord, the Lord will return them to the land promised to the fathers (vv.29 – 31).

D. God's Presence with Israel (4:32 – 40)

Just as in Ex 33:15ff. God's presence among his people marked them as a unique nation, so here Moses returns to the theme of God's presence to underscore his mercy. Moses here refers to the patriarchs (v.37). Throughout the Pentateuch the patriarchs, particularly Abraham, serve as examples of what it means to keep God's laws (Ge 26:5). Thus when the Pentateuch calls for obedience to God's "decrees" and "commands" (Dt 4:40), it should be remembered that the foremost example of one who did this is Abraham (Ge 26:5), a man who lived by faith (Ge 15:6).

IV. Cities of Refuge (4:41 – 43)

This section is a narrative insertion in the midst of Moses' speech, dealing with the allotment of cities of refuge to the tribes on the east side of the Jordan (cf. Nu 35:6, 9 – 34).

V. Giving of the Law (4:44 – 5:33)

A. The Setting of the Law (4:44 – 49)

Much of what has already been recounted in chs. 1 – 3 is here repeated in summary form. It is cast in the form of a narration about Moses and is not a part of Moses' speech. This short summary plays an important role in guiding the reader through the book. Its purpose is to distinguish between the introductory material of the first three chapters and the exposition of the law itself in the subsequent chapters.

B. The Introduction to the Law: The Covenant at Sinai (5:1 – 5)

This introduction emphasizes that God's covenant made with Israel at Sinai was the immediate responsibility of the present generation. It was not a covenant made to earlier generations ("our ancestors") but to those of the present generation who had stood at the foot of Mount Sinai and heard the voice of God. These people were children when the original covenant was given at Sinai. Moses rightfully treats them as those who were present and who could still recall vividly God's power. This generation is thus reminded that the Ten Commandments have their primary goal in preserving the worship of God throughout the future generations.

C. The Ten Commandments (5:6 – 22)

The Ten Commandments are repeated here to provide the context for Moses' explication of the law that follows (see Ex 20:1 – 17 and comments). There are a few differences between the two. (1) The concept of "rest" on the seventh day includes one's whole household and servants. (2) The motivation for keeping the Sabbath is centered in Israel's redemption from Egypt. (3) In the commandment regarding honoring one's parents, the phrase "that it may go well with you" is added (v.16). (4) The Hebrew form of the last commandment (v.21) separates it into two distinct commandments by using different words for "covet" and "desire."

D. Moses Appointed as Mediator (5:23 – 33)

Referring back to the response of the people at Sinai in Ex 20:18ff., Moses recalls and expounds on their fear at hearing God's voice and his own consequent role as mediator. The fear of the people is here seen as a positive sign. Its purpose was to provoke them to seek after God and turn away from idols. It is stressed here because within Deuteronomy, "fear" is central to the concept of divine wisdom and the foundation for obedience to God's will (e.g., 6:2).

The Lord's words in v.29, however, show that the fear exhibited at Sinai was not yet the kind of fear that would produce obedience.

VI. General Principles of Law (6:1 – 11:32)

The speeches of Moses that follow show a conscious effort to develop the central ideas of the first of the Ten Commandments — wholehearted worship of God and forsaking idols.

A. Explication of Fearing God and Keeping His Commands (6:1 – 25)

Ironically, the fear of God that produces obedience is here defined by "love": "Love the LORD your God with all you heart ..." (v.5). It is thus clear that the "fear of the LORD" does not denote a heart that flees from his presence but that longs to do his will. It is a fear that produces not obeisance but obedience, not worry but worship (v.13).

Moses begins his exhortation with a summation of one of the most central ideas in all of Scripture, "Hear, O Israel: The LORD our God, the LORD is one." Jesus referred to this statement, called the "Shema" in later Jewish tradition, as the "most important" of all the commandments (Mk 12:29).

B. Explication of Separation from the Gods of Other Nations (7:1 – 26)

Moses' main concern is with the result of joining in marriage and treaties with the Canaanites who practice idolatry, "for they will turn your children away from following me to serve other gods" (v.4). He is thus not speaking of those cases where Canaanites forsook their idols to follow the Lord. Moses also stresses that separation from these pagan gods entails a refusal to allow the practice of their religion in their midst (v.5).

Moses traces the underlying concern for Israel's worship of God back to their election. Israel was God's "treasured possession" (v.6). They were unique among the nations, just as God was unique. He alone was God, and Israel alone was his chosen people. However, lest there be any reason for Israel's pride to gain a foothold, Moses quickly adds, "The LORD did not set his affection on you and choose you because you were more numerous than other peoples, for you were the fewest of all peoples" (v.7). The basis of God's election of Israel was God's love, not Israel's greatness (v.8).

C. Warning against Forgetting the Lord (8:1 – 20)

Moses recalls God's provision for the people during their sojourn of forty years in the desert. This time was a time of affliction and testing, "to know what was in your heart, whether or not you would keep his commands" (v.2). Moses describes the Promised Land and the blessings of the people living there in terms reminiscent of the garden of Eden in Genesis (Ge 1:28). Once again, obedience to the law is the key to enjoying the blessings of the good land and of avoiding the curse of death (8:20).

D. Illustrations from Israel's Past (9:1 – 10:11)

Moses now illustrates from Israel's past to support his central lesson that they should live a life of constant vigilance before God. He turns first to the incident of the golden calf recorded in Ex 32. The earlier rehearsals of past events have focused on God's faithfulness. The present illustrations focus on Israel's failure and faithlessness. They come primarily from Exodus and thus move further back in time than the earlier historical introduction in Dt 1 – 3.

1. Introduction (9:1 – 6)

Israel's possession of the land was not a reward given them on account of their own righteousness. Rather, it was "on account of the wickedness of these [other] nations" that the land was to be taken from them and given to Israel as a fulfillment of God's promise to the patriarchs (vv.4 – 6).

Moses leaves the people — and the reader — with a clear understanding that possession of the land was based on God's grace, not on Israel's own righteousness (v.6). He thus anticipates the views of the later prophets, who based their hope in the future on God's faithfulness to his promises and not on the righteousness of "a stiff-necked people" (v.6b; see Eze 36:22 – 23).

2. The golden calf (9:7 – 29)

In retelling the story of Sinai and Israel's breach of covenant in making a golden calf, Moses stresses how quickly the people fell into idolatry (v.12). His purpose is to emphasize the need for constant vigilance. The people's hearts can turn away from God when it is least expected. Certainly their standing at the foot of Mount Sinai while the prohibitions of idolatry were being written on the stone tablets was not a likely place for instigating the idol worship. Nevertheless it happened, and thus it serves as a cogent warning of how unexpectedly the hearts of the people go astray.

Returning to the incident at Sinai, Moses recounts his prayer on behalf of the people (vv.25 – 29). That prayer serves as a general statement of his concern for the people throughout the forty years in the desert. It is significant that Moses' prayer does not stress their righteousness but rather God's righteousness.

3. The new tablets at Sinai (10:1 – 5)

In order to show that the Lord heard the prayer of Moses and reestablished his covenant with them, Moses recounts making two new tablets for the Ten Commandments. He also says that in addition to the stone tablets, he made a wooden chest (the ark) in which to keep them.

4. Parenthesis: Itinerary in the desert (10:6 – 9)

Moses is concerned to show that the priesthood of Aaron was also restored after the golden calf incident (cf. 9:20). He thus inserts this parenthetical narrative into the account of the events at Sinai. It recounts God's establishment of the house of Levi as priests before the Lord.

5. Conclusion: Dismissal from Mount Sinai (10:10 – 11)

At the conclusion of his speech, Moses states what his previous words have, in fact, already suggested, that God was gracious to the people: "It was not his will to destroy [them]" (v.10). Furthermore, God intended them to enjoy the blessings of his promises to the fathers.

E. Admonition to Fear the Lord (10:12 – 22)

Moses now drives home the lesson of the preceding narrative. God calls Israel "to fear the Lord your God, to walk in obedience to him, to love him, to serve the Lord your God with all your heart and with all your soul." For Israel to follow in God's ways means a fundamental change of heart. Such a change of heart is described as circumcision of the heart (v.16).

F. Conclusion: Call to Love God and Obey His Will (11:1 – 32)

Moses now turns to Israel's responsibility as parents and guardians of the next generation, who had not actually witnessed the great acts of God. For that generation and all subsequent ones, God's great acts would not be seen with their own eyes, but would be "seen" in the words of Scripture. Therefore Moses encourages the people to "fix these words ... in your hearts and minds.... Teach them to you children, talking about them when you sit at home and when you walk along the road, when you lie down and when you get up" (vv.18-19). The top priority is thus given to Scripture as the means of teaching the greatness and grace of God.

As a final means for driving home the importance of obedience and trust in God, Moses gives instructions for a ceremony that the people were to carry out when they entered the land (vv.29-32). They were to read the curses and blessings of the covenant on Mount Gerizim and Mount Ebal (see 27:1ff.). This ceremony was in fact initiated under Joshua in Jos 8:33ff.

VII. Instructions for Life in the New Land (12:1 – 26:19)

A. Instruction for the Life of Worship (12:1 – 16:17)

1. Central place of worship (12:1 – 32)

Moses repeats his instructions (see 7:5) about what to do with the false worship centers after the Israelites have taken possession of the land of the Canaanites. They are to "destroy [them] completely" (v.2). Furthermore, Israel is to worship the Lord at a single, central place of worship. Not just any site would do (v.13) —only that site chosen by the Lord himself (v.14).

The provision in vv.15-25 that animals may be slaughtered for food at any place in the land clarifies the provision in Lev 17:1-7. There the slaughtering of animals for sacrifice could only be done at the Tent of Meeting.

The chapter ends with an oft-repeated warning against following after the gods of the nations (vv.29-32) and thus provides an appropriate introduction to the next chapter.

2. Warning against those who entice others to follow "other gods" (13:1 – 18)

Under no circumstances were the Israelites to forsake the Lord their God even if: (1) a prophet or dreamer, even one whose predictions come true, suggests that the people forsake the Lord by following other gods (vv.1-5); (2) someone from one's own family entices him to follow other gods (vv.6-11); or (3) an entire city forsakes the Lord and follows other gods, in which case that city must be completely destroyed (vv.12-18).

3. The purity of the people (14:1 – 21)

These regulations show the measures that must be taken to maintain the holiness of the people. They are to show that Israel was "a people holy to the LORD [their] God" (vv.2, 21).

4. Tithes (14:22 – 29)

A tithe is one-tenth of one's produce, whether grain, fruit, oil, cattle, or sheep. In addition to the first tithe given to the priests, a second tithe was also to be given by each Israelite "that you may learn to revere the LORD" (v.23). This tithe was to be given out of the remainder of the produce after the first tithe. A family celebration that included the Levites was to be held out of this tithe. Anyone who lived too far away to bring his tithe to the sanctuary was to sell his tithe and purchase food and drink for the celebration when he arrived (vv.24 – 27).

5. Care for the poor (15:1 – 18)

This passage further explains the sabbath year release (see Ex 23:10 – 11; Lev 25:2 – 7). The premise of this exposition is that if the land was left unused in the sabbath year, the landowner would not have money to pay his debts. To alleviate this hardship, debts were to be postponed for one year (the sense of the word translated "cancel" is "postpone"). This provision did not apply to the "foreigner" (one who stayed temporarily in the land; v.3), but only to those who lived permanently in the land.

In vv.4 – 5 Moses qualifies his discussion of the "poor" in the land. He reminds the people that if they obeyed the Lord, they would have no need of laws dealing with the poor because God would so bless them that there would be no poor. They would, in fact, have such abundance that they would be the creditors of many nations.

6. Firstborn animals (15:19 – 23)

Laws regarding the firstborn were given in Ex 13:11 – 16; 22:29 – 30; Nu 18:15 – 18. This passage gives further regulations regarding firstborn cattle and sheep. They were not to be worked or sheared, as the other animals. Only those without blemish were to be brought to the place of worship and eaten by all of the people.

7. Feasts (16:1 – 17)

Moses now discusses the feasts during which the people were to appear before the Lord at the central worship site.

Passover (vv.1 – 8). The Passover itself required only a lamb (Ex 12:5). However, there were also additional mandated offerings during the Passover and subsequent seven days of the Feast of Unleavened Bread (Nu 28:19 – 25). Other offerings could be given as well (cf. 2Ch 35:7 – 8). In addition, what is anticipated by the completion of the tabernacle in Ex 40:17 is clarified here in vv.5 – 6: the Passover was no longer to be celebrated in each house (cf. Ex 12:46) but only at the central place of worship.

Feast of Weeks (vv.9 – 12). This feast day, also called the "Feast of Harvest" (Ex 23:16) and "day of firstfruits" (Nu 28:26), must begin seven weeks after "the sickle [is put] to the standing grain" (v.9). Depending on any particular season, this day could vary. This feast was to celebrate God's deliverance of the people from slavery in Egypt.

Feast of Tabernacles or Booths (vv.13 – 15). According to Lev 23:43, the "temporary shelters" were to commemorate the huts the Israelites lived in when they came out of Egypt. As with other feasts, it was to be a time of great joy in remembrance.

Summary (vv.16 – 17). Moses specifies that the feasts were to be celebrated only at the central place of worship.

B. Instruction for Leadership (16:18 – 18:22)

1. Judges (16:18 – 20)

The judge was to play an important role in implementing and enforcing the prohibitions listed below.

2. Prohibition of wooden Asherah poles and pillars (16:21 – 22)

The Asherah poles and pillars were mentioned in 7:5 as accouterments of Canaanite worship. They were to be destroyed when the Israelites moved into the land. In the present context the concern is that the central worship place not contain any traces of Canaanite worship.

3. Prohibition of defective sacrifice (17:1)

A defective sacrifice is "detestable" to the Lord. The description of the defects listed here summarizes Lev 1:3, 10; 22:17 – 26.

4. Penalty for worshiping other gods (17:2 – 7)

Here the implementation of the penalty given in Ex 22:20 is closely described and applied to any "man or woman." The penalty is the same as that for one who seduces another to worship idols (Dt 13:7 – 12).

5. Law cases for the priests and judges (17:8 – 13)

The system of legal administration described here represents an implementation of that form of law established during Israel's time in the desert (Ex 18:21 – 23; Dt 1:16 – 17; 19:17 – 18). There were judges at the local level throughout the land as well as centralized at the place of worship. Obedience to the law is presented as obedience to God's will. Violation of the law is seen as rebellion against God.

6. The king (17:14 – 20)

This passage anticipates the time when a king would be established over Israel and thus prescribes the kind of king they were to have. Central to this question is that he had to be one whom the Lord himself would choose (v.15), just as Israel was to worship God only at the place he chose. It is not difficult to see in these words the anticipation of King David, whose family God chose from among all the tribes (2Sa 7:18 – 24; Ps 78:70). The warnings listed here about the dangers inherent in the kingship call to mind the downfall of Solomon, David's son.

7. Offerings for the priests and Levites (18:1 – 8)

The role of the priests, chosen by God and separated apart as his servants, is summarized. Their support was to come from a prescribed portion of the offerings given to the Lord. From the animals offered they were to receive "the shoulder, the internal organs and the meat from the head." From the rest of the offerings they were to be given "the firstfruits."

8. Detestable practices (18:9 – 14)

Before introducing the office of the prophet, Moses emphatically prohibits all other means of knowing God's will. The office of the prophet was Israel's means of knowing that will; hence these other means must not be used to rival it.

9. The prophet (18:15 – 22)

Abraham is called a prophet in Ge 20:7, and the existence of prophets is presupposed in the Pentateuch (Ex 7:1; Nu 11:29; 12:6; Dt 13:2 – 3). But now, for the first time, the office of prophet becomes the specific subject of discussion.

A prophet's words were to be taken as the final authority. For this reason, strict measures were taken to ensure that false prophets would not arise among the people to lead them away from the Lord. The simple test of a true prophet was whether his words came true.

C. Instructions for Order (19:1 – 23:14)

1. Cities of refuge (19:1 – 13)

According to Nu 35:9 – 34, Israel was to establish six "cities of refuge" to prevent the escalation of blood revenge and to provide the means for a fair trial in cases of homicide. Because of Israel's continued disobedience, God never permanently increased their borders, and the three additional cities were thus not needed.

2. Boundary markers (19:14)

In the ancient world, territory was staked out through large stones bearing inscriptions that identified the owner of the property. The notion of secretly or forcefully moving a neighbor's boundary marker thus became a proverbial expression for treachery and rebellion (Job 24:1 – 2; Pr 22:28). This is a warning against violating any standard set up by the "predecessors" that has been ordained by God.

3. Witnesses (19:15 – 21)

According to Nu 35:30 and Dt 17:6, more than one witness was required for a capital offense. This passage (and 17:6) specifies that two or three witnesses were enough. But what happens if the witness is false? Moses appeals to a provision stated earlier (17:8 – 13), that difficult cases were to be taken to the judges and priests at the central worship place.

4. War (20:1 – 20)

The Israelites were to carry out warfare with nations "at a distance" (vv.10 – 15) differently than with those nations whose land they were to inherit through God's promises (vv.16 – 20). With the first group, they were first to offer terms of peace. It is assumed that the cause of the war was just and hence Israel would have been justified in destroying the city. Israel was to act mercifully with the offending nations. If the terms of peace were not met, Israel was justified in waging war. The effect of these regulations can be seen in 1Ki 20:31, for Israel was known by their neighbors as a "merciful" people in warfare.

As for the Promised Land, this was a gift from the Lord. The Israelites were not to grow rich from their warfare there, but were to "completely destroy" all the spoils (v.17; cf. Jos 7).

5. Unsolved murder (21:1 – 9)

This law is not given elsewhere in the Pentateuch. Its purpose is clear: Whenever innocent blood was shed, the people were to carry out justice and punish the offender (cf. 19:1 – 14). If the guilty party was unknown, justice could not be adequately served and thus the people were still held responsible. The present law, then, was the means whereby the people as a whole could settle an unsolved murder.

6. Treatment of captive women (21:10 – 14)

In warfare with nations that were "at a distance," the Israelites were not to take the lives of the women and children when capturing a city (20:14). The present law ensured the well-being of those captured women by giving them protection against being sold into slavery. It also provided for the assimilation of captive women into the Israelite society by allowing marriage to them.

There is no mention in the present passage of the personal faith or religion of such a woman taken into the house of an Israelite. In light of the strict warnings against the dangers of foreign women leading Israel into idolatry and false religion (7:3 – 4), most likely the woman in question here would accept Israel's covenant stipulations.

7. Right of the firstborn (21:15 – 17)

This law is not mentioned elsewhere in the Pentateuch, though the right of the "firstborn" is assumed throughout the pentateuchal narratives (e.g., Ge 25:29 – 34; 49:3). The law is intended to protect the legitimate firstborn son, even though his mother may not have been a favorite wife.

8. A rebellious son (21:18 – 21)

According to Lev 20:9, a son who cursed his father and mother was to be put to death. The present law generalizes the offense to include any kind of refusal to obey and assumes the same stiff measures. The law here, however, provides an additional safeguard. The parents were required to bring the child before a council of elders, who were to decide the case, administer the penalty, and so eliminate the evil influence of such a child from among the people (v.21). It also provided a warning to parents and children of the consequences of disobedience and rebellion.

9. Various laws (21:22 – 22:12)

After an execution, the body could hang on a tree as a public display of the consequences of disobedience (21:22 – 23). It was not, however, to remain on the tree overnight.

The general principle is then laid down that one cannot hide one's eyes from an obvious need (22:1 – 4; cf. Ex 23:4 – 5). It is one's duty to care for the lost property of a neighbor.

The next rule is sufficiently general to forbid a man's wearing any item of feminine clothing or ornamentation, or a woman's wearing any item of masculine clothing or ornamentation (v.5). The only reason given is that such a practice is detestable to the Lord.

The law in vv.6 – 7 both suggests the sense of fair play inherent in God's law and shows that God cares for the least among his creation.

In v.8 is another example of the importance of looking out for one's neighbor, even in seemingly insignificant places. No area of life fails to come under the scrutiny of God's will.

10. Marriage, adultery, and rape (22:13 – 30)

If doubt were to arise as to the virginity of one's bride, a formal accusation was to be made to the "town elders" and proof of virginity was to be given by her parents (vv.13 – 15). If the accusation was false, the husband was to pay a penalty. The proof probably consisted of a blood-stained cloth or clothing that the parents had kept since the night of the wedding.

The law prohibiting adultery in Lev 20:10 is restated here in v.22. Its purpose is further explained here by the addition of the phrase to "purge the evil from Israel."

Various conditions are given for deciding the penalty for rape. The first cases (vv.23 – 27) are those in which the young girl was already "pledged to be married." In this case she was considered a married woman, and thus the penalty for adultery applied. The second case (vv.28 – 29) deals with the rape of a young girl who was not "pledged to be married." The law protected her and ensured her continued welfare.

11. Exclusion from the assembly (23:1 – 8)

Several conditions disqualify one from entering "the assembly of the LORD" — emasculation (v.1), offspring of a forbidden marriage (v.2), off-spring of Ammonites or Moabites (vv.3 – 6), and, to a lesser extent, off-spring of Edomites or Egyptians (vv.7 – 8). It is not entirely clear what "entering the assembly" means. It may have the limited sense of exclusion from public service or marriage into an Israelite family, or, more generally, it may mean exclusion from Israel's covenant relationship with God.

12. Uncleanness in the battle camp (23:9 – 14)

In Nu 5:1 – 4 instructions were given for maintaining the purity of the whole Israelite camp. Here the concern is for the camps of the armies of Israel during the time of battle.

D. Miscellaneous Laws (23:15 – 25:19)

At the close of this section, the author has selected twenty-one miscel-laneous laws to further illustrate the nature of the requirements of living under the Sinai covenant. These laws cover such areas as fugitive slaves, shrine prostitution, usury, divorce, concern for the poor, paying of wages, equal justice, levirate marriage, and honesty in weights and measures.

E. Two Ceremonies: Firstfruits and Tithes (26:1 – 15)

1. Firstfruits (26:1 – 11)

The firstfruits of the produce of the land were to be given to the Lord (Ex 23:16; 34:26; Lev 27:30 – 33; Nu 18:12 – 13). They were to be brought to the priests as their inheritance (Dt 18:3 – 8) during the Feast of Harvest (Ex 34:22; Lev 23:15 – 17; Nu 28:26; Dt 16:9 – 10) and the Passover (Lev 2:14; 23:10). The present passage initiates a special ceremony for this event.

2. Tithes (26:12 – 15)

Tithes were discussed in 14:22 – 29. This passage describes the prayer offered at the giving of the second tithe. This prayer not only acknowledged payment of the tithe but also confessed general obedience to the Lord and an expectation of his blessing.

F. Conclusion (26:16 – 19)

Moses' concluding words hark back to the beginning of the covenant at Sinai in Ex 19:5 – 6. If Israel obeyed the covenant, they would be God's prized possession, and he would make them an exalted and holy nation.

VIII. The Covenant Ceremony in Moab (27:1 – 28:68)

A. The Instructions on the Stones and Altar on Mount Ebal (27:1 – 10)

When the people entered the land, they were to set up large stones on Mount Ebal (vv.1 – 4), along with an altar for sacrifices, fellowship offerings, and a sacred meal (vv.5 – 8). The stones were to be plastered over and prepared for writing. These stones appear to be the same ones as those used for the altar (v.8). The content of the writing is not specified; suggestions are the Ten Commandments, the blessings and curses of chs. 27 – 28, or the whole book of Deuteronomy. In Jos 8:32, when this command was carried out, Joshua "wrote on stones a copy of the law of Moses." This writing was to remind the people of the importance of obeying the covenant and its laws.

B. Twelve Curses (27:11 – 26)

A further ceremony was to be carried out when the people entered the land. In the northern territory of the tribe of Manasseh near Shechem stood two mountains, Gerizim and Ebal. Half of the tribes of Israel (Simeon, Levi, Judah, Issachar, Joseph, and Benjamin) were to stand on Mount Gerizim to recount the blessings of the covenant, and the other half (Reuben, Gad, Asher, Zebulun, Dan, and Naphtali) were to stand on Mount Ebal to recount the curses.

C. Blessings and Curses (28:1 – 68)

Another list of blessings and curses is given. These are not a continuation of the words to be recited at Ebal and Gerizim but are rather a further elaboration of the blessings and curses that would be incurred in the covenant.

Just as the curses were given more prominence in the ceremony of ch. 27, so the curses incurred by disobedience to the covenant are much more fully developed here. The writer of the Pentateuch hints that Israel would not prove faithful to the covenant (cf. Dt 31:16 – 18, 27) and thus would not enjoy its blessings.

IX. The New Covenant (29:1 – 34:12)

A. Introduction (29:1)

Here Moses is deliberately setting up a contrast between the covenant at Sinai and the covenant he envisions for Israel in the future. The past ended in Israel's failure to keep the covenant and trust in God. But there is hope for the future; to this hope Moses now turns.

B. Warnings Regarding the Covenant (29:2 – 28)

Moses reviews Israel's complete failure to see and understand God's work in their midst (v.4). It began with God's work in Egypt and continued to the conquest of the Transjordan (vv.2 – 8). Moses further grounds the work of God in the promises made to the "fathers, Abraham, Isaac and Jacob" (vv.9 – 13); thus he presupposes the lessons of Genesis.

As one example of these lessons, Moses turns to the story of Sodom and Gomorrah (v.23). His treatment of that narrative is an interesting reversal of what is found in Genesis. In Genesis, that account was intended to show not only God's wrath against the wickedness of the pagan nations but also his salvation of the righteous.

C. Conclusion (29:29)

Moses closes these remarks abruptly with a statement about the limits of God's revelation. God has not revealed the whole of his wisdom and knowledge, but he has revealed "all the words of this law," and they are given to all generations. There is no end to the "secret things" that one devises about God and his world. Moses, however, puts an end to all of them here by simply pointing to God's great act of grace in revealing his will in the law.

D. Future Blessing (30:1 – 20)

Before concluding this book, Moses takes a long look into the future of God's people. Israel's disobedience would lead to their captivity in a foreign land. At that point, they will again turn to the Lord, and the Lord will have compassion on them and restore them to the land (vv.1 – 5). The Lord will give them a new heart (a circumcised heart; v.6, cf. 10:16), and they will "love him with all [their] heart and with all [their] soul, and live."

The word "today" in v.15 shows that the perspective and focus of Moses' words have returned to the present, to the people about to enter the land. Moses closes with several allusions to the first instance of the revelation of God's will in the Scriptures, Adam in the garden of Eden.

E. Provisions for Maintaining the Leadership of Moses (31:1 – 29)

The work of Moses was to be maintained and continued in various ways after his death. The Lord himself would go before the people in battle with the Canaanites (vv.3 – 6), and Joshua would be their new leader (vv.1 – 8, 14 – 18, 23). Moses was to write down the law that God had given them and entrust it to the priests, who were to keep it in the ark of the covenant and read it publicly every seven years during the Feast of Tabernacles (vv.9 – 13, 24 – 27). Moses was also to write a song as a continual reminder of the message of the law (vv.19 – 22; see 31:30 – 32:47).

F. The Song of Moses (31:30 – 32:47)

This song is another example of the way poetry is used in the Pentateuch to teach its major themes (see also Ge 49; Nu 24). Its central theme is Israel's apostasy and God's threatening judgment. Moses closes his song with a reminder to the people to pay close attention to the words he has put before them and to teach them carefully to their children (vv.45 – 47).

G. God's Instructions to Moses to Die on Mount Nebo (32:48 – 52)

God repeats his instructions about Moses' death from Nu 27:12 – 14, only with more details. The purpose of this repetition is not clear.

H. The Blessing of Moses (33:1 – 29)

These final words of Moses to the people are introduced as a "blessing." They begin with a brief introduction (vv.2 – 5) and, after listing the blessings for each of the tribes of Israel (vv.6 – 25), Simeon excluded, they conclude with a summary (vv.26 – 29).

1. The introduction (33:2 – 5)

Moses is here portrayed as a "king" among God's people. This is important in light of the fact that in ch. 34, Moses is viewed as a prototype of the coming prophet (see 18:15). Thus at the close of the Pentateuch, the two central messianic visions of the book — that of a coming king (Ge 49:10; Nu 24:7 – 9) and of a prophet (Dt 18:15) — are united in the figure of Moses, the prophet-king.

2. Blessings (33:6 – 25)

The blessings of each tribe are similar to the words of Jacob in Ge 49:1 – 27. The Levites were given the role of teaching God's law to all Israel (vv.8 – 11), and the tribe of Joseph is pictured as enjoying the most abundant part of the land (vv.13 – 17). Clearly the intention of the blessings was to include all Israel in God's blessing.

3. Conclusion (33:26 – 29)

The final words of the blessing speak of the nation as a whole and of its enjoyment of God's good gift of the land. As we might expect, here at the end of the book, Moses pictures Israel's dwelling in the land as a reversal of the events of the early chapters of Genesis when Adam and Eve were cast out of the garden of Eden.

I. The Death of Moses (34:1 – 12)

The account of Moses' death was probably added long after his death. His burial was so far in the past that the location of his grave was uncertain to the writer. In fact, the writer says God buried him. Furthermore, a long succession of prophets had come and gone so that the writer could say, "Since then, no prophet has risen in Israel like Moses" (v.10). Though added later, this chapter plays a major role in the interpretation of the Pentateuch.

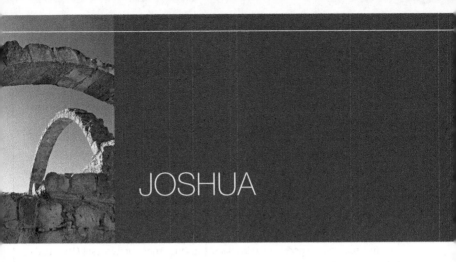

JOSHUA

Introduction

The book receives its name from its central character, Joshua son of Nun (cf. 1Ch 7:20–28). He was from the tribe of Ephraim (Nu 13:8). We first learn of him in Ex 17:8–13, where he, with God's help, defeated the Amalekites in battle. This book shows it is not Israel that took the land, but rather the Lord who regained it from the Canaanites and gave it to Israel (cf. Jos 24:13).

There are significant parallels between the books of the Pentateuch and the book of Joshua. the accompanying chart lists some significant parallels and links between them.

The Pentateuch	The Book of Joshua
(1) Crossing the Red Sea: "The waters were divided, and the Israelites went through the sea on dry ground" (Ex 14:21–22).	Crossing the Jordan River: "And the Lord said, 'Today I will begin to exalt you in the eyes of all Israel, so they may know that I am with you as I was with Moses" (Jos 3:7); "The whole nation had completed the crossing on dry ground" (Jos 3:17); "The Lord your God did to the Jordan just what he had done to the Red Sea" (Jos 4:23).
(2) Blood on the doorposts marking the houses of those who were to be saved in the Exodus (Ex 12:13).	Red cord marking the house of Rahab; anyone in the house would be saved in the conquest (Jos 2:7–20).

The Pentateuch	The Book of Joshua
(3) Israelite males were saved from the command of the king by the resourceful and courageous Hebrew midwives (Ex 1:17 – 19); Moses[2] life was saved by his mother by being hidden from the king in the reeds (Ex 2:3); in the Song of the Sea, Moses says, "The people of Canaan will melt away" (Ex 15:15); God rewarded the midwives by giving them "houses of their own" (NIV, "families") (Ex 1:21).	Israelite spies were saved from the command of the king by the resourceful and courageous Canaanite harlot (Jos 2:3 – 4); Israelite spies were saved by Rahab by being hidden from the king in the stalks of flax (Jos 2:6); Rahab tells the spies, "All who live in this country are melting in fear" (Jos 2:9); Rahab was rewarded for her deeds by sparing her family among the Israelites (Jos 6:25).
(4) Two spies gave a good report in taking the land (Nu 14:38).	Joshua sends out two spies (Jos 2:1); they return with a good report in taking the land (Jos 2:24).
(5) Moses meets the angel of the Lord in the burning bush before he leads the people out of Egypt (Ex 3:2 – 6): "Take off your sandals, for the place where you are standing is holy ground" (v.6).	Joshua meets an angel of the Lord near Jericho before he leads the people into the land (Jos 5:13 – 15): "Take off your sandals, for the place where you are standing is holy" (v.15).
(6) Moses must circumcise his son before the Exodus (Ex 4:24 – 26).	Joshua must circumcise the Israelite sons before the conquest (Jos 5:2 – 8).
(7) Moses and the Israelites celebrated the Passover before the Exodus (Ex 12:21).	Joshua and the Israelites celebrated the Passover before the conquest (Jos 5:10).
(8) Moses performed 13 signs before the Exodus (three signs, Ex 3:9; ten signs, Ex 7 – 11).	Joshua and the Israelites circled Jericho 13 times before the conquest (once each of the six days and then seven times on the last day, Jos 6:3 – 4).
(9) Moses held his staff raised until all the Amalekites were defeated (Ex 17:11).	Joshua held his javelin raised until all the Canaanites at Ai were defeated (Jos 8:26).
(10) After the victorious deliverance of the Exodus, the Israelites disobeyed God and failed in the wilderness (Nu 14).	After the victorious defeat of Jericho, the Israelites disobeyed and failed at Ai (Jos 7:1 – 5).
(11) Moses intercedes for the people of Israel after their failure in the desert: "The Egyptians will hear about it.... And they will tell the inhabitants of this land about it" (Nu 14:13 – 16).	Joshua intercedes for the people after their failure at Ai: "The Canaanites and the other people of the country will hear about this...." (Jos 7:7 – 9).

I. Israel's Entry into Canaan (1:1 – 4:24)

A. The Commissioning of Joshua as a Replacement for Moses (1:1 – 18)

The narrative opens with a reminder of the death of Moses, the servant of the Lord (v.1; cf. Dt 34:5 – 12). As Moses had received a commissioning from the Lord while in the desert of Sinai (Ex 3:10), so now, at the beginning of this book, Joshua also receives a direct commission from the Lord to lead his people in fulfillment of the divine promise to Abraham (Jos 1:6b; cf. Ge 12:1 – 3). As God had told Abraham, "Go, walk through the length and breadth of the land, for I am giving it to you" (Ge 13:17), so here God tells Joshua, "I will give you every place where you set your foot" (Jos 1:3).

B. The Reconnaissance of Jericho (2:1 – 24)

Joshua sent the spies into the land, who met Rahab. Joshua is here portrayed as a new Moses leading God's people into the land. Rahab is presented as a model of Gentile faith. Her confession is noteworthy: "The Lord your God is God in heaven above and on the earth below" (v.11). On the basis of this confession, the writer of Hebrews later wrote, "By faith the prostitute Rahab ... was not killed with those who were disobedient" (Heb 11:31).

C. The Crossing of the Jordan River (3:1 – 4:24)

Two major developments come from the crossing of the Jordan. (1) Joshua is God's new leader: "Today I will begin to exalt you in the eyes of all Israel, so they may know that I am with you as I was with Moses" (3:7). (2) Israel receives confidence that the Lord truly is able to give them the land: "This is how you will know that the living God is among you and that he will certainly drive out before you the Canaanites" (3:10).

II. The Conquest (5:1 – 12:24)

A. First Stage of the Conquest (5:1 – 8:35)

1. Final preparations for battle (5:1 – 15)

Final preparations for the conquest were made. These included the rite of circumcision and the celebration of the Passover. Just as circumcision and the celebration of the Passover preceded the exodus from Egypt (Ex 4:24 – 26; 12:1 – 13), so now they mark its conclusion.

CONQUEST OF CANAAN

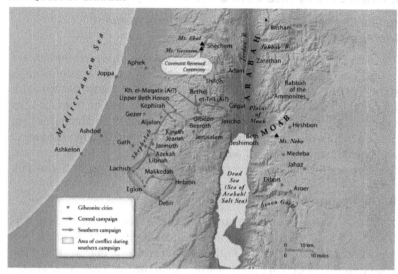

As a prelude to Israel's taking the city of Jericho and the rest of the land, we, the readers, are given a behind-the-scenes look at the real nature of the conquest. Joshua met the captain of the Lord's army. Israel would not take the land alone. They would have the help of the armies of God. Though the narrative is short and leaves us with many unanswered questions, we know that God was at work in the actions that follow.

2. The capture of Jericho (6:1 – 27)

In the battle of Jericho, the military strategy places the victory entirely in the hands of God. Even before the city was taken, the Lord had said, "See, I have delivered Jericho into your hands" (v.2). At the pitch of battle Joshua told Israel, "Shout! For the LORD has given you the city!" (v.16). The plan was dangerously simple. Israel was to circle the city silently once a day for six days. On the seventh day, they were to circle it seven times. Thus, Israel's role was purely and simply to represent the Lord before the people of the city. They had only to stand by and watch the Lord destroy the city walls. The presence of the Lord is clearly marked in the narrative by the ark of the covenant carried by the priests.

3. The overthrow of Ai (7:1 – 8:29)

When they entered the city of Jericho, Joshua had warned the people not to take from any of "the devoted things" of the city, lest they too become subject to the destruction (6:18). Achan, in disregard to Joshua's warning, took and hid a part of the plunder in his tent. As a result the Israelites suffered a total defeat at the city of Ai.

Achan's sin had a more lasting effect on Israel's conquest of the land than we might otherwise have expected. No longer would Israel merely have to carry the ark before them and the walls of the cities would fall as at Jericho. A stratagem was necessary. Though the narrative is clear that the stratagem would fail without God's help, it is also apparent that Israel's failure to obey God's leader, Joshua, had ushered in a new stage in the conquest—one that would finally result in an incomplete conquest (cf. 13:1) and failure (23:15–16).

4. Ceremony at Mount Ebal (8:30–35)

In accordance with the command of Moses in Dt 27:1–8, Joshua built an altar on Mount Ebal. Though this passage is only loosely connected with the events of the conquest, its present location in the text should be understood chronologically. Immediately after Israel had gained a foothold in the land, Joshua led the people to Mount Ebal to carry out Moses' command.

B. Second Stage of the Conquest: The Fraud of the Gibeonites (9:1–27)

1. Introduction (9:1–2)

Because of Israel's defeat of Jericho and Ai, the kings of the land are frightened. The writer surveys a territory ("all the kings west of the Jordan"—in the hill country and the lowlands from one end of the country to the other, as far as Lebanon) much larger than the one encompassed by the events of the following narrative. He thus provides a wider context for the more limited narrative that follows. He returns to this broader scope in the summary in 10:40–43.

2. Gibeonites' fraud (9:3–15)

The pact with the Gibeonites takes up the course of events following the defeat of the city of Ai (8:24–29). The Gibeonites, fearing the worst for themselves, attempted a bold plan that the author compares to the kind of ruse the Israelites were able to play on the inhabitants of Ai.

3. The consequences of the pact with the Gibeonites (9:16–27)

The events of this narrative play an important part in the larger thematic structure of the OT books. (1) Joshua's solution to the dilemma of what to do with the Gibeonites follows precisely the instruction of Dt 20:11, "[They] shall be subject to forced labor and shall work for you." (2) Joshua's words provide a link between this narrative and the curse of the Canaanites in Ge 9:25. (3) Joshua specified that the Gibeonites were to *serve* in "the house of my God" (v.23 – 25).

C. Third Stage of the Conquest: Victory over the Southern Coalition (10:1 – 43)

1. Defeat of the five kings (10:1 – 27)

The battle recounted here is between Israel and the five Amorite kings. The occasion was the peace treaty between Israel and the Gibeonites. The underlying cause was the Amorite kings' fear of Israel's victories at Jericho and Ai, as well as the fact that the Gibeonites had sided with them and now posed a formidable threat.

Led by the king of Jerusalem, Adoni-Zedek, five kings moved to punish the Gibeonites for making a treaty with Israel. In accordance with their treaty with Israel, the Gibeonites immediately appealed to Joshua for help (vv.3 – 7).

The Amorite kings were summarily routed by the Israelites only because God fought for them (vv.8 – 27). To highlight the constant faithfulness of God in coming to Israel's aid, the Lord's words to Joshua deliberately allude to those of Moses: "Do not be afraid of them; I have given them into your hand. Not one of them will be able to withstand you" (v.8; cf. Dt 20:1 – 4).

2. Defeat of the seven cities (10:28 – 43)

As this summary shows (vv.40 – 43), God fought for Israel and delivered the enemies into their hands. The number seven functions as an expression of totality or completeness. Thus the writer lists the defeat of seven cities and leaves us with the sense of total victory.

D. Fourth Stage of the Conquest: Victory over the Northern Coalition and Hazor (11:1 – 15)

The description of the battle at the Waters of Merom (vv.4 – 14) is brief and clearly designed to highlight the role of Joshua as God's obedient servant. The battle is carried out along the lines prescribed in Dt 20. The swiftness of the victory ("suddenly," v.7) is matched by the briefness of the account. The author hurries to the conclusion that victory came because "Joshua did to them as the LORD had directed" (v.9).

The account of the destruction of the city of Hazor (vv.10 – 14), though important to the author in its own right as a continuing example of the success of the Israelites in the conquest, also becomes a further vehicle to portray the nature and extent of Joshua's obedience to God.

E. Summary of Events (11:16 – 12:24)

Here we find a broad description of the conquest of Canaan that reaches far back even into events recounted in the Pentateuch (e.g., Sihon and Og, 12:1 – 6). By means of this summary the narratives of the book of Joshua are linked as a unit to those of the Pentateuch.

1. Territories taken by Israel (11:16 – 23)

The first point stressed by this summary is that the extent of the conquest included all Canaan: "So Joshua took this entire land" (v.16). The enumeration of the various geographical areas (vv.16 – 17) makes it clear that the author means to say that all the land was taken.

Second, the summary turns to the kings and cities of the land (vv.18 – 19) and assures the readers that they were all, except the Gibeonites (cf. 9:1 – 27), captured and put to death after Joshua waged war against them "for a long time." Here the author seems intent on expanding the reader's perception of the conquest beyond merely the events covered in the preceding narratives.

Third, the author makes an important theological point: "It was the LORD himself who hardened their hearts to wage war against Israel, so that he might destroy them totally" (v.20). This is a new idea in Joshua, though one mentioned in the Pentateuch (Ex 4:21; cf. chs. 7 – 12).

In vv.21 – 23, Joshua accomplishes precisely that which kept the original generation out of the land and in the desert for forty years, i.e., the defeat of the Anakites (cf. Nu 13:26 – 14:9). Earlier, Joshua, along with Caleb, had encouraged the people to trust God and take the land: "Do not be afraid of the people of the land, because we will devour them" (Nu 14:9).

2. Kings defeated by Israel (12:1 – 24)

Regarding the lands and kings east of the Jordan, the list of victories reaches back into the pentateuchal narratives to the accounts of the conquest of East Jordan. By means of this summary the narratives of Joshua are linked as a unit to those of the Pentateuch.

III. The Distribution of the Tribal Territories (13:1 – 21:45)

A. Introduction (13:1 – 7)

In each of these passages, special attention given to the old age of Israel's leader marks a transition in the leadership of God's people. Also the nature of the transition is from the ideal leadership of a godly person to that of a less than ideal situation. We should not be surprised, then, to find that just after this transition in the narrative, we read of the less than ideal conditions that prevailed among God's people, namely, that much of the land still remained to be taken.

B. The Distribution of Land East of the Jordan (13:8–33)

The passage begins with a brief description of all the land east of the Jordan allotted to half of the tribe of Manasseh and to the tribes of Reuben and Gad (vv.8–13). There is then a short reminder that the Levites were not given an inheritance of land (v.14, cf. v.33). What follows is a detailed description of the allotment of land to Reuben (vv.15–23), Gad (vv.24–28), and the half tribe of Manasseh (vv.29–32).

C. The Distribution of Land West of the Jordan (14:1–19:51)

1. Judah (14:1–15:63)

Attention is first given to the two central tribes, Judah and Joseph. A short introduction (14:1–5) explains how the parcels of land were chosen ("assigned by lot," 14:2) and by whom ("Eleazar the priest, Joshua son of Nun and the heads of the tribal clans of Israel," 14:1).

Curiously, the allotment of territory to the house of Caleb, a non-Israelite, within the region of Judah is recounted first (14:6–15). The purpose of the writer in highlighting Caleb is to show that he, along with Joshua, was the only one among the earlier generation who proved faithful at taking God at his word.

The lengthy description of the territory allotted to Judah (15:1–63) is broken up by a few short, though important, narratives. (1) Jerusalem was a part of the territory of Judah (15:8). (2) Caleb took Hebron from the Anakites (15:13–19). (3) Judah could not take Jerusalem, so that the conquest was not complete.

2. Sons of Joseph (16:1–17:18)

The introduction (16:1–4) begins with a general overview of the allotment of Joseph and ends with a reminder that this allotment was divided between Joseph's two sons, Manasseh and Ephraim (16:4). The allotment of Ephraim is listed in 16:5–10 and that of Manasseh in 17:1–13. After both lists the writer notes that the sons of Joseph were unable to drive the Canaanites completely out of the land (16:10; 17:12–13). Thus the lists conclude on the same thematic note as that of Judah (15:63), i.e., the failure of the people to drive out all of the Canaanites.

LAND OF THE TWELVE TRIBES

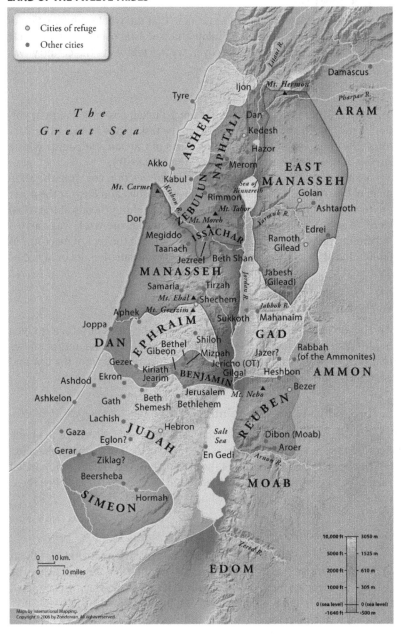

Cities of refuge
Other cities

The Great Sea

Damascus
ARAM
Pharpar R.
Litani R.
Ijon
Mt. Hermon
Tyre
ASHER
Dan
NAPHTALI
Kedesh
Hazor
Akko
Merom
EAST
MANASSEH
Mt. Carmel
Kabul
ZEBULUN
Sea of Kinnereth
Golan
Ashtaroth
Kishon R.
Rimmon
Dor
Mt. Tabor
Mt. Moreh
Yarmuk R.
Edrei
Megiddo
ISSACHAR
Ramoth Gilead
Taanach
Jezreel
Beth Shan
MANASSEH
Jabesh (Gilead)
Samaria
Tirzah
Jordan R.
Mt. Ebal
Shechem
Jabbok R.
Aphek
Mt. Gerizim
Sukkoth
Mahanaim
Joppa
EPHRAIM
GAD
DAN
Shiloh
Bethel
Gibeon
Mizpah
Jazer?
Rabbah (of the Ammonites)
Gezer
Kirlath Jearim
Jericho (OT)
Heshbon
AMMON
Ashdod
Ekron
BENJAMIN
Gilgal
Ashkelon
Gath
Beth Shemesh
Jerusalem
Mt. Nebo
Bezer
Lachish
Bethlehem
REUBEN
Gaza
Hebron
Salt Sea
Dibon (Moab)
Gerar
Eglon?
JUDAH
Aroer
Ziklag?
En Gedi
Arnon R.
Beersheba
MOAB
SIMEON
Hormah

10 km.
10 miles

Zered R.

EDOM

10,000 ft — 3050 m
5000 ft — 1525 m
2000 ft — 610 m
1000 ft — 305 m
0 (sea level) — 0 (sea level)
-1640 ft — -500 m

3. Tent at Shiloh (18:1)

The writer here inserts an important note that the whole congregation of Israel had gathered together at Shiloh and had established the tabernacle (the Tent of Meeting) there. Moreover, we are told that "the country was brought under their control."

4. Remaining seven tribes (18:2 – 19:51)

There were still seven tribes who had not yet taken possession of their portion of the land. The writer thus turns to the task of describing, in cursory form, the conquest of the remaining parts of Canaan. He begins with a survey of the land commissioned by Joshua (18:2 – 10).

A formal conclusion (19:51) is given to this section covering the allotment of the tribes (14:1 – 19:51). The names of Joshua and Eleazar the priest are repeated from 14:1, along with the mention of the "heads of the tribal clans of Israel." Moreover, we are reminded that the work was carried out "in the presence of the LORD at the entrance to the tent of meeting" in Shiloh. In this way the allotment is given official sanction. It could not be contested.

D. The Cities of Refuge Appointed (20:1 – 9)

An abbreviated description of the purpose of the cities of refuge is given here (taken from Nu 35:6 – 34; Dt 4:41 – 43; 19:1 – 13). The author shows that the people and Joshua followed God's instructions from the law and appointed cities as he had commanded.

E. The Levitical Cities Appointed (21:1 – 42)

The Israelites continued to obey God's law in their allotment of the land. Because the Levites were not given a territory of their own, they were allotted cities within the territories of the other tribes. Moses had commanded each tribe to give a portion of its land to the Levites (cf. Nu 35). Now these instructions are carried out by Joshua.

F. Summary (21:43 – 45)

The section on the distribution of the tribal territories concludes with an important summary of its meaning to the author. Here we see clearly the theological message the writer has in mind for the book. Having conquered the land and allotted it among the tribes, it could now be said that God's promises to the patriarchs had been fulfilled.

IV. Final Speeches of Joshua (22:1 – 24:33)

A. Joshua's Speech to the Two and One-Half Tribes (22:1 – 34)

1. The return of the Transjordan tribes (22:1 – 9)

The theology and basic lessons of the Pentateuch can be seen clearly in Joshua's words to the tribes of the Transjordan area — the Reubenites, Gadites, and the half tribe of Manasseh. Their obedience has led to Israel's success, and thus they can now return to their land and enjoy it as a good gift from God. When they settle down in their land, however, they must always be mindful that it is only by their faithful obedience to God's will expressed in the Pentateuch (the law) that they can continue to enjoy God's gift.

What does it mean to obey the law? Joshua's answer is taken directly from the Pentateuch: "to love the LORD your God, to walk in obedience to him, to keep his commands, to hold fast to him and to serve him with all your heart and with all your soul" (v.5; cf. Dt 30:6 – 10). With this message, Joshua blessed these tribes and sent them to their homes.

2. The altar at Geliloth (22:10 – 34)

The writer now raises the problem of the altar at Geliloth that these tribes built after they returned home (v.10). The law had clearly emphasized that only one altar was to be built and that was at the place where God had chosen (Dt 12). Shiloh was now that place, for it was there that the tabernacle had been set up (18:1).

The reply of the Transjordan tribes is interesting. Their new altar, they said, was not intended as a rival of the altar at Shiloh, but rather a reminder of the importance of all the tribes to worship God together at that one place. The altar at Geliloth was to be a "witness between us and you and the generations that follow, that we will worship the LORD at his sanctuary" (v.27). Like the stones set up at the crossing of the Jordan (4:1 – 9), this altar was to remind future generations of the importance of obedience to the will of God in the law.

B. Joshua's Speech to the Elders and Leaders (23:1 – 16)

Two more speeches follow in rapid succession at the close of the book. These serve not only as a conclusion to this book but also provide an important link to the rest of Scripture.

The first is Joshua's speech to the leaders of Israel. In it Joshua reviews the major events of the conquest and draws out the central lesson: "Be

very strong; be careful to obey all that is written in the Book of the Law
of Moses" (v.6).

C. The Covenant at Shechem (24:1 – 28)

In the last of Joshua's speeches, we find the people of Israel renewing
their covenant relationship with the Lord. He had now delivered the land
into their hands. They had been duly warned of impending dangers and
disasters. Now they gathered at Shechem, where they had been in 8:30–35,
being represented again by their tribal leaders. The form of the covenant
follows that of ancient treaty documents.

D. The Death of Joshua and Eleazar (24:28 – 33)

As the book of Joshua began with the death of Moses, so now it concludes
with the death of Joshua (v.29) and Eleazar the priest (v.33). Between the
accounts of the death of these two leaders is the notice that Israel had
faithfully carried out the instructions of Joseph in Ge 50:25 by burying his
bones at Shechem.

JUDGES

Introduction

The title of this book comes from 2:16: "Then the Lᴏʀᴅ raised up judges, who saved them out of the hands of these raiders." During the time of both Moses and Joshua, a select group of leaders in Israel were called "judges" (cf. Nu 25:5; Dt 1:16; Jos 8:33; 23:2; 24:1). According to Ex 2:14, there were already judges among the Israelites in Egypt before Moses gave the law.

This book has one of the clearest structures of any book in the Old Testament. All sections of the book work together to express one main idea, namely, the necessity of God-ordained leadership in Israel. The book functions in a series of cycles. Step 1 is the death of God's leader and the falling away of the people from following the Lord. Step 2 is the Lord's sending oppressors upon the people. In Step 3, Israel calls out to the Lord for help. Then, as Step 4, God raises up a judge to help the people and lead them in the way of the Lord.

I. Prologue (1:1 – 3:6)

A. Survey of the Battles of the Conquest (1:1 – 36)

1. Death of Joshua (1:1)

The book opens with the notice of the death of Joshua, which sets the context for the following description of the conquest of the land.

2. Judah and Simeon (1:2 – 20)

The central focus of ch. 1 is on the tribe of Judah and its conquests. This suggests that Judah has begun to replace Joshua as God's leader. Just as Judah was the first to lead the tribes away from Sinai (Nu 2:3), so Judah led in taking possession of the land. God's promise to Judah in Ge 49:8 – 12 had been that the rulership would not pass from him until the true King would come. Those promises were still intact.

3. Battles by other tribes (1:21 – 36)

These verses list a series of battles by several of the remaining tribes: Benjamin (v.21), the house of Joseph (Manasseh, vv.27 – 28; Ephraim, v.29), Zebulun (v.30), Asher (vv.31 – 32), Naphtali (v.33), and Dan (v.34). For the most part these battles ended inconclusively with the Israelites living side by side with the people of the land.

B. The Angel of the Lord at Bokim (2:1 – 5)

The failure of the Israelites to fully take the land is traced back to the covenant they made with the Gibeonites (cf. Jos 9:1 – 27). There is a marked contrast between the message of the captain of the Lord's host who met Joshua at the beginning of the conquest (Jos 5:13 – 15) and the words of the angel who met Israel at the close of the conquest (Jdg 2:1 – 4). With Joshua, it was a time of great anticipation of victory. Now, after many battles and after the death of Joshua, the angel announces the failure of God's people to obey his will and to successfully take the land. The story of the conquest concludes with Israel's weeping and offering sacrifices to the Lord for their sins.

C. The Apostasy of the Nation (2:6 – 3:6)

Within the framework of Israel's unwillingness to obey the Lord, the role of the judges is introduced. When the people found themselves "in great distress" (v.15) as a result of their unfaithfulness, the Lord raised up judges for them who "saved them out of the hands" of their enemies (v.16). For the most part, as long as they had a judge over them, the people walked in God's way. When the judge died, however, they again forsook God and followed other gods.

The most startling aspect of this section is the comment that after Joshua and his generation died, "another generation grew up who knew neither the LORD nor what he had done for Israel" (v.10). The sin of the people described here was directly attributable to the nation's knowing neither the Lord nor their history as told in their Scriptures.

II. The Judges (3:7 – 16:31)

A. Othniel and Cushan-Rishathaim (3:7 – 11)

In this short narrative the pattern of the story of the judges is clearly portrayed. Israel had sinned and fallen into idolatry. The Lord was angered and sold them into the hands of the Aramean king Cushan-Rishathaim. They served him eight years. When they cried out to the Lord, he raised up Othniel. By means of God's Spirit, Othniel defeated Cushan-Rishathaim, and there was peace as long as Othniel lived (i.e., forty years).

B. Ehud (3:12 – 30)

The story of Ehud has all the makings of an adventure story. Ehud was a genuine hero who used courage and resourcefulness to deliver God's people. Ehud used his own unique physical limitations to carry out God's work. The whole of the story is built around his being left-handed, which to the writer was a limitation. In Hebrew, being left-handed is described as "restricted in his right hand."

C. Shamgar (3:31)

Shamgar is not called a judge, but the text explicitly states that he "saved Israel," and thus he is included within the story of the judges. Like Samson, Shamgar fought the Philistines and delivered Israel by superhuman feats. Samson slew one thousand Philistines with the jawbone of a donkey (15:15), and Shamgar killed six hundred Philistines with an oxgoad.

D. Deborah (4:1 – 5:31)

The story of Deborah begins with the notice that Israel again did evil in God's sight (4:1). God then sold them into the hands of the Canaanites (v.2), and the people cried out to God for help (v.3). God answered their cry by raising up a judge, Deborah (vv.4, 9), who with Barak defeated their oppressors (vv.16, 24); the land had peace for forty years (5:31b).

E. Gideon (6:1 – 8:35)

The story of Gideon follows the essential pattern of the other judges. Once again the Israelites did what evil in God's sight (6:1a), and God gave them over to the Midianites (v.1b). The Israelites cried out to God (v.6), and God sent a deliverer, Gideon (v.14). The enemy was defeated, and the land had rest for the forty years that Gideon ruled over Israel (8:28).

As the story begins to unfold, the words of an unknown prophet (6:7–10) review for the reader that it was God alone who had brought the Israelites out of Egypt and into the Promised Land: "I [God] drove them from before you and gave you their land" (v.9). Moreover, Gideon's uncertainty and the details of his call (vv.11–24) further show that he did not go into battle in his own strength. He was, in fact, a reluctant warrior. Gideon insisted that the Lord reassure him with signs that he was with him.

Gideon's major call to action came when the Midianites and their allies amassed for battle against Israel in the Valley of Jezreel (6:33). The course of the battle itself shows that God was behind Gideon's successes (7:9–25). When the battle ensued, "the Lord caused the men throughout the camp to turn on each other with their swords" (7:22). Thus, neither Gideon nor the Israelite armies delivered Israel from the Midianites. It was God and God alone.

F. Abimelek and Jotham (9:1–57)

Though the story of Abimelek and Jotham, the two sons of Gideon, is complicated, its message is clear. God truly reigned as king in Israel despite the fact that Israel often forsook his ways and followed after other gods. This story, therefore, answers to Gideon's words in 8:23, "The Lord will rule over you." Behind this story lies the hand of God patiently and powerfully working out his just purpose.

G. Tola (10:1–2) and Jair (10:3–5)

Tola saved Israel and judged for twenty-three years. Jair had thirty sons who rode thirty donkeys and controlled thirty towns. He judged Israel twenty-two years.

H. Jephthah (10:6–12:7)

The central theme here is God's sovereign will in choosing and using whomever he pleases. Jephthah's claim to rule in Israel was not based on birth, tact, or judgment. Rather, it was based solely on his zeal to trust God and do his will.

The nature of Jephthah's vow (11:30–31) and its fulfillment (v.39) has occasioned much discussion. A common view is that Jephthah's apparent vow to sacrifice whatever or whoever came out to meet him when he returned from victory over the Ammonites meant that he sacrificed his own daughter. Such an interpretation, however, overlooks important features in the original Hebrew. The words of Jephthah in 11:31 should be rendered, "Whatever comes out of the door ... will be the Lord's, or I will sacrifice it as a burnt offering." In other words, Jephthah dedicated his daughter to the service of the Lord.

I. Ibzan (12:8 – 10), Elon (12:11 – 12), and Abdon (12:13 – 15)

Ibzan, from Bethlehem, judged Israel seven years. He had thirty sons and thirty daughters. Elon, from Zebulun, judged Israel ten years. Abdon, from Ephraim, judged Israel eight years. He had forty sons and thirty grandsons who rode seventy donkeys.

J. Samson (13:1 – 16:31)

The story of Samson is one of the most puzzling in the Bible. Clearly many things Samson did cannot be lessons of godly leadership. What stands out, however, is the zeal with which he fought against the enemies of God's people. He was primarily an example of the wholehearted zeal that God's leader was to have against God's enemies.

III. Epilogue (17:1 – 21:25)

The book of Judges closes with two extended narratives that illustrate the almost unbelievable apostasy and degradation of the nation during this time: Micah's idolatry (17:1 – 18:31) and the Benjamite war (19:1 – 21:25). Their primary thematic purpose is suggested by the recurring phrase, "In those days Israel had no king; everyone did as they saw fit" (17:6; 18:1; 19:1; 21:25). Without the kind of leadership exemplified by the king in Dt 17:14 – 20, there was little hope of the people walking in God's ways.

RUTH

Introduction

In the English Bible, the book of Ruth is generally considered an addendum to the book of Judges. Note how it opens: "In the days when the judges ruled" (1:1). In the Hebrew Bible, however, it is considered an addendum to the book of Proverbs. The character of Ruth is portrayed as a historical example of the virtuous woman of Pr 31:10–31.

The mention of David in ch. 4 suggests that this book was intended to be read in light of the role that David was to play in the monarchy. In this book, then, we have a picture of the faithful lineage of the house of David. At a time when the Israelites were forsaking the Lord and following the gods of the Canaanites and Moabites (Jdg 2:12–15), Ruth forsook those gods to follow the Lord.

I. The Sojourn from the Promised Land (1:1–22)

The book opens with an account of God's people in exile. They are in the land of Moab, it is in the days of the judges, and there is a famine in the land. Particularly the tribe of Judah is at risk, and wives for them are being sought in Moab. Judah is the tribe of David and also of the Messiah. Through the events of the story, however, God takes this hopeless situation and turns it to his purpose and glory.

II. Ruth Meets Boaz (2:1 – 23)

In ch. 2 we begin to see the hand of God at work. Naomi returned from her sojourn in Moab to the land of Israel, and Ruth accompanied her. Ruth's faithfulness and trust in God were well-known throughout the whole region (v.11), and God was about to repay Ruth for her faithfulness (v.12). The firstfruits of God's blessing came to Ruth in the form of Boaz's special treatment of her and his provision for her family (vv.13 – 18).

III. Ruth's Night at Boaz's Threshing Floor (3:1 – 18)

This chapter concentrates on Ruth's unusual night visit to Boaz at the threshing floor. Fortunately, the sketchy details of the story and the customs involved do not affect the overall meaning of the story. It appears likely that the law of the levirate marriage lies behind the actions of Ruth and Boaz (see Dt 25:5 – 10; cf. Ge 38:8).

IV. Ruth's Marriage to Boaz (4:1 – 22)

It is no surprise that the closest kin forfeited his right to redeem Ruth's inheritance (vv.1 – 6). Up to here in the story the recurring theme has been God's faithfulness to the house of David and the confluence of human events to that purpose. Therefore, when the closest of kin refused to buy Ruth's inheritance and take her as his wife, we see further evidence of God's providence.

The genealogy in vv.18 – 22 makes the final link between this story and the birth of David. It is the story of the birth of David, the king of Israel, and the story of the birth of the Son of David, the Messiah.

1 SAMUEL

Introduction

The title of this book is derived from the principal character of the book, Samuel the prophet. He was the founder of the Israelite monarchy. Since the events of the two volumes run from the final days of the judges to the final days of the life of David — over one hundred years — its author likely did not witness all of the events in the book.

I. The Period of Samuel's Judgeship (1Sa 1:1 – 7:17)

A. The Rise of Samuel and the Fall of Israel to the Philistines (1:1 – 4:22)

1. The story of Hannah (1:1 – 2:11a)

The main characters in the story are introduced in 1:1 – 3. Elkanah, Samuel's father, was from the hill country of Ephraim and had two wives, Hannah and Peninnah. Hannah was barren because the Lord had closed her womb (v.5), and Peninnah had many children (v.2b).

The climax of the story comes with Eli's announcement that Hannah's prayer had been heard (1:17). She returned to her husband "and her face was no longer downcast" (v.18). Hannah's song (2:1 – 10) is important for the interpretation of the story because, like most songs in the Bible, the author uses it to draw out thematic hot points of the story. Hannah's answered prayer was a sign that the Lord is a righteous judge. He brought down the proud (Peninnah) and exalted the humble (Hannah). The idea of the Lord's judging the proud and exalting the humble is linked to the concepts of the barrenness and the blessing of children that are central here.

2. The exile of the ark (2:11b – 4:22)

In the first segment of this story (2:11b–4:1a) the author demonstrates that the priests, Eli's sons Hophni and Phinehas, were totally bereft of the ideals of God's law. He gives two reports of their misdeeds—the first demonstrating their greed (2:12–17) and the second their promiscuity (vv.22–25). Then follow two reports of God's judgment on the house of Eli: the speech by the "man of God" (vv.27–36) and God's word to Samuel (3:1–18).

In the final segment of the story (4:1b–22), the narrative records the exile of the ark of the covenant. The Israelites met the Philistines in battle and were summarily defeated (4:1b–2). In their second encounter, the ark was captured. Though the narrative provides no explanation for these defeats, the larger context suggests that it was because of the failure of their leadership, the ungodly priests.

B. The Return of the Ark and the Revival of the People (5:1 – 7:17)

1. The ark in exile and its return (5:1 – 7:1)

After their capture of the ark, the Philistines brought it to Ashdod to put it in the temple of their god, Dagon (5:1–2). Presumably it was placed there as a trophy.

When the ark was returned, the Israelites treated it carelessly, and many died because of that (6:19). The ark was then given proper treatment according to the law of Moses, and a priesthood was appointed to care for it (6:20–7:1).

To appreciate the meaning of this story we must remember that according to the Pentateuch, the ark represented God's promise to dwell among his chosen people (Ex 25:22). The Israelites had misused this privilege by presuming upon it, and the Philistines' attempt to turn their possession of the ark into a blessing for their land also failed. The Lord's presence with the ark could not be manipulated; it was a matter of grace.

2. The lesson of obedience (7:2 – 17)

After the ark had been returned and the Israelites had mourned their losses, Samuel gathered the people to call them to obedience (vv.2–3). The people responded by obeying the words of Samuel and putting away their foreign gods to follow the Lord alone (v.4).

II. The Beginning of the Israelite Monarchy (8:1 – 15:35)

A. The Request for a King (8:1 – 22)

At the close of Samuel's life, a crisis developed over the kind of leaders Israel should have. The people, recognizing that Samuel's old age was hindering his ability to judge Israel, requested that he appoint a king over them to rule like the other nations around them (vv.4 – 5). Rather than wait for God to deliver by raising up a judge like Samuel, the people wanted to appoint a permanent leader, a king.

Samuel, however, was angered by this request and turned to the Lord for help. The Lord responded by explaining their request and instructing Samuel to acquiesce to their plan, even though the motives of the people were not right (v.7). Samuel then carried out their proposal and established the kingship in Israel with the house of Saul, though not without a solemn warning to remain faithful to the covenant and to remember that the Lord alone was the true king in Israel. The earthly monarch was merely the obedient servant of the Lord (vv.11 – 22; 12:14 – 15).

B. The Selection of Saul (9:1 – 10:16)

After a brief introduction to the family of Saul (9:1 – 2), the story begins with Saul's trek after his father's lost donkeys. Being unable to find them (vv.3 – 4), Saul sought the help of Samuel (vv.5 – 12). The next morning, Samuel privately anointed Saul as king in Israel (9:25 – 10:1). As a confirmation of his calling, Samuel gave Saul three signs that would be fulfilled (10:2 – 13), which followed the requirements for the confirmation of a prophet's words (see Dt 18).

C. The Public Appointment of Saul (10:17 – 27)

A fascinating view of Saul is presented here. Virtually all of it is positive, showing Saul's humility (v.22) and his great strength and acclaim: "There is no one like him among all the people" (v.24). Even the army he formed contained "valiant men whose hearts God had touched" (v.26). Thus the people's request for a king to lead them in war was fulfilled.

D. The Divine Confirmation of Saul (11:1 – 15)

To set the stage for the account of Saul's failure, the writer provides one more narrative to show the people's and God's initial approval of him. Saul is presented as Israel's deliverer, remarkably similar to the judges. Saul rallied the tribes, and just as during the time of the judges, the Spirit of God came on him and he defeated the Ammonites in battle. Saul's mighty deeds were known and acknowledged by the people.

E. Samuel's Speech (12:1 – 25)

Samuel called the people together at Gilgal to celebrate Saul's victory over the Ammonites and to reconfirm him as king (11:14). In Samuel's speech, he began by declaring his own innocence in both the matter of the kingship and the matter of his role as judge over Israel. He then recounted God's "righteous acts" (12:7) for Israel, as recorded in the Pentateuch, beginning with God's sending Moses and Aaron to bring the people out of Egypt and into the land (v.8). He then turned to the time of the judges, listing himself as the last judge (vv.9–11). Finally, he warned the nation that their present request for a king was a serious matter and that it greatly displeased the Lord.

In spite of the Lord's displeasure, however, there was still much hope for Israel. If they obeyed the Lord, he would bless them. If they rebelled, both they and their king would go into exile. The lesson of Samuel's speech is that of Moses in the book of Deuteronomy (e.g., Dt 4) and the prophet Ezekiel (e.g., Eze 36:22–32).

F. Saul's Failure as King of the Lord's People (13:1 – 15:35)

The clearest example of the role that the king was to play in Israel comes from the account of Saul's failure. Saul failed as king because he did not provide spiritual leadership for the nation. He overstepped his bounds within God's established pattern for the king—he did not heed the words of God spoken by the prophet (13:9–14). Saul, as it turned out, was the kind of king Israel had wanted, for he could maintain a standing army, but he was not the kind of king the Lord wanted—he did not obey God's will. Thus Saul was rejected as king and ultimately fell in defeat in battle (31:4).

1. Saul's first offense (13:1 – 15a)

This is the first of two accounts of Saul's failure to show godly leadership (see also 15:1–23). Samuel had instructed Saul to wait for him at Gilgal, and he would come in seven days to offer a sacrifice before the battle (v.8). Saul, however, feeling the threat and pressure of the Philistine forces gathered for battle, did not obey Samuel's words, and he offered the sacrifice before Samuel arrived (vv.8–9). As soon as he offered the sacrifice, Samuel arrived (v.10). Saul had preempted the authority of the Lord and had disobeyed the word of the Lord's prophet (cf. Dt 18:18). Thus, according to Dt 17:20, he could no longer be king.

2. Saul's campaign against the Philistines (13:15b – 14:52)

This narrative is positioned between the two accounts of Saul's rejection as king. Surprisingly, much of what Saul did here is positive and in line with the lessons of the Deuteronomy. Saul is, in fact, portrayed as a victorious king. Thus, this story seems intended to show that from a general point of view, Saul was a desirable king and a worthy leader.

3. Saul's second failure as king of the Lord's people (15:1 – 35)

Samuel the prophet called on Saul to engage the Amalekites in a holy war, i.e., a war to carry out divine judgment on the Lord's enemies (vv.1 – 3). Samuel's instruction was total destruction: no Amalekite was to survive (15:3). Note that Samuel's words to Saul were the words of the Lord, who was commanding him to go out against the Amalekites (vv.2 – 3).

Saul obediently went out against the Amalekites. God gave him victory, but Saul did not fully carry out the word of the Lord. He "spared Agag and the best of the sheep and cattle, the fat calves and lambs — everything that was good" (v.9). Saul had turned a solemn commission of the Lord into an occasion for his own prosperity.

Saul confessed his sin of disobedience but to no avail (vv.24 – 26). Samuel told him, "You have rejected the word of the LORD, and the LORD has rejected you as king over Israel!" (v.26).

III. The Decline of Saul and the Rise of David (16:1 – 31:13)

A. David, the Man after God's Own Heart: The Early Years (16:1 – 30:31)

With God's rejection of Saul as king, the process of the divine selection of a new king began. We are told far in advance that the new king will be one "after [God's] own heart" (13:14) — i.e., one who desired to walk in the way of the Lord. When David was selected, it was apparently this very feature that gained him God's final approval. Even Samuel was willing to accept a leader on the basis of external judgment, but not God. The Lord looks into the human heart and selects his representatives on that basis (16:6 – 7).

1. The selection of David (16:1 – 23)

The Lord instructed Samuel to go to the house of Jesse, David's father, to anoint the one whom he had chosen to replace Saul as king (vv.1 – 3). Again we see the importance of Samuel, the prophet, as the one through whom the kingship was established. God's authority came through the prophet.

Jesse had eight sons, seven of whom he brought to Samuel for the selection. David remained with his father's sheep, not even considered as a possible choice. It was, of course, this David whom the Lord had chosen all along. Thus the narrative highlights its central theme—the Lord does not look on the outside, as a human being does, but at the heart (vv.4–13).

David was immediately anointed king and received special endowment by the Spirit of God to carry out his role as king (v.13). At the same time, the Spirit left Saul (v.14)—he was thus no longer God's special representative, though he remained the "anointed" king. One of the most striking pictures of David in this book is his reluctance to force his way into his rightful position as king. He was the anointed king from 1Sa 16 on, but not until 2Sa 5 he was recognized as king over all Israel. David patiently waited for God's timing and tried as best he could to live peacefully with the jealous Saul.

2. The confirmation of David (17:1 – 54)

The next major episode in David's rise to the kingship was his slaying of the giant Goliath. The most important insight here is David's understanding of the Lord's role in a kingship. For David, Israel could not be protected by mere spears and swords (v.47). David is the key example of a leader who puts his trust wholly in the Lord.

3. The public recognition of David (17:55 – 18:16)

Three short narratives follow the account of David's slaying Goliath; they show the extent of David's growing recognition among the people. The first narrative shows the special recognition given David by Saul and his officers (17:55–18:5); the second is that of the celebration of Saul and David's victory by the women of the city (18:6–11); and the third is the summary of David's success with the people (18:12–16).

4. The beginning of opposition from Saul (18:17 – 30)

God was with David and not with Saul. Try as he might, Saul could not curb David's successes or his growing popularity with the people. Saul concocted a scheme to deliver David into the hand of the Philistines. He had to prove he was a mighty warrior to win the hand of Saul's older daughter in marriage (v.17; cf. 17:25, that anyone who killed Goliath would marry Saul's daughter). David refused Saul's first offer of his oldest daughter but accepted the offer of Michal, who loved him (18:20, 28). But Saul's plan backfired, for David managed to kill the Philistines to win Saul's daughter, and David's popularity with the people increased even more.

DAVID'S FAMILY TREE

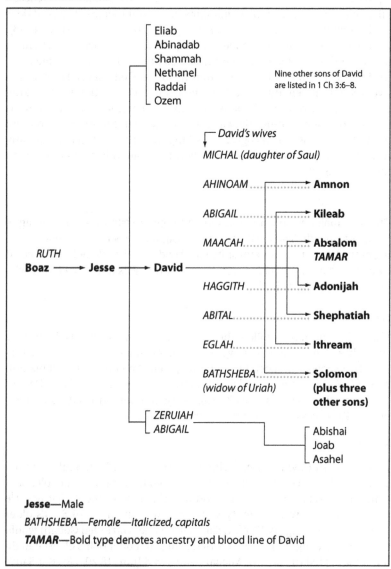

Eliab
Abinadab
Shammah
Nethanel
Raddai
Ozem

Nine other sons of David are listed in 1 Ch 3:6–8.

David's wives

MICHAL (daughter of Saul)

AHINOAM .... → **Amnon**

ABIGAIL .... → **Kileab**

MAACAH .... → **Absalom**
                        TAMAR

RUTH
Boaz ⟶ **Jesse** → **David**

HAGGITH .... → **Adonijah**

ABITAL .... → **Shephatiah**

EGLAH .... → **Ithream**

BATHSHEBA .... → **Solomon**
(widow of Uriah)   **(plus three other sons)**

ZERUIAH
ABIGAIL

Abishai
Joab
Asahel

Jesse—Male
BATHSHEBA—Female—Italicized, capitals
TAMAR—Bold type denotes ancestry and blood line of David

5. The intensification of Saul's opposition (19:1 – 24)

Saul now openly tried to have David killed. In his first attempt, Saul's son Jonathan was able to ameliorate his anger (vv.1 – 7). As David continued to have military success and gained wider recognition among the people, Saul's troubled spirit returned and his efforts to kill David were renewed (vv.8 – 17). This time it was Michal, Saul's daughter, who rescued David (vv.12 – 16). The thematic elements of the narrative are reminiscent of the early chapters of Exodus where Moses was delivered from the decrees of Pharaoh by Pharaoh's own household.

In the third phase of Saul's attempt on David's life, his plan was averted through the Spirit of God (vv.18 – 24). Saul was prevented from doing so when the Spirit of God came upon him. Saul prophesied all night while David escaped.

6. Jonathan allied with David against Saul (20:1 – 42)

This long and carefully detailed narrative shows that David, the newly anointed king, made a peaceful transition from the old dynasty. He did not gain the throne by force or rebellion. Rather, it came to him with the full acknowledgment of the legitimacy of the old regime. This idea becomes particularly important in the final narratives of 1 Samuel. When given the opportunity to take the kingdom by force, David repeatedly refused (cf. 24:1 – 22).

7. David's flight from Saul (21:1 – 27:12)

The biblical writer now gives a loosely connected account of David's marshaling of his army and of his initial rise to power. There is nothing particularly glamorous about it. Rather, David rose to power by simple trust and obedience to the Lord's guidance. The central theme running throughout these narratives is the picture of the future king, David, following the words of the prophet Gad and inquiring of God's will by means of the priests.

Throughout these chapters is an underlying comparison between David's actions and those of Saul. Saul is portrayed as disloyal to God or his people even while living in the land. David, by contrast, is portrayed as one who remained loyal to the Lord and his people even though living in exile.

8. An interlude: Samuel's final word to Saul (28:1 – 25)

As v.1 suggests, David was in exile and Saul was waging war with the Philistines. A parenthetical note tells us that Samuel was dead and that Saul had expelled all mediums and spiritists from the land. In seeking guidance for battle, Saul sought a message from the Lord through all legitimate means—dreams, Urim, and prophets—but there was no answer (vv.4-6). Thus Saul turned to an illegitimate one, the witch of Endor (vv.7-14).

Curiously, when Saul sought the Lord through the prophets, he received no word. But when he turned to the medium, he received a word from Samuel. There is clear irony here. The word from Samuel further confirmed God's original words to Saul that his kingdom would be taken away from him (vv.17-18). Moreover, Samuel's prediction of Saul's death also served to confirm the word of Samuel.

9. David is saved from fighting for (or against) Saul (29:1–11)

David had joined the ranks of the Philistines and was preparing for battle with Saul (vv.1-2). The Philistine commanders, however, raised an objection to David's participation (vv.3-5), for they did not trust this Israelite in their ranks. In 27:8-12 we were told that David had deliberately misled Achish into thinking that he was the enemy of Saul and Israel. But Achish was wrong about David; David would indeed have joined with Israel against the Philistines (v.4). The Philistines' reference to "taking the heads of our own men" likely alludes to David's taking Goliath's head (17:46, 51, 57).

10. David defeats his enemy and restores his kingdom (30:1–31)

Although still fleeing Saul, David now began to take the steps that would lead him to the kingdom. He was saving God's people from their enemies, and his successes in battle came clearly from the Lord. David took his men from near rebellion to total victory over the Amalekites. The key to his success is given in v.6b: "But David found strength in the LORD his God." This attitude is expressed also in the matter of the division of the spoils. David reminded his men that it was the Lord alone who had given them victory in the battle and who had given them all the spoils (vv.23-24).

B. The Death of Saul (31:1–13)

According to 1Ch 10:13-14, "Saul died [and lost his kingdom] because he was unfaithful to the LORD ... and did not inquire of the LORD." Twice Saul did not keep the word of the Lord that was spoken through the prophet Samuel (1Sa 13:1-23; 15:1-35), and Saul sought the counsel of a medium (1Sa 28). Behind this condemnation is the clear teaching of Dt 18:10-22. Israel was not to seek the will of God in the counsel of mediums or in the words of false prophets but in his own word, spoken by his prophets.

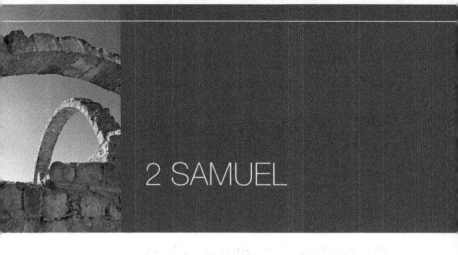

2 SAMUEL

Introduction

See introduction to 1 Samuel.

I. David's Rise to the Kingship in Jerusalem (1:1 – 6:23)

A. Saul, Abner, and Joab (1:1 – 3:39)

The last stages of David's rise to kingship over all of Israel were marked by two apparent mishaps: the death of Saul and Joab's murder of Abner (2:18 – 3:39). In both of them, however, David was innocent.

Just before David assumed the kingship, the nation of Israel was divided into two separate kingdoms. David was already ruling the southern tribe of Judah, while Saul's son Ish-Bosheth was ruling the north, the area called simply Israel.

B. The Death of Ish-Bosheth (4:1 – 12)

As is clear in the case of the Amalekite's supposed slaying of Saul in ch. 1, David did not take the kingship from Saul by force. The treacherous deed of Saul's captains, Baanah and Rekab, removed Ish-Bosheth from the throne and thus paved the way for David's rule over the northern tribes. Their action was not rewarded but severely punished by David. David's heart was right before God, and he did not seek to promote himself to the throne.

C. David Becomes King over All Israel (5:1 – 5)

David had already been anointed king over the tribe of Judah in Hebron (2:4). After the death of Ish-Bosheth, the elders of the northern tribes sought David at Hebron and there anointed him king over all Israel.

D. David Captures Jerusalem (5:6 – 25)

Though Israel had long lived in the land, the city of Jerusalem had not been permanently captured (see Jos 15; Jdg 1:2 – 20). Now David took the city for his own. Henceforth, Jerusalem was the "City of David." David also went on to defeat the Philistines.

E. The Ark Is Brought to Jerusalem (6:1 – 23)

This event teaches the seriousness and reality of God's presence. God had graciously promised to be near his people, and Moses had instructed them how the ark was to be treated (Ex 25 – 31). There was much celebration before the ark as David and the people attempted to move it to Jerusalem; however, not all was carried out as the Lord had commanded. The people were carrying the ark of God on a cart pulled by oxen (v.3). This failure to be faithful led to the great tragedy recorded here (cf. 1Ch 13:9 – 10). Uzzah put out his hand to steady the ark because the oxen stumbled, and "God struck him down" (v.7).

II. The Davidic Covenant (7:1 – 29)

David as king of all Israel had rest from his enemies and a united kingdom. He now set his mind on building a "house" (i.e., a temple) for the ark of the covenant. But the Lord had other plans. He sent the prophet Nathan to ask David, "Are you the one to build me a house to dwell in?" (v.5). David was not to build a "house" for the Lord; rather, the Lord would build a "house" for him (v.26) — that is, a continuing line of kings, a dynasty of his offspring over all Israel and the tribe of Judah.

III. The Decline of the House of David (8:1 – 24:25)

The rest of the 2 Samuel deals with several significant events from the life of David. The writer begins with a general description of his conquests.

A. David's Conquests (8:1 – 18)

David's reign appears to be shaped by the vision of Balaam in Nu 24:17–20. Balaam had prophesied that a king (Nu 24:7) would arise in Israel who would conquer Israel's enemies, the Moabites, Edomites, and Amalekites. David fulfilled much of this prophecy. It is in this sense that we should understand the description of David in v.15: "David reigned over all Israel, doing what was just and right for all his people." The Lord was with David, for he "gave David victory wherever he went" (v.6; repeated in v.14).

B. David Provided for the House of Saul (9:1 – 13)

David had promised Jonathan that he would always care for his household (cf. 1Sa 20:14). Thus, as the writer recounts David's successes against his enemies, he also recounts David's faithfulness to his word to Jonathan, particularly in caring for Mephibosheth. In this way, David's victories are cast as the fulfillment of Jonathan's words, "May the LORD call David's enemies to account" (1Sa 20:16).

C. David Defeats the Ammonites (10:1 – 19)

David subjugated the Ammonites. This battle further involved the Arameans, a group of city-states already defeated by David (cf. 8:5–6), so that in the end, David ruled over the Aramean state controlled by Hadadezer (v.19). The focus of the passage is on the Aramean states of Zobah and Damascus.

D. David's Sin with Bathsheba (11:1 – 27)

This story focuses our attention on the role of the prophet Nathan in confronting the king with his need to follow the justice prescribed in the covenant. According to Deuteronomy, the prophet was to guard the covenant responsibilities of the king; he was never to side with the king if the king disobeyed those requirements. In this story David clearly committed adultery, covered up his sin, and was ultimately responsible for the death of Uriah, Bathsheba's husband.

E. David's Repentance (12:1 – 31)

David's repentance after the incident with Bathsheba (12:1–25) shows he truly was a man after God's own heart. He listened to the rebuke of the prophet, something neither Saul nor many later in the Davidic dynasty were willing to do. David followed the prescriptions of God's law, even in times of weakness and failure. The narrative ends on the positive note of

DAVID'S CONQUESTS

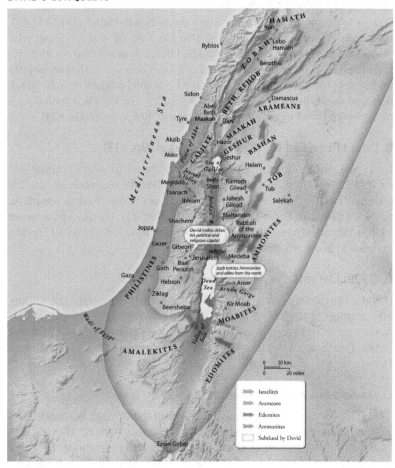

the birth of Solomon, whose name means "he has made peace." The writer adds that "the LORD loved him" and thus instructed Nathan to name him Jedidiah, "loved by the LORD" (vv.24–25).

F. Amnon and Tamar (13:1–39)

The sin of David with Bathsheba was repeated or duplicated in the lives of David's sons. Thus Amnon's rape of Tamar has its parallel in David's adultery with Bathsheba. The sins of the father are being passed on to the next generation.

G. The Wise Woman from Tekoa (14:1 – 33)

David was saved from making a fatal mistake by the words of a wise woman (cf. Abigail in 1Sa 25). This account is written in such a way that the woman's description of the events of Amnon's death at the hand of Absalom does not follow the actual account given in ch. 13, but rather the story of Cain and Abel in Ge 4. In both stories, the two sons were "in the field" and the one rose up against the other and killed him.

These parallels are intended to show that David has a heart like God. Both responded with wise compassion: God showed kindness to the murderer Cain (Ge 4:15) and David showed kindness to the murderer Absalom. David had the heart of God, and the woman acknowledged this by saying, "My lord the king is like an angel of God in discerning good and evil" (v.17).

H. Rebellion within the House of David (15:1 – 20:26)

1. Absalom's rebellion (15:1 – 19:43)

This narrative demonstrates David's trust in God's faithfulness. Even in the face of the rebellion of the offspring of his own house, David trusted God fully to secure his promise. The clearest statement of such trust is in 15:25. When driven from Jerusalem by Absalom's rebellion, David did not seek to fight for the city. He said simply, "If I find favor in the LORD's eyes, he will bring me back and let me see it and his dwelling place again." When Shimei from the family of Saul cursed David, David's left the matter in the Lord's hands (16:11). Note v.12: "It may be that the LORD will look upon my misery and restore to me his covenant blessing instead of his curse today."

2. Sheba's rebellion (20:1 – 22)

This narrative raises the question of whether David's kingdom could be replaced by someone from another tribe. Sheba, from the tribe of Benjamin, instigated a revolt against David, calling into question his right to rule all Israel. The promises to the patriarchs in the Pentateuch had specifically named the tribe of Judah as the only legitimate home of the promised kingdom (cf. Ge 49:8 – 12). As was characteristic of the Samuel narrative since the beginning, the author rests his case for the legitimacy of the house of David in the work and words of a wise woman. The wise among God's people stand behind the Davidic kingship. Only the fool like Sheba would dare question what had been so clearly promised in Scripture.

3. Peace restored (20:23 – 26)

In the end, peace is restored, and this section closes with a listing of David's government officials.

I. David Avenges the Gibeonites (21:1 – 14)

There was a famine throughout the land for three years, so David "sought the face of the LORD" — i.e., he inquired of the prophet (cf. God's command in Dt 18:14-22). David quickly responded to God's answer. This famine came because the iniquity of Saul against the Gibeonites had not been avenged. David carried out God's word from the prophet, and God honored David's response (v.14b). David's compassionate heart is also manifest (vv.13-14).

J. David's Victories against the Philistines (21:15 – 22)

In order to confirm that the Lord had forgiven David and was now again fighting for him, the writer recounts a series of victories of David and his men over the Philistines. In his descriptions of the Philistines, the writer seems to go out of his way to draw a connection between these final battles of David against the Philistines and his first battle with Goliath. One of the Philistines defeated by Abishai, for example, was Ishbi-Benob, "whose bronze spearhead weighed three hundred shekels" (v.16), bringing to mind Goliath's bronze coat of armor "weighing five thousand shekels" (1Sa 17:5). Another Philistine slain by David's men was "a huge man" (v.20), just as Goliath was described as "six cubits and a span" (1Sa 17:4; NIV note: "about 9 feet 9 inches").

K. David's Final Song (22:1 – 51)

It is fitting that the David narratives be concluded by one of his many songs from the book of Psalms — in this case, Ps 18. The psalm celebrates God's faithfulness to David and his house. Its central message falls in the final lines: "He gives his king great victories; he shows unfailing kindness to his anointed, to David and his descendants forever" (v.51).

L. The Lord's Anointed (23:1 – 7)

In these last words of David, we are shown David's own evaluation of God's promise in ch. 7 and what it means in light of the failure of his own house to fulfill it. David begins with a brief description of the "man anointed by the God of Jacob" (v. 1), about whom David wrote so many of his psalms. He makes the claim that in these psalms, the Lord spoke through him by "the Spirit of the LORD," putting his word on David's tongue (v.2). What did David write of in these psalms? He says he wrote of the Anointed One who "rules over people in righteousness ... in the fear of God" (v.3). This passage has long been understood by Christians and early Judaism to refer to the Messiah.

If this passage is read in light of the continued story of the failure of the house of David in 1 and 2 Kings, then David's words prove to be prophetic. We find that none of the historical kings fulfilled the prophetic promise of the Anointed One that David wrote of in the Psalms. Moreover, David's words fall in line with the strategy of the narratives in the books of Kings, in that they conclude on this same note.

M. David's Mighty Men (23:8 – 39)

The list of David's thirty-seven mighty warriors serves two purposes. (1) God had given David help on all sides. One cannot read these exploits without drawing the conclusion that God had given these men to King David. (2) At the same time, however, the focus on their exploits, rather than on David's, appears to push David out of center stage. It thus prepares the way for the view of David that emerges in the next chapter—the view of one who had lost his confidence in God to help him in time of trouble and who had begun to rely instead on his own strength.

It is no accident that this list of mighty warriors ends with Uriah the Hittite. The reader is reminded of David's sin with Bathsheba, his first failure to obey God's will in ruling his people. Thus we come to his last failure, the numbering of his army.

N. David's Numbering of His Army (24:1 – 25)

This chapter records David's second failure to trust God and live according to Dt 17:14 – 21. The fact that two accounts of David's failure are recorded is related to the requirement in Dt 19:15 that "a matter must be established by the testimony of two or three witnesses." Thus, David was not God's ultimate promised King.

When David saw the angel striking down the people of Israel, he quickly confessed the wrong he had done and asked the Lord to let his hand fall on him and his house (v.17). He purchased the threshing floor of Araunah where, in God's grace, the plague had been stopped. David built an altar at this location and the Lord answered his prayer (v.25). The writer puts much emphasis on this location, because it was to be the site of the temple.

Thus in this final act of David, the first step toward fulfilling the promise in ch. 7 was accomplished. God had chosen the place where his name was to dwell. Thus 2 Samuel ends with one question resolved, i.e., where the temple was to be built; but another question is unresolved, who was to build it? That question is addressed in the next book, the book of Kings.

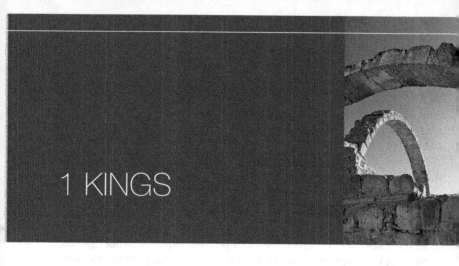

1 KINGS

Introduction

In the Hebrew Bible there is no division between 1 and 2 Kings. The date and author are unknown. Early tradition ascribed the book to the prophet Jeremiah, but there is no sound basis for that assertion. The last event recorded is the release of King Jehoiachin from prison in Babylon and the daily ration of food given him "as long as he lived" (2Ki 25:27–30). Thus the book was written a considerable period of time after the exile in 586 BC.

I. Solomon (1:1 – 11:43)

A. Adonijah's Rebellion and Solomon's Accession (1:1 – 53)

The book of Kings opens with the continuation of the question of who would succeed David as king and thus fulfill the Lord's promise in 2Sa 7:12–13, "I will raise up your offspring to succeed you.... He is the one who will build a house for my Name." With David now near death, the question of his successor was urgent. Absalom was dead, and the oldest son was Adonijah, David's fourth son (2Sa 3:4).

Adonijah conspired with members of David's court (1Ki 1:9) to take the throne. Bathsheba, Zadok the priest, Nathan the prophet, and Benaiah (v.26) the captain of the guard, however, took countermeasures to make Solomon king. While Adonijah and those with him were celebrating their impending success, Solomon was quickly escorted to the spring of Gihon (v.38) and anointed king by Zadok before all the people (v.39).

B. David's Last Words (2:1 – 12)

David's last words to Solomon (2:1–9) carry a great deal of weight in light of the message of the book of Kings. They provide a specific link to 2Sa 7 and the major theme of that book: the Davidic promise. His words also refer back to a number of unfinished incidents from 1 and 2 Samuel, clarifying and specifying two important features of the promise. (1) David raises the issue of obedience as a condition of the fulfillment of God's promise (vv.2–4). (2) As long as the descendants of David remained faithful to God's law, they would not be cut off. Hence, David's words anticipate the central theme as well as the conclusion of 1 and 2 Kings.

C. Solomon's Kingdom Established (2:13 – 46)

1. Adonijah's second rebellion (2:13 – 25)

After David died, Adonijah made another, more subtle, attempt for the throne. But Solomon was not to be fooled. He knew that Adonijah's request for Abishag, the Shunammite, was a veiled attempt to gain legitimacy to David's throne through marriage to Abishag (v.22). Adonijah was therefore executed (v.25). We should note, however, that the writer of Kings uses Adonijah's own words to vindicate Solomon's kingship. He said to Bathsheba, "The kingdom has gone to my brother [Solomon]; for it has come to him from the LORD" (v.15b).

2. Old debts are settled (2:26 – 46)

After this, Solomon dealt with those who had followed Adonijah. Abiathar was replaced as high priest by Zadok (vv.27, 35), Joab was executed (v.34), and Shimei was killed (v.46). In each of these three cases, the theme is that of fulfillment. Zadok and his lineage henceforth assumed the office of high priest in fulfillment of God's word to Samuel (1Sa 3); Joab was punished for the murder of Abner (2Sa 3:27) and Amasa (2Sa 20:10); and David was avenged for the mistreatment he received from Shimei (v.44b; cf. 2Sa 16:5–12). Moreover, in these acts Solomon also fulfilled David's last instructions to him (cf. vv.5–9).

D. Solomon's Wisdom (3:1 – 4:34)

Solomon went to Gibeon to offer sacrifices at the large "high place" erected there. The author of Kings appears somewhat apologetic for Solomon's actions, assuring us that Solomon, appearances to the contrary, loved God and was obedient to his commandments (3:3). Note how God gave Solomon great wisdom in the context of the dream, not within the context of the high place. After this dream, Solomon returned to Jerusalem and presented himself before the Lord at the ark of the covenant (3:15). The chronicler offers more details about this incident, showing that the Tent of Meeting, the tabernacle, and the bronze altar were at Gibeon at this time, and thus Solomon's sacrifices were in line with the law of Moses (see 2Ch 1:1-13).

E. Solomon's Temple (5:1 – 9:28)

The writer has two primary purposes in his account of Solomon's building the temple. (1) He directs the reader's attention to the possibility that Solomon's temple fulfilled God's promise to David (2Sa 7). In this passage it is Solomon's own words to the king of Tyre that turn our attention to God's promise to David, "I intend, therefore, to build a temple for the Name of the LORD my God, as the LORD told my father David" (5:5). Solomon undoubtedly believed he was the promised offspring; on that basis he planned to build the temple. The patient reader will learn, however, that in God's plan, Solomon was not the promised offspring (11:9-13). When the conditions for the fulfillment of the promise to David are reiterated to Solomon (see 6:12), we realize by the end of the story of Solomon that he did not meet these conditions (11:9-13).

Thus within the flow of the narrative, our attention, though initially directed to consider Solomon as a possible fulfillment of God's promise to David, is redirected to look far beyond him for the fulfillment of the promise. It is in this sense that these texts in the book of Kings are to be considered messianic texts. They develop the theme of the promised offspring of David and attempt to show that none of the historical kings in the house of David met the condition of full obedience that was to be the characteristic sign of the Promised One.

(2) Solomon's work on the temple is a picture or image of the ultimate fulfillment of God's promise to David. The promised offspring will be like Solomon when he comes. By this point in Scripture, it had long been promised that the nations, along with Israel, would play a significant role in the kingdom of God promised to David (cf. Ge 49:10c; Nu 24:7-24). With Hiram king of Tyre at the beginning of the account of the temple's building (5:1-18), and the queen of Sheba's visit at its conclusion (10:1-13), the writer portrays the nations playing an important role in Solomon's kingdom, supplying their own wealth for building the temple (cf. Hag 2:7) and appreciating its glory and splendor (cf. Isa 2:2-4).

F. Solomon's Wealth and Glory (10:1 – 11:8)

The writer presents Solomon as a figure or picture of the ideal king envisioned in Dt 17 and 2Sa 7. Though ultimately Solomon's kingship, like that of the rest of the Davidic kings, ended in ruin and division, his rule came closer to the ideal than any of the others. Thus, the writer elaborates on the glories and splendor of that kingdom. Solomon was Israel's greatest king and a picture of the promised King who would be even greater than Solomon (Mt 12:42).

The queen of Sheba, visiting the wise King Solomon, had her hard questions with which she tested his wisdom (10:1), and "Solomon answered all her questions; nothing was too hard for the king to explain to her" (v.3). The queen was overwhelmed and confessed, "Indeed, not even half was told me; in wisdom and wealth you have far exceeded the report I heard" (v.7). From the author's point of view we know that she was not merely testing Solomon's wisdom, but she was testing God's wisdom as well (cf. 4:29-34). Her response, then, was an evaluation of the source of his wisdom, i.e., divine instruction found in Scripture.

In the summary of Solomon's reign (10:23-11:8), one can clearly see the narrator's strategy. He begins by extolling the wisdom God had given Solomon, but before he finishes, we see that it was just this wealth and wisdom that led to Solomon's downfall. He was "greater in riches and wisdom than all the other kings of the earth. The whole world sought audience with Solomon to hear the wisdom God had put in his heart" (10:23-24). This summary looks back to God's earlier promise to Solomon that through the wisdom God gave him, he would "have no equal among kings" (3:12-13).

G. Solomon's Fall (11:9-43)

The Lord had commanded Moses in Dt 17:17 that the king "must not take many wives, or his heart will be led astray." Solomon clearly violated this command, and the writer has taken great pains to show it. Moreover, Solomon's transgression shows that he was *not* the "offspring" promised to David in 2Sa 7. According to that promise, David was to have a son who would rule after him and build a temple in Jerusalem (7:12-13). What better candidate for fulfillment of that promise than Solomon, who built the temple? But Solomon's unfaithfulness to God's law demonstrates that he was not the promised offspring.

After the death of Solomon, Rehoboam his son succeeded him as king (11:43).

II. The Divided Kingdom (12:1 – 22:53)

A. Israel 1: Jeroboam (12:1 – 14:20)

After the death of Solomon, his kingdom was divided. The northern tribes rebelled against the Davidic dynasty in Jerusalem and established an independent kingdom. Jeroboam the son of Nebat, from the tribe of Ephraim, who had once rebelled against Solomon (11:26), was chosen as king (12:20). The divided kingdom was the result of a foolish decision of the young king Rehoboam. The elders who had counseled his father, Solomon, advised him to "be a servant to these people and serve them and ... they will always be your servants" (v.7). Rehoboam, however, rejected their counsel and followed the harsh advice of "the young men who had grown up with him" (vv.10–14).

Still, the writer makes it clear that behind this act of folly were the workings of the sovereign hand of God: "The king did not listen to the people, for this turn of events was from the LORD, to fulfill the word the LORD had spoken to Jeroboam" by the prophet Ahijah (v.15). Moreover, when confronted with a second word from God (vv.22–24a), Rehoboam wisely "obeyed the word of the LORD" and thus averted more calamity (v.24b).

In contrast to the Davidic king Rehoboam, who proved obedient in the end, the king of Israel, Jeroboam, began an apostasy that was to plague the northern kingdom throughout all its years, ultimately leading not only to the ruin of his own dynasty (13:34), but to the destruction of the entire northern kingdom (2Ki 17:21–23). Jeroboam established two rival worship centers, one at Bethel and the other at Dan (1Ki 12:25–33). At these centers he established a new priesthood and new feast days "of his own choosing" (v.33), and he set up two golden calves (cf. Ex 32:4) before which the people offered sacrifices. All this was intended to rival the true worship of God at Jerusalem (v.27).

B. Judah 1 (14:21–15:24)

The writer devotes most of his attention to the ruin and loss in the Davidic kingdom after the death of Solomon. There was much apostasy in Judah (14:22–24). Not only did Rehoboam lose most of his father's kingdom, he also lost most of his father's wealth (vv.25–28). Moreover, there was continual warfare between Israel and Judah during this time (vv.29–31).

Conditions did not improve during the subsequent reign of Abijah (15:1–8). The heart of this king was "not fully devoted to the LORD his God, as the heart of David his forefather had been" (v.3). David was the standard by which all the subsequent rulers of Judah were judged. The very survival of the kingdom during this time was due only to God's faithfulness to his promise to David (v.4; cf. 2Sa 7:16).

The kingship of Asa (15:9–24) represents a turn for the better. He "did what was right in the eyes of the LORD, as his father David had done" (v.11). Consequently, he gained the upper hand against the northern kingdom of Israel and had peace with his neighbors (vv.16–22). The only drawback to

Asa's reign was that he failed to remove the "high places" (v.14) from the northern kingdom, i.e., the false worship centers at Bethel and Dan. The writer mentions this not to find fault with Asa, but to reinforce the word of the man of God who had prophesied that Josiah would be the one to remove them (13:2).

C. Israel 2 (15:25 – 22:40)

This long narrative returns to the events of the kings of Israel in the north. Embedded in this section is the account of the prophet Elijah (1Ki 17:1 – 2Ki 2:12), who waged what appears to be a one-man battle against the apostasy of Ahab's kingdom. For the writer of Kings Elijah represents everything that was good and necessary in God's establishment of the office of prophet (Dt 18:14 – 22). He followed the script of the Pentateuch so well that he virtually spoke and acted as Moses would have, had he lived in that time.

The fact that Elijah lived as an outsider, in constant threat of imprisonment and persecution, witnesses to the state of apostasy in the land. When God told him that there were 7,000 others like him "whose knees have not bowed down to Baal" (19:18), we, the readers, are as surprised as Elijah.

D. Judah 2: Jehoshaphat (22:41 – 50)

Jehoshaphat, like his father Asa, was a good king. Also like his father, he did not remove the "high places" (v.43) — the false worship centers at Bethel and Dan set up by Jeroboam. The chronicler (2Ch 17 – 20) devotes much attention to Jehoshaphat because of the many good aspects of his reign. The writer of Kings passes over Jehoshaphat rather quickly, for unlike the chronicler, his interest is more on the failures of these kings than on their successes.

2 KINGS

Introduction

See the introduction to 1 Kings.

I. The Divided Kingdom (Continued) (1Ki 22:51 – 2Ki 17:41)

A. Israel 3 (1Ki 22:51 – 2Ki 8:15)

1. Ahaziah (1Ki 22:51 – 2Ki 1:18)

The book of 1 Kings closed with a brief notice of the reign of Ahaziah (1Ki 22:51–53), who "did evil in the eyes of the Lord" by following in the ways of Jeroboam (v.52). What the writer means by this is that he continued to maintain and encourage the priests, ceremonies, and worship centers established by Jeroboam at Bethel and Dan (1Ki 12:25–33).

2. Elisha (2:1 – 13:10)

After Elijah departed (2:11–12), the writer has inserted a major section of narratives dealing with the acts of his successor, Elisha (2:13–8:15). When Elisha asked Elijah for a "double portion of your spirit" (2:9b), he was not only asking to continue the work of Elijah but to increase it as well. To show that his wish was granted, the writer has structured and selected the narratives about Elijah and Elisha so that there are twice as many miracles recorded for Elisha (sixteen in all) as those of Elijah (eight in all).

3. Joram (Jehoram) (3:1 – 9:26)

After a brief report on the wickedness of Joram (3:1 – 3), the writer incor-porates a major portion of the story of Elisha into the account of his reign. For the most part, Joram remains in the background, described here only as "the king of Israel" (e.g., 5:6; 6:10). In fulfillment of the word of the Lord spoken by Elijah to his father Ahab (1Ki 21:29), God ultimately brought judgment on the house of Ahab in the death of his son Joram. This came by the hand of Jehu (2Ki 9:24 – 26), God's chosen agent of judgment (1Ki 19:16).

4. Hazael (8:7 – 15)

In 1Ki 19:15 the Lord had commanded Elijah to anoint Hazael as king over Aram. Though it is not recorded in the book of Kings, the present text, which records Elisha's journey to Hazael in Damascus, assumes that Elijah did, in fact, anoint him. From Elisha's troubled response to the prospect of Hazael's kingship (8:12), it is apparent that Hazael had been anointed to inflict judgment on Israel. In that sense he was like the "adversaries" that the Lord raised up against Solomon (1Ki 11:14, 23) and the Assyrians whom God would use to judge Israel for their idolatry (2Ki 17:7 – 23). The writer of Kings makes frequent mention of the hardships that Hazael inflicted on Israel and Judah (8:28 – 29; 9:14 – 15; 10:32b; 12:17 – 18; 13:3, 22).

B. Judah 3 (8:16 – 9:29)

1. Jehoram (Joram) (8:16 – 24)

The attention of the writer now shifts to the kingdom of Judah and the reign of Jehoram son of Jehoshaphat. Jehoram married a daughter of Ahab and thus followed the ways of the house of Ahab (8:18). His treachery served as an occasion for the writer to recall God's faithfulness to his promise to David: "for the sake of his servant David, the LORD was not willing to destroy Judah. He had promised to maintain a lamp for David and his descendants forever" (v.19; cf. 2Sa 7:16). This is the heart of the theological message of the book of Kings: God's faithfulness to the house of David and the hope in the eternal kingdom.

2. Ahaziah (8:25 – 9:29)

Ahaziah, like his father Jehoram, was related to the house of Ahab (8:27), or as the writer reminds us, the house of Omri (v.26; cf. 1Ki 16:21 – 28). In the account of Ahaziah's reign, the writer of Kings has inserted the narra-tives that treat Jehu son of Jehoshaphat, the son of Nimshi.

C. Israel 4: Jehu (9:1 – 10:36)

Jehu son of Jehoshaphat, the son of Nimshi, had been singled out as an instrument of God's judgment already in 1Ki 19:16. Now he would carry out that task under the aegis of the prophet Elisha. Thus he was anointed king of Israel with the specific task of destroying the rest of the house of Ahab (2Ki 9:1 – 13).

First, Jehu killed Joram (9:14 – 26) and Ahaziah (vv.27 – 29). Then he went after Jezebel, the wife of Ahab, and, with the help of the inhabitants of Jezreel, killed her (vv.30 – 37). With Jezebel's death the word of the prophet Elijah was fulfilled (v.36; cf. 1Ki 21:23 – 24). Then follows the account of Jehu's total eradication of the house of Ahab, including Ahab's seventy sons in Samaria (2Ki 10:1 – 10) and all who remained in Jezreel, including "his chief men, his close friends and his priests" (v.11). He traveled through the countryside executing any survivors (vv.12 – 17). Jehu then turned against the priests and the servants of Baal and destroyed Baal worship in Israel (vv.18 – 29).

D. Judah 4: Joash (11:1 – 12:21)

When Ahaziah was killed (9:27), his mother, Athaliah, assumed the throne in Jerusalem, thinking she had killed all possible rivals (11:1 – 3). However, Joash son of Ahaziah had been hidden away in the temple, and there he remained until he was old enough to rule (vv.3, 21). When Joash reached the necessary age, Jehoiada, a priest at the temple (cf. v.9), secretly executed a plan to make the young crown prince king and thus secure his rightful throne (vv.4 – 21). This plan was successful, and Athaliah was put to death (vv.15 – 16). Jehoiada then made a covenant between the Lord and the people, and the temple of Baal, with its priests and its altars, was destroyed (vv.17 – 18a).

Because of the godly instruction of Jehoiada, the young king "did what was right in the eyes of the LORD" (12:2). As had all the kings who preceded him in Judah, however, Joash failed to remove the "high places" at Bethel and Dan (cf. 10:29; 1Ki 12:25 – 33); thus he never lived up to the ideal of David in uniting the people in the worship of God at Jerusalem.

E. Israel 5 (13:1 – 25)

1. Jehoahaz (13:1 – 9)

Jehoahaz was the son of Jehu (v.1). Like those before him, he did not remove the high places at Bethel and Dan that Jeroboam had set up (v.2); thus God sent Hazael king of Aram against him (v.3; cf. 8:12; 1Ki 19:15).

Jehoahaz, however, repented and sought the Lord, and God sent Israel a deliverer (2Ki 13:4–5). The writer of Kings was not so much interested in the identity of the deliverer as he was in the fact that God sent him. It may be that Jehoash son of Jehoahaz was understood as the deliverer in that he "recaptured from Ben-Hadad son of Hazael the towns he had taken in battle from his father Jehoahaz" (v.25). He did this because "the LORD was gracious to them and had compassion" (v.23). A similar situation occurred during the reign of his son, Jeroboam II (14:25–27). God had compassion on Israel in spite of their sins.

2. Jehoash (13:10–25; 14:15–16)

Though in the estimation of the writer of Kings, Jehoash did not rise above the other kings of Israel, he records several important events during his reign. Elisha became ill and died during the reign of Jehoash. The king's sorrowful response to Elisha's illness is a witness to the high regard with which he was held even by a king who did evil in God's eyes. When he saw the deathly ill Elisha, Jehoash exclaimed, "My father!... The chariots and horsemen of Israel!" (13:14) — apparently with the sense of "You are worth more to Israel than all her chariots and horsemen combined." A testimony to the unusual power of Elisha is found in the brief episode of the dead man disposed of in haste in Elisha's grave (13:20b–21).

The writer interjects a lesson in the midst of his account of Jehoash that sheds much light on the entire history of God's dealings with Israel. Israel was oppressed by Hazael, king of Aram, during the reign of Jehoash, but God was "gracious to them and had compassion" on Israel. Thus he did not let Hazael destroy his people. God's actions were not motivated by anything Israel had done. It was rather "because of his covenant with Abraham, Isaac and Jacob" (v.23). Thus the writer of Kings reaches back into the earliest sections of the Pentateuch for his lesson on God's work with his people. In his patience and longsuffering with Israel, God was being faithful to his promises.

F. Judah 5: Amaziah (14:1–22)

As with many of the kings of Judah, Amaziah did a number of good things, but he failed to end the false worship centers in Bethel and Dan. Only one king did this — Josiah (23:15).

The writer specifically mentions that in his administration of the kingdom, King Amaziah obeyed the "Book of the Law of Moses," quoting Dt 24:16. Amaziah thus approximated in his life the ideal of the kingship as spelled out in Dt 17:18–19. Having mentioned his obedience to the law, the writer then notes that Amaziah defeated the Edomites, another sign that he was approximating the ideal king (see comments on 2Ki 8:16–24).

Amaziah was subsequently defeated by Jehoash, the king of Israel (14:8–14), and fell prey to an internal conspiracy (vv.19–20). Amaziah's downfall came as a result of pride and arrogance (v.10).

G. Israel 6: Jeroboam II (14:23 – 29)

Jeroboam II followed in the footsteps of his namesake, Jeroboam son of Nebat. The prophet Jonah lived during his reign and had given a prophecy regarding God's compassion on his people Israel (v.25). God fulfilled the prophecy through Jeroboam II.

By inserting such notes about the early work of the prophets, the writer of Kings prepares the reader for the lesson of ch. 17. When, at last, God rejected Israel and sent them into exile, the writer assures us that it was only after much patience and compassionate warnings on God's part: "The LORD warned Israel and Judah through all his prophets and seers" (17:13). God had sent Israel a continuous line of prophets to warn the nation of the consequences of their sin and idolatry, but Israel failed to take heed.

H. Judah 6: Azariah (15:1 – 7)

Azariah obeyed God but did not remove the false worship places at Bethel and Dan. He was stricken with leprosy in the latter part of his life, which the writer of Kings saw as the result of divine judgment (v.5).

I. Israel 7 (15:8 – 31)

Zechariah (vv.8–12) was the fourth generation of the house of Jehu. His assassination at the hand of Shallum fulfilled God's word to Jehu (10:30). As a reward for his father Jehu's obedience to his divine commission (1Ki 19:16–17; 2Ki 10:30), God had allowed Jehu's dynasty to remain four generations. With Zechariah, however, Jehu's dynasty ended.

After Zechariah, the leadership of the northern kingdom began to disintegrate. Shallum (2Ki 15:13–16), Zechariah's assassin, was himself assassinated by Menahem after only one month (v.14a). Israel endured the hard rule of Menahem (vv.17–22) for ten years. During his reign the king of Assyria, God's appointed instrument of judgment, first came on the scene (v.19). Peace could now only be obtained with the price of silver and the taxation of every Israelite, particularly the wealthy.

With Pekahiah (vv.23–26), Pekah (vv.27–31), and Hoshea (17:1–6), the northern kingdom of Israel came to an end. These kings fared no better than their predecessors. They continued to encourage the false worship of the golden calves at Bethel and Dan. Pekahiah was assassinated by one of his chief officers, Pekah (v.25). In Pekah's day the Assyrian king Tiglath-Pileser captured a major portion of his territory (v.29). Pekah was assassinated by Hoshea, who succeeded him as king (v.30). The fall of Hoshea's kingdom to the Assyrians is given in ch. 17.

J. Judah 7 (15:32 – 16:20)

Jotham, the son of Uzziah (or Azariah; cf. 2Ki 15:7), did what was right in the eyes of the Lord — i.e., he obeyed the law and the word of the prophets (vv.32 – 38). Like the kings of Judah before him, however, he did not remove the calf images and sanctuaries Jeroboam had built in the northern kingdom.

Jotham resisted an initial attack on Judah's northern border from Pekah, king of Israel, and the Aramean king Rezin (v.37). After Jotham's death (v.38), Ahaz became king of Judah (16:1 – 20). During his reign Pekah and Rezin attacked Jerusalem and besieged the city (v.5). Ahaz, a wicked king in the eyes of the writer of Kings (vv.2 – 4), appealed to the Assyrian king, Tiglath-Pileser, for help (v.7). This king complied and, after being paid off with the silver and gold from the temple at Jerusalem (v.8), he attacked and defeated Damascus (v.9; see also Isa 7:1 – 8:18). Ahaz eventually put a foreign altar like that of the Assyians in the Jerusalem temple.

K. Israel 8 (17:1 – 41)

The last king to reign in Israel was Hoshea (vv.1 – 6), who did evil in God's sight, "but not like the kings of Israel who preceded him" (v.2). This perhaps means that the actions of kings like Pekahiah and Pekah who preceded Hoshea had reached such depths that it was impossible to sink any lower. The fall of the northern kingdom came during the reign of Hoshea (vv.7 – 41). A brief description of the event is given in vv.3 – 6, followed by the writer's lengthy lesson on its cause (vv.7 – 23) and aftermath (vv.24 – 41).

Caught in a political crossfire between Assyria and Egypt, Hoshea was attacked and imprisoned by the new king of Assyria, Shalmaneser V (vv.3 – 4). After a long siege of Israel's capital city, Samaria, and a wholesale invasion of the land, the Assyrians captured the city and sent the Israelites living in the northern kingdom into exile.

The Assyrians resettled the northern kingdom with people from other parts of their empire (v.24). The writer of Kings is aghast at the religious syncretism of the resettled population (vv.25 – 34a). His purpose, however, was not to denigrate this new group of settlers, who he suggests could not have known any better (e.g., v.27), but rather to drive a lesson home to his readers, who were familiar with the Scriptures and the law of God (vv.34b – 41).

II. Judah after the End of the Northern Kingdom (18:1 – 25:30)

A. Hezekiah (18:1 – 20:21)

Hezekiah receives high marks in the text (18:1 – 8). He was king of Judah when the Assyrians attacked and deported the northern kingdom (vv.9 – 12). During his reign, the Assyrians also invaded Judah and captured many cities (v.13), threatening even to lay siege to Jerusalem (18:14 – 19:34). God intervened and the Assyrians were defeated (19:35 – 37). The story of Hezekiah's courage and trust in God serves as a backdrop for the writer's central message.

In the story of Hezekiah's illness (20:1 – 11), the writer shows how God hears the prayers of the righteous and gives them years of blessing if they call on him. The prophet first said to the king, "You will not recover" (v.1b), but after Hezekiah's prayer, the Lord told Isaiah to go back to Hezekiah and tell him, "I have heard your prayer and seen your tears; I will heal you" (v.5). Surely these words from God are directed as much to the reader as they were to Isaiah.

B. Manasseh (21:1 – 18)

The last days of Judah have come. Manasseh led the people in such apostasy (vv.2 – 11) that the Lord determined to bring destruction and exile on Judah and Jerusalem (vv.12 – 16). The writer of Kings makes it clear that the basis of God's complaint against Judah was their failure to keep the law of Moses (vv.8 – 9). A measure of the severity of God's anger against Manasseh can be seen in that when Judah later repented and put away their idolatry during the time of Josiah (chs. 22 – 23), God did "not turn away from the heat of his fierce anger, which burned against Judah because of all that Manasseh had done to arouse his anger" (23:26).

C. Amon (21:19 – 26)

Amon was a carbon copy of his father Manasseh. He fell victim to a conspiracy and assassination (v.23) after only two years on the throne (v.19).

D. Josiah (22:1 – 23:30)

Josiah was a good king in the eyes of the writer (22:1 – 2). He was actively engaged in the upkeep and repair of the temple (vv.3 – 7). In the process of cleaning the temple, the high priest, Hilkiah, found "the Book of the Law" (v.8). This book was apparently a copy, or the copy, of what we now have as the Pentateuch (cf. 23:25). When the book was brought before the king and read, it caused an instant revival (22:9–11). The king set out at once to obey the words written in the book and to avert the anger of the Lord so clearly spelled out in it (vv.12–13).

The first thing Josiah did was to send for Huldah the prophetess (v.14), to inquire of the meaning of what he had read in the book. Huldah replied first that the Lord was about "to bring disaster on this place and its people, according to everything written in the book" (v.16). She then added that the Lord had heard and seen the repentance of Josiah and thus judgment would not come in his days (vv.18–20).

Josiah read the "Book of the Covenant" (Ex 24:7) before all the people (23:1–2), and they renewed their covenant with the Lord (v.3). The temple was cleaned out, all foreign objects of worship were burned outside Jerusalem, and the ashes were taken to Bethel (v.4). All forms of pagan religion were removed from Jerusalem (vv.5–7). Josiah then sent word throughout his kingdom that all pagan worship was to be totally eradicated (vv.8–20).

In the process of clearing away the foreign altars, Josiah came to Bethel and "even that altar and high place he demolished" (v.15). He defiled these altars with the bones of the nearby tombs, just as the man of God had foretold (v.16; cf. 1Ki 13:2). With this act, Josiah distinguished himself from all other kings in Israel and Judah. Josiah also led the people in the celebration of the Passover (2Ki 23:21–23) and followed all the commandments of the law of Moses (vv.24–25; cf. Jos 1:7).

E. The Last Kings of Judah (23:36–25:7)

Jehoahaz (23:31–35) reigned as king in Judah only three months. He was displaced and imprisoned by the Egyptian pharaoh Necho. The pharaoh appointed Eliakim son of Josiah as king, changing his name to Jehoiakim (23:36–24:7). During his reign, King Nebuchadnezzar of Babylon first invaded Judah (24:1). The Lord also sent other raiders—Babylonian, Aramean, Moabite, and Ammonite—against Judah during his reign "because of the sins of Manasseh" (vv.2–4). These things were happening to Judah just as the prophets had long ago foretold (v.3).

Though Jehoiakim's son, Jehoiachin, reigned in Jerusalem only three months (24:8–25:30), he continued as "king of Judah" well into the Babylonian captivity (25:27–30). Jehoiachin surrendered Jerusalem to Nebuchadnezzar and his army (24:10–12a) and was taken prisoner to Babylon (vv.12b, 15). Nebuchadnezzar removed the royal treasures and temple artifacts to Babylon, along with all but the poorest inhabitants of the city. He then made Mattaniah, Jehoiachin's uncle, king in Judah, changing his name to Zedekiah (v.17).

F. Exile to Babylon (25:8 – 26)

The last days of the kingdom are recounted almost matter of factly. During the reign of Zedekiah (24:18 – 25:7), Nebuchadnezzar returned to plunder and destroy Jerusalem (25:1 – 17). The temple and the royal palace were burnt (v.9), the walls were broken down (v.10), and the people were taken into exile (v.11). All of the valuable utensils and temple equipment were taken to Babylon, including the precious metals from the temple decor (vv.16 – 17). The chief priest and the leading men of the city were executed (vv.18 – 21).

Nebuchadnezzar appointed Gedaliah (vv.22 – 25) as governor over the people who remained in Judah, but he was quickly assassinated (v.25). Fearing Babylonian reprisals, those who had remained in the land fled to Egypt (v.26).

G. Epilogue (25:27 – 30)

For the writer of the book of Kings, the destruction and judgment of the exile was not the last word. There was still hope in God's promises to the house of David because it was an eternal promise (2Sa 7:16). Thus, at the close of this book, he turns to the future, noting that the house of David was not only still intact but flourishing in the house of the king of Babylon. Jehoiachin, the heir to the throne of David and the promises of God, was sitting on "a seat of honor higher than those of the other kings who were with him in Babylon" (v.28). Clearly this was meant to inspire hope in God's faithfulness to his promises.

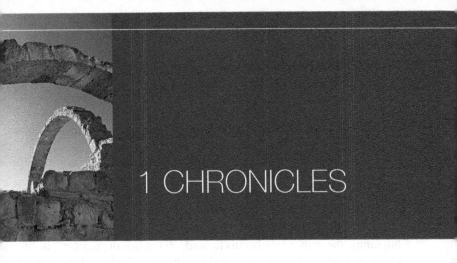

1 CHRONICLES

1. Introduction

The earliest title known for the books of Chronicles is "The Things Left Behind." This seems to mean that these books contained material not included in the other historical books. But that title was also taken more positively to mean that the books contained important summaries of other biblical books. They were a condensed version of the rest of the OT historical books.

To their own generation, the books of Chronicles were a vivid reminder of the hope that rested in the faithfulness of God. They were reminders that the Lord had made a promise to the house of David of peace and prosperity. The channel of the fulfillment of that promise was the covenant people of God, Israel. In that setting, these books called for trust and obedience on the part of God's people (see 2Ch 7:14).

I. Names and Genealogies (1:1 – 10:14)

A. The Lineage of David (1:1 – 3:24)

The writer begins by introducing the house of David. The use of genealogical lists to set the stage of historical narrative is well-known in both the OT (Genesis) and the NT (Matthew and Luke). Just as Luke's gospel traces the lineage of Jesus (the Son of David) back to Adam (Lk 3:38), so also this writer traces David's lineage to Adam.

One of the overarching themes of 1 and 2 Chronicles is that the Davidic kingship is to be the instrument of God's promised salvation and blessing.

In these genealogies the writer seems especially concerned to show that this salvation and blessing are not just for God's people, Israel, but for all humanity as well. Here, at the outset, it becomes clear that the house of David is of the house of Abraham, a descendant of Adam. By working through the descendants of David, God is reaching to the entire human race. By recognizing the house of David as also of the lineage of Adam, the chronicler is close in his thinking to the apostle Paul, who saw in Jesus Christ "the last Adam" (1Co 15:45).

B. The House of Israel (4:1 – 7:40)

Having placed the line of David firmly within the context of the families of humanity, the author now begins to mark off the line of promise. The line of the promise is that elect nation through whom God intended to bring blessing and salvation to a lost world. He takes great pains to tell us that the nation is Israel, the descendants of the sons of Jacob.

1. The family of Judah (4:1 – 23)

The list of the sons of Israel begins with the family of Judah. According to the prophecy of his father Israel (Ge 49:8 – 12), Judah was to be the leader of the families of Israel, and the promised blessing was to come to Israel and the nations through that family. With that promise in mind, the chronicler begins his enumeration of the household of Israel. That the Davidic dynasty represents that chosen leadership is central to Chronicles. The stage is being set here, and the actors in the great drama to follow are given their proper introduction.

2. The family of Simeon and the Transjordanian families (4:24 – 5:26)

Simeon and his descendants come next in the list, probably because the family of Simeon shared the territory allotted to the family of Judah (Jos 19:9).

The chronicler then gives a short history of the families that settled along the eastern banks of the Jordan. When the Israelites settled in the land of Canaan, three families remained on the east side of the Jordan: those of Reuben, Gad, and half of Manasseh (Nu 32; Jos 13:8 – 33).

3. The family of Levi (6:1 – 81)

The list of the names of the family of Levi is carefully constructed. Its purpose is to make clear the line of descent of the priests and Levites. The list begins with the Levitical line that traces its descent from Aaron, the first priest (6:1 – 15). The chronicler begins with this line because only those Levites (descendants of Levi) who were descended from Aaron could legitimately do the work of a priest at the temple (6:49; Nu 3:5–38) and could carry out the duties of the sacrificial system. The importance of that distinction is seen after the rebuilding of the temple during the return from exile. If a priest could not establish that he was a descendant of Aaron, he could not serve in the new temple as a priest (Ne 7:63–65).

The next section is a general enumeration of the Levitical family (vv.16–53). Several descendants are selected and emphasized: Samuel, Heman, Asaph, and Ethan. These men and their descendants were the prophets who served God at the temple (1Sa 3:21; 1Ch 25:1). They are the counterparts of the priests. Together with the priests, those prophets and their descendants maintained the relationship and fellowship between God and Israel at the temple.

4. The remaining families of Israel (7:1–40)

The chronicler ends his genealogical and historical survey of the families of Israel by tracing briefly the descendants of Issachar, Benjamin, Naphtali, Manasseh, Ephraim, and Asher.

Two families are omitted: Dan (Ge 30:1–6) and Zebulun (Ge 30:19–20). The writer is concerned to show that the house of Israel still consists of the twelve families of the sons of Jacob. Since he has counted the half tribe of Manasseh as a complete family (5:23–24) and has counted the Levites as part of the twelve families (6:1–81), the omission of Dan and Zebulun is required to maintain the number twelve.

C. The House of Saul (8:1–9:44)

The last list of names serves as a transition into the first narrative section, the death of Saul (10:1–14). Continuing the genealogical style, the chronicler prepares the way for the opening of his narrative by giving the lineage of Israel's first king, Saul (8:1–40). He does so in a unique way. In both chapters, those descendants who "lived in Jerusalem" (8:28; 9:34) are distinguished from those who lived in Gibeon (8:29; 9:35). The purpose of that distinction is to show that Saul was from that part of Benjamin that was from Gibeon, not Jerusalem.

D. The Death of Saul (10:1–14)

Saul was Israel's first king. He was anointed by Samuel (1Sa 10:1) and fought valiantly against the Philistines and other enemies of God's people. Saul's kingship, however, ended in defeat as he proved to be a king not worthy to lead God's people (1Sa 13:13–14). Because the house of Saul was not God's chosen instrument of salvation, the chronicler is interested only in the last and most significant event in Saul's reign as king: the defeat of Saul and his army by the Philistines at Gilboa. The account is almost a verbatim report of Saul's defeat in 1Sa 31.

An important recurring lesson in the books of Samuel and Chronicles is the importance of the leaders of God's people to follow the word of the Lord. Leadership is serious business. There is no room for only partial obedience.

II. David (11:1 – 29:30)

David is a central figure in 1 and 2 Chronicles. The theme of salvation and blessing was personified in his reign over Israel. As a result, David became the standard by which all future kings were measured. A good king was one who did "just as his father David had done" (2Ch 29:2). Moreover, David was the king who most epitomized the promised Messiah. For many of the biblical writers, to talk of David was to talk of the Messiah (e.g., Eze 34:23 – 24). Judging from some of his own psalms (e.g., Ps. 22), David even entertained that view about himself.

Such a view of David seems also to have been the viewpoint of the chronicler. As he writes about David and evaluates later kings by the standards of David, he has in mind not just the David who was king, but also the "David" who would yet be king, the Messiah. In that sense much of the perspective of Chronicles is messianic. These books look forward with anticipation to the coming King who will bring in God's final salvation and blessing.

A. David Becomes King over Israel (11:1 – 3)

David's struggle to rise to power and his setbacks under King Saul that loom so large in 1 Samuel are passed over, except for a simple comment from those who had gathered to make David king (see v.2). David's kingship found confirmation in three ways: (1) the consent of God's people (vv.2 – 3); (2) the word of the prophet Samuel; and (3) the victories he received from the hand of God.

B. The Capture of Jerusalem (11:4 – 8)

With David in possession of Jerusalem, the kingdom was given a centrally located capital with the best natural defenses in the area. Mount Zion, the city of David, became a citadel that symbolized God's eternal care and protection of his people. Psalmists often sang the praises of God and his holy city (e.g., Ps 48:1 – 3).

C. David's Mighty Men (11:9 – 12:40)

A person is known by the company he or she keeps. That is the idea behind the enumeration of the mighty men who surrounded David and aided his establishment of the kingship. The chronicler has already described the mighty deed of David's commander, Joab. Now he turns to describe David's army. The list of mighty men is given in three sections: the chiefs among David's men (11:10 – 25), the mighty men in David's army (11:26 – 47), and the mighty men who joined David in Ziklag while he was still fleeing Saul (12:1 – 40).

The point of the detailed enumeration of the names and exploits of those men is to show that David was a leader who had gained the full confidence and support of the best men in Israel.

D. David and the Ark of the Covenant (13:1 – 16:43)

The ark of the covenant plays a central role in these chapters. The ark was a wooden chest overlaid with gold. The pattern for building the ark was given to Moses at Mount Sinai, and it became one of the most important components of Israel's worship (Ex 25:9 – 22). By means of the ark, the invisible presence of the God of the covenant was visualized. The ark was the place where God had chosen to center his presence among his people (Ex 25:22).

1. Removing the ark from Kiriath Jearim (13:1 – 14)

The first stage of David's moving the ark to Jerusalem teaches the seriousness and reality of God's holy presence among his people. That presence is not to be taken lightly. God had graciously promised to be in the midst of his people. His presence was real and not to be treated as merely symbolic. God's holiness can never be treated with mere empty ritualism.

It was a failure to be faithful in one little matter that led to the great tragedy in vv.9 – 10: the death of Uzzah as he touched the ark when the oxen stumbled. Things happened so unexpectedly that David responded in anger and fear, not knowing whether to carry on or to postpone moving the ark. Having decided out of apparent desperation for the latter option, he left it at the home of Obed-Edom, along the way to Jerusalem.

2. Restoring fellowship with God (14:1 – 17)

Not only had the Lord restored the blessing of his presence at the ark in the house of Obed-Edom (13:14), but David's kingdom was again experiencing God's blessing. The chronicler singles out three events from David's life to show that the Lord was blessing his kingdom. These events in ch. 14 are to be read as a direct consequence of David's taking proper care for the ark of God. Blessing from God follows obedience to God's Word.

3. The ark rests in Jerusalem (15:1 – 16:43)

With the events of chs. 13 and 14, David had learned many important lessons. He now returns to his original intentions of moving the ark to Jerusalem and restoring the presence of God to its rightful place — in the midst of God's people. Chapters 15 and 16 now stress three important points: (1) the centrality of the priests and the Levites (15:1 – 15); (2) the joy of God's presence (15:16 – 16:6); (3) telling God's glory among the nations (16:7 – 43).

E. David and the Promise (17:1 – 29:30)

In these chapters we find the single most important event in the life of David — God's covenant promise to give him an eternal kingdom. By sheer repetition (three times), it is clear that the house of David is God's chosen vehicle for bringing salvation to the nations. The Messiah will be the Son of David.

1. The first account of God's promise to David (17:1 – 21:30)

The chronicler throws light on the fulfillment of the specific promises to David in his own lifetime. In other respects, however, the promises concern a descendant who will do for Israel far more than his father David. By showing God's faithfulness in his promises to David, the chronicler is giving a basis for trust in God's faithfulness concerning the future Son of David, the Messiah, who is in the center of the message of hope.

First Chronicles 17:8 – 9 helps to show the outline that follows the first account. In v.8 God promised to give victory to David over all his enemies, so the account of David's victories is recorded in chs. 18 – 20. In v.9 God promised that through David he would establish a place for his people, Israel. As the following verses and Dt 12:1 – 11 make clear, the Lord had in mind primarily a place for his temple. Thus, ch. 21 records the events leading up to the selection of the site for the temple — the threshing floor of Araunah.

God's choice of the temple site was carried out through his servant David. The occasion of the selection of that site is recorded in great detail, because the events point out in remarkable clarity the ultimate purpose for the temple: God's salvation for his people.

David had angered God by numbering his army (21:1 – 7). That was apparently a reflection of David's lack of trust in God to save his people. Although David confessed his sin, he was required to bear the consequences of that sin (vv.8–12). After thousands fell by the plague that the Lord had sent upon his people, he was grieved and called his messenger of destruction to a halt (v.15).

At the site where the messenger halted, the threshing floor of Araunah the Jebusite, David fell down before the Lord and pled to let the punishment fall on him and his house rather than on the people (vv.16–17). But God commanded David to build an altar there and offer up the sacrifice he had provided in his law. On that site God chose to build his house (21:18–22:1). In a dramatic and climactic way, the purpose of the building of the temple was given: not to be a religious shrine, but the place where sinful human beings would meet with a righteous and holy God and where God would genuinely show that his mercies were great.

2. The second account of God's promise to David (22:1 – 27:34)

In this second account of the promise to David, David himself made preparations for the fulfillment of those aspects of the promise that extended beyond his own reign. David prepared for the future fulfillment of the promise in concrete, specific terms: he gathered the material for building the temple (22:1–19) and appointed the officials who would administer the kingdom after him (23:1–27:34).

Embodied in David's zealous activity is an important lesson: the preoccupation of God's people with the hope of his promise. David's uppermost desire was to see God's promise fulfilled. The focus of the promise was the building of the house of God.

This section concludes with an account of the organization of the princes of Israel (27:1–34): his army (27:1–15), tribal leaders (27:16–24), administrators (27:25–31), and counselors (27:32–34).

3. The third account of God's promise to David (28:1 – 29:30)

The chronicler's primary concern in recounting events in the life of David has been the promise of a coming King to reign over God's people. God made a promise to David that one of his descendants would rule over his kingdom forever and build a house for him. In his own day the promise had not yet been fulfilled. In this third account of God's promise, it is to be announced to a congregation of the leaders of Israel (28:1).

In both the second (22:7–13) and third accounts, Solomon is taken to be the descendant of the promise by virtue of his being a man of peace and his building the temple. From David's perspective there seemed little doubt that God's promise was about to be fulfilled in the reign of Solomon (28:5–7). Certainly the preparations made for building the temple showed that David had little doubt that Solomon was the one.

If the chronicler was still waiting in hope for the fulfillment of the promise to David, then he, contrary to David, certainly did *not* believe Solomon was the son promised. Solomon was "a son" of David and he built a temple, but he is not "the Son" of David. As the chronicler sees it, a future temple is yet to be built (2Ch 36:23).

2 CHRONICLES

Introduction

See introduction to 1 Chronicles.

III. Solomon and the Descendants of David (1:1 – 36:23)

Solomon's major accomplishment was building the temple in Jerusalem. We see the chronicler's interest in that aspect of Solomon's reign by comparing the account of his reign here and in 1Ki 1:1 – 11:43. The Chronicles account is a shorter work overall, and with few exceptions it includes only those events that show Solomon's concern and care for building the temple. In this way, the chronicler's treatment of Solomon is similar to his treatment of David and of the Davidic dynasty in the remainder of the book. In recounting the deeds of the kings of Israel and Judah, he is concerned primarily with their care for the temple of God.

A. Solomon (1:1 – 9:31)

By any standards, Solomon was a great king. David had bequeathed to him a large and stable kingdom. Here the major interest is in how Solomon went about his task of building the temple. Whatever his weaknesses, Solomon had true greatness, and that greatness was seen in his devotion to the worship of God at the temple. He devoted himself to providing for the presence of God among his people. In that respect Solomon was like the promised King.

1. Solomon's preparation (1:1 – 17)

The first official act of Solomon was his journey to Gibeon with his entou-rage since "God's tent of meeting" was there (v.3). Therefore, Solomon's first official act was one of worship. The chronicler carefully points out that worship at Gibeon was legitimate because all the accoutrements of worship prepared by Moses' instruction, except the ark, were kept here.

The wisdom and wealth that characterized Solomon's kingship were a gift from God. He asked for wisdom and knowledge "that I may lead this people" and "govern" them (v.10). Both the chronicler and the writer of 1Ki 3 had in view here the requirement of the king in Dt 17:18–20. The king was expected to know the law of God, fear God, and observe God's will as expressed in the law. In the words of Moses in Dt 4:5–8, the law is wisdom and understanding.

2. Preparations for building the temple (2:1 – 18)

Although the chronicler enumerates some details of the construction mate-rials, his primary interest in the temple preparations lies clearly in the written exchange between Solomon and Hiram of Tyre. Solomon's letter to Hiram provides a telling glance into his intention in building the temple. He saw the temple not as a place to contain the God of the universe, but as a place where he and his people could celebrate God's presence. Solomon's letter also reveals his purpose for wanting the best craftsmen and the most precious materials: "The temple I am going to build will be great, because our God is greater than all other gods" (v.5).

3. The temple is built (3:1 – 5:1)

The site of the temple, Mount Moriah, is identified both with the thresh-ing floor of Araunah, which David purchased (1Ch 21:18–30), and with the mountain where Abraham offered up his son Isaac (Ge 22:2, 14). Since in Ge 22:14 the theme was God's provision of a substitutionary sacrifice, the chronicler is reminding his readers that Solomon's temple site was on the same mountain. For sinful humanity to come into God's presence, a sacrifice was necessary. By grace, God provided the sacrifice in David's final Son.

No accurate picture of the temple can be drawn from Chronicles, since the account here is merely a rough sketch. The structure was about 90 feet long, 30 feet wide, and a little over 40 feet high—about the size and shape of a large suburban home. The glory of the temple lay not in its impressive size but in the quality and craftsmanship of its construction and furnishings.

4. The dedication of the temple (5:2 – 7:11)

The chronicler gives the account of the temple dedication in four parts. (1) *The ceremony of the ark* (5:2 – 14). David brought the ark to Jerusalem (1Ch 15 – 16), and now Solomon brings it into the temple. (2) *Solomon's speech* (6:1 – 11). Once more the Davidic covenant promise was repeated (see 1Ch 17). This time Solomon expressly applied the promise to himself and his completion of the temple (vv.4, 10). (3) *Solomon's prayer* (6:12 – 7:3). The point of Solomon's prayer is clear: God is present among his people and hears their prayer when they, in obedience, call out to him (cf. 6:14, the prayer's beginning). (4) *The dedication ceremony* (7:4 – 11). A seven-day feast for the dedication of the altar was coupled with the seven-day Feast of Tabernacles. The number of animals sacrificed during the dedication, though large, is not improbable. Even larger numbers of animal sacrifices are known from ancient times.

5. Solomon's night vision (7:12 – 22)

Solomon received a confirmation of his prayer in a night vision. But he also received a stern warning of the importance of obeying God's will. Solomon's kingdom would be established if he obeyed that will; if not, the nation would be exiled and the temple destroyed.

The chronicler certainly knows that the Davidic kings were not obedient. His history has helped to make that fact indelible. But his purpose is not to rub salt in old wounds; rather, it is to show how to avoid the consequences of disobedience. When the nation suffers because of disobedience, the proper recourse of the people is repentance. God's people can always pray, repent, and seek forgiveness; he is always ready to hear and forgive (7:14 – 15).

6. Solomon's kingdom is established (8:1 – 18)

The Lord had appeared to Solomon and had reaffirmed the Davidic promise to him. When the chronicler recounted the initial promise to David (1Ch 17:1 – 21:30), he stressed several features of David's kingdom that demonstrated God's fulfillment of specific promises in the life of David. After the Davidic promise was reaffirmed to Solomon, the chronicler recounts several features of Solomon's realm that demonstrate the Lord's words "I will establish your royal throne" (7:18). Narratively, the chronicler has shown that God is faithful to his word.

7. Solomon's wealth and wisdom are acclaimed (9:1 – 28)

Not only had the Lord given Solomon a great kingdom in fulfillment of the promise to David, but he also had given Solomon much wealth and wisdom, as he had promised at Gibeon (1:12). Solomon asked first for wisdom, and God also gave him wealth.

Behind the wealth of Solomon lay a clearly defined hope in what God will again do through the Davidic kingship. One like Solomon will come some day, and the nations will bring their wealth to him (see the prophecy in Ps 2:7–8).

8. Solomon's death (9:29–31)

What is surprising about the portrayal of Solomon is that it concludes without any notice of the misfortune that befell him in his later years (see 1Ki 11). The chronicler's reason for omitting those details involves two factors. (1) He assumes the reader knew the details from 1 Kings and felt no need to repeat them since they were not important to his overall purpose. (2) His interest in Solomon was primarily exemplary. Solomon was an example of the promised descendant of David who, in the chronicler's day, had not yet come. Insofar as the reign of Solomon represented the reign of the Promised One, the chronicler's interest was served. He was content to let the other biblical writers give the more rounded picture. His goal was to build hope for the future rather than to lament the past.

B. Rehoboam (10:1 – 12:16)

Following his death Solomon's kingdom was divided. Ten tribes to the north rebelled against the Davidic dynasty in Jerusalem and established an independent state. For the most part the chronicler concentrates only on the Davidic kings in Jerusalem. He was seeking not a comprehensive understanding of the past but a theological perspective on the present and future.

1. The rebellion of the northern tribes (10:1 – 11:4)

Two interesting lessons can be drawn from this account, taken almost verbatim from 1Ki 12. (1) Solomon's son Rehoboam did not act wisely and lost his kingdom. Taking counsel from the young men and rejecting the counsel of the elders are the ultimate in the lack of wisdom. (2) The king did not listen to the people (10:15).

2. Rehoboam's kingdom (11:5 – 23)

This material has no parallel in the other historical books. The section gives an important glimpse of the chronicler's evaluation both of the northern kingdom, Israel, and of the southern kingdom, Judah. The northern kingdom was led into apostasy by their new king, Jeroboam (v.15). Thus, no one who still professed to seek the Lord could be a part of such worship. They had to come to worship God at Jerusalem (v.16).

3. Shishak's invasion (12:1 – 12)

The invasion of the southern kingdom by the Egyptian army under Shishak offers two lessons: (1) Unfaithfulness brings punishment if you are God's people; (2) God looks on a repentant heart with grace (cf. Ps 51:17b).

4. The conclusion to Rehoboam's reign (12:13 – 16)

The summary of Rehoboam's reign is to the point: "He did evil because he had not set his heart on seeking the LORD" (v.14). That is, he did not properly worship the Lord by caring for the temple and leading his people in God's law.

C. Abijah (13:1 – 14:1)

In contrast to the brief notice of the reign of Abijah in 1Ki 15:1 – 8, the chronicler takes special interest in his short reign. The writer of 1 Kings grouped Abijah along with those kings who "committed all the sins his father had done before him" (1Ki 15:3). The chronicler, however, puts Abijah in a better light by virtue of his concern for the temple, the priests, and the Levites. He undoubtedly concurred with the assessment of the writer of 1 Kings, but that did not prevent him from pointing to at least one redeeming act of Abijah.

D. Asa (14:2 – 16:14)

1. General character of Asa's reign (14:2 – 8)

The 1 Kings account of the reign of Asa is considerably expanded here. Both authors agree at the start that "Asa did what was good and right in the eyes of the LORD his God" (14:2; cf. 1Ki 15:11). The chronicler finds several features of Asa's reign that both support that general view and, to some extent, temper it with the picture of a reign characterized by spiritual defeat. The strength of Asa's reign lay in his concern for the renewal of the temple and its worship and the courageous faith that Asa had in his Lord.

2. The invasion of Asa's kingdom (14:9 – 15)

The invader Zerah was a Cushite (Ethiopian), probably in the service of the Egyptians who held nominal control over the southern borders of Asa's kingdom. The chronicler is interested in one aspect of the invasion—its demonstration of the power of God to deliver his people from the enemy. Although Asa was clearly outnumbered, he recognized in those unfortunate odds the opportunity to trust in the power of God to deliver (v.11). The chronicler's summary statement tells the rest of the story: "The LORD struck down the Cushites before Asa and Judah. The Cushites fled" (v.12).

3. Asa's revival (15:1 – 19)

As with many religious revivals, the revival in Asa's day was started by the words of the prophet Azariah. His message was straightforward: seek the Lord while he can be found (v.2). Azariah drew his lesson from the past and evidently had in mind the period of the judges, although his description could fit many periods in Israel's history (vv.3 – 7).

Asa's response to Azariah's message was immediate. He rededicated the temple and celebrated the renewal of the covenant of the Feast of Weeks (Pentecost), which later Jewish tradition also used for commemorating the covenant. The emphasis was the direct connection between the king's spiritual leadership and his concern for the worship of God at the temple. Here, Asa's actions were an intimation of the final work of the One who is to come (Jn 2:15 – 16).

4. War with the northern kingdom (16:1 – 10)

Again the chronicler adds considerable detail to the account of 1Ki 15:17 – 22, casting a shadow across Asa's victory over the northern kingdom. The account of the war between Judah and Israel in 1 Kings is given without much editorializing on the part of the chronicler. His inclusion of the prophecy of Hanani (vv.7 – 9) shows that he, too, considers Asa's alliance with Ben-Hadad to have been an unfortunate mistake. As with the invasion by Zerah the Cushite, Asa should have trusted in the Lord, for the Lord would have delivered him (v.8).

How easy it is, in Asa's shoes, to forget the help of God in the past and to falter in our trust in him today. The prophet's words remain our only source of comfort as they should have been to Asa: "The eyes of the LORD range throughout the earth to strengthen those whose hearts are fully committed to him" (v.9). Asa was angry at the prophet's suggestion that he had acted foolishly. His lack of trust in God resulted in despotic oppression of his own kingdom (v.10).

5. The conclusion of Asa's kingdom (16:11 – 14)

This conclusion calls to mind the final failure of the Davidic kings as a whole, again reminding the reader that Israel's hope was in One yet to come. Why did Asa's reign end in the shadow of God's judgment rather than in the light of God's help? The answer is given in the statement about Asa's diseased feet: "Though his disease was severe, even in his illness he did not seek help from the Lord, but only from the physicians" (v.12). Asa again failed to trust God.

E. Jehoshaphat (17:1 – 20:37)

Jehoshaphat's name means "the Lord will rule [judge]." The account of his reign seems to be governed by that theme. Everything he accomplished was based on the reality of a living God actively at work among his people, instructing them in the way they should go and defending them when they put their trust in him.

1. Introductory summary of Jehoshaphat's reign (17:1 – 6)

The account of Jehoshaphat's reign begins with an assessment of the king that measures him by the deeds of David. According to accounts, Jehoshaphat did well.

2. Jehoshaphat's administration of the kingdom (17:7 – 19)

Here we find a survey, not included in 1 Kings, of the administrative accomplishments of King Jehoshaphat. He was concerned that his kingdom be properly instructed in the law of God. He wanted God's law to rule among his people, so he appointed officials and Levites to travel throughout Judah to teach them that law (vv.7 – 9). As he built walls to fortify his cities, so also he built spiritual walls to ensure obedience to God. Although those walls were not made of stone and mortar, they would still be standing long after the last bricks had crumbled in his fortified cities, for "the word of our God endures forever" (Isa 40:8).

The evidence of the Lord's approval of Jehoshaphat's reign is given by the description of the fear his enemies had for him. They did not make war on him because they feared the Lord. Their ancient enemies the Philistines even brought Jehoshaphat "gifts and silver" (v.11).

3. Jehoshaphat and King Ahab (18:1 – 34)

This chapter describes a war between Ahab's northern kingdom and the Arameans over the disputed Transjordan lands around Ramoth Gilead. The battle ended with Israel's defeat and Ahab's death.

Jehoshaphat first made his mark on the situation when he insisted that Ahab inquire for a word from the Lord before he went into battle (v.4). Jehoshaphat wanted to do only the will of God. Not convinced that Ahab's four hundred prophets had really spoken God's will, Jehoshaphat insisted further that a "prophet of the Lord" be found (v.6). Reluctantly, Ahab had the only prophet of the Lord available to him, Micaiah, brought before them and, as he had guessed, Ahab heard only an evil report from that prophet. Clearly the Lord was not with Ahab (vv.16–22). Ahab's defeat in battle confirmed that the words of Micaiah were true.

4. Jehoshaphat's appointment of judges (19:1–11)

Jehoshaphat returned home safely after a close brush with death in his alliance with Ahab. When he returned home, the prophet Jehu son of Hanani was waiting with a word from the Lord: "Should you help the wicked and love those who hate the LORD? Because of this, the wrath of the LORD is on you" (v.2). Jehu's words clearly referred to Jehoshaphat's alliance with Ahab and his close call with death. In light of Jehoshaphat's appointment of judges in this chapter, the chronicler also intended Jehu's words to apply to his present task, for his prophecy is a fitting statement of the theme of ch. 19: Jehoshaphat's appointment of judges.

5. Jehoshaphat's war with the Moabites and Ammonites (20:1–30)

This event, recorded only here, typifies Jehoshaphat's reign and name: "The LORD will rule [judge]." The salvation of God is put in its clearest light in this narrative. As the prophet Jahaziel put it, "You will not have to fight this battle. Take up your positions; stand firm and see the deliverance the LORD will give you, Judah and Jerusalem" (v.17).

The account of Jehoshaphat's prayer is reminiscent of Solomon's dedication of the temple (6:12–42). The nation was in danger of attack by its enemies, and the king rallied the people at the temple to ask God's help. The basis of his prayer was God's promise to be present at the temple and to give the land to Abraham's descendants (vv.5–9). Jehoshaphat's request can be applied to the godly in any age: "Our God, will you not judge them? For we have no power to face this vast army that is attacking us. We do not know what to do, but our eyes are on you" (v.12). Jehoshaphat was not asking for vengeance; he was only calling on God for help.

The reply of Jahaziel reinforced Jehoshaphat's reliance on the Lord: "The battle is not yours, but God's" (v.15). In those words we can hear not only the prophet speaking to Jehoshaphat and his people, but also the chronicler speaking to his own day: "Have faith in the LORD your God and you will be upheld; have faith in his prophets and you will be successful" (v.20). Surely God's people today need to hear that same word.

F. Jehoram (21:1–20)

Jehoram's reign is a classic example of forsaking the Lord. He murdered his own brothers for no apparent reason and followed the idolatrous practices of the kings of Israel to the north, to whose family he was related by marriage (v.6). His kingdom began to crumble as kingdoms on the east and west of him rebelled (vv.8 – 10) and invaded his own kingdom (vv.16 – 17). His life ended with a terrible illness, and when he died it was "to no one's regret" (v.20). All this was the result of Jehoram's forsaking the Lord and doing evil in God's sight.

G. Ahaziah (22:1 – 9)

Ahaziah, like his father, Jehoram, and his mother, Athaliah, had close ties with the northern kingdom. His mother was the granddaughter of the wicked Israelite king Omri and was the daughter of Ahab. The influence of his close relationship with Israel and with his own mother ultimately meant destruction for Ahaziah (22:4).

This is a greatly abbreviated story of the end of the dynasty of Ahab as recorded in 2Ki 9 – 10. The chronicler has given only the facts relevant to Ahaziah's death. Because of his close association with Ahab's son Joram, Ahaziah was slain along with Joram by Jehu, God's anointed. That meant that Ahaziah's death was also from God (v.7).

H. Athaliah (22:10 – 23:21)

At the beginning of Athaliah's reign she killed all the heirs to the throne of David, with the unintended exception of Ahaziah's young son, Joash. This young boy was hidden in the temple by his aunt Jehosheba, the wife of the high priest Jehoiada. Chapter 23 takes up the events that marked the end of Athaliah's six-year reign and the enthronement of Joash. Because she was not a son of David, the chronicler is not interested in her reign.

The events of ch. 23 are crucial to the message of 1 and 2 Chronicles. For the most part, the chronicler has paid attention to the role of the Davidic king in protecting and caring for the proper worship of God at the temple. When the true, promised King comes, he will build the house of the LORD.

I. Joash (24:1 – 27)

The account of the reign of Joash, tragic as it is, provides a classic example of the lesson the chronicler has had in mind: God will fulfill his promise of peace by sending a son of David to reign successfully on the throne; his success will depend on his obedience to God's will; and that obedience will be measured in terms of concern for the worship of God at the temple. The priests and Levites were to play a central role in the promise because through their teaching of God's law to the king and the people, obedience was accomplished. Jehoiada, the godly priest, was able to lead the young king in God's will as long as he was alive. But when he died, the king and his kingdom fell into apostasy (vv.2, 15 – 18).

Yet when the people fell away, God did not abandon them; he sent prophets to warn them that they would be given over into the hands of their enemies as punishment (vv.20–22). When the king and the people rejected the word of the prophets, God's warning of punishment came true (vv.23–24).

Behind the tragedy of Joash's reign, however, a message of hope pervades. If the people would only listen to the prophets and turn to God, the Lord would restore their blessing, and their latter glory would be greater than the former glory (cf. 6:24–25).

J. Amaziah (25:1 – 28)

At first glance the account of Amaziah's reign appears sketchy and disjointed. A closer look, however, reveals three carefully collected events from his reign that deal with the issue of obedience to God's will (cf. vv.3–4; 25:5–13; and 25:14–24). They teach the familiar lesson of this book: God helps his people when they obey; but when they disobey, God's people can expect punishment.

K. Uzziah (26:1 – 23)

In 2Ki 15:1–7 we have only a bare sketch of the reign of Uzziah (or Azariah), noting that "the LORD afflicted the king with leprosy until the day he died" (2Ki 15:5). The chronicler has included much more material regarding Uzziah's leprosy to show that it was a result of the king's pride and presumption.

L. Jotham (27:1 – 9)

Jotham was a good king. He cared for the temple (v.3), and his reign was recognized even by his neighbors (v.5). In summary, "Jotham grew powerful because he walked steadfastly before the LORD his God" (v.6). All of that should have added up to an important and influential reign. It is, however, surprising that the chronicler has devoted so little to the reign of this king. One clue may lie in the comment that "the people ... continued their corrupt practices" during his reign (v.2). Such a reign does not serve to build hope in the fulfillment of the Davidic promise. Jotham was a great king, but in his day there was no revival of his people. The kings that interest the chronicler are those who bring revival.

M. Ahaz (28:1 – 27)

The reign of Ahaz provides the first evidence of the chronicler's response to the question of the purpose of the exile. This account is supplementary to the one recorded in 2Ki 16:1–20.

Although Ahaz fell far short of God's will, he did not turn to God in repentance when chastisement came, as other kings had done. On the contrary, God's chastisement served only to harden him in his unfaithfulness: "In his time of trouble King Ahaz became even more unfaithful to the LORD" (v.22).

N. Hezekiah (29:1 – 32:33)

Although much material is devoted to Hezekiah's reign, the main point is simple: when the son of David cares for the temple and the worship of God there, God brings peace to his kingdom. The length of the chronicler's treatment of Hezekiah's reign is due to his concern for detail, which is his way of driving home his point. He gives a detailed account of the rededication of the temple (29:1 – 36), the celebration of the Passover (30:1 – 27), and the reestablishment of the orders of priests and Levites (31:1 – 21). This revival of the worship is followed by a most stunning victory of God — the defeat of the Assyrian Sennacherib (32:1 – 33).

1. The temple rededication (29:1 – 36)

Ahaz had closed the doors of the temple (28:24) and set up worship centers throughout Jerusalem and the other cities of Judah. Hezekiah's first important task was to open the temple for worship and reconsecrate it with a solemn assembly.

2. The Passover (30:1 – 27)

The revival that began in the heart of the king spread to the leaders and was proclaimed throughout the land. For those remaining in the north and for those still in need of repentance in the south, the celebration of the Passover would mark the establishment of a renewed covenant and a return to the "God of Abraham, Isaac and Israel" (v.6).

Hezekiah's proclamation to the north shows that repentance would mean a return from exile of many of those captives in Assyria (v.9). The basis of his call for repentance was the appeal to a God who is "gracious and compassionate. He will not turn his face from you if you return to him" (v.9).

Hezekiah's prayer for the people (vv.18 – 20) allows a helpful glimpse into the heart of both this godly king and the chronicler. Both were sincerely concerned for the proper exercise of worship at the temple. Carelessness in this regard would be the last thing either would tolerate. At the same time they were both concerned ultimately with the question of a right heart attitude. Mere ritualism is not the goal of temple worship (30:19; cf. Ps 15).

3. The priests and the Levites (31:1 – 21)

Like David and Solomon before him, Hezekiah took a personal interest in the organization and welfare of the priests and Levites. The chronicler's particular interest seems to show that when the people tithe, there is abundance, with plenty left over (v.10).

4. The invasion of Sennacherib (32:1 – 33)

The Assyrian king Sennacherib was one of that country's most powerful kings. He led several military campaigns against the lands around Judah, and on more than one occasion his armies threatened the kingdom of Judah. Sennacherib recorded his version of the events in ch. 32 in his own royal archives.

Hezekiah's encouraging words strengthened not only those in Jerusalem in his own day, but continue to give courage to failing hearts in every age: "Be strong and courageous. Do not be afraid or discouraged because of the king of Assyria and the vast army with him, for there is a greater power with us than with him. With him is only the arm of flesh, but with us is the LORD our God to help us and to fight our battles" (vv.7 – 8).

O. Manasseh (33:1 – 20)

Manasseh's reign represents one of the most dramatic turnabouts in 1 and 2 Chronicles. He began as an extremely evil king and consistently led the hearts of the people away from the Lord (vv.2 – 9). Other biblical writers see his reign as the point of no return, leading to the exile (see 2Ki 23:26; Jer 15:4). The chronicler, however, gives an account of Manasseh's repentance and the reparations that resulted from his tortuous exile to Babylon. What happened to him personally in Babylon would soon happen to the whole nation.

P. Amon (33:21 – 25)

The reign of Amon was short; the chronicler devotes little time to it. Its primary significance lay in Amon's failure to repent as his father Manasseh had. That failure was a direct result of his father's earlier sins. In other words, Manasseh's sins continued to affect God's people and, in particular, his own son.

Q. Josiah (34:1 – 35:27)

The reign of Josiah was tragic. He was one of the few godly kings of the line of David. He ushered in widespread reform throughout his kingdom, including the land to the north (34:6). At the peak of his reign, he was slain

in battle (35:22 – 24). The account of Josiah's reign emphasizes two important events: (1) the discovery and reading of the law of Moses (34:14 – 33),
and (2) the celebration of the Passover (35:1 – 19).

1. The law of Moses (34:1 – 33)

The loss of the law of Moses in Josiah's day was not a new problem. In fact,
the problem appears to have been at the very root of Israel's failure to keep
her covenant obligations. Already in the earliest stages of her history as a
nation, after the death of Joshua and his generation, "another generation
grew up who knew neither the LORD nor what he had done for Israel" (Jdg
2:10). A new generation cannot live on a legacy. They must learn afresh
who the Lord is and what he has done for them. When the law of Moses
was read to the king, its words became God's final sentence against his
disobedient people: "My anger will be poured out on this place and will
not be quenched" (34:25) — a reference to the coming Babylonian exile
(36:17 – 21).

2. The Passover (35:1 – 19)

Again the intensity of the chronicler's interest in Josiah's care for the
worship of God at the temple can be measured in his attention to detail.
Josiah's reign pictures vividly the reign of the coming King. When he
comes, he will be like Josiah and will lead his people in the worship of
God at the temple.

3. The death of Josiah (35:20 – 27)

The chronicler is not concerned with the details of the battle that resulted
in Josiah's death. The battle at Carchemish involved two major empires
of the ancient Near East, Babylon and Egypt. Josiah met his end while
attempting to oppose the Egyptian forces en route to the battle. Because
he did not listen to Necho's message, he was killed. Josiah, a great king
whose reign was characterized by obedience and godliness, in the end did
not heed God's warning and fell in battle. At this last moment in his book,
the chronicler reminds his readers that the Promised Seed of David has
not yet come. Even Josiah failed to obey God's will. The words of David
regarding the promise of an eternal kingdom lie behind Josiah's tragic end:
"If you seek him, he will be found by you; but if you forsake him, he will
reject you forever" (1Ch 28:9).

R. The Conclusion (36:1 – 23)

The chronicler ends with a cursory review of the last kings who reigned
over the kingdom of their father David (vv.1 – 13), a short sermon on the

cause of the exile (vv.14–21), and Cyrus's edict, which marks the start of the temple rebuilding (vv.22–23).

1. The last kings (36:1 – 13)

The chronicler's emphasis in recounting the days of the last Davidic kings is to show that their dominion was finished and that the real power now rested in the hands of foreign empires—Egypt and Babylon. What a great distance from the expectation that the Son of David would rule from sea to sea with the nations as his inheritance (Ps 2). The point is that the historical kingdom of David was not the reign envisioned in the promise to David. That kingdom ended in failure. To explain that further, a concluding sermon is added to this account of the last kings—kings whose reigns typified much of the house of David before them.

2. The chronicler's sermon (36:14 – 21)

The theme of the chronicler's concluding remarks is expressed awesomely in v.16: "They mocked God's messengers, despised his words and scoffed at his prophets until the wrath of the LORD was aroused against his people and there was no remedy." God gave his people over into the hands of their enemies, and those enemies burned the house of God (v.19) and carried his people into captivity in Babylon (v.20). All that is the opposite of what the chronicler hoped for. The past lay in ruins, but the future lies in the promise of God as stated in 7:14. When the temple is again rebuilt and the people pray, even though they are in exile (6:36–39), God will hear their prayer and restore their peace. All is made to rest on the rebuilding of the temple.

3. The edict of Cyrus (36:22 – 23)

The last two verses of 2 Chronicles ultimately determine the mood of both books. They are not about human failure but about the power and promises of God. Out of the ruins of human effort, the chronicler shows that God's purposes can never fail and that all he intends to do will be accomplished (see Isa 9:7). The exile and the destruction of the temple may have seemed to put an end to the promise that God would rule his people through the house of David, but the chronicler's purpose has been to show that God is still at work and that the hearts of the mightiest rulers are in his hand.

EZRA

Introduction

The date and authorship of the book of Ezra are unknown; see introduction to Nehemiah.

I. The Return (1:1 – 6:22)

A. Rebuilding the Temple in Jerusalem (1:1 – 4:24)

1. Cyrus allows Jews to return to Jerusalem (1:1 – 4)

This book begins with a fulfilled prophecy from Jeremiah, who had foretold that Judah would go into exile to Babylon (Jer 25:8 – 10) and that this exile would last for seventy years (25:11). At the end of this period, Judah would return to the land (29:10 – 14). The writer of Ezra, referring to Jeremiah's prophecy, sees its fulfillment in the first group of Jews who returned to Jerusalem under the leadership of Zerubbabel and Jeshua the high priest. Their primary task was to reconstruct the temple. Part of the strategy of this book is to show that though there was initial fulfillment, much more remained of God's promises in the future.

2. Preparation for the return to build the temple (1:5 – 2:70)

The leaders of the exiles made the necessary preparations for the journey and the construction of the temple (1:5 – 6). This included regaining possession of the original utensils of the temple that had been taken by Nebuchadnezzar (vv.7 – 11). These treasures were put in the care of Sheshbazzar (v.8; 5:14), who was appointed governor of the region (5:14).

Some indication of the extent of the undertaking can be seen in the list of returning exiles (2:1–67). At the head of the list were twelve leaders, including Zerubbabel and Jeshua, the high priest (v.2). These are followed by a list of "the men of the people of Israel" (vv.2b–20, 70b; cf. 3:1). This group included a remnant of the original "Israel" that once occupied the northern kingdom. The return is pictured as a comprehensive return of God's people. A list of priests (vv.36–39), Levites (v.40), singers (v.41), gatekeepers (v.42), temple servants (vv.43–54), and descendants of the servants of Solomon (vv.55–58) follows. There were also many whose lineage could not be clearly established (vv.59–60), even from among the priests (vv.61–63).

When they arrived in Jerusalem, the returning exiles and their leaders were eager to begin work on the temple. They gave freely from their own wealth (vv.68–70).

3. Beginning the work (3:1–13)

The first act of restoration was the rebuilding of the altar at the site of the temple (vv.1–6), accomplished under the leadership of Zerubbabel and Jeshua. Zerubbabel had royal Davidic blood through his father Shealtiel (v.8), and Jeshua was the high priest (Hag 1:1; Zec 3:1).

There was great celebration with the laying of the foundation (vv.10–11). Those who had seen the former temple, built by Solomon, wept in sorrow, while others shouted for joy (vv.12–13). Already Solomon's temple was being idealized, and the present one could not match it. Though there was joy in what God had done in the present, there was still room for hope that greater blessing was possible in the future.

4. Opposition to the rebuilding of the temple (4:1–24)

When Zerubbabel and those working on the temple refused to allow the local inhabitants of the land to participate in the building, "officials" were bribed to "frustrate their plans" (v.5). This effectively halted the work on the temple throughout the reign of Cyrus and into the reign of the next king, Darius (vv.4–5, 24; 5:16b).

B. Renewal of the Rebuilding of the Temple (5:1–6:22)

After a long delay, the rebuilding of the temple was again underway. There were two causes for this renewed effort. The first was the prophetic encouragement of Haggai and Zechariah (5:1–2). The second was a letter sent to Darius (5:3–6:12). The writer clearly intends us to see a link between these two causes. When the people followed the words of the prophet (cf. Dt 18:18), God brought them success.

The temple was completed in the sixth year of Darius (6:13–15). The Levitical priesthood was installed during an elaborate dedication of the temple (6:16–18), and in the same year they celebrated the Passover (6:19–22).

II. Ezra (7:1 – 10:44)

A. Ezra Prepares to Leave for Jerusalem (7:1 – 14)

Ezra was a priest of the house of Aaron (7:1–5) who was "well versed in the Law of Moses" (v.6). Apparently because of his wisdom and knowledge of Israelite law, he enjoyed the favor of the king (v.6). Ezra came to Jerusalem with a letter of introduction from King Artaxerxes, commissioning him to administer the land of Judah according to God's law (7:11–28). He was accompanied by a large company who returned with him to Jerusalem (8:1–36).

B. Problem of Intermarriage (9:1 – 10:44)

A major problem facing Ezra's administration of the law was that the people, especially their leaders, had "not kept themselves separate from the neighboring peoples with their detestable practices" (9:1). Although the problem involved intermarriage (v.2) with the sons and daughters of the nations, the difficulty lay with their "unfaithfulness" to God (vv.3–4).

Ezra, in his prayer of confession (ch. 9), cast this sin of the people within the larger context of Israel's covenant relationship with God. The people had been warned by God's prophets (vv.10–12), but they had disregarded God's words and were guilty (v.15). God had remained faithful to his promises, and the people had found grace in their return from captivity (vv.8–9). But now they once again joined in apostasy with the people of the land. God's people were no further along than in the days of Joshua when they disobeyed God and made a covenant with the Gibeonites (Jos 9).

The people eventually agreed to put away their foreign wives.

NEHEMIAH

Introduction

The date and authorship of Nehemiah are unknown. Though Nehemiah speaks in the first person throughout the book, there is no direct evidence that he is the author since he is also a part of the narrative (e.g., 8:9). In the Hebrew text, the books of Ezra and Nehemiah are a single book; hence the heading "The words of Nehemiah son of Hacaliah" (1:1) marks a section of the book only. It is not a title.

I. Nehemiah's Return (1:1 – 4:23)

This book opens with the godly Nehemiah hearing of the despicable condition of the city of Jerusalem (1:1–4). The walls lay in ruin and the gates were torn down. Because he held a high office in the court of the Persian king Artaxerxes I, Nehemiah was able to do something about it—but not without the Lord's help. He went immediately to prayer (vv.5–11).

Having obtained permission and assistance from Artaxerxes to return and rebuild the city of Jerusalem, Nehemiah left for Judah (2:1–9) and inspected the walls (vv.11–16). But there was trouble brewing among the enemies of God's people; Sanballat and Tobiah "were very much disturbed that someone had come to promote the welfare of the Israelites" (v.10).

As the rebuilding of Jerusalem began (2:17–18), opposition immediately arose (vv.19–20). The people were mocked and taunted by their enemies, but it served only as an occasion for Nehemiah to give a renewed commitment to the faithfulness of God: "The God of heaven will give us success" (v.20). As a demonstration of the truth of Nehemiah's confession, the writer records, at length, the success of the builders (3:1 – 32). The report of further opposition only highlighted the success that the Israelites were enjoying from the hand of God (4:1 – 23).

II. Problems among the People of God (5:1 – 19)

The writer now inserts two brief narratives that show the quality of Nehemiah's godly leadership. The first deals with the fact that some Israelites were charging interest to their fellow Israelites, which led to poverty and economic slavery (5:1 – 13). Nehemiah took strong action.

Nehemiah's godly leadership is further exemplified in his not requiring the food allotment that was rightfully his as governor of the province (5:14 – 19). Though previous governors had insisted on their allotment and had thus placed heavy demands on the people, Nehemiah did not (v.18).

III. Conspiracy against Nehemiah (6:1 – 7:3)

The narrative resumes the opposition of Sanballat and Tobiah to Nehemiah's work (vv.1 – 14). Nehemiah refused to be intimidated by the threats and antics of his enemies. He met each case of opposition by trusting God and striving to be obedient to his word. He let God take care of the opposition (v.14). Hence the wall was completed in fifty-two days (vv.15 – 16) — a vivid demonstration to the nations that the work had been done with the help of God (v.16). Even though important leaders in Judah and men close to Nehemiah had sided with the opposition (vv.17 – 19), God gave him success and thwarted all their plans. Jerusalem was protected (7:1 – 3).

IV. Registration of Families: List of Returnees (7:4 – 73)

The city walls now complete, Nehemiah turned to the problem of restoring the city itself. He began by taking a census of the people living in the land who had returned from Babylon. The writer includes the original list of those who had returned to rebuild the temple (vv.6 – 73), a virtual duplicate of the list in Ezr 2. For the next three chapters, the writer devotes his attention to the religious life of the city and the growing importance of the law of Moses among the people. In ch. 11 the narrative returns to Nehemiah's efforts to restore city life in Jerusalem.

V. Ezra and the Law (8:1 – 10:39)

A. Ezra Reads the Law (8:1 – 12)

On the first day of the seventh month Ezra stood on a high wooden plat-
form and read aloud the "Book of the Law of Moses." This book was apparently the same document as our Pentateuch. This day was a special day of
rest (Sabbath) and was celebrated as the Feast of Trumpets (Lev 23:23 – 25;
Nu 29:1 – 6). All the people stood as Ezra read the book, and "he read it
aloud from daybreak till noon" (8:3). The people wept as they listened
to the words of the law (v.9); the Levites (Jeshua and the twelve) also
explained it to the people who were standing nearby, "giving the meaning
so that the people could understand what was being read" (v.8). Thus the
people celebrated "with great joy, because they now understood the words
that had been made known to them" (v.12).

B. The Response of the People (8:13 – 10:39)

Ezra continued to teach the law to the people (8:13), fulfilling the task for
which he had been sent to Jerusalem (cf. Ezr 7:10, 25b – 26). Moreover, he
led them in the celebration of the Feast of Booths (8:13 – 18). As a result of
their reading the law of Moses, a special day of fasting and repentance
was called on the twenty-fourth day of the same month. On this day the
Israelites "stood in their places and confessed their sins and the sins of
their ancestors." The writer appears intent on showing that by this time
the people had reached the same state of repentance and godly sorrow as
Nehemiah had at the beginning of the book (cf. 1:4 – 11).

VI. Residents of the New Land (11:1 – 13:3)

A registration of families who had returned from Babylon apparently
showed that far too few people had settled in Jerusalem. Nehemiah thus
provided for an orderly resettlement in the city by casting "lots to bring one
out of every ten of them to live in Jerusalem" (11:1).

This incident shows the nature and extent of Nehemiah's godly leadership. The "great trouble and disgrace" of the "Jewish remnant that had
survived the exile" in Jerusalem (cf. 1:1 – 11) have now been cared for, and
Nehemiah's visit was successful. Thereupon the wall of the city of Jerusalem (12:27 – 43) was dedicated. Once again order was restored in Jerusalem
and worship was carried out as "in the days of David" (v.46).

VII. Nehemiah's Final Reforms (13:4 – 31)

The last words of the book focus ironically on God's blessing of Nehemiah, "Remember me with favor, my God" (v.31b), and decidedly not on the people as a whole. The reader has learned that though there were godly persons like Nehemiah among God's people, the nation as a whole was not any different than it had been in the days of King Solomon, who "was led into sin by foreign women" (vv.26 – 27).

ESTHER

Introduction

The date and authorship of Esther is unknown. Tradition ascribed the book to the "Men of the Great Synagogue," but there is no independent confirmation. The central part of the book is devoted to telling the story of Esther, the Jewish queen of Persia (1:1–9:17), and the last section deals with the origin of the Jewish Feast of Purim (9:18–10:3).

I. The Story of Esther (1:1 – 9:17)

A. Royal Banquet (1:1 – 22)

The story opens with a royal banquet given by the Persian King Xerxes (vv.1–9). During this banquet Queen Vashti refused the request of the king to attend and thus was removed from her claim to the throne (vv.10–22).

B. Esther Becomes Queen (2:1 – 18)

Within the course of telling the story, the writer carefully introduces Esther to his readers. Not only are we told that Esther "had a lovely figure and was beautiful" (v.7), but also we see that her beauty and charm were immediately recognized by Hegai, the one in charge of the king's harem (v.9a). His excessive concern for her (v.9b) leaves no doubt in the reader's mind that she will be chosen by the king. It is really no contest.

C. The Moment of Crisis (2:19 – 5:8)

Ironically it was Mordecai's refusal to pay honor to Haman that incited him against the Jews (3:1–15). Thus the story teaches more than persever- ance through suffering. As in the book of Daniel, this story teaches stead- fast loyalty to one's beliefs, even in the face of recriminations. Mordecai's refusal to bow before Haman bears similarity to the equally bold refusal of Shadrach, Meshach, and Abednego to bow down to Nebuchadnezzar's golden image (Da 3:16–18), or Daniel's continued daily prayers in the face of Darius's prohibition (Da 6:10). All of these people were willing to accept the consequences, yet trusting that God would intervene.

D. Haman's Consequences (5:9–9:17)

Haman's boasting and preparation for the death of Mordecai led to God's honoring Esther's courage through a series of "coincidences" (5:9–14; cf. 7:9–10). All too quickly, for Haman's sake at least, the crucial pieces of his fate fell into place. By his own selfish words to the king, he pronounced a blessing on Mordecai and the Jews (6:6–13), reminiscent of Balaam's constrained blessings of Israel in the days of Moses (see comments on Nu 22–24). Haman was hanged on the gallows he had designed for Mordecai (7:1–10), his estate was put into the hands of Esther and Mordecai (8:1–2), his plans to destroy the Jews were reversed (8:3–17), and the Jews were given free rein to protect themselves against their enemies (9:1–17).

In mounting up such a multilayered set of "coincidences," the writer builds his case that God is at work in the world both to will and to do his good pleasure (Php 2:13), and that all things work together for good for those who trust in him (see Ro 8:28; cf. Ge 50:20).

II. The Feast of Purim (9:18–32)

The writer of Esther now turns to the meaning of the Jewish festival Purim. So great was the deliverance of God's people that an annual feast was com- missioned for its remembrance.

III. A Final Word about Mordecai (10:1–3)

Curiously, the book concludes with a final word about Mordecai rather than Esther. Though Esther was the crucial link in the working out of God's blessing for Israel, the writer concludes by saying that it was Morde- cai who "worked for the good of his people and spoke up for the welfare of all the Jews" (v.3b).

JOB

Introduction

The book of Job is named for its principal character, Job. The name means "the persecuted one." The author of the book is unknown, as is the time of its composition. It has been attributed both to Moses and to Solomon, but with little solid evidence for support. This book and its central themes are a part of the wisdom books of the OT. Job is presented as a nearly perfect example of a wise man. What happens to him and what he learns from it serve as a model for the life of the people of God.

Rather than look at all of the individual passages in the book, we will summarize the argument of the book as a whole.

Summary of the Argument of the Book

This book presents Job as an example of a perfectly wise man. The Lord himself describes him as "blameless and upright, a man who fears God and shuns evil" (1:8). What especially marked Job as a wise man was that he feared God (1:8–9). The fundamental and essential quality of biblical wisdom is "the fear of the LORD" (cf. Ps 111:10; Pr 1:7).

As the perfect example of the kind of wisdom that God intended his people to seek and to have, Job became the target of a great challenge. Satan attacked God in the first chapter of the book by challenging the validity of divine wisdom. Like Goliath (1Sa 17), Satan challenged the validity of true godly wisdom.

It is generally held that the primary purpose of the book is to explain why God's people suffer or why the righteous suffer. Though there are such lessons, that is not its main focus. Strictly speaking, the book explains only why Job suffered. Because of his wisdom, Satan attacked him; Job was a test case for divine wisdom.

The theme of the quality and motivation of Job's wisdom is developed in the book along two lines. (1) There was the challenge and the test of Job's wisdom, recorded in the prologue. Job was tested twice (1:13 – 19; 2:7 – 10), and on both occasions he proved by his actions that he feared God; his wisdom was genuine (1:20 – 22; 2:10).

(2) In the main body of the book of Job, we see Job learning deeper lessons about God and one's relationship to him. These lessons all point to the central theme: true wisdom, true godliness, comes from complete submission to God's rule, regardless of temporary rewards or suffering. Job echoes this conclusion in the final scene of the book: "I know that you can do all things; no purpose of yours can be thwarted.... My ears had heard of you but now my eyes have seen you. Therefore I despise myself and repent in dust and ashes" (42:2 – 6).

The series of discourses between Job and his friends is based on a common assumption they shared. All four were convinced that Job's suffering came from God and that there was a lesson to be learned from it. But this assumption was only partially correct. The writer of the book forces us to evaluate critically the various positions of Job and his friends; we are pulled into the discourse since we know more than the participants themselves.

In response to his three friends' advice, Job persistently maintained his innocence. He was convinced that he had done nothing to merit the magnitude of his troubles (9:21; 16:12; 23:10 – 12; 27:2, 4 – 6). Job, for his part, wanted a hearing with God (13:3, 14; 23:3 – 5). As readers we know that Job's suffering was not caused by sin, but we learn from the text itself that his continuous accusations against God came dangerously close to attributing injustice to God.

The truly wise man, like Job, is one who submits to God's will and does not call God's justice into question. God is the Creator, human beings are the creatures, and in the final analysis, their role is to submit to the divine authority. The book teaches that God always does justice, even though we cannot always see it from our limited perspective. As represented in the character of Job, the proper response of God's people is to submit to God's will and wait for the return of divine blessing.

PSALMS

Introduction

The book of Psalms can be read as a single book with each individual psalm intentionally arranged within the book in a meaningful way. Underlying that arrangement is the view that they are to be read as pointing to the messianic King. (See also *The Essential Bible Companion to the Psalms*.)

I. Introduction (1 – 2)

Psalm 1. This psalm serves as an introduction to the whole book. It establishes the central theme of Psalms: meditation on Scripture as the way of the righteous. In God's written Word, the righteous will find blessing.

 Psalm 2. This psalm is attached to Ps 1 as a means of further qualifying its central theme. It is a messianic psalm based on the promise to David in 2Sa 7:16 (see comments on 2Sa 7). Meditating on Scripture ultimately leads to trusting in the Messiah (v.12).

II. David and the Promised Seed (3 – 9)

Psalm 3. The link to Ps 1 – 2 is provided by the superscription, "A psalm of David. When he fled from his son Absalom." This title suggests that Ps 3 continues the theme of the messianic promise to David in 2Sa 7:16. How did David himself understand God's promise when his own son Absalom rebelled against the house of David (2Sa 15)? David did not waver in his trust in God's promise, even in the face of a grievous obstacle to the fulfillment of that promise. In spite of overwhelming odds, David says, "From the Lord comes deliverance" (v.8). This psalm thus encourages readers to imitate David's faith in God's promises and not to let their faith in God waver even though God's promised Messiah had not yet come.

Psalm 4. Continuing from Ps 3 (see comment), this psalm shows David's constant pleading for God to act on his behalf — "Answer me when I call to you, my righteous God. Give me relief from my distress" (v.1). David's words express his own longing for the coming of the promised Messiah. This theme continues throughout the book.

Psalm 5. David, the king, addresses God, the King, waiting in eager expectation of God's reply. Here he asks that his enemies, who "have rebelled against" God (v.10b), be brought to their knees. The superscriptions of Pss 3 and 7 have helped identify David's plight historically as Absalom's rebellion. Psalms 1–2, however, have directed the reader to understand David's words in light of the promised Messiah. The righteous for whom David prays in 5:12 are thus the "blessed" ones who take refuge "in him" (2:12), i.e., the Lord's "anointed" (2:2).

Psalm 6. David returns to the theme of waiting patiently for God's response. He is in anguish as he waits for God to act, "How long, Lord, how long?" (v.3). Yet still he knows that God has promised to save him (v.4) and that the Lord has heard his prayer (v.9). The terminology that David uses in v.4, "because of your unfailing love," shows that his thoughts are on God's promise to send an eternal King in 2Sa 7.

Psalm 7. The superscription here provides the key to the links between the first several psalms. This psalm represents David's response to the word of Absalom's death, which he heard from the Cushite (2Sa 18:21–33). David was greatly distressed and said, "O my son Absalom! My son, my son Absalom! If only I had died instead of you" (2Sa 18:33). In a similar fashion here, David disclaims all guilt in the matter, saying, "If I have repaid my ally with evil ... let him trample my life to the ground and make me sleep in the dust" (Ps 7:4–5). David appeals to God, the "righteous judge" (v.11), and turns his eyes toward God's final judgment of the ungodly (v.13). At the close of the psalm, David vows to "sing the praises of the name of the Lord Most High" (v.17), which introduces Ps 8.

Psalm 8. The NT writers saw this psalm as a prophecy of Jesus Christ (Heb 2:6–8). Perhaps the compiler of the psalms also understood it messianically, for the phrase translated here "human beings" (v.4b) is sometimes translated "son of man." If so, this phrase can be understood in light of "the Son" in Ps 2:12, as Hebrews sees the connection. In such a context, this psalm is to be understood as a praise of the "Son of man" who, "crowned ... with glory and honor," was "a little lower than God" (8:5, see NIV note). He is thus a royal figure, much like the "son of man" in Da 7:10–14, and has dominion over all God's creation (v.6).

Psalm 9. In light of the messianic and eschatological sense that this psalm has within Psalms, it is fitting that the theme of Ps 9 is the eternal kingship of God: "The LORD reigns forever; he has established his throne for judgment. He will rule the world in righteousness" (vv.7–8). Moreover, the theme of Zion as the place of God's kingship, an essential part of the Davidic promise (2Sa 7), plays an important role in this psalm (Ps 9:11, 14). Its central theme is the judgment of the wicked nations (vv.15, 17, 19–20) and the divine salvation of the righteous (vv.9, 18); it ends on a high note of triumph and praise. As we will see, however, the next psalm takes a sharp turn in another direction and hence shifts the thematic focus of the book as a whole.

III. Times of Trouble for the House of David (10–41)

Psalm 10. The opening lines of this psalm set the tone for the next series of psalms: "Why, LORD, do you stand far off? Why do you hide yourself in times of trouble?" (v.1). In stark contrast to the victorious praise of Ps 9, the focus of Ps 10 is the trouble one experiences when the wicked prosper (vv.1–11). There is hope at the end of the psalm, however, and it consists of the same hope in the coming kingdom of God: "The LORD is King for ever and ever; the nations will perish from his land" (v.16).

Psalm 11. Like Ps 10, this psalm focuses on the question of what the righteous should do during the times of trouble when the wicked prosper (see v.3). The answer lies in the patient expectation of the righteous for the coming of the divine King (vv.4–7). The opening line of the psalm, "In the LORD I take refuge," refers back to the introductory theme of trust in God's promise to send the Anointed One (2:2, 12).

Psalm 12. This psalm too focuses on times of trouble for God's people (vv.1–4). Rather than looking into the future to the time of the establishment of God's kingdom, however, it stresses God's present comfort and care for the righteous (vv.5–8): The Lord "will keep the needy safe and will protect us" (v.7).

Psalm 13. This psalm looks internally at the heart of the righteous, who must wait patiently for God's salvation. It expresses the despair that often accompanies such waiting: "How long, O LORD? Will you forget me forever?" (v.1). The psalm concludes by recalling God's "unfailing love" (v.5), which in Hebrew links the psalmist's hope to God's promise of a deliverer from the house of David (2Sa 7:16).

Psalm 14. As in the introduction to the book of Psalms (Pss 1–2), hope in God's messianic promises to the house of David is cast in terms of the wise man and the fool. The "fool" is one who has given up hope that God will punish the wicked and deliver the righteous (vv.1–5a). The wise, however, continue to long "that salvation for Israel would come out of Zion!" (v.7a). The fool's words, "There is no God," are not those of an atheist, but rather of the wicked, who think they can get away unscathed with their evil deeds. The psalmist expresses confidence in his presence, "for God is present in the company of the righteous" (v.5b).

Psalm 15. Having raised the question of the righteous who wait for the fulfillment of God's promise in Ps 14, the compiler now offers a description of true righteousness (vv.2–5a).

Psalm 16. As a model of faithfulness and trust in God's messianic promise, the compiler includes one of David's own reflections on the Davidic promise (2Sa 7:16). At the center of his thoughts is David's confidence in the resurrection. David contemplates his own trust in God (vv.1–4) and the blessing he received from God's hand (vv.5–6; cf. 2Sa 7). The source of his rejoicing is God's promise of eternal blessings (vv.7–11). David knows that God will not abandon him and his descendants in the grave, and he keeps the promise of an eternal King and kingdom before him at all times (v.8). David's confidence in his own resurrection stems from his trust in the resurrection of his Promised Seed: "nor will you let your faithful one see decay" (v.10).

Psalm 17. The content of this prayer of David focuses the reader's attention on the theme of resurrection. The psalm recalls the laments of David as he was being pursued by his enemies. At its close, however, David looks beyond his immediate enemies, resting his hope in the fact that one day he will see God's face (v.15b).

Psalm 18. The superscription locates this psalm to the time when David fled from Saul (see the same psalm in 2Sa 22). It begins with David's expression of trust in God (vv.1–3) and follows with a lament (vv.4–5), a call to God for help (v.6a), and God's answer (v.6b). The central part of the psalm consists of a description of God's rescue of David, cast in the form of a theophany, i.e., an awesome display of God's power as Creator (vv.7–19). In the rest of the psalm, David casts himself as a figure of the promised messianic King, God's "anointed" (v.50), seeing in his own divinely wrought victories a portrait of his eternal descendant (v.50b).

Psalm 19. Two themes come together in Ps 19: the revelation of God in creation (vv.1–6) and the revelation of God in his Word (vv.7–14). God's glory is displayed in creation and God's grace is displayed in his Word. Three major psalms stress the importance of God's revelation in his Word:

Pss 1, 19, and 119, each of which is immediately followed by a messianic psalm or group of psalms (Pss 2, 20–21, 120–133). The compiler balances the one theme, God's Word, with that of the other, God's Anointed—the Messiah. The Word of God and the Anointed One, the Messiah, are God's two primary means for bringing salvation and redemption. God's Word is "more precious than gold" (v.10) because it points to the Redeemer (v.14b).

Psalm 20. This psalm is a blessing (vv.1–5) in behalf of the Anointed King of the house of David (v.6). Its aim is the fulfillment of the promises to David as described in Ps 2 and 2Sa 7:16. This psalm functions as a thematic marker within the structure of the whole book. It establishes the context of the surrounding psalms by linking them to the messianic themes of Pss 1–2 and to the messianic promise in 2Sa 7.

Psalm 21. This psalm takes up the theme of the king's trust in God (v.1) introduced in Ps 20:7 (compare also 20:4 with 21:2). In addition, Ps 21 links with several of the preceding psalms insofar as it elevates the portrait of the "king" taken up from the preceding psalms to a much higher plane. In this way Ps 21 focuses the reader's attention on the future of the house of David instead of on its past. For the Davidic king, the time of the fulfillment of the hope expressed in the Psalms still lies in the future, in the coming of the Messiah.

Psalm 22. The first part of the psalm (vv.1–22) is a lament of "the afflicted one" (v.24a). Though David is its author, he must not be understood as the one who is speaking in the psalm itself. David as author begins to speak only at v.23, where he addresses the congregation about the "suffering of the afflicted one" (v.24); God "has listened to his cry for help" (v.24b). In v.25 he turns to address the "afflicted one": "From you comes the theme of my praise in the great assembly." By speaking *about* the Lord, not *to* him, in vv.25–26, the author shows that he is actually addressing the Afflicted One. Moreover, David affirms that "all the families of the nations will bow down before [you]" (v.27b), using an image that recalls the "son of man" in Da 7:13–14. David concludes: "Posterity will serve him; future generations will be told about the Lord. They will proclaim his righteousness" (vv.30–31).

Psalm 23. Following closely on the heels of the Afflicted One in Ps 22, who feels "forsaken" by God at his moment of trial (22:1), the present psalm is centered on the theme of God's presence in the face of death. The psalm is about the "anoint[ed]" one (v.5) who enjoys God's presence forever (v.6). In the Hebrew text of this psalm, the speaker says, "I will return to the house of the LORD," rather than "I will dwell in the house of the LORD." The "house of the LORD" refers to the temple in Jerusalem. This psalm thus looks forward to the time when the Anointed One returns to the temple. Within the OT, this is a common messianic image (cf. Zec 9:8–9). This prepares us for the next psalm.

Psalm 24. This psalm celebrates the victorious return of the glorious King to the temple in Jerusalem. His kingdom is "the world, and all who live in it" (v.1). The King is met by those who have a pure heart (v.4) and are blessed of the Lord (v.5). They sing that the gates of Jerusalem and the temple may open for the victorious King. The King is identified as the Lord himself. It is common in the Bible to refer to the King Messiah as God (cf. Ps 45:6; Isa 9:6).

Psalm 25. During the time that the book of Psalms was being compiled in its final form, a prominent theme in Israel's messianic hope was that Israel and the nations would return to Jerusalem with its temple and would there be taught God's truth, the law (cf. Zec 8:20–23; see also Isa 2:2–3). The placement of Ps 25 after Ps 24 reflects this messianic picture. Having come to the temple in Jerusalem to receive "the King of glory" (Ps 24), the psalmist now asks, "Guide me in your truth and teach me, for you are God my Savior, and my hope is in you all day long" (v.5). The psalm, written as an acrostic of the Hebrew alphabet, repeatedly raises the request for the Lord's instruction. The last line expresses hope for the coming of Israel's Redeemer (v.22).

Psalm 26. Continuing the theme of the enjoyment of God's presence in the temple, the psalmist praises God for his protection and care. He loves God's house, the temple, where God's glory dwells (v.8). Echoing the themes of God's instruction from Pss 1 and 25, he confesses that he walks in God's truth and does not "consort with hypocrites" and "the wicked" (vv.3–5). The psalmist stresses the importance of sincerity of heart in worship (vv.6–11).

Psalm 27. As in Ps 23, the psalmist focuses on God's presence in the temple and his loving protection of the righteous. He looks forward with expectation to the time when he will again "dwell in the house of the LORD all the days of [his] life" (v.4; cf. 23:6). An exhortation at the end of this psalm gives a note of urgency: "Wait for the LORD; be strong and take heart and wait for the LORD" (27:14). David wants the reader to follow his example.

Psalm 28. This psalm plays a key thematic role in the psalms. It not only takes up the theme of God's presence in the temple (found in the preceding psalms), but also ties it into the overarching theme of hope in the coming of the Messiah. The preceding psalms admonish readers to be like David and to place their hope in God. In this psalm, that hope is focused in God's sending his Anointed One (v.8). David's own words here appear to conclude with the confession in v.7, "The LORD is my strength and my shield ... and with my song I praise him." The psalm then applies these words to a specific situation in the life of the people, namely, their waiting for the salvation and blessing of the "anointed one" (vv.8–9).

Psalm 29. In Ps 28:7 David says, "With my song I praise [the Lord]." This prepares us for Ps 29, where David sings that praise to God. The Lord is praised here both as the Creator and Sustainer of all creation (vv.1–9a) and as the King who dwells among his people in his temple (vv.9b–11).

Psalm 30. This psalm was used "for the dedication of the temple." We should pay close attention to these titles since they often show the linkage of the psalms. Since Ps 23 referred to a divine rescue of David and his return to the temple, the mention of the dedication of the temple here most naturally recalls the return of the Israelites from exile and the rebuilding of the temple in Jerusalem. God's rescue and restoration of David after a season of trials thus becomes a picture of Israel's recovery from exile (see also Ps 51).

Psalm 31. As in Ps 30, David's prayers for help from the Lord are presented as exemplary models of faithfulness. David took refuge in the Lord (vv.1–9), and though he suffered greatly (vv.10–13), he did not lose heart (vv.14–22). At the close of the psalm, the "saints" of the Lord are addressed in terms reminiscent of the first psalm: "The Lord preserves those who are true to him, but the proud he pays back in full" (v.23; cf. 1:6). Its final words, "Be strong and take heart" (v.24), recall God's challenge to Joshua, "Be strong and courageous" (Jos 1:6).

Psalm 32. David rejoiced in God's forgiving grace (vv.1–2). It did not come easy, however. He agonized greatly before openly confessing his need for God's forgiveness (vv.3–5). His joy at God's forgiveness leads him to call on others to seek the Lord's grace while he can still be found (vv.6–10; cf. 95:7b). At the end of this psalm David applies his words to the "righteous" and the "upright in heart" (v.11). The "righteous" are those to whom the book of Psalms as a whole is addressed (cf. 1:6).

Psalm 33. This is linked to Ps 32 by addressing its readers as "righteous" and "upright" (v.1; cf. 32:11). It praises (vv.1–5) God the Creator (vv.6–9) and the sovereign Lord of the nations (vv.10–19). At its end we hear God's people respond to the word of praise: "We wait in hope for the Lord; he is our help and our shield" (vv.20–22). These words of praise express the people's hope for future deliverance from the Messiah.

Psalm 34. David was fleeing from Saul and sought refuge with the Philistines. God delivered him from both. This psalm is an alphabetic acrostic on the theme of God's deliverance. The final line (v.22) focuses the reader's attention on God's redemption of his servants who take refuge in him. In doing so, this line links the psalm to the larger messianic theme established in Ps 2:12, "Kiss his Son. . . . Blessed are all who take refuge in him."

Psalm 35. This psalm is concerned almost entirely with the theme of the Lord's vindication of his faithful servant (v.27). The psalmist does not find the source of his hope in his own righteousness but in God's concern for the poor and the weak (v.10) and for the unjust treatment he has received (vv.11–18).

Psalm 36. The psalmist's attention turns from the righteous sufferer in Ps 35 to the wiles of the wicked (vv.1–4) and God's protection of the righteous (vv.5–12).

Psalm 37. This psalm is a wisdom psalm; that is, it is concerned with proper actions and outlooks among God's people. Its message is "Do not fret because of those who are evil" (v.1), and "Trust in the LORD and do good" (v.3). The Lord will work all things out for the good of the righteous, and the wicked will not succeed. The optimistic tone of the psalm is tempered, however, by the way in which it postpones the reward of the righteous and the judgment of the wicked. The righteous are directed to "wait patiently" for the Lord to act (v.7). The wicked, though they now prosper, will be cut off in "a little while" (v.10). Ultimately, the vindication of the righteous and the punishment of evil will come in the day of the final judgment, known only to the Lord (v.13).

Psalm 38. Here is a vivid example of David's own "fretting" over evil men (vv.12, 16–20), the very attitude warned against in Ps 37. Psalm 37 closed with the promise that the Lord will "help" and "deliver" and "save" the righteous, and Ps 38 closes with the desperate call to the "Savior" to come quickly to "help" (v.22). In the midst of his lament, however, David sees the hand of God (v.2b), even in his afflictions (vv.1–11). David has resolved to "wait" for God to answer him (38:15).

Psalm 39. David's afflictions are here viewed from a new vantage point, that of eternity. When David saw how short were his days (v.4) and the vanity of human life and wealth (v.6), he could not but confess his hope in God alone (v.7) and his sense of alienation from this world (v.12b). The psalm ends on a note of despair (v.13), but that note is followed in Ps 40 by God's answer to David's prayer and the reassurance of God's promise to send a deliverer.

Psalm 40. David begins by recounting deliverance from the Lord (vv.1–3a), seeing his salvation as an example to others to "put their trust in the LORD" (v.3b). He then raises his own experience to a general principle: "Blessed is the one who trusts in the LORD" (v.4a). Moreover, he views his experience of deliverance in light of God's great "wonders" accomplished for his people in the past (v.5a) and yet promised for the future (v.5b).

With the mention of God's future deliverance, David recalls what was written "in the scroll" of the book about God's promised deliverer (vv.6–8).

He does so by speaking, in the first person, in behalf of the deliverer. The "scroll" refers to the Pentateuch, the book of Moses. In it, Israel was taught that God did not desire "sacrifice and offering" but rather service, exemplified by the sign of piercing the ear of a slave to denote his devotion to his master (Ex 21:6). Such obedience comes from the heart (40:8; Dt 30:6).

David confesses God's faithfulness and salvation before the great assembly (v.10). On this basis, he calls out for God to accomplish salvation for his people and the defeat of their enemies (vv.11–17).

Psalm 41. Following the call for help and deliverance in Ps 40, the compiler of the Psalms concludes the first major section with a psalm of trust. Here David expresses the unfailing faithfulness of the Lord in behalf of his own. God is closer than a trusted friend (v.9–10). The final praise unit of this psalm (v.13) is part of the structure of the book of Psalms. This recurring phrase divides the Psalms into five sections (cf. 72:19; 89:52; 106:48).

IV. The Prayers of the Sons of Korah (42–49)

Psalm 42. This psalm is the first of eight songs "of the sons of Korah." There is a thematic development in these psalms. In Ps 42 the psalmist has been cast away from God's presence and longs to return to him and "go to the house of God under the protection of the Mighty One with shouts of joy and praise among the festive throng" (v.4). Though his soul is downcast (vv.5, 11), he strengthens himself in the hope that he will yet praise God among the worshipers at the temple.

Psalm 43. This psalm continues Ps 42, a castaway seeking to return to God's presence (see esp. 42:6a, 11 and 43:5a; 42:9 and 43:2; these two psalms were probably intended as a single psalm). The psalmist is "oppressed by the enemy" (43:2b). In Ps 42 he saw himself as "forgotten" by God (42:9a), but now he adds that he has actually been cast away by God himself: "You are God my stronghold. Why have you rejected me?" (v.2). The cause of this separation lies in divine rejection, implying fault on the part of the psalmist. With this added sense of guilt, the psalmist's notion of God as "Savior" (43:5b; cf. 42:11b) implies the further need of divine forgiveness. In the next psalm, his laments focus precisely on the question of human guilt.

Psalm 44. This psalm begins with the words of the congregation, "We" (v.1), which reflects back on God's deliverance and help of their fathers (vv.1–8). In the midst of these reflections, the psalmist inserts his personal thoughts and provides an explanation of God's past help: "You are my King and my God, who decrees victories for Jacob" (v.4), and "I put no trust in my bow, my sword does not bring me victory" (v.6). These two insertions help explain the unusually strong complaint against the Lord expressed by the congregation in the rest of the psalm (vv.9–26): "But now you have rejected and humbled us" (v.9; cf. 42:9; 43:2).

The congregation complains that God has rejected and humbled them (vv.9–16) for no apparent reason (vv.17–25). They have been faithful to his commandments and have not fallen into idolatry (v.20). In spite of this, God had hidden his face and forgotten them (v.24). But if we read their complaint in light of v.6, "I put no trust in my bow," we can conclude that, though outwardly obedient, they still lack trust in God. In this respect the psalm is similar to 51:16–17. The congregation's call for divine redemption (v.26) is answered by the promise of a divine Redeemer in the next psalm.

Psalm 45. The call of God's people for divine redemption in Ps 44:26 finds its answer here. Using the image of an ideal earthly king, the psalmist envisions the coming of the divine King (45:6) to defeat the enemies of his people. He first describes the excellence and glory of the Warrior-King (vv.2–3), who will "ride forth victoriously in the cause of truth, humility and justice" (v.4) and will defeat the enemy (v.5). He then describes the King as the one who occupies the eternal throne of God (v.6) and rules exalted over other royal figures as the Anointed of God (vv.7–9).

Psalm 46. Following the portrayal of the coming of the ideal King (Ps 45) is a description of the King's city, Jerusalem. When God dwells in his temple in Jerusalem, there is no reason to fear, for "the LORD Almighty is with us" (v.7a).

Psalm 47. This psalm states that God's reign as King in Jerusalem extends beyond that of his own chosen people to include all the earth. God, who "is seated on his holy throne" (v.8; cf. 45:6), "reigns over the nations" (v.8).

Psalm 48. The description of Jerusalem at peace under God's protective care continues Pss 46–48. Jerusalem, like Sinai, is God's holy mountain (vv.1–3). It is safe from all threats (vv.4–7), and his people live there securely (v.8). Within God's protective care, his people meditate on his "unfailing love" and rejoice over his judgments (vv.9–11). Jerusalem is secure with God as their guide, even unto death (vv.12–14; NIV, "the end").

Psalm 49. Having raised the question of God's care and protection "even to the end" (48:14b; i.e., "death"), this "wisdom" psalm extends the promise of God's care *beyond* the grave. Human beings cannot redeem their own lives (vv.7–9). They cannot add any days. Wise people and fools alike will die (vv.10–14). But the godly need not worry in the face of death (v.5), because "God will redeem me from the realm of the dead; he will surely take me to himself" (v.15). The key to life is "understanding" (v.20), for wealth and glory will quickly fade away (vv.16–19). This is the "wisdom" (v.3a) the psalmist calls upon all to hear (v.1).

V. The Prayer of Asaph (50)

Psalm 50. The psalm has two parts, the first being addressed to the righteous (vv.1–15) and the second to the wicked (vv.16–23). To the righteous, the Lord says two things. (1) God will come in judgment to punish the wicked and gather to himself the "consecrated people, who made a covenant with [him] by sacrifice" (vv.1–6). This refers to the covenant sacrifice at Sinai (Ex 24:4–8). (2) In light of the role of sacrifices in establishing the covenant, the psalmist warns the people against undue dependence on them (vv.7–15). God does not need our sacrifices (vv.8–13). What he wants from his people is simple trust (v.15).

Turning to the wicked, God warns them against undue trust in the law and the covenant (v.16). Though they may give sacrificial offerings, their hearts are disobedient and their tongue speaks evil (vv.17–20). What pleases God is a grateful heart (vv.21–23). This theme leads into David's prayer in the next psalm.

VI. The Prayers of David (51–65)

Psalm 51. David wrote this psalm when the prophet Nathan rebuked him after he had committed adultery with Bathsheba (see the superscription). David calls to God for mercy (vv.1–3). He confesses his guilt against God's law (v.4) and sees it as a part of a guilt that extended back through his parents, before his own birth (v.5). David cries out to God for remission of sin: "Wash me, and I will be whiter than snow" (v.7). He knows the only remedy is a new heart and a new spirit (vv.8–13). In these words David expresses the living hope of the new covenant (cf. Dt 30:6; Jer 31:31–34; Eze 36:24–27).

Psalm 52. The evil one whom David addresses here is Doeg the Edomite (see 1Sa 21:7; 22:9–23), though the story sheds little light on this psalm. The note about Doeg is probably intended to bring David's words into the larger messianic picture of the fall of the house of Edom (cf. Nu 24:18). It had long been an important part of the messianic hope of Israel that the Messiah's coming would lead to the destruction of Israel's enemies, especially the Edomites (e.g., Am 9:12; Ob 18). Edom was singled out for a literary reason, for Edom represents all humanity (the Hebrew word for

"Edom" is similar to the word for humankind, "Adam"). The defeat of Edom (v.5) is therefore God's judgment of all humanity. That is why the next psalm focuses on God's universal judgment of humankind.

Psalm 53. The psalmist, who sees that "mankind" (v.2) has turned away from God and does not fear his judgment (vv.3–5), concludes that they are "fools" (v.1). When they say, "There is no God," they mean that God will not punish their sins with judgment. They ignore his laws and oppress his people (vv.2–4); but to their surprise, God does act by putting to shame those who attack his people (v.5). In light of his confidence in God's care for Israel, the psalmist calls for God to fulfill his messianic promise to David (cf. 2Sa 7:16), "Oh, that salvation for Israel would come out of Zion!" (v.6).

Psalm 54. David wrote this psalm when he had been betrayed to Saul by "the Ziphites." David calls these men "strangers" and "ruthless people ... without regard for God" (v.3). They are thus identified with the "fool" in 53:1 who says, "There is no God." By contrast, David confesses, "Surely God is my help; the Lord is the one who sustains me" (v.4).

Psalm 55. David calls out for help from the Lord (vv.1–2a) amid deep periods of anguish and rejection (vv.2b–11). Even his own closest friends have turned against him (vv.12–14, 20–21). As the psalm progresses, however, his mood shifts from one of despair to one of trust and resolve to put his confidence in the Lord (vv.16–19). David concludes by admonishing others to imitate him and put their trust in God (vv.22–23).

Psalm 56. Having called on others to always trust God despite the severity of their situation, David now recalls a specific time in his life when he had to do this very thing: "when the Philistines had seized him in Gath" (cf. 1Sa 21:10–15). On that occasion, David did not hesitate to call out to God for help (vv.1–2), and God heard his call (v.13). He acknowledged his fear (v.3a) as well as his trust in God (vv.3b–5). This theme can be applied to any difficult situation. The psalm's recurring theme is the contrast between God's faithfulness ("In God I trust," vv.4, 11) and human powerlessness ("What can mere mortals do to me?" cf. vv.4b, 11b).

Psalm 57. David sang this psalm when he "had fled from Saul into the cave" and found deliverance (1Sa 24:1–4). In the dangers of fleeing from the enemy (vv.1–6), David remained firm in his trust in the Lord (vv.7–11).

Psalm 58. As if turning to address the enemies who have pursued him in the two previous psalms, David begins by asking, "Do you rulers indeed speak justly?" (v.1a). His answer is based both on his knowledge of human nature and on his own sense of innocence: "In your heart you devise injustice" (vv.2–5). Thus, David asks God for help, using bold imagery (vv.6–9). His purpose is to set before the reader a vivid picture of God's righteous vindication of the oppressed (v.10a) and to encourage them in the faith that "there is a God who judges the earth" (v.11b).

Psalm 59. Within this psalm, David is cast as one hiding from evil and violent men (cf. vv.6, 14). But David knows he is safe because he lies within the mighty fortress of a "loving God" (vv.9–10, 16–17). He is confident he has done no wrong (v.4); thus God will deliver him (vv.5, 10) and will severely punish these unjust men (vv.11b–13). God's wrath has come upon the ungodly because of their sin and pride (vv.12–13).

Psalm 60. David confesses Israel's transgressions and acknowledges God's righteous anger against them (vv.1–3). Nevertheless, he has hope for the faithful that God will save them (vv. 4–5), a hope grounded in God's faithful care for his chosen people Israel (vv.6–7) and his ultimate judgment of their enemies (vv.8–12).

Psalm 61. Having raised the notion of God's final victory over his enemies in Ps 60, David prays in behalf of God's eternal King: "May he be enthroned in God's presence forever" (v.7). David reflects on God's promise in 2Sa 7:16 — the promise of an eternal kingdom and an eternal King. This is the decree of the Lord mentioned in Ps 2:7. As in 2:8, David pictures the domain of this King in universal terms: "From the ends of the earth I call to you" (v.2).

Psalm 62. Continuing his focus on God's promise to the house of David (2Sa 7:16), David turns his attention to God's faithfulness and power: "My soul finds rest in God; my salvation comes from him" (v.1). As it now stands, this psalm does not mention the messianic king, though the notion of salvation (vv.1–2, 6–7), God's loyal love (v.12), and future reward (v.12) bring it within the thematic range of the messianic hope found in the Psalms. David points to the future salvation of God's people and the promise of a Messiah.

Psalm 63. David wrote this psalm "when he was in the Desert of Judah," which provides the setting for the imagery of the psalm. The notion of David in the desert leads to his thirsting after God "in a dry and parched land where there is no water" (v.1). Moreover, his waiting for God in the desert recalls the imagery of Israel's sojourn in the desert and their hope of entering the Promised Land. Thus, this psalm testifies to the larger picture of salvation and redemption for Israel, and certain words echo those of Moses and the Israelites in the desert. When David says, "My soul will be satisfied as with the richest of foods" (v.5), he recalls Israel's daily enjoyment of the divine provision of manna (Ex 16). When David says, "Those who want to kill me will be destroyed; they will go down to the depths of the earth" (v.9), one cannot help but think of the fate of those who opposed Moses in the desert (Nu 16:32–33). Finally, the sudden mention of "the king" brings to mind the Pentateuch's focus on the victorious King of the future, who would arise from the tribe of Judah and bring salvation to God's people (Ge 49:8–12; Nu 24:7, 17).

Psalm 64. David begins with a prayer in his own behalf (vv.1–6), expressing confidence that God will rescue him (vv.7–8). This leads him to an expression of confidence that one day "all people" will fear God and proclaim his wonderful works (v.9). He thus concludes by calling on "the righteous [to] rejoice in the LORD and take refuge in him" (v.10). These last words bring David's psalm into alignment with the central theme of Psalms: "Kiss [pay homage to] [God's] son.... Blessed are all who take refuge in him" (2:12).

Psalm 65. Taking up the theme from 64:9 of God's universal rule, David writes a song of praise to God who dwells in Zion (i.e., Jerusalem) and who rules over all the earth. "All people will come" to Zion (v.2) and will be forgiven their transgressions (v.3). God will be the "Savior, the hope of all the ends of the earth and of the farthest seas" (v.5). He is the Creator (v.6), the Redeemer (v.7), and the Sustainer of his people (vv.8–13).

VII. Anonymous Psalms (66–67)

Psalm 66. Following David's description of God's universal reign in Ps 65, the compiler inserts two anonymous psalms. This first one calls on the whole world to sing praises to God for his wonderful deeds (vv.1–4). The psalmist, recalling the theme of the exodus, tells of what God did for his people in delivering them from bondage in Egypt (vv.5–12). This recalls God's salvation of Israel and his gift of the Promised Land and Jerusalem. While bringing his burnt offering before the Lord at the temple (vv.13–15), the psalmist acknowledges his need to confess his sin (vv.16–18) and praises God for his answer to prayer (vv.19–20).

Psalm 67. God's salvation of the nations reaches its full expression. This psalm opens with a blessing, "May God be gracious to us and bless us and make his face shine on us" (v.1). It then turns to the theme of the salvation of the nations, "that your ways may be known on earth, your salvation among all nations" (v.2). This theme then extends to God's universal reign over the entire world: "May the nations be glad and sing for joy, for you rule the peoples with equity and guide the nations of the earth" (v.4). The God of Israel is the God of all the earth (vv.5–7).

VIII. Prayers of David (68–72)

Psalm 68. Psalms 66–67 pave the way for the central theme of Ps 68, the coming of the universal King to Zion. David opens with a call for the coming of the divine King (v.1a) and the defeat of his enemies (vv.1b-2). Turning to the righteous people of his own nation, David calls on them to sing praises to the Lord, who is in his holy dwelling (vv.3-6). He then recounts the appearance of the Lord in his glorious victories in behalf of his people (vv.7-10) when he gave them the Promised Land (vv.11-14). The conquest was great indeed (v.15), but it paled in comparison to God's triumph over Zion, "the mountain where God chooses to reign" (v.16). When he has conquered Zion, all nations will come to worship him and bring their gifts (vv.17-18). They will sing praises to God, the King and their Savior (v.19), who will give them life (v.20). The enemy will be destroyed (vv.21-23); the Lord will be accompanied by a great procession into the sanctuary (vv.24-26), which will include not only his people Israel (v.27) but also the kings of the earth (vv.28-31).

With this hope in view, David calls on the kingdoms of the earth to praise the Lord, the God of Israel, who is awesome in his sanctuary (vv.32-35).

Psalm 69. At first glance, this psalm seems to contrast sharply with Ps 68. But when one reads through the entire psalm, it becomes apparent that the two psalms are similar—they both express a fervent desire for God's salvation of Zion and the establishment of his kingdom (vv.34-36). In other words, both look back to God's promise to David (cf. Ps 2:7; 2Sa 7:16) and eagerly await its fulfillment in Zion.

David first focuses his attention on his miserable state as a representative of God's people as they await the fulfillment of the promise. They, like David, have sunk "in the miry depths, where there is no foothold" (vv.1-3) and have many enemies (v.4). They are willing to admit their guilt (v.5) and place their hope in the Lord (vv.6-12). They call out for deliverance (vv.13-18) but find no one to comfort them (vv.19-21). Thus they beseech the Lord for the destruction of their enemies (vv.22-28). In the end, they, like David, will rest content in the hope that "God will save Zion and rebuild the cities of Judah ... and those who love his name will dwell there" (vv.29-36).

Psalm 70. This psalm serves as a fitting request for a speedy answer to David's call for salvation in Ps 69. David begins with an anxious call to God for help in v.1, and he concludes on the same note in v.5. In isolation from its context within Psalms, this psalm is a simple call for help in an unnamed emergency. When read in the context of Ps 69 and Pss 71-72, it is a call for God's swift return to establish his universal kingdom and to send his eternal King.

Psalm 71. The section of Psalms that recounts the prayers of David is now drawing to a close (cf. 72:20). This is the last prayer of David; Ps

72 is by Solomon. David, now as an old man (vv.9, 18), looks back over a lifetime of God's faithfulness (vv.5 – 6, 17). Though he still has enemies (vv.4, 11, 13) and still needs God's protection (vv.1 – 3, 12), his long years of trusting God assure him that God will care for him. Thus he praises the Lord (vv.14 – 16) and proclaims his righteousness (vv.19 – 24). Just as this section began in Ps 3 with David's expression of trust in God's promise (Ps 2; cf. 2Sa 7), so now it concludes with a similar statement of trust.

Psalm 72. The psalm begins with a request for justice and righteousness on behalf of the King (vv.1 – 4) and is reminiscent of Solomon's own request for wisdom to rule God's people (1Ki 3:9). The psalm then turns to a request that shows the psalmist can only be thinking of the future eternal Messiah: "May he endure as long as the sun." He then describes the earthly reign of the messianic King (vv.6 – 14), which he envisions as a time of universal prosperity (vv.15 – 17). In the book of Revelation, John depicts this rule as a one-thousand-year reign of Christ, the millennium. The psalm concludes with praise to God (vv.18 – 19).

IX. Psalms of Asaph (73 – 83)

Psalm 73. Beginning with the overall thought of the psalm, "Surely God is good to Israel, to those who are pure in heart" (v.1), Asaph turns his attention to the seemingly endless prosperity of the rich and famous in contrast to the suffering and daily misery of the common person (vv.2 – 12)! What good does it do for us to live for the Lord and keep a pure heart (vv.13 – 16)? But Asaph, a choir leader at the temple, stops himself and recalls the true state of the matter represented by God's presence at the temple. When he entered the temple and contemplated God's presence there, it was clear to him that the rich and famous have a passing treasure, "like a dream when one awakes" (vv.17 – 20). God is with his people, and he is their strength forever (vv.21 – 26). What a contrast to the godless who will ultimately perish apart from God (v.27)! Thus, it is "good to be near God" (v.28).

Psalm 74. In stark contrast to the assurance of God's presence expressed by Asaph in Ps 73, the psalmist begins with the despairing words, "O God, why have you rejected us forever?" (v.1). The cause of his despair is that the temple has been destroyed and now lies in ruins (vv.3 – 8). His chief problem is God's apparent lack of help: "We are given no signs from God; no prophets are left, and none of us knows how long this will be" (v.9). The psalmist has no doubts that God can and will act to vindicate his promises to Israel (vv.11 – 17). He has made a covenant with them (v.20), and thus he prays for God's quick action on their behalf (vv.21–23). God's response comes in the following psalm.

Psalm 75. This psalm responds to the lament of Ps 74. Here Asaph recounts God's words, "I choose the appointed time; it is I who judge with equity" (v.2). Though God's people should call out to him for salvation (Ps 74), they must remember that he acts according to his own time schedule (Ps 75). Both psalms show vividly that God always acts in response to the prayers of the upright. God in effect tells Asaph to keep praying until the appointed time comes.

Psalm 76. This psalm picks up the previous ones and describes God and his time for judgment. With Ps 73, he is the God whose dwelling place is Zion, the site of the temple. With Ps 74, he is the God who comes in judgment on those who have oppressed the godly. Here he is the God who acts at his appointed time and thus is the one who is to be feared (v.11).

Psalm 77. The psalmist expresses confidence in the midst of his prayers for divine action. Though there were no miraculous deeds in his own day (cf. 74:9), he resolves to meditate on God's glorious deeds in the past (77:5–12) and will continue to seek God's justice in the present. The psalm concludes with a brief description of God's past deeds as recorded in Scripture (vv.13–20). The next psalm records God's past deeds on Israel's behalf (Ps 78).

Psalm 78. This psalm, which recounts in poetic form the major events of the biblical narratives, picks up Ps 77, where the psalmist vowed to remember and meditate on God's past deeds. His purpose is clear: "I will utter hidden things, things from of old" (v.2b) in order to "tell the next generation the praiseworthy deeds of the Lord, his power, and the wonders he has done" (v.4). In other words, he is going to recount the narratives of Scripture for his children.

Psalm 79. As a sequel to Ps 78, in which the rejection and exile of the northern kingdom is recounted along with God's special care for Judah and the temple at Jerusalem, Ps 79 recounts the ultimate downfall of the southern kingdom and the destruction of the temple. In other words, neither kingdom proved faithful to God; both were subject to God's judgment.

Psalm 80. This psalm turns directly to the question of the restoration of the house of David in the postexilic period. The psalmist calls out for God's help and deliverance. His focus is on the restoration of the Davidic kingdom, which had flourished in the preexilic period like a lush vine planted by God. At the center of his hope is the "son of man," whom God was to raise up himself (v.17). The hope and expectation of this psalm is virtually identical to that of Da 7 and together with it forms an important basis for the NT's understanding of the Messiah.

Psalm 81. In response to the prayer for help and salvation in Ps 80, the Lord replies in Pss 81–82. If his people want deliverance, they must obey his word (vv.13–14). Israel has been disobedient and God has given "them over to their stubborn hearts to follow their own devices" (v.12). If they only would follow him, says the Lord, "You would be fed with the finest of wheat; with honey from the rock I would satisfy you" (v.16).

Psalm 82. The Lord continues (from Ps 81) to reply to the prayers of Israel, calling on them to obey his word. This psalm reminds us of the theme heard many times in the prophets that obedience to God's will should produce acts of kindness and mercy (vv.3–4; cf. Mic 6:8).

Psalm 83. This psalm concludes the Asaph psalms (Pss 73–83) by again calling on God to deliver his people (the central theme of these psalms). The temple lies in ruins (74:7), and the city of Jerusalem is bare (79:1). Thus the psalmist cannot keep quiet until God has acted on their behalf and destroyed the enemy (vv.2–17). Behind the psalmist's call for vindication lies the hope that in their judgment, the nations may come to know that God alone is "the Most High over all the earth" (v.18).

X. Psalms of the Sons of Korah (84–85)

Psalm 84. The psalmist expresses the excitement and anticipation of the pilgrimage to the temple to celebrate the annual feast days (cf. Lev 23). It recounts the journey to Jerusalem (vv.5–7) as well as former visits to the temple (vv.1–2). The psalmist even envies the sparrow who makes his nest in the rafters of the temple and raises her young there. She is always near to God's altar (vv.3–4). In its present context within Psalms, this psalm expresses the longing hope for the rebuilding of the temple and the exhortation to prepare for it. Humility (vv.8–10), godliness (v.11), and trust (v.12) are prerequisites for enjoying God's presence and protection.

Psalm 85. This psalm voices hope for God's ultimate restoration of his people. Salvation is near for those who fear him, but there is a need for righteousness to prepare for his coming. God has forgiven Israel their transgressions, and thus there is a basis for hope in the future. The psalmist takes great comfort in knowing that God's anger against his people will not last forever.

Note how this psalm casts the specter of hope into the more remote future, with expressions such as, "Will you be angry with us forever? Will you prolong your anger through all generations?" (v.5). The psalm looks to a more seasoned hope in God's deliverance. Salvation is near, but only to those who fear him (v.9). Before the salvation of the Lord occurs, righteousness must prepare the way (v.13). The example of David is given in the next psalm.

XI. Psalm of David (86)

Psalm 86. The compiler of Psalms may well have intended this Davidic psalm as an example of how God heard the prayers of the righteous in the past and answered them with deliverance. Thus he has inserted it in the midst of the Korahite psalms. Here David expresses the central themes of Pss 84–85, divine forgiveness for the righteous: "You, Lord, are forgiving and good, abounding in love to all who call to you" (v.5; cf. 85:2).

David's words also provide a pattern for obtaining divine forgiveness: "Teach me your way, Lord, that I may rely on your faithfulness; give me an undivided heart, that I may fear your name" (v.11). If one longs for God's mercy, one must long to walk as David did before the Lord. David is an example of a truly godly Israelite, in the same way that he serves as an example of a truly godly king in the book of Kings. The past is presented as the pathway to the future.

XII. Psalms of the Sons of Korah (87–88)

Psalm 87. This psalm gives us a glorious picture of a restored Zion. In that day, says the psalmist, even Babylon and Philistia, the two archenemies of Jerusalem, will acknowledge God's presence in Zion. This song embodies the hope set forth throughout the Psalms of the restoration of Jerusalem in the days when God fulfills his promises to David (cf. 2Sa 7). Hence the meaning of the phrase, "Glorious things are said of you, city of God," refers to the time of the Messiah's reign in Jerusalem over the nations of the world.

Psalm 88. Heman the Ezrahite, one of the sons of Korah, opens with a lament for his suffering from divine judgment (vv.1–9a). He says to the Lord, "You have put me in the lowest pit.... Your wrath lies heavily on me" (vv.6–7). Though he acknowledges that his "troubles" come from God, he still calls out to God for deliverance (vv.9b–14). The depth of his torment can be seen in his statement, "From my youth I have suffered" (v.15). He continues, "Your wrath has swept over me; your terrors have destroyed me" (v.16), and he concludes on a note of despair, "The darkness is my closest friend" (v.18).

XIII. Psalm of Ethan the Ezrahite (89)

Psalm 89. Psalm 89 opens with a praise of "the Lord's great love" (v.1). The compiler of the Psalms wants the readers to look beyond the suffering expressed in Ps 88 to the joy that awaits the faithful when God sends the deliverer to Zion (cf. Ps 87). This praise song is thus to be read in anticipation of that fulfillment and serves to comfort those who, like the psalmist in Ps 88, have not yet experienced God's fulfilled promises.

Midway through the psalm, however, there is a break in the mood of praise and expectation. The psalmist suddenly turns to the sorrows of his own day (vv.38–39). He has in mind the destruction of Jerusalem and the exile. Reflecting over the glories of the past in the days of David and the sorrow and rejection of his own day, he calls on God to act in restoring Zion to its former glory. This honest prayer becomes the voice of the countless generations of God's faithful who long to see his kingdom established and the enemy silenced (v.51).

XIV. Psalm of Moses (90)

Psalm 90. At this point in Psalms, the reader is in need of comfort and reassurance in God's eternal care. This psalm of Moses provides such a word. Just as in writing the Pentateuch, in his picture of God's power and care, Moses reflects on the creation (vv.1–2; cf. Ge 1), the fall of humankind (vv.3–6; cf. Ge 3), divine judgment (vv.7–9; cf. Ge 6–9; 19), and human frailty (v.10; cf. Ge 47:10). In light of such a view of God and the human condition, Moses calls on God to have compassion on his people and send a deliverer (vv.13–17).

XV. Anonymous Psalms (91–100)

Psalm 91. Following on the theme of Ps 90, "Lord, you have been our dwelling place throughout all generations" (90:1), Ps 91 gives a word of comfort for those who have not yet seen the fulfillment of all of God's promises: "Whoever dwells in the shelter of the Most High will rest in the shadow of the Almighty" (v.1). Rather than call for an end to the ever-present threat to God's people, this psalm calls on its readers to seek refuge in the Lord in the middle of their troubles. Readers need to settle in for the long term. Though they pray earnestly for the Lord to send salvation to Zion, as in the earlier psalms, we should also seek comfort and protection in trusting the Lord. God will protect us even while we wait for his deliverance.

Psalm 92. With Pss 90 and 91 the mood and focus of the psalms have shifted to that of extolling God's greatness and grace. This psalm carries that theme to a new height and prepares the way for the theocratic hymns that follow (Pss 93–99). In Ps 92 the psalmist looks at God's love and faithfulness (vv.1–3), his power in the created world around him (vv.4–5a), and the profundity of his thoughts in God's Word (v.5b), which the foolish do not understand (vv.6–7). In light of these certainties of God's provision, the godly need not fret over the deeds of the wicked (vv.9–11). They will flourish because God is their Rock (vv.12–15).

Psalm 93. The Lord's eternal rule over the world is now celebrated (Pss 93–99). This psalm focuses on God's rule over the great powers of creation, specifically the waters of the sea (vv.3–4). It ends by reminding us of the steadfastness of God's eternal Word (v.5). God, like the earthly king in Dt 17:18–20, is pictured as one who rules according to his own divine statutes.

Psalm 94. God is the "Judge of the earth" (v.2). An important implication of God's kingly rule is his judgment of the wicked (vv.3–11). God's work in the world turns on what he has revealed in his Word: "Blessed is the one you discipline, LORD, the one you teach from your law" (v.12). To avoid God's judgment we must seek to live by the principles of his Word (vv.13–15). Consolation, strength, and joy come from meditating on that Word (vv.16–19). In this way, the godly take refuge from the wicked (vv.20–23).

Psalm 95. This psalm begins in a usual way, calling on God's people to praise him as their eternal King (vv.1–7a). He is "the Rock of our salvation" (v.1; cf. 92:12–15), the Creator (vv.3–5), and the One who is to be worshiped as our Maker (vv.6–7). At v.7b, however, the psalm takes an abrupt turn from praise to warning, calling on us to obey God's Word and not rebel as Israel had in the desert (vv.7b–11). God's power and grace are great, but the most important implication for his people is obedience to his will. Note how this psalm follows the basic outline of the Pentateuch, beginning with the portrayal of God as Creator, then moving to the response of his people in worship, and ending on a note of their failure to trust in him.

Psalm 96. Once again in this psalm the twin themes of God's theocratic rule and divine judgment come together. The psalm begins by calling all the nations to praise and worship the eternal King (vv.1–13a); it closes with a warning that when he comes, he will "judge the world in righteousness" (v.13b). Divine kingship requires a response of both praise and obedience.

Psalm 97. The psalm begins like the other theocratic psalms with a celebration of God's kingly rule: "The LORD reigns, let the earth be glad" (v.1). It turns quickly to the theme of judgment: "Clouds and thick darkness surround him; righteousness and justice are the foundation of his throne" (v.2). The righteous should rejoice at his coming (vv.8-12), but the wicked should tremble at the thought (vv.3-7).

Psalm 98. This psalm continues with the theme of the rejoicing of the righteous at the coming of the Lord. God's judgment of the wicked means salvation for the righteous (vv.1-3). Therefore all creation should rejoice to see God's righteous judgment of the wicked (vv.4-9).

Psalm 99. This psalm marks an important transition within the book of Psalms. The theocratic psalms (Pss 93-99) have concentrated on God's universal rule over all creation. Now the focus shifts to the special and unique care God has taken for his chosen people Israel. The focus turns to God's universal reign "in Zion" (v.2) and his election of the patriarchs (v.4), Moses and Aaron (v.6a), and the prophets (v.6b). We see this also in the psalms that follow.

Psalm 100. The eternal and universal King praised in the Pss 93-99 is now extolled as the God of Israel, his chosen people. Universal creation is seen in terms of the divine election of Israel: "It is he who made us, and we are his; we are his people, the sheep of his pasture" (v.3). Praise of God comes from the courtyards of his temple in Jerusalem (v.4). His covenant with Israel is celebrated as an eternal manifestation of his love (v.5).

XVI. Psalm of David (101)

Psalm 101. In keeping with his focus in this part of Psalms, the compiler has included a personal, pietistic psalm of David. We do not see David the king here. Rather, we see David the individual believer, seeking to do God's will in his everyday life. The love and justice of God that were celebrated in universal terms in the theocratic psalms (Pss 93-99) are pictured in the godly life of one of God's chosen people (see esp. v.2). The virtues he extols are humility, honesty, and goodness (vv.3-8).

XVII. Psalm of an Afflicted Man (102)

Psalm 102. Again a psalm notes the restoration of the city of Zion. Between two Davidic psalms, this psalm of an anonymous sufferer expresses the yearning for the Lord to "rebuild Zion and appear in his glory" (v.16). It was to David that the original promise to restore Zion and to send the Messiah was given (cf. 2Sa 7). The insertion of a "Zion song" that focuses on personal piety blends together the two themes of personal godliness and eager anticipation of God's work in the world—two themes often found together in the Bible. God's people are to wait eagerly for the coming of the Lord; yet, while doing so, they are to live as though he were already here.

XVIII. Psalm of David (103)

Psalm 103. Taking its lead from the Scriptures themselves (Ex 34:6), this psalm of David focuses the reader's attention on God's great love. Its chief concern is the Lord's forgiveness of the sins (v.3) of those "who keep his covenant and remember to obey his precepts" (v.18). God, whose throne is in heaven (v.19), will not "harbor his anger forever" (v.9). Forgiveness will come for a disobedient people, but it will come only because of God's great compassion (v.13).

XIX. Anonymous Psalms (104 – 107)

Psalm 104. This is a hymn of praise to God as the Creator and the Sustainer of all life. The psalmist begins by extolling God's work of creation (vv.1–9). He then recounts the many ways in which God continues to sustain his creation. He gives water to all his creatures (vv.10–12) and to his creation (v.13), so that the earth brings forth food and shelter for the animals and for people (vv.14–18). The sun and the moon mark off the seasons of human life (v.19). Even the time of darkness provides the means whereby some animals receive their food (vv.20–21), leaving the daytime safe for human beings and their work (vv.22–23). There is a "wisdom" in all this that the psalmist wants his readers to see (v.24) — a wisdom that is a constant reminder of God's power and care for his creation (vv.25–30). It is this wisdom that gives occasion for displaying God's glory in the present psalm (vv.31–34).

Psalm 105. This psalm summarizes the message of the Pentateuch. It centers on God's promise to Abraham to give his descendants the land of Canaan (Ge 15:18–21). It begins by recounting that promise (vv.1–11) and ends by recounting its fulfillment, or lack of fulfillment, in Israel's conquest of the land (v.44). There is some uncertainty at the end of the psalm because of the sudden mention of obedience (v.45). The Israelites were brought into the land to obey God. Does the psalmist see the conquest of Canaan as the fulfillment of the Abrahamic promise? Or does his mention of obedience suggest he sees the conquest as a failure of the people to fully claim the promise? Perhaps it is both. Although the people entered the land in fulfillment of God's promise, they did not "keep his precepts and observe his laws" (v.45). The psalmist assumes his readers were aware that Israel failed (cf. Jos 24:19–20).

Psalm 106. Like Ps 105, this psalm is a poetic summary of Pentateuch. The key to understanding lies in the statement: "We have sinned, even as our ancestors did" (v.6). The psalmist writes when Israel was under divine judgment for their disobedience. He looks back at the Pentateuch to find parallels for his own day. His final plea is that somehow things will turn out differently in his day. He concludes by calling out to the Lord for the salvation of his people, though he acknowledges that God is just in punishing them. Like Daniel (cf. Da 9:4–19), the psalmist prays in the midst of exile that God will restore his people to their land (v.47).

Psalm 107. The previous psalm closed with a call for God to gather his people from the nations (106:47). The present psalm, appropriately, expresses the thanksgiving of "those he gathered from the lands, from east and west, from north and south" (vv.1–3). As in the days of the desert wandering, when the people cried out to the Lord, he heard their cry and "led them by a straight way to a city where they could settle" (v.7). Similarly, this psalmist acknowledges that God was just in sending his people into exile (v.11). But when they cried out to him, he heard their prayer and "brought them out of darkness, the utter darkness, and broke away their chains" (v.14). The psalmist illustrates this from several biblical examples.

XX. Psalms of David (108 – 110)

Psalm 108. This psalm begins with praise (vv.1–5) and moves quickly to a request for help in the midst of defeat (v.6). David's experience in this psalm is a model for the righteous at all times. God answered his prayer (vv.7–9), and thus all Israel knows that they "will gain the victory" when he tramples down the enemy (v.13).

Psalm 109. David calls for God's righteous judgment against "people who are wicked and deceitful" (v.2). He asks that God send someone to do to them what they have done to him. David is not trying to get even with those who have mistreated him. He only wants God to act and "not remain silent" (v.1) in the face of injustice. The poetic imagery used in this psalm has many overstatements and exaggerated metaphors. He says of the wicked, for example, "May his children be fatherless and his wife a widow" (v.9). David is not wishing evil of innocent children and wives. Rather, he employs picturesque, even graphic, language to make his point; but he is writing poetry, not prose. His words should not be taken literally here, anymore than when he says, "My heart is wounded within me" (v.22) or "I fade away like an evening shadow" (v.23).

Psalm 110. The last Davidic psalm in this series of three focuses on the messianic promise that God made to David in 2Sa 7. This was a promise of a royal descendant and an eternal kingship. As in other psalms of the same theme (e.g., Pss 2; 72), this one views David's kingship in universal and victorious terms: "Rule in the midst of your enemies!" (v.2b). But its focus is not on the kingship of the Davidic Son alone. David also develops the theme of the priesthood of his descendant, "You are a priest forever, in the order of Melchizedek" (110:4b). In 2Sa 7 God had told David that his promised descendant would build "a house" (i.e., a temple) for the Lord (2Sa 7:13); according to Chronicles, God also promised to establish this descendant over both his "house" (the temple) and over his kingdom (1Ch 17:14). Like Melchizedek (Ge 14:18), the coming Son of David would be a king-priest.

XXI. Anonymous Psalms (111 – 121)

Psalm 111. This psalm is an acrostic, whose purpose is to expand the psalmist's exposition of a single theme. In effect, it forces the psalmist to repeat a single idea twenty-two times, one time for each letter of the alphabet. The theme of this psalm is God's faithfulness to his covenant. It plays an important role after the account of the Davidic covenant in Ps 110.

Psalm 112. This psalm is also an acrostic, centering on God's faithfulness to the righteous. Though David is not mentioned in the psalm, its context within the Psalms suggests that the composer of the book had David in mind. The psalm is thus a reassurance of God's faithfulness to the house of David: "Their children will be mighty in the land ... and their righteousness endures forever" (vv.2 – 3).

Psalm 113. This hymn praises God for his gracious care of his people. It focuses on God's choosing a leader for them by raising him out of the humblest circumstances and seating him with princes. This must without doubt refer to David's words in 2Sa 7:18, "Who am I, Sovereign LORD, and what is my family, that you have brought me this far?"

Psalm 114. This brief psalm links God's deliverance of Israel from Egypt (v.1), the conquest of Canaan (vv.3 – 6), and the establishment of the temple in Jerusalem (v.2) in a continuous seam of divine activity on Israel's behalf. It also links these divine acts with "the God of Jacob, who turned the rock into a pool, the hard rock into springs of water" (vv.7b – 8). Thus, the three major covenants in the OT (Abrahamic, Ge 15; Mosaic, Ex 24; and Davidic, 2Sa 7) are united and identified with the "springs of water" that God gave Israel in the desert (v.8).

Psalm 115. Here the "God of Jacob" of Ps 114 is contrasted with the idols of the nations (vv.4–8). The nations may ask, "Where is their God?" (v.2), but the psalmist knows that God cannot be seen by human eyes. He is not made of "silver and gold" (v.4). The true God dwells "in heaven" (v.3) and is sovereign over all his creation (v.3b). In his grace, God has created "[the] earth" (v.15) and has given it to human beings as their place to live (v.16).

Psalm 116. The psalmist, facing a danger, looks back at God's gracious deliverance (vv.1–10). Though others have failed him (vv.9–11), God has proved faithful (vv.12–16) and is thus the focus of the psalmist's hope (vv.17–18). In v.19 Israel's hope lies in the restoration of the temple, the house of God, in Jerusalem. The hope thus expressed in this psalm is that of the fulfillment of the Davidic covenant (see 2Sa7).

Psalm 117. The previous psalm focused the reader's attention on the fulfillment of God's promise to David through the coming of the Messiah. This one shows that the scope of that promise is all the nations of the world. The promise to David was of a universal kingdom. Thus the psalmist calls on all the nations to sing praises to God. His great love is toward all.

Psalm 118. This psalm opens on the same note as it closes: God's love for Israel and the nations "endures forever" (vv.1, 29). The speakers within the psalm are identified first as Israel (v.2), then as the priests (v.3), and finally all "those who fear the LORD" (v.4). Thus the words of the psalm apply to the nations as well as to Israel. The key is whether the nations fear the Lord (v.4) or fight against him (vv.5–12). If they are on God's side, then they, like Israel, can put their hope in God's deliverance (vv.13–14). The righteous of this psalm are thus defined as those who fear the Lord and call out to him (vv.15–21). Their salvation has come about because of the "stone the builders rejected" (v.22). This stone has become the "cornerstone" of the new gates of the temple in Jerusalem (vv.22–26). He is the Blessed One who comes in the name of the Lord (v.26a). Though the psalm itself does not identify this person, the larger context of Psalms makes it clear that he is the Promised Seed of the house of David, the Messiah. It is why this psalm is quoted frequently in the NT (Mt 21:42; Mk 12:10–11; Lk 20:17; Ac 4:11; Eph 2:20; 1Pe2:7).

Psalm 119. The central theme of Ps 119 is simple: it celebrates God's gift of the law (the Torah) to his people. It is an acrostic, containing twenty-two sections of eight verses, each verse of each section beginning with a letter of the Hebrew alphabet in sequence. The term "law" should be understood as the Hebrew Scriptures themselves—i.e., the Pentateuch, the prophetic books, and even the book of Psalms (cf. Ps 1). This psalm thus celebrates God's gift of the Scriptures. Through reading and studying them we grow in our relationship with God. Walking with God means reading his Word. God's Word is a light along the pathway of one's life (v.105). Through it one may "keep his way pure" (v.9).

XXII. Psalms of Ascents (120 – 134)

Psalm 120. The Psalms of Ascents must be read within Psalms as an expression of the hope of God's faithfulness to David and the fulfillment of his messianic promise. Psalm 120 picks up with the theme with which Ps 119 curiously ended, the picture of a "lost sheep" who has strayed from the Lord. The psalmist finds himself dwelling in Meshech, "among the tents of Kedar" (v.5). Like the psalmist in Ps 119, he is lost and calls out to the Lord in his distress (v.1).

Psalm 121. The psalmist here affirms his hope and trust in the Lord, the Creator of the heavens and earth (v.2). His hope is not in the mountains (v.1), but in the One who made the mountains. Though lost and in need of deliverance, he remains confident in the Lord's salvation.

Psalm 122. The salvation hoped for in Ps 121 is depicted here as rebuilding of city of Jerusalem and the house of David—that is, the fulfillment of the Davidic covenant (2Sa 7). To pray for the peace of Jerusalem (v.6) is to pray for the coming of the Promised Seed of David, the Messiah.

Psalm 123. The psalmist is confident that only the Lord himself can bring salvation. He waits patiently for any and every act of God on behalf of his promise. He is like a servant who waits intently for any movement of the master's hand. His hope is filled with eager anticipation.

Psalm 124. This psalm repeats the previous one. God alone is the One who will bring Israel's salvation. Just as he saved Israel from the waters of the Red Sea (Ex 14 – 15), so their future redemption will come before their enemies destroy them.

Psalm 125. The future blessing of God's people is pictured in terms of the Davidic covenant, i.e., the restoration of Jerusalem (vv.1 – 2). The eternal restoration of that city was promised to David along with the reign of an eternal Seed (2Sa 7). A renewed and rebuilt Jerusalem is thus the centerpiece of Israel's future hope. "The LORD will banish" the wicked and bring peace to Israel.

Psalm 126. The psalmist raises the specter of Israel's return from captivity. But the picture of the return from Babylon used here is an image drawn from Israel's *past*. It was, indeed, a time of great rejoicing and celebration—so much so that it now has become a picture of Israel's future blessing. Just as Israel went into captivity in weeping and returned with songs of joy, so also when God finally restores their fortunes, they will again be like "those who sow with tears" and "reap with songs of joy" (v.5).

Psalm 127. Although the sense of this psalm has a personal application in the life of every parent ("children are a heritage from the LORD"), the context of the Psalms of Ascents suggests that the house of David and the Promised Seed are meant. God alone will raise up that house and watch over Jerusalem. God's people cannot hurry the coming of the Messiah. They can only wait for the Lord to act and establish his kingdom. It is vain to attempt to do otherwise.

Psalm 128. In this psalm, a personal blessing (vv.1–4) becomes an expression of hope for the coming of the Messiah (vv.5–6). The key phrase is "may you see the prosperity of Jerusalem" (v.5b). It is one thing to have a prosperous life and large family (vv.2–3), but it is another thing to enjoy such blessings within the context of the reign of the Promised Seed of David (v.5b). The psalm uses imagery from the former to express the latter.

Psalm 129. The psalmist expresses the hope of God's people: "They have greatly oppressed me from my youth, let Israel say … but they have not gained the victory over me" (vv.1–2). Just as the Lord has remained faithful to the psalmist, so he will not neglect his promises to Israel.

Psalm 130. The psalmist presents his own patient waiting on the Lord (vv.1–6) as a model for Israel's hope in their own redemption (vv.7–8).

Psalm 131. The psalmist again calls on Israel to hope in the Lord's promised redemption (v.3), using his own patient waiting as their example (vv.1–2).

Psalm 132. This psalm is the centerpiece of the Psalms of Ascents. The focus of Israel's hope is God's promise to David: "LORD, remember David" (v.1). The psalm follows closely the account of the Davidic covenant in 2Sa 7. David, wanting to make a place for God to dwell (vv.2–10), received an oath from the Lord that his own descendants would rule over his throne forever (vv.11–12). David's descendants were not faithful, however, and were thus removed from the throne. But God had chosen David and the city of Jerusalem (Zion), and thus he promised to raise up a future Seed to the house of David, the Anointed One, the Messiah (vv.13–17). Psalm 132 reminds us that God's promise to David remains intact and is the basis for Israel's hope. When the Chosen Seed of David comes, God promises, "I will clothe his enemies with shame, but his head will be adorned with a radiant crown" (v.18).

Psalm 133. Using the terse imagery of this psalm, the compiler of Psalms interweaves several basic themes. Following Ps 132, it is clearly to be read as an expression of the blessing that the Promised Seed of David will bring to his people. When he comes, "God's people live together in unity" (v.1), no doubt hinting at the united kingdom that Israel enjoyed during the reign of David and will once again enjoy during the reign of the Messiah. Moreover, the coming of the promised Seed will mean a return of the glorious worship of God on Mount Zion (v.3), pictured here in the image of precious oil running down the beard of Aaron (v.2). Most important, the blessing that the Promised Seed will bring to God's people is an eternal blessing—the gift of "life forevermore" (v.3; cf. Jn 3:16).

Psalm 134. This psalm concludes the Psalms of Ascents. It calls on all who worship God at Zion to praise the Lord, the Creator, and to look for his blessing from Zion. Its call for praise (v.1) is answered in the following two psalms (135–136).

XXIII. Anonymous Psalms (135–137)

Psalm 135. In response to the call of Ps 134:1, this psalm recounts God's greatness as seen in creation (vv.5–7) and his grace as displayed in delivering Israel from Egypt and in giving them the land (vv.8–12). It closes with a reminder of the futility of idolatry (vv.13–18).

Psalm 136. In further response to Ps 134:1, this praise psalm also recounts God's greatness displayed in creation (vv.4–9) and his grace displayed in delivering Israel from Egypt (vv.10–16) and giving them the land (vv.17–22).

Psalm 137. This psalm returns to the exile and despair expressed in Ps 120. The purpose of these two psalms is to clarify for the reader that this psalm must be read within the context of Israel's return from exile. Thus, this psalm expresses Israel's renewed hope for the fulfillment of the Davidic covenant. Even though God's promise to David to rebuild his kingdom and send the Messiah did not find its fulfillment in the return from exile, that return did provide a renewed basis for hope in the ultimate fulfillment of the promise. God was still at work among his people, and he would remain faithful to his Word. Though present events were difficult and were like those of the captivity itself, Israel could remember earlier days when God proved faithful.

XXIV. Psalms of David (138–145)

Psalm 138. David calls on his own people at the temple to sing praises to God (vv.1–3) and on "all the kings of the earth" (vv.4–5) to sing as well. The scope of the Davidic covenant is thus extended far beyond the borders of ancient Israel (cf. 2:8–12). At the end of this psalm David renews his hope in the fulfillment of God's promise: "The LORD will vindicate me; your love, LORD, endures forever" (v.8). David's faith is a model for the reader. In spite of all his sins and difficulties, David's faith in God's promised Messiah never wavered!

Psalm 139. Why does David have such faith in God? In Ps 139 we receive an intimate look at the substance of David's faith in God. We hear in his own words about the God in whom David put his trust. This psalm offers David's own description of that God. As Moses gave a poetic description of God in Ex 15, so here David gives a poetic "theology" of God and his omniscience, omnipresence, and omnipotence.

Psalm 140. Following closely on David's lament against evil people at the end of Ps 139, this psalm develops the portrait of David as the righteous sufferer who is content to leave the wicked in God's hands for judgment. After lamenting the slanderous deeds of ungodly men (vv.1–11), David concludes by voicing his confidence that "the LORD secures justice for the poor and upholds the cause of the needy" (vv.12–13).

Psalm 141. This psalm is a model of simple piety and trust in God. It is an example of how the readers of the Psalms can respond to evil in their own world. Here David laments the unjust treatment he has received at the hands of the wicked. He knows that God is just and that the deeds of these people will ultimately come back to judge them. In the meantime, David is content to fix his eyes on the Lord and "let the wicked fall into their own nets" (v.10).

Psalm 142. The theme of this psalm is the same as others in this section. David has come to the end of his rope, but his faith and trust in God have not wavered. Though his spirit grows faint within him, he waits for God to act and anticipates the time when the righteous will prevail.

Psalm 143. This psalm adds significantly to the overall message of Psalms. (1) It adds the dimension of seeking God's will amid trials and troubles. Here David not only laments his troubles, but he also meditates on God's Word, seeking to understand his ways (v.5; cf. Ps 1, where meditating on God's Word day and night is the means of finding success and blessing in this life). (2) This psalm adds the notion of God's leading by his Spirit (v.10). Throughout the Scriptures we are taught that the godly must depend on God's Spirit for guidance, wisdom, and strength. In this psalm, David is a model of such dependence (cf. Eze 36:27; Ro 8:4).

Psalm 144. Continuing in the same vein as Pss 140–143, David now calls on the Lord to come to the rescue of the righteous. There is a clear note of imminency in this psalm, coupled with a widening of his vision of God's intervention. Psalms has increasingly focused our attention to the imminent hope of the coming of the Lord. The psalmist wants us to share the same hope of the Lord's glorious and victorious return to establish a kingdom of peace and prosperity unequaled by anything Israel had yet experienced (144:12 – 15).

Psalm 145. This is the last Davidic psalm in the book. It is a praise psalm — unlike any that David has sung before! In it David lists and extols the mighty attributes of God. He begins by instructing each generation to continue to proclaim the greatness of God (vv.1 – 7). God's people are to commend his works to another (v.4a) by telling of his "mighty acts" (v.4b). They are to meditate on his "wonderful works" (v.5b) and celebrate his "abundant goodness" (v.7a).

XXV. Anonymous Psalms (146 – 150)

Psalm 146. The book of Psalms appropriately ends on the note of praise. In Ps 146 all the major themes of this book are repeated; God's power as demonstrated in his creation and care of the universe (v.6); God's grace in his love and care for his people (vv.7 – 9); God's kingdom that he has promised to David (v.10) and will establish in Zion (v.10).

Psalm 147. In his praise of God's grace and care for his people, the psalmist turns to the picture of Jerusalem at the time of the return of the people from captivity (v.2). God's act of deliverance is a continual reminder of his special care for Israel (vv.3 – 11). A second reminder is the fact that he gives peace and prosperity to Jerusalem (vv.12 – 18). A final reminder is that God has given Israel "his word" (v.19). This emphasis on God's Word picks up the same theme introduced in Ps 1:2 and throughout the book (cf. Pss 19; 119). God has revealed his will to Israel in his Word.

Psalm 148. All creation must praise God. The focus of his praise is the "horn" that God has raised up for his people (v.14). The identification of this "horn" is not certain within this psalm. In light of other psalms, the psalmist is clearly referring to the Promised Seed of David (cf. 110:7). This book is both a literary work and thoroughly messianic in purpose. This is how Jesus and the NT writers read the book of Psalms (Lk 24:44; Ac 2:25 – 31).

Psalm 149. The central theme of this psalm is the praise and celebration of the Israelites at the time of the restoration of Zion and the establishment of the kingdom (v.2). Zion is restored, the King is ruling, and the nation has set out "to inflict vengeance on the nations and punishment on the peoples" (v.7). This is the same vision depicted so eloquently in Da 7 and so dramatically in the book of Revelation. This psalm enables the entire book to end with an expression of celebration of the restoration of Zion and the return of her King.

Psalm 150. Psalms ends with this praise psalm. God in his sanctuary (v.1) is surrounded by the praises of his saints. This is precisely the picture of the reigning king in Rev 4 and Da 7:27. The psalms are not placed randomly within the book. They show a clear focus and intention to present the hymns of Israel as expressions of the hope that God will fulfill his promises to David and send the Messiah.

PROVERBS

Introduction

The title of the book of Proverbs in the Hebrew Bible is "The Proverbs of Solomon." There are, of course, proverbs in the book not written by Solomon (cf. 24:23; 30:1; 31:1). Thus the title indicates that it was written as a showpiece of the wisdom of Solomon; a major part of the book consists of his own proverbs. According to 1Ki 4:32, Solomon wrote at least three thousand proverbs. Some three to four hundred of these have been preserved in this book.

The lack of a literary context within the book forces the reader to provide a context for interpretation from his or her own life. Behind the apparent randomness of the book, therefore, is the goal of applying the wisdom of the proverbs to one's own life. This is consistent with the overall purpose of biblical wisdom, i.e., the application of divine truth to everyday life.

I. Prologue (1:1 – 7)

The prologue clearly sets forth the intent of the book: "for gaining wisdom and instruction ... for giving prudence to those who are simple, knowledge and discretion to the young" (vv.2 – 4). From the beginning the prologue makes it clear that the wisdom intended here is divine wisdom: "The fear of the Lord is the beginning of knowledge" (v.7).

II. Apologetic for Wisdom (1:8 – 9:18)

This defense of the importance of seeking wisdom is cast in the form of parental counsel. Those addressed are called "sons," and the counsel given is referred to as "your father's instruction" and "your mother's teaching" (1:8). The word for "teaching" is the Hebrew word *torah*, a word used to refer to God's "law." Parental instruction has a character analogous to divine instruction.

III. Collection of Solomonic Proverbs (10:1 – 29:27)

A. Proverbs of Solomon (10:1 – 24:22)

The first collection of proverbs consists of a loose grouping of nearly fifteen chapters of individual proverbs. This collection provides a sample of wise sayings and judgments on all aspects of human life: relationships among family members, business partners, neighbors, friends, and enemies. All levels of human social activities are covered.

This section closes with the admonition to "fear the LORD and the king," because the destruction of the wicked will arise suddenly and without warning (24:21 – 22; cf. Ps 2:12). The everyday deeds of God's people, whether good or bad, are viewed from the eternal perspective of a holy God intent on bringing the entire human race into account for their rebellious deeds — a new outlook on the wisdom sayings from the first part of the book, but a familiar theme in biblical literature in general.

B. Sayings of the Wise (24:23 – 34)

This short addition to the words of Solomon is attributed simply to "the wise" (or possibly "for the wise"). These sayings elaborate on the words of Solomon. Their focus is on the practical affairs of everyday life: the courtroom (24:23b – 25, 28 – 29), interpersonal relationships (24:26), domestic work (24:27), and business (24:30 – 34). They provide a few test cases for applying the general wisdom statements that preceded them. In this respect they resemble many of the laws in the Pentateuch; they do not so much express the general rule, but rather illustrate it by example.

C. More Proverbs of Solomon (25:1 – 29:27)

This collection of wise sayings is prefaced with a rare notice of its authorship: the proverbs of Solomon gathered by court officials during the reign of King Hezekiah (25:1). It is thus noteworthy that nearly all of these sayings relate to political rule or governance, though they can also be applied to private life. One could entitle this section "Principles of Leadership." Once again, there is little recognizable structure to aid in the interpretation of each saying; thus, the reader must search within the context of his or her own life for an application.

IV. Sayings of Agur (30:1 – 33)

In the last three sections, we see wisdom embodied through the lens of the lives of three individuals; they become the model for the reader's own life-application of wisdom. Agur's sayings are by far the most unusual in the book. In fact, more than merely "wisdom sayings," they are also called "an inspired utterance" (30:1). Whereas a wisdom saying is a conclusion drawn from the observation of everyday life, an "inspired utterance" is a word from God.

V. Sayings of Lemuel (31:1 – 9)

Lemuel's words are, like Agur's, called an "oracle," given to him by his mother. It focuses on the practical application of the general principles embodied in Proverbs. Unlike most of the sayings in Proverbs, the oracle of Lemuel's mother focuses on only a couple of brief themes: the dangers of a profligate life (vv.1 – 7) and defending the rights of the poor (vv.8 – 9).

VI. Poem to a Virtuous Woman (31:10 – 31)

Proverbs closes with an ode to a virtuous woman. Throughout the book, a central theme has been the personification of wisdom as a virtuous wife (3:13 – 18; 5:15 – 23; 8:1 – 21; 9:1 – 11). It is thus fitting that the book should close with an extended example of such a wife. The poem itself is an acrostic; each line begins with a different letter of the Hebrew alphabet. The first line begins with the question "A wife of noble character who can find?" (31:10). Apart from the book of Proverbs, the term "wife of noble character" is used also in the book of Ruth (Ru 3:11), where Boaz calls Ruth "a woman of noble character" (same Hebrew phrase as used here). In the Hebrew Bible, the book of Ruth follows Proverbs directly. As the ancestress of David, Ruth is treated as an historical example of the virtuous woman mentioned here.

ECCLESIASTES

Introduction

The Hebrew title of the book means "the preacher" and is rendered in English by way of the Greek word for "preacher," *ekklesiastes*. The preacher is the primary character of the book. While not expressly stated, he is probably to be identified as Solomon, "son of David, king in Jerusalem" (1:1).

The Message of Ecclesiastes

Ecclesiastes is concerned with the major themes of OT wisdom. At its heart is the notion of the fear of the Lord and its value in everyday life. Moreover, the book clearly has a "this-worldly" orientation. It is concerned with the practical application of God's law in the life of the righteous. Furthermore, it evaluates different life patterns. Wisdom literature in general was keenly aware of varying ways of living and often sought to determine the "best" way.

In the last analysis, however, there are only two ways: the way of the righteous and the way of the wicked (cf. Ps 1). The way of the righteous consists not so much in finding wisdom per se, as in finding wisdom in obeying God's law. Underlying the "wisdom" taught here is the biblical idea of the fear of the Lord as taught, for example, in Ex 20:18–20: The fear of God is intended "to keep you from sinning."

There are two levels of assessment of wisdom in Ecclesiastes. First, the author compares wisdom with other ways of life as they are seen "under the sun." Second, there is a view of true wisdom seen from God's perspective. Human wisdom appears to offer little beyond those other ways that human beings have devised for themselves. The preacher states, "Then I said to myself, 'The fate of the fool will overtake me also. What then do I gain by being wise?' I said to myself, 'This too is meaningless'" (2:15). "Like the fool, the wise too must die!" (2:16b). His ultimate conclusion is to "fear God and keep his commandments" (12:13).

SONG OF SONGS

Though the first verse of the book is usually translated "Solomon's Song of Songs," it could be understood either as a song that Solomon wrote or a song about Solomon (cf. Ps 72:1). In light of the fact that Solomon is referred to within the book itself (e.g., 3:7), it seems more likely that it is a poem about Solomon and one of his young lovers (cf. 1Ki 11:3).

The book's straightforward depiction of human love in all its aspects gave rise to various figurative interpretations at an early stage in its history. Jewish interpreters of this book understand it as a picture of God's relationship to his beloved Israel, whereas Christians have commonly seen it in terms of Christ and his church. In modern times there have been many interpreters of the book who have understood it "literally" and simply as an ode to human love.

Although it is, on the face of it, just that — an ode to human love — one must ask whether it was originally intended to be read this way. Some indications within the book suggest it was not. For example, the book is poetic, and much of its visual imagery is intended to portray themes and ideas that lie outside the range of the poetic images themselves. The book is a poetic drama of a lover's longing for his beloved and of her willing complicity, but we must not confuse the poetic imagery with the purpose of the poem.

ISAIAH

Introduction

Isaiah is the first book in what is called the prophetic literature in the Bible. The prophets were messengers of the covenant God. Sent to a disobedient people, they were like modern-day revivalists, calling the people back to the faith of the fathers, the faith of the covenant promises to Abraham, Moses, and David.

In their day, God's people largely failed to keep his commands. Over and over they fell away from him and his covenant. They mistook the blessings of the covenant (God's presence at the temple) for the requirements of the covenant (their own obedience). They felt that because the Lord was in their midst, nothing bad would happen.

In the face of such false security, the prophets brought the startling word that God was not on the side of his own covenant people. Since they had forsaken his covenant, he would send judgment. A dominant theme, then, in the rest of the books of the Old Testament is that one day all of Israel's objects of comfort and religious support would be taken away and God would judge them for their disobedience.

The book of Isaiah is an anonymous work. Its title, "The vision ... that Isaiah son of Amoz saw," does not indicate its authorship so much as it does its content—the prophetic words of the prophet Isaiah. The author intends it to be read, however, from the perspective of its original context in Isaiah's own day. Both his naming of the Persian King Cyrus and the prediction of his release of the Jewish captives in Babylon long before its time form a central part of the message of the book (cf. chs. 44–46). That these prophecies are authentic, therefore, is essential to their meaning.

I. Introduction of Isaiah (1:1)

Isaiah the prophet prophesied from the days of King Uzziah (791 – 740 BC) to those of Hezekiah (716 – 687). His call to be a prophet came in the year that Uzziah died (6:1).

II. Judgment and Salvation for God's People (1:2 – 12:6)

This book begins with the rebellion and apostasy of God's people, Israel (1:2 – 6:13). Israel had forsaken God and thus stood in danger of divine wrath. In the face of impending judgment, God called the prophet Isaiah. He was taken into the very throne room of the holy God (6:1 – 13), where he was purified and commissioned to speak God's words of judgment and salvation. He was warned, however, that God's people would not heed his words, and his message would only serve to harden them further and seal them for divine judgment. Yet a "holy seed" (6:13) would survive God's day of wrath and a remnant would return.

The writer inserts a brief narrative of Isaiah's confrontation with King Ahaz of Judah (7:1 – 25). Ahaz was under attack by King Rezin of Aram and King Pekah of Israel, the northern kingdom. Isaiah's message to Ahaz was to trust in God (v.9), but the king did not. He rejected God's offer to give him a sign under the guise of piety: "I will not put the LORD to the test" (v.12). God, however, responded with a show of his own faithfulness. He gave Ahaz and the house of David a sign to prove his determination to deliver his people from trouble, namely, the promise of a son of David born of a virgin. The child would be born in a time of distress for God's people when they would be under the rule of an oppressor (vv.14 – 17).

Another sign was given to Ahaz, but it was a sign of impending and swift judgment (8:1 – 3): the birth of Isaiah's own son, "Maher-Shalal-Hash-Baz," whose name means "quick to the plunder, swift to the spoil." The birth of this son would mark the impending destruction of the northern kingdom of Israel (Samaria) and the Aramean kingdom of Damascus (v.4), as well as the devastation and subjugation of Judah by the Assyrians (vv.5 – 8).

Because God was with Judah, however, Assyria's plans to destroy Jerusalem would not succeed (vv.9 – 15). Israel, the northern kingdom and enemy of Jerusalem, however, would perish (9:8 – 10:4). God had continually warned them, yet they would not turn back to him. Moreover, Isaiah's prophecies looked beyond the punishment brought on by the Assyrians to a time when the Lord would turn in judgment against Assyria (10:5–11, 13–19, 23–34) and thus bring peace to his people again (vv.12, 20–22).

The future salvation of Jerusalem is seen most clearly in the prophecies of 11:1–12:6. Here Isaiah describes the coming of the Son of David (11:1), filled with God's Spirit (v.2). He would judge the nations in righteousness (vv.3–5) and bring peace to the world (vv.6–9). When he came, he would gather the lost remnant of Israel from among all the nations (vv.10–13) and reclaim the Promised Land to its original boundaries from Assyria to Egypt (vv.14–16; cf. Ge 15:18). In that day Israel would sing praise to God for his great salvation (12:1–6).

III. Judgment and Salvation for the Nations (13:1 – 23:18)

The time when God would punish the nations and bring peace to Israel involved not only the Assyrians but all the nations of the world (chs. 13–23). The judgment of these nations would one day result in establishing a final peace (cf. 18:7; 19:21–25).

The writer of this book begins his selection of divine judgments against the nations with Isaiah's oracle against Babylon (13:1–14:23). The Lord would bring a mighty nation against Babylon (13:1–8), which would destroy Babylon in a mighty conflagration (vv.9–16). Isaiah identified this nation as the Medes (vv.17–19). Babylon would never rise again (vv.20–22). At that time, Israel would again dwell in their own land (14:1–2) and sing taunt songs against Babylon, their former oppressor (vv.3–23).

In the same way that Babylon would fall by God's hand, God would also destroy Assyria (14:24–27), Philistia (14:28–32), Moab (15:1–16:14), Damascus (17:1–14), Cush (18:1–8), Egypt (19:1–17; 20:1–6), the Desert by the Sea (21:1–10), Dumah (i.e., Edom; 21:11–12), Arabia (21:13–17), Jerusalem (22:1–25), and Tyre (23:1–16). In the midst of these prophecies of judgment, however, Isaiah includes a word of salvation and blessing for the nations: Moab (16:5), Damascus (17:7), Cush (18:7), Egypt (19:18–25), and Tyre (23:17–18).

IV. Isaiah's Apocalyptic Vision (24:1 – 35:10)

Having enumerated the destruction of Israel's historical enemies, the writer now turns to an apocalyptic vision of the destruction of all nations and humankind. At this time God's kingdom will be established in Jerusalem and "the LORD Almighty will reign on Mount Zion and in Jerusalem" (24:23). In response to his vision of the future reign of God's King, Isaiah breaks out into praise. He envisions the time when God will establish his kingdom on Mount Zion and hold a great banquet for all the nations.

Isaiah then turns to Ephraim, the northern kingdom, which was about to be taken into exile by Assyria. His oracle warned them of God's impending judgment. Israel would not listen to God, so he brought against them a nation that spoke "with foreign lips and strange tongues" (28:11).

Next, Isaiah addresses an oracle of woe to "Ariel," i.e., Jerusalem, the city of David. It too would be besieged by Assyria, the instrument of God's wrath. But unlike the kingdom of the north, God would rescue Judah and Jerusalem for the sake of his promises to David. When God did this wonderful work of salvation among them, however, those in Jerusalem would be blinded to it as if they were in a "deep sleep" (29:10). Thus, Isaiah pronounced judgment on Jerusalem for their failure to trust God. They would rather look to the strength of Egypt, but Egypt would bring them "only shame and disgrace," and their help would be utterly "useless" (30:5).

Isaiah was instructed to record his oracles of judgment against Jerusalem in writing as "an everlasting witness" (30:8) against the rebellious people of Judah. The people in Isaiah's own day did not want to hear the words of the prophets, so the words were written down for a future generation to read. Included in God's words of judgment were also words of comfort and salvation. A time would come when the people of Jerusalem would "weep no more" (30:19).

All nations are warned of the day when God would bring retribution on them "to uphold Zion's cause" (34:8). The prophet singles out Edom in particular as Israel's archenemy. When this judgment came upon Edom and the nations, the "scroll of the LORD" would testify that all these things had been foretold and came to pass just as it was written.

V. Isaiah's Historical Insertion (36:1 – 39:8)

The Assyrian invasion of Judah marked an important moment for Isaiah's prophecies, for God began to turn against Assyria, the instrument of his wrath, and would bring destruction upon it (37:36 – 38). That which Isaiah had announced in 10:12 now seemed to be happening.

However, the end that Isaiah had seen coming at this time did not come. Therefore, at this point in the book of Isaiah, the writer must address this central question that the prophecies of Isaiah have inevitably raised: When would these things happen? Was the prophet speaking of events in his own day? Or did he look forward to a future judgment and salvation of God's people?

He answers that question with this lengthy insertion of historical narrative into the words of Isaiah (chs. 36–39). The narrative inserted into Isaiah goes beyond the time of the Assyrian invasion of Jerusalem and ends with Isaiah's warning of a future exile of Jerusalem to Babylon (39:6). Babylon, not Assyria, is the actual focus of the narrative.

VI. Prophecies Relating to the Return From Babylon (40:1 – 55:13)

Looking now at events that lay far in the future, Isaiah begins to describe the coming of a mighty king who would do God's work of judgment upon the nations and return Israel to their land (41:1–3). In this chapter the identity of this king remained veiled: "Who has stirred up one from the east, calling him in righteousness to his service?" (41:2; but see 45:1).

In 41:8 God calls Israel "my servant." In 42:1–4, this "servant" is a single individual who would "bring justice to the nations" (v.1b) by establishing "his justice" among all the peoples of the world (v.4b). As described here, this servant would be a new Moses who, like Moses in the desert, would give God's law to the people. Having described the messianic Servant of the Lord who was sent to open the eyes of the blind, Isaiah returns to the image of Israel as God's servant and identifies them as the blind and the deaf (vv.18–20). It would be their eyes whom the messianic Servant would open, and he would release them from captivity (cf. vv.19, 21–25).

Though Israel would suffer divine punishment, they would not be forsaken (44:1–2). A time of great blessing and restoration awaited them in the future (vv.3–5). God would pour out his Spirit on Israel and bless their descendants (v.3b). This would happen in the day that the Lord raised up the Persian king Cyrus (v.28; cf. Ezr 1–3). Cyrus would be God's anointed one, chosen to redeem God's people from captivity and rebuild the temple (45:1).

The prophet's vision now turns to Babylon, the nation that would take Israel from Jerusalem and into captivity (47:1–15). God used Babylon against the nation of Judah as an instrument of his wrath (v.6), but Babylon was a proud and wicked nation. With the rise of Cyrus, their glory would come to an end. Their ruin would be evident to all.

The two servants of the Lord now speak. In light of the preceding prophecies of judgment against God's people, the first servant, Israel, confesses, "I have labored in vain; I have spent my strength for nothing at all" (49:4). By way of contrast, the Servant who speaks in vv.5–7 cannot be

Israel because he was called "to bring Jacob back to him and gather Israel to himself" (v.5a). This Servant would not only restore Israel (v.6), but also God would make him a "light for the Gentiles" to bring "salvation ... to the ends of the earth" (v.6). This Servant would take Israel from captivity and restore them in the land (vv.8–26).

The Lord now addresses a disobedient Israel as the son of a divorced wife (50:1–3). They were sold into slavery because of their own sins (v.1b), not because their Father was unable to ransom them (v.2b). God would send a Redeemer to Israel, the Servant, but they would reject him (vv.4–11). Nevertheless, God would send his salvation to those who would "listen" to him, "pursue righteousness," and "seek the LORD" (51:1): "The LORD will surely comfort Zion and will look with compassion on all her ruins" (v.3).

God's future redemption of Israel would be like his great acts of creation and redemption in the past (51:9–16). Therefore, though they would suffer much at the hand of the Lord for their transgressions, those who lived in Jerusalem should rejoice in the expectation of their salvation (vv.17–23). When God sent their deliverance and cleansed the city, Jerusalem would never be defiled again (52:1). It would be oppressed, but the Lord would return to Zion and proclaim peace and salvation (vv.2–9). When that happened, "all the ends of the earth" would see "the salvation of our God" (v.10).

Israel's salvation would be the work of God's Servant (52:13–53:12). He would accomplish his goal and be highly exalted (52:13), but in the process the Servant would be marred and so disfigured that many would be as appalled at him as they were of Israel in their captivity (v.14). He would offer himself as an atonement sacrifice for Israel and the nations (v.15). In his own day, no one would believe his message, though they would later turn to him and marvel at their former unbelief (53:1). He would be ignored (v.2), rejected (v.3a), and despised (v.3b). Yet he would take upon himself the afflictions and sorrows of others and give his life as a sin offering (vv.4–12).

By means of the offering of his Servant, the Lord would redeem Israel and the nations. When they turned to him in faith and trust, the Lord would never again cast them off (54:1–17). His "covenant of peace" with Israel and the nations would last forever (vv.10). Thus the invitation is given to all nations to accept the Lord's offer of life through his "everlasting covenant" with David (55:1–3; cf. comments on 2Sa 7). Through the messianic Seed of David and the eternal kingdom promised him, the Lord would have mercy on all nations (vv.4–7). God's word never fails, and his promises achieve their purpose (vv.8–13).

VII. Isaiah's Final Prophecies (56:1 – 66:24)

Because God's salvation was close at hand, he would call on his people to "maintain justice and do what is right" (56:1). For the Israelite who lived under the Mosaic covenant, this meant strict observance of the Sabbath day of rest (v.2). Even foreigners and others excluded from the people were to be included in Israel's worship if they kept God's Sabbath and his covenant (vv.3 – 7). God's salvation extends to more than a select few (v.8).

In Isaiah's day, the Israelites did not show much sign of repentance (56:9 – 12). Only a few lived righteously (57:1), and those who did suffered for it (v.2). The rest had forsaken the Lord and followed after idols (vv.3 – 11). When the day of distress came upon God's people and they were carried off in exile, their only refuge would be their trust in the Lord (vv.12 – 13). God would look upon their contrite heart and forgive them, but if they persisted in their wickedness, there would be no peace for them (vv.14 – 21). The kind of repentance God required of his people is a contrite heart and a life of good works. There was little value in fasting if one's life did not reflect compassion and obedience to the will of God (58:1 – 14).

Israel's troubles were not due to God's inability to help them. Rather, their sins had separated them from God (59:1 – 8). In behalf of God's people, Isaiah acknowledges their guilt (vv.9 – 15). Israel could not help themselves, so God himself would come to their defense (vv.16 – 19) and send his Redeemer to Zion (v.20). That Isaiah's prophecy has the new covenant (Jer 31:31; Eze 36:26) specifically in mind here is clear from what the Lord says in 59:21: "'This is my covenant with them,' says the LORD. 'My Spirit, who is on you ... and my words that I have put in your mouth will always be on your lips, on the lips of your children ... forever,' says the LORD."

When God established his covenant with Israel and sent his Spirit on them, all the nations would see their light and stream into Jerusalem (60:1 – 14). Isaiah's oracle in vv.1 – 4 is an expansion of his vision in 2:2 – 4. In that day Israel, though once poor and destitute, would receive great wealth from the nations, and Jerusalem would be rebuilt (60:15 – 18). God himself would dwell among his people in Jerusalem, and all his people would be righteous (v v.19 – 22).

In that day one anointed by God's Spirit would come "to proclaim good news to the poor" (61:1) and "to proclaim the year of the LORD's favor and the day of vengeance of our God" (v.2). This would be a time of restoration and rebuilding of Jerusalem (vv.3 – 4) and great reward for God's people (vv.5 – 9). The Anointed One would make Jerusalem a place of righteousness and praise before all the nations (vv.10 – 11). This city would be known among the nations as the new bride of the coming Savior (62:1 – 12).

When the Savior arrived, he would trample over Jerusalem's enemies as one treads a winepress (63:1–6). Yet the Lord would be kind to the house of Israel (vv.7–8), just as he had been with them in the past (v.9). But the Lord would turn and become Israel's enemy if they rebelled against him (v.10). At this point, the writer inserts a lengthy recollection of God's dealings in Israel's past and present (63:11–65:16). The perspective is that of the exiles in Babylon (see comments on 39:1–7): "Lord … for a little while your people possessed your holy place, but now our enemies have trampled down your sanctuary" (63:17–18). "Even Zion is a wasteland, Jerusalem a desolation" (64:10). "Our holy and glorious temple … has been burned with fire" (v.11). They acknowledged their guilt and called upon God for help (64:1–7, 12).

In the past, God pleaded with them to turn from their wicked ways (65:1–7). God, however, still saw a good remnant among the people in Israel, and he determined not to destroy all of them (v.8). The faithful remnant, his "servants," will yet enjoy God's blessing (vv.9–10), but the rest "who forsake the Lord and forget [his] holy mountain [Zion]" (v.11) will be destined for the sword and will be forgotten (vv.12–16).

In God's future for Israel and the nations, he will create "new heavens and a new earth" (v.17a), and "the former things will not be remembered" (v.17b). God will delight in Jerusalem. As in the early chapters of Genesis (Ge 5), human life will be extended so that "the one who dies at a hundred will be thought a mere youth" (65:20). There will be peace and harmony in God's creation as it was in the beginning (v.25).

At that time God will not seek the one who worships in the temple with sacrifices (66:1–4). True worshipers will be "those who are humble and contrite in spirit, and who tremble at [his] word" (v.2). The peace of Jerusalem will flow like a river (v.12). It will be the place where all nations will see God's glory (vv.18–21). Those who repent and turn to the Lord will live forever (v.22) in God's presence (v.23), but those who rebel against him will perish (v.24).

JEREMIAH

Introduction

Jeremiah prophesied from the time of Josiah to the time of the Babylonian captivity (cf. 1:2). The leading political power in his day was Babylon under King Nebuchadnezzar. The end of the Assyrian Empire had come with the fall of Nineveh (612 BC) and the battle of Carchemish (605 BC). The last kings of Jerusalem (Jehoiakim, Jehoiachin, and Zedekiah) were defeated by Babylon, and Jerusalem was destroyed in 587 BC.

I. Introduction (1:1 – 19)

A. Title (1:1)

The title of this book is descriptive of its contents—the "words," or "matters," of Jeremiah. According to 36:32, Jeremiah dictated to his scribe, Baruch, much of the material in this book. Moreover, "many similar words were added to them." These "words" (1:1) are divided into two sections, 1:2 – 39:18 and 40:1 – 51:64a. The subscription, "The words of Jeremiah end here" (51:64b), marks the end of that segment of the book that begins with "the words" of Jeremiah (1:1). The book itself, however, is extended by a further account of the fall of Jerusalem (52:1 – 30) and the release of Jehoiachin after the exile (52:31 – 34).

B. Summary (1:2 – 3)

The book opens with a brief chronological note regarding the time of Jeremiah's ministry. He prophesied from the thirteenth year of Josiah to the exile to Babylon. There are many other historical notes throughout the book. The author's purpose with these notes is to make sure that the reader views Jeremiah's message within the context of the exile to Babylon. In so doing, the book raises the question of whether the prophecies of Jeremiah, both the judgments and the anticipated blessings, were to be understood as fulfilled in his own day or find their reference in future events.

For the most part, the NT writers saw Jeremiah's prophecies concerning the future as relating to the time of the coming of Jesus Christ. We will see that this was also the viewpoint of the author of the book. Jeremiah's strategy in relating his words to historical events of his own day shows how these events came and went, and yet his words were not fulfilled in them. Their fulfillment related to an event still to come, namely, the appearance of the Messiah.

C. Jeremiah's Call (1:4 – 19)

Jeremiah's message is summarized in his call. He was chosen before he was born and charged with announcing the impending divine judgment against Judah and Jerusalem. There would be an overwhelming defeat of the nation by "the peoples of the northern kingdom" (1:15). This is pictured in the destruction of Jerusalem by the Babylonians. But before we reach its end, we learn that God's words look far beyond that historical event to a time of judgment for Israel identified later in the book of Daniel as the "abomination that causes desolation" (Da 9:27).

II. Prophecies of Doom against Judah, Jerusalem, and the Nations (2:1 – 25:38)

Jeremiah 2 begins with a lengthy indictment of the unfaithfulness of the people of Israel, beginning with the early days when God cared for them in the desert, but concentrating on the sins of Judah and Jerusalem in Jeremiah's own day (2:1 – 3:5). Judah did not heed the lesson of the destruction of the northern kingdom (3:6 – 10) and thus, in God's sight, was more guilty than Israel whom God had cut off (v.11).

Two central themes stand out amid Jeremiah's many words of judgment. (1) God's people were "uncircumcised in heart" (9:26). (2) Israel had been involved in idolatry (10:1 – 16). The same power God had demonstrated in creation would one day be turned against his own disobedient people.

Jeremiah, however, had learned from the example of the potter who refashioned his ruined pot that God would relent his plans of judgment and bless his people if only they would repent and hearken to his warning (18:1 – 12). Israel did not repent, however (vv.13 – 17). Instead, they made plans to kill the prophet so their own wise men and prophets would prosper (vv.18 – 23). Jeremiah responded by renewing his message of judgment against Jerusalem (19:1 – 15).

In the midst of this word of judgment, however, Jeremiah spoke a word of hope — there would come to the house of David "a righteous Branch, a King who will reign wisely and do what is just and right in the land" (23:5 – 8). Here Jeremiah looked forward to a return of God's people from their captivity (v.3). At that time a Davidic King would again reign over them in Jerusalem. Judah and Israel would be reunited as in the days of David.

In the vision of the two baskets of figs (24:1 – 10), Jeremiah was shown what would happen to two groups of exiles in Judah. The first group were those who had been taken to Babylon with the Davidic king Jehoiakim in the first deportation by Nebuchadnezzar (24:1; cf. 2Ki 24:15 – 16). This group would return to the land and find God's blessing after the exile (Jer 24:4 – 7). Though not stated directly by Jeremiah, the basis of this promise of future blessing was the Davidic covenant (2Sa 7). God had promised an eternal kingdom to the house of David, and thus the final word for the Davidic kingship could only be blessing. In light of this prophetic word, it is significant that this book concludes with a word about King Jehoiachin and his release from prison during the last days of the exile (52:31 – 34).

There was no word of hope for the second group of exiles, however (24:8 – 10) — the group that remained in the land with Nebuchadnezzar's puppet king, Zedekiah (v.8; cf. 2Ki 24:17); they would perish outside the land. Before Jeremiah ends, we learn that Zedekiah died a humiliating death at the hands of the Babylonians (Jer 52:7 – 11), and all those who remained in Judah were exiled (vv.12 – 30). This stands in stark contrast with the blessing of King Jehoiachin (52:31 – 34).

Chapter 25 starts a major turning point in Jeremiah. Using the words of the prophet's earlier oracles (25:1), the focus is beyond the immediate events of the destruction of Jerusalem by Nebuchadnezzar to the return of God's people and the punishment of the Babylonians. The writer's use of earlier prophecies from the days of Jehoiakim is occasioned by the fact that during the reign of Jehoiachin, Jehoiakim's son, God had warned all prophets not to speak oracles in his name (23:33 – 36). Jeremiah had earlier prophesied a time limit to the judgment of God's people by Babylon — seventy years (25:11). After that time, Babylon itself would be destroyed (v.12), just as the other nations who had cursed God's people (vv.13 – 38).

III. Prophecies of Salvation for Israel and Judah (26:1 – 35:19)

When Jeremiah had prophesied his earlier oracles (26:1), there was still hope for God's people if they repented (vv.2–6). They had not repented, however; moreover, the priests and prophets now set out to kill Jeremiah because of his strong words of judgment (vv.7–15). He was rescued by an appeal to the example of Hezekiah's reverential treatment of the prophet Micah (vv.16–19).

Jeremiah's prophecies (27:1–22), given during the reign of Jehoiakim, raised the heat of his words against Judah one more notch. Not only had the people been warned of the coming destruction of their land through the Babylonians, but now they were also being told to submit willingly to the yoke of Babylon. They were to take their punishment by Babylon as from the Lord. Now even more punishment would come for refusing to accept God's judgment (v.8). Submitting to Babylon would be a sign of trust in God's faithfulness to Jerusalem (vv.11–12).

Jeremiah met head-on with the false prophet Hananiah over the issue of the return of the temple vessels. Hananiah claimed to have received an oracle after the time in which God had ceased giving them (23:34–38). The text, then, has already marked his words as his own and not God's.

In conformity to his words against the false prophets, Jeremiah sent a letter to the exiles in Babylon (29:1–23). They could not expect to return quickly, as Hananiah and the false prophets had said. They should "build houses and settle down; plant gardens and eat what they produce" (vv.4–5). They would be in Babylon for seventy years (v.10). Added to the stark reality of Jeremiah's words of prolonged judgment (vv.4–9, 15–23, 24–32), there were also words of comfort and promises of eventual blessing (vv.10–14).

In ch. 30 Jeremiah breaks out into a full description of the divine blessings that lay ahead for Israel and Judah. Jeremiah adds to his vision of Israel's future blessing the notion of a "new covenant" (31:31). Just as God had brought Israel out of Egypt and entered a covenant with them at Sinai (Ex 19), so when he restored them to the land again it would be on the basis of a covenant. This new covenant would not be like the Sinai covenant. In that covenant, Israel had been given the law on tablets of stone. Moreover, in the incident of the golden calf, they had broken the covenant and Moses dashed into pieces the tablets of stone (v.32; cf. Ex 32). But in the new covenant, Israel would be given the law written on their hearts.

In ch. 33 the writer links Jeremiah's words about the new covenant with his earlier emphasis on God's promise to David (2Sa 7:16): "In those days and at that time I will make a righteous Branch sprout from David's line; he will do what is just and right in the land" (Jer 33:15). In those days there would be both an eternal kingship and an eternal priesthood (vv.17–18). God's covenant with David was as certain and eternal as his appointment of the times of day and night (vv.19–22). Through his promise to David, God would restore all the descendants of Abraham, Isaac, and Jacob (vv.23–26).

IV. Baruch's Narrative of the Suffering of Jeremiah (36:1 – 45:5)

The account of the first edition of Jeremiah's book (36:2) sheds much light on the purpose and strategy of the present edition. God had spoken many times to the inhabitants of Judah, but they had not heeded his words. Jeremiah was thus instructed to write out in full all the words that he had spoken from the days of Josiah to those of Jehoiakim. Perhaps the cumulative effect of all these words would have a more lasting effect on them (v.3). This need for a cumulative effect helps explain the unusually complete record of divine judgments against Judah and Jerusalem in Jer 1–35. That it achieves this goal is clear to anyone who reads through them in a single sitting. King Jehoiakim, however, takes the composite book and burns it (ch. 36).

The added narratives about the life and ministry of Jeremiah begin with the story of his imprisonment (ch. 37). After Zedekiah had been placed over Judah by Nebuchadnezzar, Jeremiah's fate took a turn for the worse. Since his message had always been that the Babylonians were the instrument of divine wrath and that the Israelites should submit to their rule, it appeared to many that he had sided with the enemy, Babylon, and was attempting to discourage any further resistance. Jeremiah was thus imprisoned on what amounted to a charge of treason (37:11–15; 38:1–6).

The fall of Jerusalem finally came in Zedekiah's ninth year (39:1–10). At this point, the writer's primary interest lies both in the fact that God's word through Jeremiah was fulfilled and Jeremiah himself, along with those who had sided with him, escaped the fate of the others. As if to add insult to injury, the fulfillment of Jeremiah's own words against Jerusalem is stated by the general of the Babylonians, Nebuzaradan: "The LORD your God decreed this disaster for this place. And now the LORD has brought it about; he has done just as he said he would" (40:2–3).

Those from Judah left behind by the Babylonians recognized Gedaliah as their leader. This man had been appointed by the Babylonians as an overseer of the region (40:5). Though he was well liked among the Jews (vv.7–16) and the people were beginning to prosper under his leadership (vv.10, 12), Gedaliah was assassinated and many leaders were killed by an Ammonite-led rebellion against Babylon (41:1–12). Through the leadership of Johanan son of Kareah and his remnant of an army, the survivors were liberated.

These Jewish survivors, led by Johanan, banded together with Jeremiah to serve the Lord and obey his word (41:16–42:6) — intent on fleeing to Egypt to escape Babylonian reprisals (41:16–18). Through Jeremiah, however, the Lord warned these people not to go down to Egypt, but rather to remain in the land and seek the Lord's help and protection from the Babylonians (42:7–18). If they fled to Egypt the same divine judgment that had overtaken Jerusalem would come to them in Egypt. Jeremiah himself pleaded with them to heed God's word (vv.19–22).

As if they had learned nothing from the events of the immediate past, the people forsook Jeremiah's word and went to Egypt (43:1–7) anyway, forcibly taking Jeremiah with them (43:6). En route, Jeremiah prophesied that Nebuchadnezzar would destroy Egypt on account of the Jews who had taken refuge there (44:8–14, 20–30). The people, however, did not listen to his words (44:19). Only Baruch (45:1–5) and a small remnant (44:28) would survive the divine wrath about to come upon the people in Egypt.

V. Prophecies of Doom against the Nations (46:1 – 51:64)

The last major section of Jeremiah consists of a series of judgments against the enemies of Israel: Egypt (46:1–26), the Philistines (47:1–7), Moab (48:1–46), Ammon (49:1–6), Edom (49:7–22), Damascus (49:23–27), Kedar and Hazor (49:28–33), and Elam (49:34–38). This series culminates in an extended word of judgment against Babylon (50:1–51:64a), in which the rise of the empire of the Medes is specifically foretold (51:11, 28). The enumeration of these various judgments against Israel's enemies was a way to express the certitude of God's promise of salvation for Israel (49:2b; 50:4–8, 17–20, 33–34; 51:5–6, 10, 24, 35–39, 45–53). But these words also express the certitude of divine blessing and salvation for Israel. Interspersed in these words of judgment are words of hope and salvation for Israel (46:27–28) as well as for Moab (48:47), Ammon (49:6), and Elam (49:39).

VI. Conclusion (52:1 – 34)

Jeremiah closes with two narratives from 2 Kings. The first reiterates the fall of Jerusalem (52:1–30), taken almost verbatim from 2Ki 24:18–25:21. This puts the preceding prophecies of judgment against Babylon (50:1–51:58) in their proper perspective. Even though Babylon was an instrument of judgment in God's hand (51:7), they had destroyed Jerusalem and God's temple (v.11b), and thus God was raising up the Medes to punish them (50:41–44; 51:11).

The second (52:31–34) is a verbatim account of the restitution of the royal prerogatives of King Jehoiachin in the palace of the Babylonian king Awel-Marduk (taken from 2Ki 25:27–30). Its purpose is to show that God's purposes for Israel and his promises to David (2Sa 7) were still being carried out, even though the city had been destroyed and the king was living in exile in Babylon. The promised Redeemer had not yet arisen, but one could see in the events of this brief narrative that God was still at work. This book thus ends on a note of hope and expectancy of the fulfillment of God's blessing for Israel.

LAMENTATIONS

Introduction

The impact of the exile on the thought and life of the Jewish people is best seen in the document that came directly from the time of the fall of Jerusalem, the book of Lamentations. The writer is not identified in the text; it may have been Jeremiah (based on 2Ch 35:25, though the "laments" mentioned there for King Josiah are not the laments in this book).

Lamentations is a theological explanation of the exile and destruction of Jerusalem. The days of Israel's reliance on the Lord's covenant, established with Israel at Sinai, were over. The covenant, or rather, Israel's disobedience, had led to the punishment of the exile.

I. The City of Jerusalem (1:1 – 22)

The author begins by describing Jerusalem as it lay in ruins after the Babylonian destruction (vv.1–4). Jerusalem, like a forsaken widow, weeps bitterly in the night, with no one to comfort her (1:1–2). There were no more appointed feasts (v.4), all her gates were desolate (v.4), her priests were groaning (v.4), and she had become the slave of her enemies (v.5). The author points out, however, the reason behind Jerusalem's misfortune: "The Lord has brought her grief because of her many sins" (v.5).

II. Israel's Enemy (2:1 – 22)

In ch. 2 the author gives full vent to the notion that Israel's enemy has now become the Lord himself: "The Lord is like an enemy; he has swallowed up Israel. He has swallowed up all her palaces and destroyed her strongholds. He has multiplied mourning and lamentation for Daughter Judah" (v.5).

III. Despair and Comfort (3:1 – 66)

In ch. 3 the author again expresses the idea that it was the Lord himself who brought on the destruction of Jerusalem; this brings him to the brink of despair (3:17 – 18). At this very point, however, the writer pauses to remember that not all hope is lost. There is one final source of comfort — God's loyal love, his covenant faithfulness, and his compassion never cease (v.22). "This I call to mind," he says, "and therefore I have hope" (v.21). Out of the midst of the deepest despair of the exile spring new rays of hope: "Great is your faithfulness" (v.23). With this hope comes a new call to life and faith in the Lord.

At the present time, however, the exile is real. The judgments must be endured. But a new way of life is called for in the light of this new hope in God's promises — a life of waiting silently for the salvation of God (vv.26 – 31). Thus in vv.39 – 42, the writer calls for repentance and confession of guilt, and then lapses again into the grief of the present hour — the horror of the exile and of the destruction of Jerusalem (vv.43 – 48).

The last sections of ch. 3 record a new note amid the voice of ruin, a call for God to recompense those who brought on this destruction (i.e., the Babylonians): "LORD, you have seen the wrong done to me. Uphold my cause!" (v.59); "Pay them back what they deserve, LORD, for what their hands have done" (v.64; see also v.66).

IV. Anticipation of Return (4:1 – 22)

In ch. 4 the poet continues to describe the tremendous devastation of the Promised Land, concentrating especially on the effects of the siege of Jerusalem on the people. But there is also the anticipation of a return from this exile: "Your punishment will end, Daughter Zion; he will not prolong your exile" (v.22a).

V. The Poet's Prayer (5:1 – 22)

The final chapter is in the form of a prayer. The author asks the Lord to look on what has been happening to his people. He acknowledges that it was decades of sin that caused this pain and suffering (v.7). He closes his prayer by asserting God's eternity (v.19) and by asking God to restore and renew his chastised people (vv.20 – 22).

EZEKIEL

Introduction

Ezekiel began his prophetic ministry in the fifth year of Jehoiachin's exile (1:2; 592 BC); the latest date in the book is the twenty-seventh year of Jehoiachin's exile (29:17; 570 BC). Ezekiel was living among the exiles in Babylon and carried out his prophetic ministry there.

The historical events that are important in the book are the rise of the Babylonian Empire and the rise of the land of "Magog" — the next Gentile ruling nation of importance. Gog is mentioned as the "chief prince of Meshek and Tubal" in 38:2 (Rosh in NIV note), but it is not easily identified from historical records. It may be intended as a symbol of a great empire that was yet to rise and take a stand against God's people in the prophet's own day or in the eschatological future.

As Ezekiel opens, the first wave of exiles to Babylon had taken place and the second was pending (cf. 1:2; 2Ki 24:12ff.).

I. Introduction (1:1 – 3)

For the most part the book of Ezekiel is written in the first person, with the prophet himself as the narrator. Although that is also the case in 1:1, the next two verses are clearly the work of someone other than the prophet, for he writes: "The hand of the LORD was on him [Ezekiel]" (v.3). His purpose of interrupting Ezekiel was to clarify the otherwise ambiguous date in 1:1, "in [the] thirtieth year." The NIV interprets this year as referring to Ezekiel's age when he first received his vision. In any case, five years after the first exiles were taken from Judah, Ezekiel saw the heavens opened and received "visions of God."

The first group of visions contains mostly words of judgment against God's people who still remained in Judah and Jerusalem. These were the people who would later be taken captive by Nebuchadnezzar. Interspersed in these words of doom and judgment are also many words of comfort and hope. Beginning in ch. 34, these become the major focus of the book.

II. Judgment against God's People Israel and Judah (1:4 – 24:27)

A. Ezekiel's Call (1:4 – 3:27)

The book opens with a description of Ezekiel's divine call. From the midst of "a windstorm coming out of the north," Ezekiel saw the appearance of God's glory (1:4 – 28). Falling facedown, he heard a voice saying that he was to go to the rebellious nation of Israel (2:1 – 8) and proclaim to them the words of "lament and mourning and woe," written for him on a scroll (2:9 – 3:11). Ezekiel was then taken by the Spirit "to the exiles who lived at Tel Aviv" (3:12 – 15), where he was told to be a "watchman" for the people. The guilt of the people was upon his shoulders if he failed to warn them of their need to repent (vv.16 – 27). He was allowed only to speak when God put his words in his mouth (vv.26 – 27). After Jerusalem was destroyed, when God had words of comfort for his people, Ezekiel's mouth was opened (33:22).

B. The Announcement of the Fall of Jerusalem (4:1 – 7:27)

Ezekiel's first words of warning come as a series of symbolic acts, each picturing some aspect of the impending destruction of Jerusalem. He first laid siege to the city inscribed on a clay tablet (4:1 – 3). He then lay on his side for 430 days (vv.4 – 8), eating wheat and barley to symbolize the defiled food the Israelites would eat while living among the nations in exile (vv.9 – 17). Then he shaved his hair and beard, burning a third, striking a third with a sword, and scattering the rest in all directions (5:1 – 4), symbolizing Jerusalem's destruction and scattering among the nations (vv.5 – 17). The small portion of hair that Ezekiel was told to "tuck … away in the folds of [his] garment" (v.3) apparently was meant to symbolize the eventual salvation of a remnant after God's anger against Israel had subsided (v.13).

In graphic detail, the prophet describes the impending destruction of Judah and its structures of idolatry (6:1 – 7:27). The destruction would come from "sword, famine and plague" (6:11) — an "unheard-of disaster" that would mark "the end" of Israel's possession of the land (7:5-6). Ezekiel presumably had in mind the final destruction of the kingdom by "the most wicked of the nations to take possession of their houses" (v.24) — Babylon, though not mentioned by name. Ezekiel may already be viewing the destruction of Jerusalem in eschatological terms and not merely in terms of the immediate destruction by Nebuchadnezzar. That Ezekiel has a perspective on the final days of history is clear from chs. 36-39.

C. The Temple Vision (8:1 – 12:20)

In the sixth year of the first wave of exiles, Ezekiel envisioned the various forms of apostasy within Jerusalem (8:4-18). There was an idol at the entrance north of the gate of the altar (vv.5-6). Seventy elders were in the temple, each with a shrine to his own idol (vv.7-13). Women were mourning for Tammuz, a foreign deity (vv.14-15), and twenty-five Israelite men were bowing down to the sun in the east (vv.16-18). This is why the Lord was angry with Israel and determined to bring down his wrath (v.18).

As a result, the glory of the Lord departed from the temple (9:1-11:25). When Solomon built the temple and the ark of the covenant was brought into it (1Ki 8:1-9), "the glory of the LORD filled his temple" (1Ki 8:11). Now, because of the extreme wickedness and apostasy of the people, that glory was taken away. Ezekiel first saw God's glory gradually move from above the cherubim to the threshold of the temple (9:3), and then to the entrance of the east gate (10:18-19), where it left the temple and the city (11:22-25). It was through the same east gate that the glory of the Lord would eventually return to the temple in the last days when Israel was restored and the temple rebuilt (43:4).

After the vision, Ezekiel packed his belongings and, in full view of the people, set out on a journey to symbolize the coming exile of Jerusalem (12:1-20). He dug through the walls of the city and carried his belongings on his shoulders (v.7). To the curious onlookers, Ezekiel explained the meaning of his act: " 'This prophecy concerns the prince in Jerusalem and all Israelites who are there.'... As I have done, so it will be done to them" (vv.10-11).

D. Popular Sayings Explained (12:21 – 19:14)

The next major section of this book gathers together a series of responses to popular sayings among the exiles apparently used by those in exile to justify their complacency in following God's law. Ezekiel thus sets out to refute these sayings and thereby to turn the people's attention back to God.

Saying 1. "The days go by and every vision comes to nothing" (12:21–23). This saying was intended to call into question the validity of the prophet's word of judgment since Jerusalem still lay intact and unharmed. But Ezekiel's word was that God would soon "put an end to this proverb" (v.23). The day of judgment was near; "it shall be fulfilled without delay" (v.25).

Saying 2. "These men have set up idols in their hearts and put wicked stumbling blocks before their faces. Should I let them inquire of me at all?" (14:1–11) The saying is cast in the form of a question, a puzzle. Its answer is ironic. Such idolatrous people may inquire of the Lord, but the Lord would answer them with severe judgment.

Saying 3. "Even if these three men — Noah, Daniel and Job — were in it, they could save only themselves by their righteousness" (v.14). The saying assumes that the people were relying on the righteousness of some among them or of their forefathers for their security with God. God's response, however, is that divine judgment cannot be averted merely by the righteousness of a select few. The righteous will be saved but the wicked will perish (vv.12–23).

Saying 4. "How is the wood of a vine different from that of a branch from any of the trees in the forest?" (15:1–8). This saying assumes a knowledge of the value of the wood of a vine and that of a tree. The wood of a vine, like Jerusalem, is good for nothing but burning.

Saying 5. "Your father was an Amorite and your mother a Hittite" (16:3, 45). This saying introduces an extended allegory of God's dealings with Judah and Jerusalem (vv.1–63). They are seen as part and parcel of their Canaanite and pagan neighbors. The section ends with a recalling of God's covenant promises of blessing to Israel "in the days of [their] youth" (v.60). Thus, it ends on the positive note of a prophecy of hope (vv.60–63).

Saying 6. Chapter 17 consists of an allegory (vv.1–10) with an interpretation (17:11–21). Within the allegory, the first eagle is Babylon, the vine is Israel taken into captivity, and the second eagle is Egypt, to whom Israel looked for help instead of trusting in God. But this image gives rise to another allegory, picturing a redeemed Israel as a young shoot of a cedar tree planted "on a high and lofty mountain" (17:22–24; cf. Isa 4:2).

Saying 7. "The parents eat sour grapes, and the children's teeth are set on edge" (18:1–32). This saying appears to acknowledge the validity of the prophet's announcement of impending judgment, expressing a fatalistic interpretation of it: What can the sons do about divine judgment if it comes because of the sin of the fathers? Ezekiel countered this saying with another: "The one who sins is the one who will die" (v.4). God's judgment could be averted through repentance (see vv.31–32).

Saying 8. "What a lioness was your mother among the lions!" (19:1–9). This saying, and the one that follows, are based on an ironic application of the prophecy of Jacob in Ge 49:8–12 to the kings of Judah. Ezekiel recalls that Judah did become a young lion (Eze 19:3; cf. Ge 49:9), but, he adds, Judah was soon carried off to Egypt with no hope of wielding the scepter. Another strong lion came from the tribe of Judah, however. This was the house of David.

Saying 9. "Your mother was like a vine in your vineyard planted by the water" (19:10–14). In Ge 49:8–12 Jacob had pictured the mighty ruler from the tribe of Judah tethering "his donkey to a vine, his colt to the choicest branch" (49:11). Thus, looking at the kingship in the time of David, Ezekiel says of Judah, "Your mother was like a vine.... Its branches were strong, fit for a ruler's scepter" (Eze 19:10–11). But now in the exile, the house of David "was uprooted in fury and thrown to the ground.... No strong branch is left on it fit for a ruler's scepter" (vv.12–14).

E. God's Dealings with Israel (20:1–44)

Ezekiel now surveys Israel's history with a view toward "the detestable practices of their fathers" (20:4b). He begins with the time of Israel's sojourn in Egypt (20:1–9). According to Ezekiel (though this is not noted in the Pentateuch), the Israelites had forsaken God and followed after the gods of Egypt during their sojourn there. They had set their eyes on "the vile images" and "the idols of Egypt" (v.7).

The situation was no better during their time in the desert (vv.10–26). The people rebelled against God, rejected his laws, and did not follow his decrees (v.13). When Israel entered the Promised Land, the situation went from bad to worse (vv.27–29).

Turning to his own day, Ezekiel envisioned a new exodus for God's people (vv.30–38), one that included both judgment (vv.34–36) and the hope of salvation in the form of a new "covenant" (vv.37–38). This time is not a return from exile; rather, it is a time of purging God's people of "those who revolt and rebel" against God (v.38).

F. Impending Judgment (20:45–24:27)

Having presented the main lines of judgment and salvation that awaited God's people, Ezekiel now turned to describe the specific aspects of the divine judgment. He looked first at the judgment about to fall on the southern regions of the land, i.e., the land of Judah (20:45–49). He then centered his prophetic word on the city of Jerusalem and the temple (21:1–27).

The judgment Ezekiel had in view was the destruction of the city by the Babylonians (21:19). The king of Judah would be removed until the true King came to claim the throne promised him long ago in the days of the forefathers (v.27; cf. Ge 49:10). Why was Jerusalem singled out among the other nations? Because it was a "city of bloodshed," and its people had not kept God's laws (22:1–16). The first commandment in the Sinai covenant was the prohibition of idolatry (Ex 20:2–6). Thus Ezekiel's indictment of the people was that they had become defiled by the idols they had made (22:4). Furthermore, Ezekiel charged them with breaking virtually all of the Ten Commandments (vv.6–12).

Turning to the remnant of the "people of Israel," Ezekiel describes the fate they would share with the inhabitants of Jerusalem (vv.17–22) as the result of the sins of the rest of "the land" (vv.23–31). With this broader perspective of the sins of the whole nation in view, Ezekiel recounts an extended allegory of the "two sisters," Oholah and Oholibah (ch. 23). Oholah (the northern kingdom) means "she who dwells in her own tent [tabernacle]." It thus views that kingdom from the perspective of the false worship centers set up by Jeroboam I (cf. 1Ki 12–13). Oholibah (the southern kingdom) means "My tent [tabernacle] is with her," which looks at the fact that the true temple of God was in Jerusalem. Oholah and Oholibah are portrayed as promiscuous young women flirting with their foreign lovers, Assyria and Babylon. In disgust, God had given them over to their lovers, and their lovers had brutally abused them (23:1–49).

The visions of Ezekiel regarding the divine judgment against Jerusalem and the temple close with a striking image of the horror and disbelief of the people on hearing of the temple's ruin. The temple was "their stronghold, their joy and glory, the delight of their eyes, their heart's desire" (v.25). The numbness that Ezekiel felt on hearing of his wife's death, "the delight of [his] eyes," was intended to symbolize the people's own quiet groaning (v. 17) on hearing of the ruin of the temple (vv. 15–27).

III. Judgment against the Nations (25:1 – 32:32)

Ezekiel now announces divine judgment against the nations for their mistreatment of Israel. The basis of his oracles was God's promise to Abraham, "whoever curses you I will curse" (Ge 12:3). The nations enumerated in this list of oracles were to be destroyed because they rejoiced at the destruction of God's people: Amnon (25:1–7), Moab (vv.8–11), Edom (vv.12–14), Philistia (vv.15–17), Tyre (26:1–28:19), Sidon (28:20–23), and Egypt (29:1–32:32). Imbedded in these oracles is a reminder of the hope that still lay ahead for the people of Israel (28:24–26); this section anticipates the theme of the second half of the book (chs. 33–48).

IV. Future Blessing for Israel (33:1 – 48:35)

A. Summary (33:1 – 20)

Chapter 33 restates and summarizes the two central themes of the preceding chapters. Ezekiel's role as a watchman for Israel is recast in 33:7 – 9 as a virtual restatement of 3:17 – 19, and the expression of God's desire for repentance (33:11 – 20) is repeated from 18:23 – 29. Thus, Ezekiel returns to the importance of Israel's repentance. The basis of his grounding Israel's salvation in their repentance is found in the theology of Ge 18:19: if the descendants of Abraham would "keep the way of the LORD by doing what is right and just," God would fulfill his promises to the fathers. This is the theology of the new covenant so clearly expressed in the second half of Ezekiel (cf. 36:27).

B. Restoration of the House of David (34:1 – 35:15)

With the announcement of the fall of Jerusalem (33:21 – 33) and thus the fulfillment of Ezekiel's oracles of divine judgment, the prophet's visions turn to that of the restoration of the house of David (34:1 – 31). The fulfillment of Ezekiel's oracles serves to demonstrate the validity of his role as a prophet (33:33). That, in turn, serves as a basis for the reader's hope in the fulfillment of Ezekiel's words of blessing.

Based on God's promise to David in 2Sa 7:16, Ezekiel saw a time when God's people would be regathered from among all the nations and return to the land (34:13 – 22). God would place his servant David over them as shepherd (v.23) and prince (v.24). Undoubtedly Ezekiel used the notion of the kingship of David as a figure of the Messiah. This is particularly clear in the idyllic scene described in 34:25 – 31, a virtual return to the conditions of the garden of Eden.

In keeping with the picture of David's kingship as a messianic figure, the writer records a prophetic oracle against Edom (35:1 – 15). Not only was David the king who successfully conquered and ruled over Edom (2Sa 8:14), but also this was specifically prophesied of the Messiah in Nu 24:18. Thus by focusing on the ruin of Edom here, the writer shows that the prophecy in Nu 24 still had its fulfillment in the future.

C. Restoration of the People of God (36:1 – 39:29)

The house of David would be restored, Israel's enemies would be defeated, and God's people would return to the land and receive a new heart (36:1 – 38). This is the new covenant, pictured here as a fulfillment of God's promise through Moses in Dt 30:4 – 6 (e.g., "The LORD your God will circumcise your hearts and the hearts of your descendants, so that you may love him with all your heart and with all your soul, and live").

The restoration of God's people is graphically pictured in the scene of the valley of dry bones (37:1–10) and its explanation (37:11–14). All Israel would again be united in a new Davidic kingdom (37:15–28). In those days Israel's enemies would be sorely defeated (38:1–39:24) and God's people would enjoy peace and safety at last in their own land (39:25–29).

D. Restoration of the Temple (40:1 – 48:35)

Ezekiel's final vision is that of the new temple in Jerusalem. The writer includes much detail, holding the grand picture of this temple before the eyes of the reader as long as possible. The restoration of the temple meant the culmination of all God's promises of blessing and fellowship. One can sense the same intensity of feeling for the new temple here in Ezekiel as in the depiction of the new Jerusalem in Revelation. Both are pictures of the same reality—the human race's enjoyment of God's presence and fellowship. It is a return to God's original intent for the human race in the garden of Eden (Ge 1–2).

For the writer of Ezekiel this could only be expressed in terms of the Mosaic covenant—the tabernacle and the temple. For John in Revelation, however, this was expressed by the incarnation of the Lamb of God and the replacement of the temple with the new Jerusalem (see Rev 21:22). He saw that God was present with his people (21:23–27), not merely in the temple, as is depicted in Ezekiel (Eze 48:35). The two visions of Ezekiel and John express the same ideas, but use different imagery. Note how John's images are derived from the OT.

The description of the new temple and its environs is given with little comment. From the mere description of it one gets a sense of its majesty and glory. The design and magnitude of the temple is left to speak for itself. Unlike the old temple that was destroyed by the Babylonian army, from which God's glory had departed (10:18–19), the glory of God filled this new temple (43:1–11). Like the old temple, however, this temple also was decorated with images of God's garden in Eden (41:17–19; 47:1–12; cf. comments on 1Ki 6).

DANIEL

Introduction

The prophet Daniel was a contemporary of Ezekiel. He is even mentioned in Eze 14:14, 20; 28:3. Although Daniel lived earlier than Esther, the events in his life were similar to hers. Both Daniel and Esther (and Joseph too) rose to a place of high position in the court of a foreign king. God used their positions to save his people from annihilation. In the lives of these three individuals we can see God's hand at work in the details of everyday life.

I. An Introduction to the Book (1:1 – 21)

Daniel 1 clarifies a number of features of this book and gives a broader context to the events recorded. The abrupt change in language from Hebrew to the language of the Chaldeans (Aramaic) in 2:4, for example, is anticipated by the story of Daniel and his friends learning this language (see 1:4b). Moreover, the chief characters of the book—Daniel, Shadrach, Meshach, Abednego, and Nebuchadnezzar—are each inducted into the court of King Nebuchadnezzar.

II. Nebuchadnezzar's Dream (2:1 – 49)

The narrative of ch. 2 contains the account of Nebuchadnezzar's dream and Daniel's interpretation. This dream with its interpretation provides the conceptual framework for most of the events and visions that follow. According to Daniel's interpretation, God has shown in Nebuchadnezzar's dream not only the whole panorama of the future of his and subsequent human kingdoms in this world but also the plan that God has for his own chosen people.

FIGURE 1

The Vision (Da 2:31–35)	The Interpretation (within the passage)
– A huge shining statue. – Head of pure gold. – Chest and arms of silver. – Belly and thighs of bronze. – Legs of iron. – Feet of iron and pottery. – Rock cut out, not by human hands; it struck the statue on the feet of iron and clay and crushed them. – The whole statue was pulverized and was swept away by the wind. It could no longer be found. – The rock became a large mountain and filled the whole land.	– Nebuchadnezzar represents world domination (2:37-38). – Another kingdom (downward or limited) (2:39a). – A third kingdom which will be over all the world (2:39b). – A fourth kingdom which will be stronger than the others (2:40). – A divided kingdom will arise, still characterized by the strength of iron but weakened by being part pottery in the [ten] toes (2:41–42). – There will be mixing of the seed of man and lack of cohesion in the kingdom (2:43). – "In the days of those kings" God will raise up an eternal kingdom (2:44a). – God's kingdom will destroy "all kingdoms" and will stand forever (2:44b). – Daniel and his three friends given authority over all of Babylon just as the saints in God's kingdom will take over the authority of the four kings (2:48-49). – The fact that Daniel was able to recount the dream shows that God is revealing these future events and that the interpretation is true (2:45).

The statue in Nebuchadnezzar's dream represented the flow of events of human history up to and including the time when God would destroy all the kingdoms of the earth and establish his own eternal kingdom. It should be noted that only Nebuchadnezzar's reign is identified by Daniel—he was the head of gold. Though numerous attempts have been made to identify the other kingdoms, the text itself does not do so. Rather than attempting to identify each of the four kingdoms, it makes more sense to take the entire statue as a representation of all earthly kingdoms and ask what Daniel's interpretation says about these kingdoms.

A common interpretation has been to identify the four metals with the kingdoms of Babylon, Medo-Persia, Greece, and Rome. The fifth kingdom, then (the falling rock that became a huge mountain), happened during the time of the Roman Empire—often seen as the birth of Jesus and the establishment of the church.

A better approach is to view the statue and the kingdoms simply as images of failed human attempts to find God's blessing. This is why the various aspects of the statue show a marked deterioration in value and strength. The metals decrease in value; the second kingdom is "inferior" (v.39) to the first; the last kingdom is a mixture of iron and clay and "will not remain united, any more than iron mixes with clay" (v.43). Thus, humanity's efforts to unite and find divine blessing become increasingly weaker and more chaotic until the end comes, when God's kingdom will replace human kingdoms. God's kingdom will remain forever.

III. Nebuchadnezzar's Image (3:1 – 30)

In ch. 3 the statue set up by Nebuchadnezzar seems intentionally linked to the dream in ch. 2. In doing so, the author casts the events of ch. 3 so that they become an instance in the larger meaning of the dream. In the events of ch. 3 we see a picture of what is required of the faithful who must wait patiently for the coming of God's kingdom. While waiting, God's people are to be like Shadrach, Meshach, and Abednego and not bow the knee to any human kingdom.

The readers, in the face of the worsening conditions of humankind forecast in the dream of ch. 2, receive the example of these three men. Their words to Nebuchadnezzar are a thematic reminder of the message of the book as a whole: "If we are thrown into the blazing furnace, the God we serve is able to deliver us from it, and he will deliver us from Your Majesty's hand" (v.17). Even if God did not rescue them, they would still not serve Nebuchadnezzar's gods (v.18).

There may also be a link between the events in ch. 3 and the vision in ch. 7. In ch. 3 the men who cast the faithful three into the furnace are consumed by the fire, while in ch. 7 the fourth beast who makes war with the saints is destroyed by fire. Moreover, in ch. 6 the king's counselors are crushed and destroyed by the lions just as the nations are crushed and destroyed by the fourth beast in ch. 7.

IV. Nebuchadnezzar's Second Dream (4:1 – 37)

Nebuchadnezzar's kingdom is likened in ch. 4 to a tree that grows till "it [is] visible to the ends of the earth" (v.11). It is thus contrasted with the kingdom of God, which begins as a stone and becomes a mountain that fills the whole earth (2:34 – 35).

There are also striking parallels between Daniel and King Nebuchadnezzar here and Joseph and the pharaoh in Ge 31 – 42. For example, just as Pharaoh was given two dreams to underscore the certainty of their fulfillment (Ge 41:32), Nebuchadnezzar also had two dreams, each signifying the same basic idea: the contrast of the kingdom of God and human kingdoms. Both Pharaoh's dreams and Nebuchadnezzar's are centered on a period of divine blessing and abundance followed by a period of divine judgment. Both conclude with a warning about a period of seven years of judgment (Ge 41:27). Finally, both the pharaoh and Nebuchadnezzar must acknowledge that their greatness has come only through the grace and power of the God of heaven (Ge 41:32 – 39; Da 4:27): "The Most High is sovereign over all kingdoms on earth and gives them to anyone he wishes" (4:17).

V. Belshazzar's Feast (5:1 – 31)

Belshazzar's kingdom "is divided and given to the Medes and Persians" (v.28), which suggests an intentional link with the "divided kingdom" of iron and clay in Nebuchadnezzar's dream (2:41). Moreover, in his interpretation of the handwriting on the wall, Daniel contrasts Belshazzar's divided kingdom with the splendor and glory of his father Nebuchadnezzar's (vv.18 – 23). Thus, like the dream in ch. 2, the "greatness and glory" of the kingdom of Nebuchadnezzar are contrasted with the "divided" and "wanting" kingdom that marks the end (2:41 – 43; 5:27 – 28).

VI. Daniel in the Lion's Den (6:1 – 28)

At the close of ch. 6, Darius proclaimed that God "is the living God and he endures forever; his kingdom will not be destroyed" (v.26). These words, similar to those in Daniel's interpretation of Nebuchadnezzar's dream in 2:44, link the events of this chapter to that interpretation. Just as the focus of

Daniel's interpretation was God's eternal kingdom, so the focus of the series of narratives that follows is also the eternal kingdom of God. The message of the narratives thus continuously reinforces Daniel's interpretation in ch. 2.

There is also a link between the events of ch. 6 and Daniel's vision in ch. 7. Just as Nebuchadnezzar dreamed of a statue with a golden head (ch. 2) and then made a golden statue (ch. 3), so also in ch. 6 Daniel was thrown into a den of lions and then, in ch. 7, saw a vision of wild beasts, the first of which was a lion. Moreover, Daniel is rescued from the wild beasts, just as the saints of the Most High are to be rescued from the fourth beast (7:21–22).

FIGURE 2

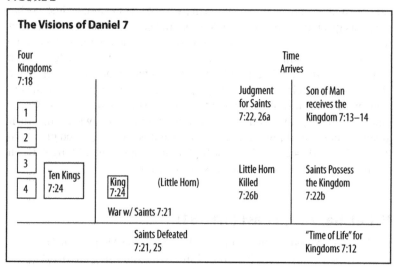

The Visions of Daniel 7

Four Kingdoms 7:18			Time Arrives	
1			Judgment for Saints 7:22, 26a	Son of Man receives the Kingdom 7:13–14
2				
3	Ten Kings 7:24	King 7:24 (Little Horn)	Little Horn Killed 7:26b	Saints Possess the Kingdom 7:22b
4		War w/ Saints 7:21		
		Saints Defeated 7:21, 25		"Time of Life" for Kingdoms 7:12

VII. The Visions of the Four Beasts, the Son of Man, and the Ancient of Days (7:1 – 28)

The visions in ch. 7 are not only central in importance to the book of Daniel, but they also provide the basis for much of the eschatological and messianic hope in the remainder of the Bible. Almost anywhere in the Bible where the Messiah is spoken of, one will find that the basic imagery and central concepts are shaped by the visions of this chapter. Central to these visions is the appearance of the "son of man" coming in the clouds to receive the eternal kingdom from "the Ancient of Days" (vv.13–14). The imagery and ideas found here are not new. They are taken from earlier biblical texts in the Pentateuch and the historical books. Chief among these is 2Sa 7, the promise of an eternal kingship in Jerusalem that God made to the house of David.

In general terms the visions of ch. 7 show a contrast between human kingdoms and the kingdom of God. The four beasts, which represent human kingdoms, rise up from the sea. By contrast, the "one like the son of man" descends out of the clouds. The description of the four beasts is viewed, as it were, from sea level, the perspective of one standing on earth, whereas we look upon the scene of the "son of man" and "Ancient of Days" as if we ourselves were standing in the throne room in heaven.

A. The First Vision (7:1 – 6)

The imagery of the four winds of heaven blowing over the great sea (v.2) has many parallels in the OT (cf. Ge 1:2; 8:1; Ex 14:21; 15:10; Eze 1:4); thus, a certain appreciation for the rest of the OT seems prerequisite to the vision. The four beasts arising out of the great sea, each one different from the other (v.3), contrast with that of the son of man, who arises out of heaven.

The first beast was like a lion, with eagle's wings (v.4). As Daniel watched, the beast's wings were plucked out, it was raised off the ground and set upon feet like a human being, and a human heart was given to it. No further description of the first beast is given, nor is there a subsequent interpretation of this beast. If correlated with the vision in ch. 2, this beast is the head of gold, Babylon (Nebuchadnezzar; cf. 2:38). Perhaps the lifting of the lion upon the feet of a human being is an allusion to the image in ch. 2 that stood upon its feet.

FIGURE 3

The Vision (Da 7:1–6)	The Interpretation (within the passage)
– Four winds blowing into the sea. – Four beasts rising out of the sea (3). – 1st like a lion with eagle's wings. – Wings plucked out; lifted off ground; stood on ground like a man; heart like a man given to it. – 2d like a bear; one side lifted; three ribs in its mouth. They said to it, "Eat much flesh." – Another (3d) like a leopard; four wings on its back; four heads; authority given to it.	– These are four kingdoms rising from the land (7:17).

The second beast, resembling a bear (v.5), is often identified with Persia or Medo-Persia (cf. 8:20). It was perhaps raised on one side because after the fall of Babylon, the kingdom of Persia waited one year for the reign of the Medes. There is no standard interpretation for the three ribs in its mouth.

The beast with four wings and four heads (v.6) is commonly identified as Alexander the Great, whose kingdom was divided into four when he died. Others identify this beast with Persia. The text does not identify the king or the kingdom represented by this beast, nor is there any indication that we are to seek an identification. The beasts, like the metals in the statue in ch. 2, appear only collectively to represent human government in its entirety. It is to this kingdom that the kingdom given to the Son of Man stands in opposition.

B. Elements of the Second Vision(s) (7:7 – 12)

1. Part 1: The fourth beast (7:7 – 8)

The fourth beast has no likeness to a known animal. Perhaps something like the beast in Isa 27:1 is in view. Perhaps the vision of the fourth beast occurs on a different night than the previous three ones (cf. v.7). Some say that the ten horns represent the ten kings of Rome preceding Vespasian, who destroyed the second temple, and that the little horn is Titus who, according to tradition, defiled the temple.

2. Part 2: The Ancient of Days (7:9 – 10)

This is God who now sits in judgment on the fourth beast and those that preceded it and who have oppressed him. The "books" contain the transgressions and evils they have committed.

3. Part 3: The Beast Slain (7:11 – 12)

The little horn speaking proud words is removed, and the kingdom of the rest of the kings is removed. Some relate this part to Rev 19:20, where the Beast and the False Prophet are cast alive into the lake of fire at the time of Christ's second coming. It appears in v.12 that the rest of the beasts are still around after the destruction of the fourth beast. A time in life is given to them until the appointed day of the battle of Gog and Magog. According to others, v.12 precedes v.11 so that by the time the fourth beast is destroyed, the other beasts have used up their extension of time. The sense is that each kingdom has its time of rule, followed by a survival after its downfall and transition to the next kingdom.

C. Elements of the Third Vision (7:13 – 27)

FIGURE 4

The Vision (Da 7:7–22)	The Interpretation (within the passage)
– Fourth beast exceedingly dreadful.	– Fourth kingdom will be in the land (23a).
– Large iron teeth.	
– Claws of bronze (7:19).	– Will consume, tread, crush (23b).
– Consuming, crushing the others with its feet.	– Will be different (23a).
– Different from the others.	– Ten kings will arise (24a).
– Ten horns.	– Another king will arise among the ten kings (24b).
– Another, little horn, coming up among the ten horns.	– He will defeat three of the kings (25b).
– Little horn uprooted three of the ten horns.	– He will speak against the most high (25a).
– Little horn has eyes like a man.	– He will wear away (harass) the saints (25a).
– Little horn speaks great (words).	
– Little horn made war with the saints (7:21).	– He will intend to change times and law (25b).
– Little horn prevailed against saints (7:21).	– The saints will be put in his hands for a time, times, half a time (25b).
– Thrones set up; Ancient of days sits.	– Judgment will sit (26a).
– Ancient of days wears white garments and has hair white as wool.	
– His throne surrounded by fire; has wheels of fire and a river of fire.	
– Multitudes surround the throne.	
– Judgment (court) sits.	
– Judgment given for the saints (7:22).	
– Books are opened.	

1. The kingdom given to the Son of Man (7:13 – 14)

The one like "a son of man," the Messiah, comes to the Ancient of Days, who is sitting in judgment on the nations. The kingdoms of the nations are given to this same person. He is likened to the beasts (possessing all dominion), and the Israelites are likened to the son of man, humble and pure.

Some recognize that the figure of the son of man in ch. 7 does not entirely fit a collective interpretation (i.e., the Israelites as a whole); they argue that this chapter is the result of a reinterpretation of an original individual figure and its application to the nation as a whole. The nation is viewed in the figure of the eschatological individual.

Note first that, according to v.14, the kingdom is given to the son of man. In v.18, however, it is "the holy people of the Most High" who are to receive the kingdom. When, in v.22, the vision of vv.13–14 is reiterated, we are told that judgment is given to the people of the Most High and that they are to possess the kingdom. Thus, in v.22, additions are made to the original vision of v.14 that correspond to the subsequent interpretation in v.18.

The further interpretation of v.14 that follows in this chapter (v.27) is inconclusive. First, it may be read either as (lit.) "the people of the saints of the Most High" are to be given the kingdom, or "the people, the saints," are to be given the kingdom (v.27). The first reading suggests that the people and the saints are not the same and thus, if the saint(s) of the Most High is the son of man, then the people of the son of man are given the kingdom. The clearest indication that an individual divine figure is in view in v.14 is the fact that the one to whom the kingdom is given will be worshiped by "all nations and peoples of every language" (v.14). It is unlikely that Daniel would envision this for the people of the kingdom.

2. The interpretation (7:15 – 27)

We offer two classic interpretations here. An older Jewish interpretation sees Israel as taking the land from Edom, which is the fourth kingdom, Rome. The horn of v.8 made war with Israel (the saints). The ten horns are ten kings from the same kingdom. After these kings, another will arise, who is Titus. He will oppress Israel and attempt to get them to transgress their feast days and laws. No one knows how long this will prevail ("a time, times and half a time").

A modern interpretation sees the "holy people" as the saved of all ages as well as the holy angels. The kingdom possessed by "the saints of the Most High," while eternal, may easily include the millennial kingdom and the eternal rule of God that follows. The little horn is the outstanding person at the end of the ages who will be destroyed when the kingdom comes from heaven. "A time, times, and half a time" refer to the last three and one-half years preceding the second advent of Christ, who will bring in the final form of God's kingdom on earth. There is nothing in ch. 7 of Daniel to alter the conclusion that the fourth empire is Rome, that its final state has not yet been fulfilled, and that it is a genuine prophetic revelation of God's program for human history.

FIGURE 5

The Vision	The Interpretation (within the passage)
– Little horn speaking great words.	– His authority removed (26b).
– The (4th) beast is killed; his body destroyed; thrown into fire.	– He is destroyed until the end (26b).
– The other beasts lose their power and are given a time of life "until a time, times, and half a time."	– Saints receive the kingdom (7:18).
– Until the time arrives (7:22b).	– The kingdom and authority are given to the people of the saints (27a).
– One like a son of man comes in the clouds.	– All authorities will worship him (27b).
– He comes up to the Ancient of days.	– His kingdom is forever (27b).
– Authority and kingship are given to him (7:14).	
– Saints possess the kingdom (7:22).	
– All nations worship him.	
– His authority is forever.	
– His kingdom will not pass away.	

VIII. Additional Visions (8:1 – 27)

The goat with four prominent horns is interpreted as four kingdoms from a nation, but without that nation's power (v.22). The parallel sense of "power" in ch. 7 is political "authority" (7:6, 12). The leopard with four heads "was given" its political authority. Since this authority is not mentioned of the other beasts in ch. 7, it appears to match the special mention of "not by his own power" in the present chapter. This suggests that the four kingdoms are not all considered from the authority and power of this one nation and hence leaves open the identity of at least one of the four kingdoms as not from the lineage of the one nation, Greece. If so, then the little horn that comes from one of these four kingdoms in ch. 8 may be the same as the little horn of ch. 7, which comes from the fourth beast, Rome. This would solve the problem of having to identify the four kingdoms with a particular moment in time when the rulers of Greece were in fact, four (usually, the number of Greek rulers during this period exceeded four); thus the four kingdoms here may have been determined from the general schema of four kingdoms throughout Daniel.

FIGURE 6

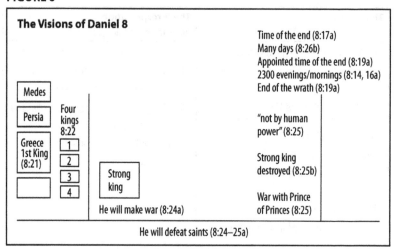

The Visions of Daniel 8

Time of the end (8:17a)
Many days (8:26b)
Appointed time of the end (8:19a)
2300 evenings/mornings (8:14, 16a)
End of the wrath (8:19a)

Medes

Persia — Four kings 8:22

Greece 1st King (8:21) — 1, 2, 3, 4

Strong king

"not by human power" (8:25)

Strong king destroyed (8:25b)

War with Prince of Princes (8:25)

He will make war (8:24a)

He will defeat saints (8:24–25a)

FIGURE 7

The Vision (Da 8:1–14)	The Interpretation (within the passage)
– A ram with two horns, beside the canal. One horn longer.	– Vision for time of the end (8:17).
– Ram charged west, north and south.	– What will be at the end of the wrath (8:19).
– Goat with prominent horn came from the west.	– Ram is kings of Medes and Persia (8:20).
– Goat charged ram in great rage, shattering his two horns, knocking him to the ground and trampling on him.	– Goat is king of Greece, the big horn is first king (8:21).
– Goat became great, but large horn was broken off.	– It was broken (8:22).
– Goat grew four prominent horns in its place.	– Four kingdoms from a nation (8:22).
– A little horn came out from them and grew large.	– At end of their kingdom, when transgressors have finished (it = their kingdom), a strong king will arise (8:23).
– It became great to the hosts of the heavens.	– In his heart he became great (8:25a).
– It caused to fall from the hosts some of the stars and trampled them.	– He will destroy mighty men and holy people (8:24b).
	– When they are at rest, he will destroy many (8:25a).
	– Against the Prince of princes he will stand (8:25b).

– It grew until it reached the starry hosts.	– He will cause astounding devastation, will succeed in whatever he does (8:24).
– The continual offerings were removed.	
– The holy place was destroyed.	– In 2300 evenings and mornings, the holy place will be sanctified (8:14).
– God's people and the daily sacrifices were given over to the little horn.	– Without hands he will be destroyed (8:25b).
– It cast truth to the ground and made great success.	
– How long? (8:13)	
*Vision of the offering.	
*Transgression that destroys.	
*Giving of Holy place.	
*Trampling of the host.	

A little horn came out from them and grew large (v.9). This is interpreted that when the reign of the four kings ends, a strong king will arise and will increase in wickedness (v.23). Some identify the transgressors as Israel, and the end of their kingdom and the completion of their transgression as the destruction of the second temple in AD 70. If so, then the strong king is Titus. Others see "their kingdom" as Israel but see the strong king as Antiochus IV Epiphanes.

Note that the ram with two horns refers to the two kings of Medes and Persia (v.20) — thus one animal but two king(dom)s.

IX. The Messiah Is Cut Off (9:1 – 27)

Up to this point, the writer has focused on the theme of the establishment of God's eternal kingdom. His emphasis has been on the gradual decline of human kingdoms and the expectation of the sudden rise of the divine kingdom. When will this be fulfilled? Will it be at the return from Babylonian captivity, as may have been suggested by Jeremiah's prophecy? Or, will it come at a much later period? Daniel now provides the answer by extending the seventy years of Jeremiah's prophecy by a multiple of seven. An anointed one will come to establish an eternal kingdom after a time of seven and sixty-two weeks. With this chapter also comes a new idea of a delay in the establishment of the divine kingdom. When the Anointed One does come to establish the kingdom, he will be cut off; thus the fulfillment of the vision in Jeremiah is to be extended still further into the future, to the seventieth week.

It is important to note the major themes in Daniel's prayer of confession (vv.5–19), for they provide the basis not only for the delay in the fulfillment of God's promises but also for God's continued faithfulness to his promises. Daniel opens his prayer with a reminder of God's continual watchfulness over his people and his promises. He then recounts the sin of the people of Israel and their continued disobedience to God's covenant. Repeatedly, Daniel returns to the themes of the Pentateuch, particularly to Deuteronomy, stressing that Israel had failed to listen to the warnings of God's prophets and had thus been cast off from the land in exile. Daniel also acknowledges that Israel deserved the exile. But God is faithful and compassionate. He has chosen this people and the city of Jerusalem, and he will not abandon them now. Daniel thus earnestly prays for divine forgiveness and restoration of his people and his city Jerusalem.

The words of the angel Gabriel (vv.20–27) are a direct response to Daniel's prayer. God will forgive and restore Jerusalem, but it will not be at the end of the exile, i.e., in Daniel's own day. It will come in the distant future, after seventy weeks of years, in which the full measure of God's judgment of Israel will be expended.

Moreover, when Jeremiah's vision is fulfilled, it will still not mark the final fulfillment of the visions of Daniel, i.e., the establishment of the eternal kingdom of God. Unlike what we might have expected from the visions of the book so far, particularly Da 7, when the king comes, he will not receive the kingdom; rather, he will be cut off (vv.25–26). In the final week of years, the seventieth week, one final enemy will come who will destroy Jerusalem and the temple and commit a great sin of sacrilege against the God of heaven. The optimistic visions of the earlier part of the book of Daniel and the prophecies of Jeremiah are thus tempered by the realistic hope presented in this chapter. Much remains of the suffering and sorrow, but the end of the enemy "is decreed" (v.27) by an all-knowing and all-powerful God.

What is to be made of the time period covered by the sixty-nine weeks of years referred to in this passage? If we know how to identify the starting time, it is not difficult to calculate the time of the coming of the "Anointed One," but the starting point is not specified. It says merely, "From the time the word goes out to restore and rebuild Jerusalem until the Anointed One, the ruler, comes, there will be seven 'sevens,' and sixty-two 'sevens'" (v.25). Fortunately, the author of Nehemiah has provided a link between the events of his book and those here in Daniel. By alluding to this prophecy, Nehemiah provides the date of the twentieth year of King Artaxerxes (445 BC) as the time when the word was issued to rebuild the city of Jerusalem (Ne 2:1–9).

X. The Last Vision (10:1 – 11:45)

A. Introduction (10:1 – 11:1)

The vision in ch. 11 is given a lengthy introduction in ch. 10. Its purpose is stated succinctly in v.14, "I have come to explain to you what will happen to your people in the future, for the vision concerns a time yet to come." Thus not only is the vision about the future, but it is specifically about the eschatological future, the last days.

FIGURE 8

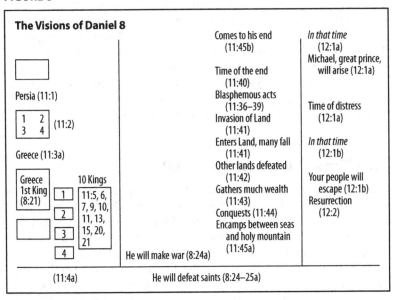

The Visions of Daniel 8

		Comes to his end (11:45b)	*In that time* (12:1a)
			Michael, great prince, will arise (12:1a)
Persia (11:1)		Time of the end (11:40)	
1 2 / 3 4 (11:2)		Blasphemous acts (11:36–39)	Time of distress (12:1a)
		Invasion of Land (11:41)	
Greece (11:3a)		Enters Land, many fall (11:41)	*In that time* (12:1b)
		Other lands defeated (11:42)	
Greece 1st King (8:21)	10 Kings 1 — 11:5, 6,	Gathers much wealth (11:43)	Your people will escape (12:1b)
	2 — 7, 9, 10, 11, 13,	Conquests (11:44)	Resurrection (12:2)
	3 — 15, 20, 21	Encamps between seas and holy mountain (11:45a)	
	4	He will make war (8:24a)	
(11:4a)		He will defeat saints (8:24–25a)	

B. The Vision Itself (11:2 – 45)

The vision begins with four kings who appear to parallel the four kingdoms of the earlier visions. These kings are all from the empire of Persia, followed by the kingdom of Greece. As in ch. 8, the vision focuses on the one strong Greek king and the subsequent division of his kingdom into four parts. The major political events of these four kingdoms are then enumerated through the reigns of ten kings (vv.5–35). There seems little disagreement that the fulfillment of this part of the vision came during the history of Israel in the Hellenistic age. The last of the ten kings is Antiochus IV, or perhaps Rome.

At the conclusion of the vision (vv.36–45), Daniel's attention is directed to another king, distinct from the kings of the North and the South who have thus far been the concern of the vision. This king will exalt himself against God and seek to overcome the other kingdoms and the Holy Land itself. The time of the coming of this king will be "the time of the end" (v.40). He is thus to be identified with the final king and kingdom in the other visions as the "little horn" (ch. 7), the "strong" king (ch. 8), and the statue that fell when the uncut stone struck it (ch. 2). At this time he will engage in a great war against the other nations and God's people (vv.40–45).

The fact that he is not to be identified with Antiochus IV or any of the kings of the previous period can be seen in the fact that in v.40, this king engages in war with both "the king of the North" and "the king of the South." This king is thus neither the king of the North or of the South. He thus cannot be Antiochus IV, who was a king of the North. Moreover, according to ch. 12, "at that time" there is to be a great distress and a resurrection in which Daniel's people will be delivered. This seems to point far beyond Antiochus IV or any period in Israel's history.

XI. A Time of Distress (12:1 – 13)

The angel continues to speak in ch. 12; he expressly refers to the time of the events of the vision in ch. 11 as "at that time" (12:1). In the days of the last king there will be a time of distress for Daniel's people, but they will be delivered by a great resurrection (v.2). With this, the vision of the end is abruptly halted and sealed "until the time of the end" (v.4).

In a final segment of the vision, the question of the time of the fulfillment of the vision is raised: "How long will it be before these astonishing things are fulfilled?" (v.6). An enigmatic answer is given, "When the power of the holy people has been finally broken" (v.7); this is linked to the oft-repeated phrase "a time, times and half a time." To this Daniel himself replies, "I heard, but I did not understand," and he is instructed again to seal up the vision until the time of the end. A final clue is given to "those who are wise" (vv.10–11). The numerical pattern of this clue refers the reader back to Gabriel's explanation of Jeremiah's seventy weeks in 9:26–27, thus showing that the fulfillment will come in the second part of the seventieth week.

As an example for all believers, Daniel is told to carry on until the time of the end when he will be resurrected with the rest of those who will receive their eternal reward.

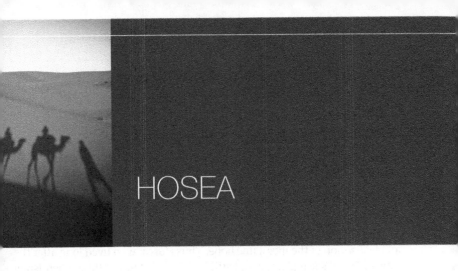

HOSEA

Introduction

In the Hebrew Bible, the last twelve prophetic books (the Minor Prophets) are considered as a single book. Hosea is the first of these prophets. He began his prophetic ministry during the reign of Jeroboam II (cf. 1:1; 2Ki 15:8–31). The book records the Lord's relationship to Israel in terms of Hosea's own unfortunate marriage. The Lord had a loyal love, a determined, steadfast love for his chosen people. It was a love that was determined to remain faithful to the covenant, regardless of Israel's unfaithfulness.

I. Hosea's Marriage (1:2–3:5)

A. Hosea's First Marriage to a Harlot (1:2–2:23)

Hosea's first marriage symbolized Israel's and Judah's apostasy. The faithfulness of Hosea to his wife, however, symbolized God's faithfulness to Israel.

Chapter 1 is not only a programmatic introduction to the book, but it is also a fitting introduction to the Minor Prophets. Israel had sinned and would be cast away from God's presence (1:4). Moreover, in the coming judgment on the northern kingdom, Judah would be delivered from Israel's fate (v.7). But in the future, God would have compassion on Israel and regather them from among the nations and, together with Judah, they would again dwell in the land (v.11).

Chapter 2 gives more details about both the judgment introduced in 1:4 and the salvation mentioned in 1:11. Israel had forsaken God to follow Baal

(2:1–13), but God would allure her back to himself, "as in the day she came up out of Egypt" (vv.14–23). As in other prophetic literature, the exodus becomes a picture of Israel's future salvation.

B. Hosea's Second Marriage to the Harlot (3:1 – 5)

The prophet's second marriage to the harlot was intended to cure her of her harlotry, which symbolized God's use of the exile to cure Israel of apostasy. Verses 4–5 introduce the theme of Israel's messianic hope, which runs throughout the Minor Prophets. This was the messianic hope derived from God's promise to David in 2Sa 7:16, that the Messiah was to be a king of the house of David; when he came, he would rule like David. David was an idealization of the messianic hope. Thus Hosea, who lived long after the time of David's kingdom, could still look forward to the time when Israel would "return and seek the LORD their God and David their king" (3:5).

II. Israel's and Judah's Present Sins (4:1 – 9:9)

This section catalogues Israel's sins, interspersed with the reminder of God's faithfulness and future redemption for Israel (5:15–6:3). For Hosea, Israel's sin consisted primarily in their looking to other nations for help rather than looking to the Lord. In 7:11, for example, Israel was said to seek the help of Egypt and Assyria. In 8:8–9 they sought Assyria's aid, and in 8:13 the exile is called a "return to Egypt." Israel was to go into exile to Assyria — seen as a return to the bondage of Egypt (8:13; 9:3, 6; cf. 11:5).

III. Israel's and Judah's Past Sins (9:10 – 14:9)

The past sins of Israel and Judah provide the context for viewing their present sin and for showing God's long-suffering love for his disobedient people. God had long endured them, but his love still remained. In spite of Israel's past sins, their future remained hopeful because God would not forsake them (11:8–11). The future held for Israel a "new exodus" from Egypt (11:11; cf. 12:13).

Hosea thus deliberately casts the future messianic age in imagery drawn from Israel's past deliverance from Egypt (see esp. 12:10). The Messiah would be a new Moses, who would once again lead God's people out of the land of their bondage and captivity (12:9). In his use of this imagery, the writer follows the lead of the writer of the Pentateuch (see comments on Nu 24), where the future is an antitype of the past.

Furthermore, in 3:5 this future messianic leader will be of the house of David (see the divine promise in 2Sa 7). At the conclusion of the book, the writer calls us to understand his book with wisdom and discernment (14:9). The books of the Minor Prophets, then, appear to be directed specifically to the "wise" among the people of God (cf. also introduction to Joel).

JOEL

Introduction

It is not possible to assign a date to the time of Joel's ministry. The fact that it stands between Hosea and Amos suggests that its message should be read in context with the message of those two books. Joel begins with a call to the wise ("elders") to seek understanding and pass it on to their children (1:2 – 3; cf. Hosea's admonition to the wise in Hos 14:9). Throughout Joel the reader is continually reminded of the impending "day of the LORD," a phrase that unifies the book (1:15; 2:1, 11, 31; 3:14).

I. Introduction (1:1 – 3)

These verses cast the book in the form of wisdom instruction. It addresses the readers as "elders," calling on them to "tell it to [their] children" (1:2 – 3).

II. Locust Plague (1:4 – 20)

The devastation of a locust plague is a symbolic anticipation of the coming day of the Lord (v.15). As in Hos 12:10, the great events of the past are images of the future. The point of Joel's description is that all the normal divine provisions that Israel enjoyed were to be removed in an instant. As in Ps 37, Joel's admonition to prepare for the coming judgment was directly to the wise and the discerning (cf. also Da 12:3); they must repent (Joel 2:13 – 15).

III. Invasion (2:1 – 11)

The day of the Lord would soon come like a military invasion that overtook the land by surprise (v.1b). In his description, the prophet's words reach epic proportions: "Before them fire devours, behind them a flame blazes" (v.3). Such a description assures the reader that God's mighty hand lay behind this scene. The earth shook, the sky trembled, "the sun and moon [were] darkened, and the stars no longer [shone]" (v.10). This was the army of God (v.11); it was the "day of the LORD" (v.11b).

IV. Call to Repentance (2:12 – 20)

The only way for Israel to avert the impending divine judgment is to repent and turn to God (vv.12 – 13). The book addresses all generations of God's people as they await the coming of divine judgment. The basis of Joel's call to repent is the wonderful grace and compassion of God: "He is gracious and compassionate, slow to anger and abounding in love" (v.13b). If the people repent, the Lord will "take pity on his people" (v.18) and drive the northern army far from them (v.20).

V. Future Salvation (2:21 – 27)

In spite of the impending doom, there was still hope for Israel, for God would restore their blessing. There was no need for fear and sorrow. God had not forsaken his people. Hence, the "people of Zion" should rejoice and be glad (v.23); "never again will my people be shamed" (vv.26 – 27).

VI. The Coming of the Spirit (2:28 – 32)

Before "the day of the LORD," God would pour out his Spirit on the entire human race. Salvation would come from Zion, i.e., Jerusalem. God's future work would be marked by a new outpouring of his Spirit on all people. As in the days when Israel was in the desert (cf. Nu 11), God would again pour out his Spirit, and his people would prophesy (Nu 11:25), dream dreams, and see visions (cf. Nu 12:6). God would also give evidence of his power through signs in the heavens and deliverance for Jerusalem (2:31 – 32; see also Eze 36:24 – 27).

VII. Judgment of the Nations (3:I – 16c)

With blessing restored to Israel, God would judge the nations for their treatment of Israel (cf. Eze 38–39). This would fulfill God's promise to Abraham: "I will bless those who bless you, and whoever cursed you I will curse" (Ge 12:3). The nations had mistreated Israel, and God would repay them with judgment in the "Valley of Jehoshaphat" (v.12).

VIII. Salvation for Zion (Jerusalem) (3:16d – 21)

Two themes dominate this section of Joel: (1) salvation and blessing would come from Zion (cf. Ge 14; 2Sa 7), and (2) the Lord was present in Zion (cf. Ps 133). The emphasis on Zion as God's habitation stems from the promise that God made to David in 2Sa 7. In Zion he would establish his kingdom and dwell in his temple. This promise was never fulfilled in David's day, nor was it fulfilled during the times of their kings. The basis of Israel's hope lay in the eternal faithfulness of God to this promise. Coupled with this promise was the further hope that God's original purposes in creation would once again come to pass. Thus Joel ends on a reflective note of the return of God's blessings in Eden (v.18) and the final destruction of the enemies of God's people (vv.19–21). This theme of God's judgment against the nations is continued in Amos.

AMOS

Introduction

The prophet Amos was a sheepherder from Tekoa, in Judah, whom God called to prophesy to the people of Israel (7:15) in the days of Jeroboam II (1:1; cf. 2Ki 14:23–29). Amos carried out most of his mission at the worship center at Bethel—a sanctuary of the king (Am 7:13). Amos preached fearful words of impending doom, summarized by the priest Amaziah: "Jeroboam will die by the sword, and Israel will surely go into exile, away from their native land" (7:11).

I. Introduction (1:1 – 2)

The book picks up remarkably well from the book of Joel (Joel 3:16), where the theme was God's judgment against the nations.

II. Oracles against the Nations (1:3 – 2:16)

The theological basis of these judgments is Ge 12:3. The irony of Amos's words, however, is that Israel and Judah were themselves included among those who would be judged. Amos was trying to show how far Israel and Judah had strayed from the covenant; they would be treated like those outside the covenant.

III. God's Word against Israel and Judah (3:1 – 4:13)

This series of sayings draws out the implications of the previous oracles against the nations. If God would punish the nations for their wickedness, how much more Israel and Judah, who ought to have known better, given their special status before God (3:1 – 2, 7).

IV. Three Woes (5:7 – 6:14)

The first woe (5:7 – 17) is an enumeration of the sin of injustice and a call to repentance. The second woe (5:18 – 27) enumerates the sin of hypocrisy in worship and issues a call to repentance. The third woe (6:1 – 14) focuses on the sin of arrogance.

V. Five Visions (7:1 – 9:15)

The first vision (7:1 – 3) portrays the devastation of the land by swarms of locusts. In the second (7:4 – 6) the land is destroyed by fire. The third (7:7 – 9) shows the Lord measuring the deeds of the people of Israel just as a builder, using a plumb line, measures the wall of a city. The fourth vision (8:1 – 3) is of a basket of ripe fruit, indicating to Israel that the time was ripe for the coming of judgment. The fifth vision (9:1 – 15) is the utter devastation of God's people of Israel. The book does close, however, with a message of salvation.

In the midst these five visions, the author has placed an important narrative of Amos's prophetic ministry (7:10 – 17). This narrative provides a historical reference point for the prophecies that precede and follow it. Amos's words refer to the sins of the king (Jeroboam) and his false worship center at Bethel, as well as the failure of the prophets to speak out against them. That is why God called a Judean farmer to deliver these words. The narrative, moreover, shows that the reference to Amos's words was the impending exile (7:17); thus, Israel's hope lay still in the future, beyond the time of captivity they were facing (cf. Isa 36 – 39).

The final vision in the series (9:1 – 15) stands in marked contrast to the first four visions in that, in addition to judgment, there is also a promise of salvation. This word of salvation is based on God's promise to David in 2Sa 7 (the Davidic covenant). "David's fallen shelter" (Am 9:11) would rise up again at a time of future blessing and salvation. This refers to the restoration of the Davidic house and the coming of the messianic king. Amos sees the kingdom of Judah as being destroyed and the house of David decimated. There was hope, however, because God had made an eternal promise to the house of David.

At that time Israel would "possess the remnant of Edom and all the nations that bear my name" (9:12). The nations, here pictured as Edom, would one day be a part of God's kingdom. Edom was often used to represent the "nations" in the OT. For Israel "to possess" the nations is the same as for the nations "to seek" the Lord.

OBADIAH

Introduction

Within the context of the Minor Prophets, the words of Obadiah against Edom (v.1) pick up the lead of Joel 3:19 and Am 1:11–12. In these two books, the people of Edom represented the nations who were the professed enemies of God's people. This also follows from Hos 12, where Jacob was presented as representative of the people of Israel in his struggles with his brother Esau (Edom, Hos 12:3). Obadiah portrays God's judgment on these nations. By contrast, the book of Jonah, which follows Obadiah, portrays God's blessing and salvation of the nations. Thus, together, the two books give the full picture of God's dealings with the nations: judgment and blessing.

I. Judgment against Edom (1 – 16)

This first section recounts the words of God's judgment against the nation of Edom for their mistreatment of the people of Judah. The Edomites had rejoiced to see destruction come upon Jerusalem and Judah. They "stood aloof while strangers carried off [Israel's] wealth and foreigners entered [their] gates and cast lots for Jerusalem" (v.11). They actually waited "at the crossroads to cut down their fugitives" (v.14).

II. Deliverance for God's People (17 – 21)

Obadiah then turns to the salvation and deliverance for God's people. Here we find a common theme in the prophets: salvation will come to Zion (v.17a) and God's people will receive their due inheritance (v.17b). On that day, Israel will turn the tables on Edom and conquer them (v.18). This will fulfill the prophecy of Balaam in Nu 24:18 and will thus signal the coming of the messianic age. The picture of Israel's conquering Edom demonstrates that Edom, and thus all "nations," will, in that day, become a part of God's kingdom. When the Deliverer who rules on Mount Zion governs the mountains of Edom (v.21a), it will mean that Edom has become a part of God's kingdom (cf. comment on Am 9:12).

JONAH

Introduction

The book of Jonah narrates one prophet's dealings with God and the nations. Its focus is on Jonah and on what his call and response reveal about God's character. Its central message contains several points. (1) God answered the prayers of confession of the pagan sailors as they cried out for help in a time of need. (2) God's plan to reach Nineveh with his word of judgment could not be thwarted by Jonah's disobedience. (3) God had mercy on the Ninevites when they repented and believed, and he rebuked his own (Jonah) for his hardness of heart.

I. Scene One: Jonah's Adventure (1:1 – 17)

A. Jonah's Call (1:1 – 2)

The book opens with God's call to Jonah to preach against the wickedness of Nineveh. This city represents the great kingdoms of this world that stand in opposition to God's people and his kingdom.

B. Jonah's Response (1:3)

Jonah disobeyed God's call by setting out in the opposite direction, heading for Tarshish (v.3). Why? We tend to suppose he was afraid to carry out God's plan because Nineveh was a "great city" (v.2). The real reason, however, is revealed in ch. 4: Jonah disobeyed God because he did not want Nineveh to receive God's grace (4:2).

C. God's Response (1:4 – 17)

God responded to Jonah's disobedience by throwing up obstacles in his way. He hurled (v.4) a great storm into the sea where Jonah was fleeing. As a result, Jonah himself was hurled (v.15) into the sea, only there to be found by a great fish that God had appointed "to swallow Jonah" (v.17). God is in control of his world, and Jonah could not hide from him. His disobedience, in fact, became the very means whereby God's grace was extended to the Gentiles. When they saw God's calming of the sea on Jonah's behalf, "the men greatly feared the LORD, and they offered a sacrifice to the LORD and made vows to him" (v.16). That is, the people put their trust in God, and God saved them.

II. Scene Two: Jonah's Rescue (2:1 – 10)

The second scene takes place in the belly of the great fish, where we overhear Jonah's rejoicing at being rescued. The words of his psalm clearly show that Jonah saw the great fish as an instrument of God's salvation, and so he gave thanks to God. The psalm also comments on what Jonah's salvation meant: "Those who cling to worthless idols turn away from God's love for them" (v.8). This refers to the sailors who forsook their trust in idols and turned to the living God. To such people God will be gracious. There is, then, a broad scope to God's salvation. It stands in sharp contrast to the narrow self-interest exhibited by Jonah. The irony of the story is that Jonah, blinded to God's grace, did not seem to appreciate the sense of his own words.

III. Scene Three: The Salvation of Nineveh (3:1 – 10)

Jonah did not have to preach long before the entire city of Nineveh turned from their idols and put their trust in God. Literally, the narrative says, "The Ninevites believed God" (v.5). This is a strong statement in the OT narratives, similar to Ge 15:6, where Abraham, the father of the nation of Israel, "believed the LORD" and was thereby counted as righteous. The genuineness of the Ninevites' response was characterized in their repentance and fasting (vv.5b – 9). They even put sackcloth on their cattle (v.8). When God saw such sincere repentance, "he relented and did not bring on them the destruction he had threatened" (v.10).

IV. Scene Four: Jonah's Lesson (4:1 – 11)

It was now time for Jonah to learn his lesson. Here we read the real motive behind his reluctance to obey God: "That is why I tried to forestall by fleeing to Tarshish. I knew that you are a gracious and compassionate God, slow to anger and abounding in love, a God who relents from sending calamity" (v.2). No wonder God forgave them when they repented (cf. v.10); God is a compassionate and gracious God.

Jonah's words also show the shortsighted vision of the prophet himself. Jonah was focused on himself and his own people. His petty concern for the vine that shielded him from the sun (vv.6–8) was a picture of Israel's own self-pity and lack of concern for the nations. God's question at the close of the book, "Should I not have concern for the great city of Nineveh?" (v.11), confronts each reader. While we may be tempted to inveigh against Jonah for his petty selfishness, we must also be aware that we are looking at our own frailties.

MICAH

Introduction

Micah was a contemporary of Isaiah. Like Amos, Micah was particularly forceful in his denunciation of the social morality in Judah. His prophecies attack the mere externality of the people's worship.

Micah's warning to Judah was that "Zion [Jerusalem] will be plowed like a field, Jerusalem will become a heap of rubble, the temple hill a mound overgrown with thickets" (3:12). Thus, like Isaiah and the other prophets, Micah envisioned a time when the temple in Jerusalem would be destroyed. Likewise, he put much emphasis on Israel's hope in the future. The central passage in this regard is 5:2 (quoted in Mt 2:5–6).

I. Introduction (1:1)

This verse introduces us to Micah and to the time in which he prophesied.

II. Judgment against Israel (1:2 – 2:11)

The book begins with the image of the Lord as the Judge of all the earth coming to judge his own people, Israel. Micah confronted the sins of idolatry (1:5ff.) and injustice (2:1ff.). Like Isaiah, he saw the instrument of God's wrath as the nation of Assyria. The identity of this nation, however, was concealed in the first pronouncement of judgment. In 1:15 Assyria is called "a conqueror" (cf. 5:5). The punishment awaiting sinful Israel was exile from the land (1:16; 2:3–5). The people were to live so that their "ways are upright" before God (2:7; cf. 6:8).

III. Salvation for Israel (2:12 – 13)

Abruptly the book turns from judgment to salvation, pictured as the return of the people from exile. Micah envisioned a time when Israel would return from captivity, led by their King, the Lord their God (cf. Isa 40:3ff.).

IV. Judgment against Israel (3:1 – 12)

Just as abruptly the book returns to judgment against the unjust and against the leaders of God's people who presumed upon God's grace (v.11). Again the punishment was exile (v.12).

V. Salvation for Israel (4:1 – 5:15)

This section consists of five pronouncements of salvation: salvation for the nations at Zion (4:1 – 5); salvation for the regathered remnant (vv.6 – 7); salvation for the victorious remnant (vv.8 – 13); salvation for the ruler of the remnant (5:1 – 5a); and salvation for the nations of the earth (vv.5b – 9).

The promised ruler in 5:1 – 5a would come from Bethlehem and lead the victorious remnant in defeat of the enemy. The theme of this section expresses the idea that the small would overcome the mighty "in the strength of the LORD" (v.4).

The nature of Assyria's guilt is clearly described in 5:10 – 15 and is summed up in the phrase "on the nations that have not obeyed me" (v.15b). Any nation (Assyria or Israel) that did not obey God would be judged.

VI. Judgment against Israel (6:1 – 7:6)

This section contains several short sayings against the wickedness of Israel. These sayings contrast their sins with the simplicity of pleasing God: "to act justly and to love mercy and to walk humbly with your God" (6:8).

VII. Salvation for Israel (7:7 – 20)

There are several components in the meaning of this final section. (1) One must wait for God's salvation. Salvation for God's people did not lie on the immediate horizon; it lay in the future (v.7). (2) Judgment had to precede salvation because God's people had sinned grievously (v.9). (3) The enemy would ultimately be destroyed (v.10). When that time came, however, all the nations would enjoy God's salvation (v.12). This future salvation was as sure as Israel's past salvation because God is faithful to his promises (vv.14–20).

Note that the book closes with a reference to the Abrahamic covenant, God's promise to Abraham of a great nation and possession of the land (7:20; cf. Ge 12:1–9). The basis of Micah's hope is thus the message of the Pentateuch: God's promises are sure. He will fulfill them just as he has promised the fathers "in days long ago."

NAHUM

Introduction

This book is about the prophet Nahum, who prophesied in the southern kingdom of Judah during the last decades of their kings. Little else is known about him and his ministry. It begins with a short poetic message, proclaiming the Lord as a mighty and righteous God who rules not only among his own people but also over his entire universe (1:1–14). Thus Nahum saw God's relationship to Israel through the lens of both covenant and creation. Nahum proclaimed comfort (his name means "comfort") to Judah in his message that the Lord would judge their bitter enemy, the Assyrians.

I. Introduction (1:1)

This first verse introduces us to the book of Nahum the prophet, whose words and message become the focus of the book. The prophet saw a great vision regarding the destiny of the nation of Assyria, particularly the city of Nineveh.

II. Hymn (1:2 – 11)

The book opens with a hymn depicting the glory of the Lord coming in judgment. The hymn is an acrostic (alphabetic psalm). It has been altered by the addition of vv.9 – 11 midway through the hymn — three verses that apply the message of the hymn to God's judgment of Nineveh. Thus, the general theme of God's judgment of the nations is particularized in his judging of Nineveh. It is fitting that this book is grouped along with Jonah and Micah, two books that also focus on the destiny of Assyria.

III. Salvation for Judah (1:12 – 2:2)

Nineveh's destruction meant the salvation of Judah. God's universal judgment of the nations would result in deliverance for his own people (1:15; 2:2). There is always a note of salvation in the midst of God's threats of judgment. Here the reader's attention is directed to the "one who brings good news, who proclaims peace" (1:15). This focus on an individual deliverer "who proclaims peace" draws on the imagery and hope firmly established in the earliest of the OT books (cf. Ge 49:10; Isa 9:6).

IV. Destruction of Nineveh (2:3 – 13)

These verses portray in graphic detail the destruction of Nineveh and of the Neo-Assyrian Empire. They emphasize that it was the mighty hand of God who had brought this against them: "'I am against you,' declares the LORD Almighty. I will burn up your chariots in smoke'" (v.13). Moreover, the book shows that God had done this great thing in order to "restore the splendor of Jacob" (v.2). That is, behind the events of history stood the sovereign power of God, and behind that power stood God's purpose. The nations had mistreated Israel, and God would not let that go unpunished. This was the lesson of God's covenant with Abraham (see Ge 12:3).

V. Destruction of Nineveh (3:1 – 19)

The fall of Nineveh is again recounted in order to put it in the context of God's ongoing work of judgment against the nations (3:8 – 19). What God had done to Nineveh was merely an example of his actions among other nations. No nation, not even mighty Assyria, could escape the chastening hand of God. Assyria had scattered God's people, and now they themselves were "scattered on the mountains with no one to gather them" (v.18).

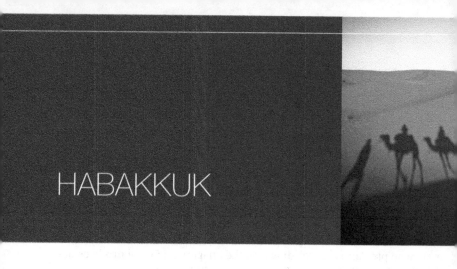

HABAKKUK

Introduction

As far as can be gathered from this book, Habakkuk lived and proclaimed his words during the time of the downfall of the Assyrian Empire and the rise of Babylon.

Two tensions surfaced in the prophet's mind as he surveyed the scene before him. (1) He saw the wickedness of his own nation Israel, which seemed to go by unpunished (1:2–4). (2) God is using a wicked nation, Babylon, to punish his own people (1:5–17).

Habakkuk's response is a model for the righteous of all ages. As he looked at the evil around him, he called out to God for action, but he then waited on God, who he knew would do what was right (2:1).

I. The Laments of Habakkuk (1:1 – 17)

The book opens with a short account of Habakkuk's laments (vv.1–4). Looking around him, he saw nothing but violence and distress. By speaking in only the most general of terms, Habakkuk's words are applicable to all times. The prophet spoke for any and all righteous ones who are distressed by the rampant disregard of God's law. His central concern was to know "how long" God was going to tolerate such evil without sending judgment.

Habakkuk's lament was interrupted by a word from God, in which he said, "I am going to do something in your days that you would not believe, even if you were told" (v.5). These words challenged even Habakkuk to look more closely at what he was lamenting to see if he might not see something of God's work already being accomplished in his midst. That "something" is not clearly defined. In the immediate context it consists of God's sending a great and fearful nation against Habakkuk's own country-men (vv.6 – 11) as a work of judgment (v.12b).

Later biblical writers identify this work of God with the coming of the Messiah and his sacrificial death on the cross (Ac 13:41). Since the book of Habakkuk itself links the work of God in v.5 with the messianic eschato-logical "work" of God in salvation (3:2; NIV, "deeds"), the NT interpretation of this passage appears correct. Habakkuk, like the faithful in every age, was being challenged to wait patiently and faithfully for God to fulfill his promise to send the deliverer, the Messiah.

II. God's Response (2:1 – 20)

Thus the revelation that Habakkuk received from God awaited "an appointed time" and would "not prove false" (v.3). Evil men and mighty nations would come and go (vv.5 – 19). The Lord would see to it that they reaped the wages of their wicked deeds (vv.13, 16b).

III. A Hymn of Praise (3:1 – 19)

At that time the Lord would come in great glory and bring final salvation to the faithful (vv.3 – 15). Habakkuk called on God to do it in his own day (v.2). Though he called for God's action now, Habakkuk was willing to "wait patiently" (v.16b) because the Lord was his strength (v.19). The final lesson of the book is for the godly to wait. God is already at work. The faith-ful can see God's hand in the events around them. Their task is to wait for God's appointed "day" (v.16) and rejoice in his salvation.

It is fitting that the following book, Zephaniah, is devoted to the theme of "the day of the LORD" — the same day recounted here at the close of Habakkuk.

ZEPHANIAH

Introduction

Zephaniah prophesied in the days of King Josiah (639–609 BC). The central theme of his book is the announcement of the coming "day of the LORD." This book appropriately follows Habakkuk; the description of this day in 1:14–18 is remarkably similar to Hab 3:3–15.

I. Introduction (1:1)

The book of Zephaniah is a literary work about the prophet and his message. These words are arranged within the book in order to convey a message to the reader.

II. The Day of the Lord (1:2–18)

The book opens with the announcement of the impending "day" of judgment against "all who live on the earth" (v.18). The focus of the pronouncement, however, is that Israel too, along with Jerusalem, stood under God's wrath (vv.10–11). This book is thus for all God's people. In God's plan there is a future for the whole of the seed of Abraham (cf. Ge 12:2–3).

The cosmic scope of divine judgment begins with a series of allusions to the creation account in Genesis. Just as God filled the whole of his creation with animals, birds, fish, and human beings (Ge 1), so also in judgment he will wipe out all of these creatures, including the human race (Zep 1:2–3). Just as the focus of the creation account in Genesis is the "land," so also here the focus of God's judgment is the land (vv.4 – 13). Judah stood under God's wrath because they had forsaken him and followed after gods of their own making (vv.5, 9b).

III. Call to the Righteous (2:1 – 3)

At the conclusion of the description of the "day of the LORD" is a brief call to the righteous to seek the Lord and find refuge in him from the wrath to come (v.3). As in Habakkuk, the righteous are those who put their trust in God. They wait for the "appointed time" to come by seeking righteousness and humility (v.3b).

IV. Judgments against the Nations (2:4 – 15)

The nations are now brought into the sphere of the day of the Lord. God's judgment extends beyond his people to all the nations. The nations that have historically oppressed Israel are warned of the coming day of divine wrath: Philistia (vv.4 – 7), Moab and Ammon (vv.8 – 11); Cush, i.e., Egypt (v.12), and Assyria (vv.13 – 15).

V. Woe to Jerusalem (3:1 – 7)

The prophet turns to Jerusalem, which "does not trust in the LORD" (v.2b). God's people have not learned from the experiences of the other nations, and so they too will suffer God's judgment (v.7). A righteous God dwells within their midst (v.5), and thus they are as subject to his wrath as are the rest of the nations (vv.5b – 7).

VI. Salvation to the Nations (3:8 – 13)

The purpose of divine judgment is salvation. God plans to purify the nations "that all of them may call on [i.e., worship] the name of the LORD" (v.9). In that day, the nations will be purified of the proud and arrogant and only the humble will remain along with the remnant of Israel (vv.12 – 13).

VII. Salvation to Israel (3:14 – 20)

After judgment comes salvation. Israel's blessing will be restored, and the exiles will return to Jerusalem (v.20). The focus of the message of salvation, therefore, is the hope of the return from exile. The hope expressed in the book, however, extends far beyond that return. As is true of most of the prophetic literature, the return from Babylon is used as an image of the future coming of the messianic age. The book of Haggai, the next book, is devoted specifically to the question of the return from Babylon and the fulfillment of God's messianic promises. Haggai, along with Zechariah and Malachi, show that the time of the return did not bring in the messianic age because the people of Israel did not respond in faith.

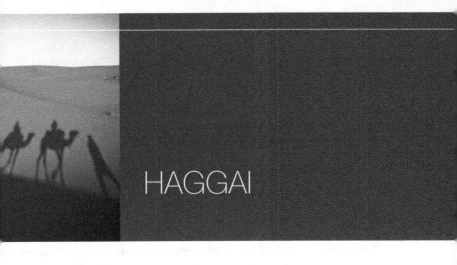

HAGGAI

Introduction

The book records the prophecies of the prophet Haggai, who preached to those who had returned from Babylon and were living in Jerusalem (ca. 520 BC). It also portrays him as a model of faithfulness and commitment to God's work. Haggai knew that God had promised that the Messiah would come when the temple was restored.

I. First Oracle (1:1 – 11)

This oracle immediately sets the tone for the interpretation of the return from the exile. God's people had returned to Jerusalem, but the temple still lay desolate (v.9). In other words, the Israel who returned from the exile was really no different from the Israel who had gone into exile. Both stood under God's judgment (vv.10 – 11).

II. Narrative (1:12 – 15)

In response to Haggai's word, Israel's leaders (Zerubbabel and Joshua) and the remnant began work on the temple. These faithful few served as a model for what had to be done to receive God's promised blessing.

III. Second Oracle (2:1 – 9)

As the remnant worked on rebuilding the temple, the second oracle developed a renewed hope for them. A temple even more glorious than Solomon's would be built from the wealth of the nations (vv.6–9). The second oracle makes the future rebuilding of the temple the focus of Israel's trust and confidence in God and his promises.

The oracle was addressed to Zerubbabel son of Shealtiel, who was the scion of the house of David and thus heir to the messianic promise (2Sa 7:14–16). The time was ripe for fulfillment. The oracle was also addressed to the high priest, Joshua. According to Zec 6:9–15 (cf. Ps 110:4), the high priest would also play an important role in fulfilling the Davidic promise in the messianic age. The Messiah was to be a king and a priest. The connection between these two came from the fact that the central role of the king was to care for the temple, the house of the Lord. Both Solomon and David were models of the Messiah in this regard.

The concern for the building of the temple in the messianic age can be seen in the prophetic word of vv.6–7: "'In a little while I will once more shake the heavens and the earth, the sea and the dry land ... and what is desired by all nations will come, and I will fill this house with glory,' says the LORD Almighty." The prophet had the future messianic kingdom in view here. But what is "desired by all nations?" Some take this to mean simply the gold and precious materials gathered from the nations used to build the temple. But most likely this refers to the Messiah himself, the one whom all nations desired. The rebuilt temple would signal his coming.

IV. Third Oracle (2:10 – 19)

This oracle provides the important interpretive clue to the relationship between the present temple and the future, or eschatological, one. The present temple was not the temple of the future because the present remnant (returned Israel in Haggai's day) was not yet like the future, eschatological remnant. The present remnant was unclean, and so was the work of their hands, the present temple (v.14). Thus, for Haggai, the long-awaited blessing was still future (v.19). Nevertheless, the present temple was a concrete, physical sign that the future temple would surely be built (vv.15, 18).

V. Fourth Oracle (2:20 – 23)

As the present temple had become the focus of the future temple, so also the present leader (Zerubbabel) was the sign of the future leader (the Messiah). Thus, the return from exile in 539 BC and the rebuilding of the temple by Zerubbabel did not fulfill the hope of the prophets (e.g., Isa 40;

Zep 3:20). The Israel of the historical return was "defiled" (unfaithful); but in their response to the words of the prophet and their willingness to work on the temple, they were a model of the faithful remnant of the future, who would one day follow the Messiah and rebuild the temple in Jerusalem; at that time all the promises of the prophets would be fulfilled.

For a fuller understanding of the sense of this book we need to look at Zechariah.

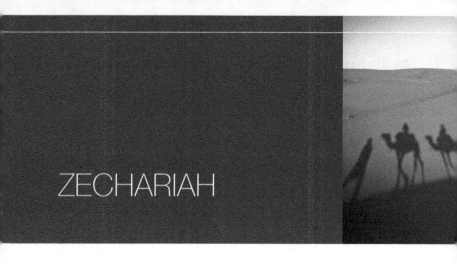

ZECHARIAH

Introduction

Zechariah was a contemporary of Haggai. The book of Haggai concludes, curiously, with the possibility that one of Israel's present political leaders (Zerubbabel) may have been *the* Messiah. Zechariah shows that the Messiah would come only when Israel had completely obeyed God's will. The fulfillment is conditional: "This will happen if you diligently obey the LORD your God" (6:15). Since the Israel and Jerusalem of his own day failed to meet that standard, Zechariah leaves us with the message that the coming of the Messiah and the promised "return" from captivity was to be reckoned as something yet to happen.

I. Introduction (1:1)

This verse introduces us to the time of Zechariah's prophecy and thus provides an important link to the preceding book, Haggai (cf. Hag 1:1).

II. Warning to Repent (1:2 – 6)

Immediately following Haggai's great expectations (Hag 2:20 – 23), Zechariah shows the true nature of the present return from the exile. The nation that returned from Babylon to the Promised Land resembled those who lived before the exile. They had to turn from their wicked ways and live righteously if God was to dwell in their midst. This warning sets the stage for the rest of the book: the blessing of the messianic age would come only when God's people had turned to him in obedience and righteousness (cf. Zec 3:7; 6:15; 7:9 – 14; 8:14 – 17).

III. Eight Night Visions (1:7 – 6:8)

(1) *The man on the red horse (1:7 – 17).* The seventy years were nearly complete and the temple was about to be rebuilt.

(2) *Four horns/four craftsman (1:18 – 21).* Israel's enemies would be destroyed.

(3) *The measuring line (2:1 – 13).* Jerusalem would be rebuilt as a habitation for all nations.

(4) *New garments for Joshua (3:1 – 10).* Israel must obey God to enjoy the promised blessing (cf. Hag 2:13 – 14; also Ge 18:19).

(5) *Gold lampstand/two olive trees (4:1 – 14).* The work of God in establishing his kingdom would be by the power of his Spirit (v.6; cf. Ge 1:2; Ex 31:3 – 6).

(6) *The flying scroll (5:1 – 4).* Justice would be administered throughout the land.

(7) *The woman with an ephah (5:5 – 11).* Wickedness would be removed from the land and taken to Babylon.

(8) *The four chariots between two bronze mountains (6:1 – 8).* God's wrath would be vented against the land of the north (Babylon/Assyria).

IV. The Crowning of Joshua (6:9 – 15)

Joshua, the high priest, was a symbol of the "priest-king" who was yet to come. His title was "the Branch." All of God's promises to the house of David, which included a "priest-king" ruler (Ps 110), would happen when Israel obeyed the will of God (6:15).

Here we see that the fulfillment of the messianic promise is conditional. That fulfillment required a king who would obey God's will perfectly. Zechariah is here building on the theme of 1Ki 6:12, where Solomon himself was told by the Lord that the fulfillment of the promise to David was contingent on his obedience. Solomon, of course, did not fully obey God's laws, and thus the Lord did not reckon his building of the temple as fulfilling the promise to David (see 1Ki 11:11). Nevertheless, the promise of God remained intact (1Ki 6:12 – 13), just as God had said it would (2Sa 7:14b – 16).

V. Judgment of Israel (7:1 – 14)

Immediately following the call for obedience in 6:15, the book turns to Zechariah's accusation that the people of his day were just as disobedient as those who went into exile. Those who returned to Jerusalem in Zechariah's day and their leaders (e.g., Zerubbabel and Joshua) were not the final fulfillment of God's promises; a future fulfillment yet awaited them.

VI. Salvation for Israel (8:1 – 23)

Zechariah now elaborates on the true nature of the kingdom yet to come. This chapter presents a panoramic view of the events in the messianic age. The prophet foresaw that God would again dwell in Jerusalem and that Jerusalem would again be called the "Faithful City" (v.3). This city would be a place of joy and salvation (vv.4 – 8), peace (vv.9 – 11), prosperity (v.12), and blessing (v.13). Worship of the true God would be restored to Zion, and peoples from all nations and tribes of the world would come to Jerusalem to worship him (vv.20 – 23).

VII. Judgment and Salvation for the Nations (9:1 – 7)

God would purge the nations so that they too would become his people. His judgment on them was a prelude to the coming of the King (cf. Isa 9:1 – 6). It should be noted just how little attention has been given to this theme in Zechariah. Its predominant emphasis lies on the salvation of Israel and Jerusalem.

VIII. Salvation for Israel (9:8 – 10:12)

At the center of Zechariah's vision of salvation for Israel was the coming of the King to Jerusalem—the King who would rule the nations in peace and righteousness (9:9 – 10; cf. Pss 2; 72). This picture of the coming King derives from the prophecies of the Pentateuch. The King riding on a donkey was that lion of the tribe of Judah who would rule the nations and God's people (Ge 49:8 – 12). Zechariah also borrowed part of his imagery from Isa 63:1 – 6 (cf. Mt 21:5; Rev 19:11 – 16).

The central theme here is Israel's coming victory over their enemies at the hand of this victorious King. These images can ultimately be traced back to the promise to Eve in Ge 3:15—the victorious "offspring" of the woman who would crush the head of the enemy.

IX. The Shepherds (11:1 – 17)

This chapter opens with a poetic prelude to the theme of Israel's shepherds (vv.1 – 3). The shepherd represents the divinely appointed leaders of the people. At first God appointed a good shepherd to rule his people. This shepherd is represented by Zechariah, who guided the people with two staffs, "Favor" and "Union." The primary focus of the passage is on a shepherd yet to come. But the people did not want to be ruled by this good shepherd. They rebelled against him for "thirty pieces of silver" (v.12). The picture is fulfilled in the rejection of Christ.

Zechariah was then appointed to represent the rule of "a foolish shepherd" (v.15), whom God would appoint over his people after their rejection of the good shepherd (v.16). This worthless shepherd would lead them to slaughter as part of God's judgment against his disobedient people because of their rejection of the good shepherd. That judgment is identified with the treatment given to the Jewish people under the Roman Empire.

X. Jerusalem and the Nations (12:1 – 14:21)

A day was coming when God would restore the peace of Jerusalem, as in the days of David; that day would be preceded by a great battle. Jerusalem would be surrounded by many nations, but God would deliver his city and people for the sake of the promise made to David (2Sa 7). At this time God's people would look back at their treatment of the rejected shepherd, and there would be great weeping (12:10 – 13:6).

At this time, events would happen much like those connected with the return from Babylonian captivity in Zechariah's day. It would be preceded by an attack on Jerusalem by all the nations, but God would defend his city against them (14:1 – 15).

The book concludes with a picture of eternal peace and blessing enjoyed by all the surviving nations (14:16 – 21). They would come to Jerusalem to worship God at the temple (vv.16 – 19). The whole world would be God's people, and all Jerusalem would be holy (vv.20 – 21). Even the cooking pots in Jerusalem would be like the sacred bowls of the temple.

Zechariah's mention of "the angel of the LORD" who would go before the people of God preparing the way of salvation (12:8b) provides the link to the next book, Malachi, which means "my angel" or "my messenger." That book focuses precisely on the role of this angel.

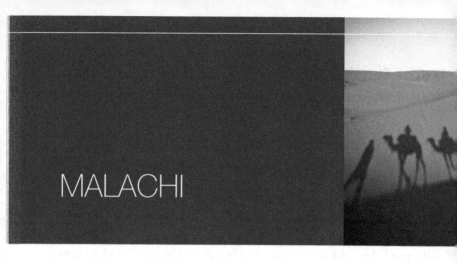

MALACHI

Introduction

Malachi carried out his prophetic work after the return from Babylonian exile. The name Malachi ("my messenger") anticipates the prophecy regarding the final messenger announced in 3:1 and the prophecy about the return of Elijah in 4:5. This future prophet would be like the present Malachi in that he would prepare the nation for the coming of God's kingdom.

The book is arranged around a series of disputes between Malachi and the people during the time of the return from exile. In these disputes, the prophet was building a case against them, which demonstrated they were not yet ready for the coming of the promised King.

I. Introduction (1:1)

The material in this book must be read as a "prophecy." Malachi, whose name means "my messenger," is the name of the prophet, which signifies the role he would play. His role anticipated that of the future prophet who would prepare the way for the coming of the Messiah. At the close of the book, that prophet is identified as Elijah; in the NT he is identified as John the Baptist.

II. Disputes (1:2 – 4:3)

The case Malachi presents against the people of God consists of six "disputes."

Dispute 1 (1:2–5). God had cared for Israel throughout the past, but Israel did not recognize or appreciate God's care. Israel was ungrateful.

Dispute 2 (1:6–2:9). Israel treated their offerings carelessly and thus dishonored God.

Dispute 3 (2:10–16). Israel profaned their covenant with God by marrying pagan women.

Dispute 4 (2:17–3:5). Though Israel might think that God would never carry out his plan of judgment against unrighteousness, God would soon send his messenger.

Dispute 5 (3:6–12). Israel withheld their tithes and offerings from the Lord. If they gave to God, he would abundantly bless their land.

Dispute 6 (3:13–4:3). Israel was tired of waiting for God's blessing, but those who did wait would have a part in the divine blessing to come.

III. Warning (4:4–6)

The time of judgment was yet to come. There was hope, however, for those among God's people who feared his name. Waiting consisted in obediently trusting God to fulfill his promises and send his future prophet—the prophet who would prepare the people for the coming of God's kingdom.

MATTHEW

Introduction

Although the title of the gospel, "According to Matthew," is found with the earliest complete manuscripts, that description probably goes back only to about AD 125. The gospel itself gives no clear indication of its date of composition or author. Since it was quoted by two early Christian writers, Ignatius (c. 35–c. 107) and the Didache (c. 100), thus we can be assured it was already in existence before the second century AD.

This gospel has a clearly marked structure: an alternation of narratives about the life of Jesus and five discourses of his teaching. Each discourse section closes with a similar formula that introduces a narrative section: "When Jesus had finished saying these things …" (7:28; 11:1; 13:53; 19:1; 26:1).

Matthew's gospel had two primary functions within the early church community. (1) It served as a collection of Jesus' sayings and actions that were a part of the community worship of the early church. (2) It was also a manual for teaching Christian leaders in the early church.

I. The Beginning (1:1 – 4:11)

A. Early History (1:1 – 2:23)

The book of Matthew begins with a genealogy of Jesus (1:1 – 17), tracing his lineage back through David to Abraham. This showed that Jesus was the son of David (hence, a legitimate heir to the title of Messiah; cf. Ps 2) and a descendant of Abraham (hence, a legitimate heir to the blessing of Abraham; cf. Ge 12:1 – 3). The author then gives an account of the birth of

Jesus. His primary focus is on the virgin birth (1:18–25) and the worldwide recognition of this birth, i.e., the Magi from the east (2:1–12).

In ch. 2 Matthew shows the Lord's protection of the young Jesus. Like Israel in the OT, Jesus sojourned in Egypt. When Jesus, with his family, came up out of Egypt, Matthew saw the providential hand of God not only in protecting him from Herod's murderous attempt, but also in fulfilling the words of the prophet Hosea (Hos 11:1): "Out of Egypt I called my son." Matthew thus saw in Israel's exodus from Egypt a picture of God's future redemption. In this respect, Matthew was like Moses, the author of the Pentateuch, who also recorded Israel's exodus as a picture of God's future work of redemption (see Nu 24:8).

Herod's brutal order to "kill all the boys in Bethlehem and its vicinity who were two years old and under" (2:16) parallels the order of Pharaoh, "Every Hebrew boy that is born you must throw into the Nile" (Ex 1:22). The similarity is not lost on Matthew. Through these events in his early life, Jesus is a new Moses, prepared in Egypt to lead his people into the Promised Land and thus to fulfill the blessings of Abraham.

B. Preparation (3:1–4:11)

Three events prepare for Jesus' ministry. (1) John the Baptist preached that the kingdom of heaven was near (3:1–12). (2) Jesus, now as an adult, was ready to do God's work and was baptized by John in the Jordan (3:13–17). (3) Jesus was tempted by the devil (4:1–11).

II. Jesus in Galilee (4:12–20:34)

A. The Sermon on the Mount (4:12–7:29)

Jesus preached in synagogues throughout Galilee (4:23–25). His message was, like that of John the Baptist, one of repentance and the nearness of the kingdom of heaven (v.17). Matthew summarizes Jesus' message with the title "good news," i.e., the gospel (v.23). In Jesus' Sermon on the Mount, Matthew shows the nature of the content of Jesus' teaching.

Jesus begins his sermon with the OT theme of "blessing," a pattern visible in Psalms (e.g., Ps 1:1). The kingdom Jesus announces is one for which its members must suffer in the present, but they will find great reward "in heaven" (5:12). That kingdom, which was being established by Jesus, would find its ultimate victory only after a time of suffering and ignominy.

In view of the notion of waiting for the consummation of the kingdom, Jesus teaches his disciples how to live in God's blessing and joy. Such a life, Jesus says, should serve as a beacon to the world, giving glory to the heavenly Father (5:16). Such a life does not abolish the teaching of the Scriptures, but rather fulfills God's intentions in giving his Word to Israel.

God's Word calls for a righteousness that goes beyond that of the scribes and the Pharisees (vv.17–20). For example, that righteousness does not stop at the prohibition of murder. It goes beyond obvious acts of violence to the inner, secret sins of anger and slander (v.22). If it is wrong to commit adultery, it is also wrong even to "[look] at a woman lustfully" (vv.27–28). In drawing such distinctions, Jesus clearly reflects the OT's emphasis on the fundamental evil of "little sins," such as hatred and slander (see Pr 6:25, 27; 11:12–13).

Jesus' standard of righteousness is not that of human wisdom or traditional values (v.47). He states clearly at the conclusion of ch. 5 that members of the kingdom of heaven are to "be perfect, therefore, as [their] heavenly Father is perfect" (v.48).

With the call to righteous living comes the warning of self-righteousness and hypocrisy (6:1–7:5; 7:15–27). The central theme of this second half of the sermon is service to God, "who sees what is done in secret" (6:4, 6, 18), rather than service before other people. In the midst of repeated warnings against hypocrisy, Jesus calls for an absolute trust in the heavenly Father and commitment to his kingdom (6:25–34; 7:7–13).

Matthew closes this account of Jesus' teaching by describing the people's response. They were astonished by the way he taught and were struck by the difference between his authority and that of their own teachers (7:28–29).

B. Jesus' Great Deeds (8:1–9:38)

To illustrate the authority of Jesus, Matthew now records several incidents in Jesus' ministry that focus on the recognition of his authority among the people and the Jewish leaders.

In the healing of the leper (8:1–4), the man says simply, "Lord, if you are willing, you can make me clean" (v.2). There is no question of Jesus' ability to heal; all depends on his sovereign will. Jesus replied, "I am willing. Be clean!" To show that Jesus' teaching did not abolish the importance of the law of Moses, Matthew adds Jesus' instructions to the leper that he show himself to the priest, "and offer the gift Moses commanded" (v.4). But the purpose for obeying Moses' command was to be "a testimony to them [i.e., the priests]" (v.4).

Jesus' encounter with a centurion (8:5–13) demonstrates that even Gentiles recognized his authority. When a Gentile centurion came to Jesus regarding his sick servant, he said simply, "Just say the word, and my servant will be healed" (v.8). The centurion's faith in Jesus' authority amazed even Jesus, who said, "I have not found anyone in Israel with such great faith" (v.10). Thus, Jesus returned to a familiar theme throughout this gospel, namely, the rejection of Israel and the Gentiles' inheritance of the kingdom of heaven (vv.11 – 12).

In the account of Jesus' authority over diseases, Matthew stresses the power of "his word" to heal. He healed Peter's mother-in-law (8:14 – 15) and cast out the spirits "with a word" (v.16). Matthew sees this as another example of fulfilled prophecy (v.17).

Matthew then shows that Jesus demanded absolute authority over those who wanted to follow him (8:18 – 22). To the one follower who vowed to follow Jesus "wherever" he went, Jesus replied, "The Son of Man has no place to lay his head" (v.20). The commitment to follow Jesus should have no qualifiers attached to it. The presumed follower apparently assumed he would have a place to sleep at night. Similarly, a second disciple's request to bury his father before he followed was met with Jesus' call for immediate obedience, "Follow me, and let the dead bury their own dead" (v.22).

Jesus' authority extended even to the forces of nature (8:23 – 27). When he calmed the storm at sea, his disciples observed, "Even the winds and the waves obey him!" (v.27). When Jesus cast the demons out of two men and allowed them to go into a herd of swine, the whole town pleaded with him to leave their region (vv.28 – 34), because Jesus' authority was a threat to their present way of life.

In 9:1 – 8, Matthew brings out the most important implication of Jesus' authority, i.e., his power to forgive sin. What requires more power — to heal the sick or to forgive sin? Both, says Jesus, are the work of God. Thus Jesus healed the paralytic that "you [may] know that the Son of Man has authority on earth to forgive sins" (v.6).

Matthew, a tax collector, gave up all to follow Jesus (9:9 – 13). When the Pharisees questioned the character of those who, like Matthew, followed the Lord, Jesus referred to a well-known OT theme to answer their complaint (v.13): God desires mercy, not sacrifice (Hos 6:6).

In the question about fasting that immediately follows (9:14 – 17), Jesus emphasized the need to break with the traditions of the past to follow and serve Jesus. New wine must be put in new wineskins (v.17). There is a further hint in Jesus' words to the time when "the bridegroom will be taken from them" (v.15) — a reference to Jesus' death and the new covenant (26:28). Thus the contrast between the old and the new in these two proverbs should be taken as a contrast between the old covenant, established between God and Israel at Mount Sinai, and the gift of the new covenant to the church, established at Golgotha (27:32 – 56).

Matthew continues to recount stories that stress Jesus' authority in his power to heal the sick, raise the dead, and cast out demons (9:18–34). The section concludes with the opinion of two groups of eyewitnesses. The first group, the crowd who witnessed the works of Jesus, said, "Nothing like this has ever been seen in Israel" (v.33); the second group, the Pharisees, questioned the source of his power, "It is by the prince of demons that he drives out demons" (v.34). The stage was being set for the leaders of Israel to reject their promised Messiah.

Matthew closes this section with a summary of Jesus' activity during this time: "Jesus went through all the towns and villages, teaching in their synagogues, proclaiming the good news of the kingdom and healing every disease and sickness" (v.35).

C. Sending of the Twelve (10:1 – 42)

Matthew now states that Jesus "gave [the disciples] authority to drive out impure spirits and to heal every disease and sickness" (10:1). Thus, the same divine authority operative in the life of Jesus was now given to his disciples. Consistent with the notion that the people of Israel were like "sheep without a shepherd" (9:36), Jesus sent his disciples only to "the lost sheep of Israel" (10:6). Their message was that the kingdom of heaven was near (v.7), and they were to do the works of Jesus (v.8). When Israel eventually rejected their Messiah, the offer of the kingdom was extended to all nations (cf. 28:19).

Jesus sent his disciples throughout the land of Israel to announce the coming of the messianic King. Jesus' instructions to his disciples are recorded in such a way that they provided a guide to the evangelistic mission of his own readers. Thus, many of the instructions Jesus gave his disciples have a larger application in the life of the readers of this gospel. The gospel is a virtual manual for evangelism and discipleship.

D. Jesus and His Opponents (11:1 – 12:50)

Jesus now gives his own understanding of John the Baptist (11:7–15). John was the last of the line of prophets who extended from the OT period (vv.7–9a), but he was more. He was also the first of the fulfillment of that which the OT prophets promised (vv.9b–11). Thus John's mission signaled the coming of the promised kingdom of God (vv.12–15).

The shift in Jesus' message is unmistakable in 11:20–24, where he reflects back on his earlier works in the cities of Israel; like the prophets before him (e.g., Isa 1:9), Jesus turns to the imagery of Sodom (Ge 19) to describe God's judgment on Israel. In these cities Jesus did the works of

God, but the people did not repent. The only explanation of such hardness of heart, Jesus says, is God's wisdom and his good pleasure (11:26) in not revealing himself to "the wise and learned" (v.25a) but to "little children" (v.25b). God's will was being accomplished in Israel's rejection of the Messiah (cf. a similar reasoning in Paul's comments in Ac 28:28).

Chapter 12 shows the rejection of Jesus by the leaders of Israel. They first accused Jesus and his disciples of breaking the law of Moses (vv.1–14). Jesus appealed to his own authority over the law ("The Son of Man is Lord of the Sabbath," v.8), as well as to a proper understanding of the law itself ("It is lawful to do good on the Sabbath," v.12). At this point the plot to kill Jesus begins. It is the point where Jesus becomes identified as the Servant of the Lord. Henceforth, a central theme of the book is that of the death of the Servant, "in [whose] name the nations will put their hope" (12:21).

The final turning point in the ministry of Jesus came when the Pharisees attributed Jesus' works to the work of Satan: "It is only by Beelzebub, the prince of demons, that this fellow drives out demons" (12:24). Jesus responded to them not only by pointing out the desperate absurdity of their charge (v.25), but also by cautioning them of the seriousness of their rejection of God's offer (v.37). Matthew also warned his readers of the seriousness of rejecting Jesus. Such rejection means rejection of God's Servant sent to die for human sin. How much better to accept the offer Jesus gives to those who believe in him: "Come to me, all you who are weary and burdened, and I will give you rest ... and you will find rest for your souls" (11:28–29).

One cannot read Jesus' final words to the Pharisees here (12:38–45) without sensing the turning point in Jesus' message: "A wicked and adulterous generation asks for a sign! But none will be given it except the sign of the prophet Jonah" (v.39). The "sign of Jonah," Jesus explains, will be his own resurrection. As in the days of Jonah and Solomon, the nations will receive the sign and come from the ends of the earth (vv.40–42), but "this wicked generation" will go from bad to worse (vv.43–45).

Membership in God's kingdom cannot be based on family relationships or nationality (cf. Jesus' words in 10:5–6). Rather, "whoever does the will of my Father in heaven is my brother and sister and mother" (12:50). Matthew returns in 13:55–56 to Jesus' family and reiterates this same point from the perspective of those in his hometown, who do not believe in him (v.58).

E. Seven Parables of the Kingdom (13:1 – 58)

The kingdom that Jesus offered to all those who would accept it is now illustrated in seven parables: the sower (13:1–23), the weeds (13:24–30, 36–43), the mustard seed (13:31–32), the yeast (13:33–35), the hidden treasure (13:44), the pearl (13:45–46), and the net (13:47–50). Though each one adds to the reader's understanding of the kingdom, each one also expresses the same basic truth. Jesus came to establish the kingdom promised in the OT, and he was, in fact, about to fulfill his mission. That kingdom, however—a visible, universal rule of the Messiah—would begin in a small, almost imperceptible, form, as a mustard seed or as a piece of yeast in a lump of dough. There would be a delay between the coming of the King and the consummation of the kingdom. During that delay, kingdom members were to anticipate the return of the King and the final establishment of the kingdom at the "end of the age" (vv.39, 40, 49).

That this fulfilled the OT hope in a way that differed from what might have been expected is suggested by Jesus' last remarks in this section: "Every teacher of the law who has become a disciple in the kingdom of heaven is like the owner of a house who brings out of his storeroom new treasures as well as old" (13:52). Jesus' view of the kingdom has some elements that are a part of the OT's view and some that are new.

F. The Itinerate Ministry of Jesus (14:1 – 16:12)

Jesus, on hearing of the death of John, went into the desert. He was not hiding from Herod, who had killed John, but he was preparing the people in the desert for the coming of God's kingdom (cf. 3:1–3).

Jesus then entered the area of Gennesaret (14:34), where he healed many sick (14:34–36). There Jesus was met by Pharisees and teachers of the law who objected to Jesus' disciples' apparent disregard for their "traditions." Jesus answered these accusations with his own exposition of the importance of God's word over against tradition. What makes for purity is not conformity to external rules and regulations, but rather a clean heart (15:1–20).

In his brief journey to Tyre and Sidon (vv.21–28), regions outside of Israel, Jesus showed that he envisioned the kingdom of God along much the same lines as the OT prophets. He told the Canaanite woman that he "was sent only to the lost sheep of Israel" (v.24). Then, seeing the woman's great faith, Jesus healed her daughter and pointed out how her faith stood out in great contrast to that of the Jews. Even the disciples, for example, had "little faith" (14:31).

Matthew closes his portrayal of the Galilean ministry of Jesus with a summary of his healing "the lame, the blind, the crippled, the mute and many others" (15:29–31), an account of the feeding of the 4,000 (vv.32–38), and Jesus' journey to Magadan (15:39–16:12). Here, having been tested by the Pharisees and Sadducees (16:1–4), Jesus warned his disciples of the yeast, i.e., the teaching (v.12), of the Pharisees and Sadducees (vv.5–12).

G. The Church (16:13 – 20:34)

Jesus' question to his disciples, "Who do people say the Son of Man is?" marks a major turning point in this gospel. As their answer shows, the people were still in the dark about the identity of Jesus: "Some say John the Baptist; others say Elijah; and still others, Jeremiah or one of the prophets" (16:14). Peter's answer, however, was on target: "You are the Messiah, the Son of the living God" (v.16). Thus, Jesus said, on this confession ("this rock") he would build his church. The church has now come into full view in this gospel. Access ("the keys") into the kingdom of heaven would henceforth come through the church.

The following two chapters consist of a collection of Jesus' deeds and sayings that establish policies and procedures for the ongoing administration of the church. The gospel of Matthew thus becomes as a guidebook for the church after the resurrection (cf. 17:9).

The first subject is the close relationship between Jesus' kingdom and the OT prophets. The transfiguration (17:1 – 13) was a vivid reminder of the unity of God's work with Israel and the church. At the same time, it showed a distinction between these two. In the transfiguration, Moses and Elijah are witnesses to Jesus' present work but not participants. Peter's desire to build "three shelters" was rebuffed by a voice from heaven. While Peter was still speaking, the Father acknowledged only Jesus as the one in whom he is well pleased; "Listen to him!" (v.5).

When the disciples raised the question of Elijah's role in the coming kingdom, Jesus replied by saying that John the Baptist was the "Elijah" who announced the coming Messiah (v.13). Thus the church, which Jesus was now inaugurating, shares with Moses and Elijah in God's kingdom, but Moses and Elijah do not share in the church. The place of Moses and Elijah is taken by "no one except Jesus" (cf. v.8).

The story of Jesus' healing the boy with a demon (17:14 – 21) draws a further parallel between Jesus and Israel. Jesus says, "You unbelieving and perverse generation, how long shall I stay with you?" (v.17). These words evoke the image of Israel's failure to believe God in the desert (see Nu 14:11; cf. Ps 95:10). Faith was the missing factor in Israel's relationship with God, and it could be the missing factor in the church. With faith, however, "nothing will be impossible" (Mt 17:20). Perhaps Jesus' words about faith moving mountains (v.20) allude to the mountain represented earlier by Moses and Elijah, i.e., Mount Sinai or Horeb (Ex 19:1; 1Ki 19:8).

In the account of Jesus' paying taxes (17:22 – 27), Matthew teaches by precept and example that Jesus' followers were to pay taxes in order not to "cause offense" (v.27). God will provide for such faithfulness. Moreover, in the church Jesus has founded, whoever comes as a little child will be the greatest (18:1–4), and "whoever welcomes one such child" in Jesus' name, welcomes Jesus (vv.5–9). Humility and meekness are important (see also 19:14).

There will be strife among God's people, so Jesus gives specific procedures for dealing with it (18:15–17). The church as a body acts in Jesus' behalf because they have been gathered in his name (vv.18–20). The central rule that governs the various relationships within the church is that of forgiveness (vv.21–35).

Matthew seems particularly concerned to show that marriage (19:1–12) and family (vv.13–15) stand at the heart of most relationships within the church. He also shows that Jesus allowed for exceptions, such as "sexual immorality" in the case of divorce (v.9), and "to live like eunuchs for the sake of the kingdom of heaven" in the case of marriage (v.12).

Jesus' teaching regarding wealth set the pattern for the early church in Jerusalem. Jesus said, "If you want to be perfect, go, sell your possessions and give to the poor" (v.21; see Ac 2:44–45). In both Matthew and Acts, this is emphasized not as the standard but as the ideal: "If you want to be *perfect*" (v.21, emphasis mine). Though it is hard for a rich man to enter the kingdom of heaven (v.23), it is not impossible (v.26). In the last analysis, salvation does not depend on a person's wealth, or lack of it, for "with God all things are possible" (v.26).

The parable of the vineyard workers (20:1–16) shows that reward will not depend on the amount of work done, but on God's generous grace. Those who put themselves first, however, "will be last [in the kingdom of heaven], and many who are last will be first" (19:30; 20:16).

Jesus is the supreme example of his teaching in willingly giving up his own life (20:17–19). Though his disciples may want to gain equal honor with Jesus in his kingdom, only Jesus knows the real price that must be paid: "to give his life as a ransom for many" (v.28). The victorious Son of Man (Da 7:9–14) must first become the Suffering Servant (Isa 53:8).

III. Jesus in Jerusalem (21:1 – 27:66)

A. The Last Works of Jesus (21:1 – 22:46)

When Jesus arrived at Jerusalem, the crowds were ready, and he entered just as the prophets had foretold the Messiah would come: "See, your king comes to you, gentle and riding on a donkey" (21:5). But when asked who Jesus was, they revealed their lingering lack of understanding: "This is

Jesus, the prophet from Nazareth in Galilee" (v.11). Their answer stands in sharp contrast to that of Peter's: "You are the Messiah, the Son of the living God" (16:16). The importance of this difference is seen in the fact that the church is built on Peter's confession (v.18), whereas at the trial of Jesus, this same crowd shouted, "Crucify him!" (27:22).

As promised in the OT, the Messiah would be recognized for his zeal for the house of God, the temple (1Ch 17:12; Zec 6:11 – 13). The children welcomed Jesus as the "Son of David," but the chief priests "were indignant" (Mt 21:15), and sought to undermine his authority (v.23). Jesus again looked to the work of John the Baptist as the one who announced his coming (vv.23 – 27; cf. 3:1 – 17; 11:1 – 19; 14:1 – 12). The chief priests and the elders feigned repentance at the preaching of John and thus, in Jesus' parable, were like the son who agreed to work for his father but did not go out into the field (21:28 – 32). But the true members of God's kingdom were those who repented at John's preaching, like "the tax collectors and the prostitutes" (v.31).

Like a landowner who casts away his dishonest and treacherous tenants, God will cast off the chief priests and elders of Israel and give his kingdom to another people (21:33 – 46). When those invited to the wedding banquet refuse to come, the king will send his army and destroy those who refuse his invitation (22:1 – 7). He will then send his servants "to the street corners and invite to the banquet anyone" willing to come (vv.8 – 14).

Jesus' teaching provoked great opposition, both in the form of hidden plans to arrest him (21:46) and of open plans "to trap him in his words" (22:15). The first plan was to trap him with the civil authorities: "Is it right to pay the imperial tax or not?" (v.17). But they were caught in their own trap in that his reply only served to demonstrate his wisdom: "Give back to Caesar what is Caesar's, and to God what is God's" (v.21).

The second plan, that of the Sadducees, sought to trap Jesus in a matter of the Mosaic law (22:23 – 32). Again, the plan failed, and the crowds were "astonished at his teaching" (v.33).

The Pharisees then returned with a third question: "Which is the greatest commandment?" But Jesus' answer left them without any objection (22:34 – 40). Moreover, he redirected their questions about his understanding of the Mosaic law to a question about their understanding of Scripture: "What do you think about the Messiah? Whose son is he?" (vv.41 – 42). When they answered merely that the Messiah was to be the son of David, Jesus showed that their answer could not stand the test of the OT. Jesus showed that David himself called the Messiah his Lord (Ps 110:1), so how can he be merely his son (vv.43 – 45)? Jesus' understanding of himself as the Christ, the Son of God, is revealed in his answer.

B. The Last Works of Jesus (23:1 – 25:46)

Jesus now turned to the crowd and his own disciples to censure the hypocrisy of "the teachers of the law" (23:1 – 38). He acknowledged the legitimate office these teachers held as interpreters of Mosaic law (v.2). Their problem did not lie in what they taught but in their lack of obedience. As Jesus had repeatedly taught in this gospel, the law was directed to the heart (see 15:18), whereas the teachers and the Pharisees did everything for show (23:5). Jesus then drove home his point with a scathing series of seven "woes" (vv.13 – 36).

Jesus extended his condemnation of the teachers of the law and the Pharisees to all Jerusalem and the nation (23:37 – 39). They were like the nation who suffered God's judgment in the exile (2Ki 25). They had killed the prophets and rejected God's messengers. Hence, they would also be "left ... desolate" (v.38; 24:1 – 2). Jesus, however, continued to speak of a time when Jerusalem would again turn to him and say, "Blessed is he who comes in the name of the Lord" (23:39). The crowds in Jerusalem had greeted him with these words when he entered Jerusalem only days before (21:9), but at a future time the whole city would join in.

On the Mount of Olives, alone with his disciples, Jesus began to teach them about his future return (24:3 – 25:46). Before that return, many false messiahs would come, deceiving many. There would be wars, famines, and earthquakes. His followers would suffer much persecution and apostasy, but the gospel of the kingdom was to be preached throughout all the world. As Daniel had foretold (Da 9:27; 11:31; 12:11), the central event to mark the return of Christ would be a great act of sacrilege called "the abomination that causes desolation" at the site of the temple. The faithful were to wait patiently for the coming of the true Messiah, the Son of Man, who would come openly, in the clouds, as Daniel had foretold (Da 7:9 – 14). Then he would gather his own from all the corners of the world. The people of Israel, God's chosen people, would remain "until all these things have happened" (24:34).

The time of Christ's return is known to no one, "not even the angels in heaven, nor the Son, but only the Father" (v.36). Therefore, God's people must watch and remain faithful (24:42), like a homeowner guarding his house (vv.43 – 45), like a wise servant waiting for the return of his master (vv.45 – 46), like wise bridesmaids with lamps filled and ready for the coming of the bridegroom (25:1 – 13), and like the "good and faithful servant" who invests his talents while waiting for his master's return (vv.14 – 30).

When the Son of Man returns, he will judge all the nations. Those who have been faithful to him in his absence will inherit "the kingdom prepared for [them]" (25:34). Those who have rejected him will be sent "into the eternal fire prepared for the devil and his angels" (v.41).

C. The Death of Jesus (26:1 – 27:66)

The death of Jesus happened at the Jewish Passover. Jesus celebrated the Passover with his disciples on the evening he was betrayed (26:17 – 35). During the meal, he identified his own death with the bread and wine of the Passover (vv.26 – 29). At the same time he identified his death as the fulfillment of a covenant "for many for the forgiveness of sins" (v.28).

As Jesus and his disciples left for Gethsemane, Matthew stresses that Jesus was to face his death alone. He left his closest disciples and then, in the garden, anticipated his separation even from the Father. Though Jesus was fully aware of what was about to happen to him in Jerusalem, the disciples were sleepy, and they quickly fell asleep. Jesus' admonition, "Watch and pray so that you will not fall into temptation" (26:41), seems directed as much to Matthew's readers as to the disciples. His words echo the warning he gave to those awaiting his second coming, "Keep watch.... [You] must be ready, because the Son of Man will come at an hour when you do not expect him" (24:42 – 44).

Jesus voluntarily gave himself over to his enemies because he saw it as a fulfillment of Scripture (26:54, 56). He was first taken to Caiaphas, the high priest, where he was interrogated (v.57). False witnesses were brought forward to testify against him (vv.59 – 63). When asked directly by the high priest if he was "the Messiah, the Son of God," Jesus said, "You have said so" (v.64). Looking beyond his crucifixion, Jesus stated that he, the messianic Son of Man, would return, "coming on the clouds of heaven" (v.64). The high priest then condemned Jesus of blasphemy. Peter, as Jesus had foretold (vv.31 – 35), denied him three times.

The chief priests and elders then handed him over to the Roman governor, Pilate (27:1 – 2). Matthew goes to great lengths to demonstrate Jesus' innocence. Before taking his own life, for example, Judas, his betrayer, confessed he had "betrayed innocent blood" (v.4). Pilate, in "great amazement" (v.14), was unable to find a single valid charge against Jesus. Pilate's wife sent him a message to have nothing "to do with that innocent man" (v.19). The crowd called for the freedom of a murderer, Barabbas, over that of Jesus (vv.15 – 21). Finally Pilate, washing his hands before the crowd, stated, "I am innocent of this man's blood" (v.24). The crowd readily consented, "Let his blood be on us and on our children!" (v.25).

In utter humiliation (vv.27 – 31, 41 – 44), Jesus was crucified (vv.32 – 56). At the moment of his death, the curtain of the temple was torn (v.51), the earth shook (v.51), the tombs broke open, "and the bodies of many holy people who had died were raised to life" (v.52). The Roman centurion and guards, terrified, said, "Surely he was the Son of God" (v.54). These events bear a marked similarity to those of Daniel's vision of the coming of the Son of Man (Da 7:13 – 14; cf. 12:1 – 2). Matthew surely had an eye on Daniel as he recorded these events of Jesus' death (see Da 9:26).

IV. The Resurrection (28:1 – 20)

Matthew assures his readers that Jesus' tomb was secured, lest "his disciples come and steal the body and tell the people that he [had] been raised from the dead" (27:64). Thus, when he writes of the resurrection, this was no hoax. As the angel first announced the birth of Jesus to his mother, Mary (1:18), so now the angel announced his resurrection to the two Marys at the tomb (28:1 – 7). While the guards were being paid off to tell a different story (vv.11 – 15), the women, having seen Jesus on their way back to Jerusalem (vv.9 – 10), were joyfully telling the disciples what they had seen.

Jesus met his disciples in Galilee and sent them out to "make disciples of all nations," promising to be with them till the end of the age (vv.19 – 20). Matthew's gospel has reached its climax, the end toward which it was heading — the good news was now to be proclaimed to Gentiles as well as to the Jews.

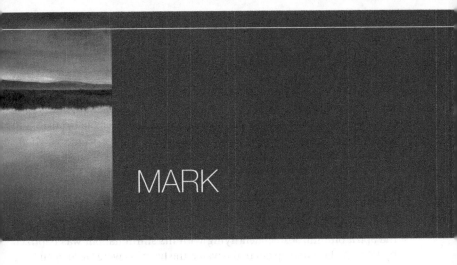

MARK

Introduction

The title of the gospel, "According to Mark," is found on the earliest manuscripts of this gospel, but these manuscripts date from the fourth century AD. The book is thus an anonymous work. The author's primary interest lies in the key events of the last week in the ministry of Jesus Christ, i.e., in his death and resurrection. The proportionally large final section of the book (chs. 11 – 16) is devoted solely to Christ's last seven days in Jerusalem.

I. The Beginning (1:1 – 13)

A. The Prologue (1:1)

Mark describes Jesus from the very start as the "Son of God" (v.1). The context suggests that Mark intended this first verse both as an introduction to the book and as a description of its first major section, the ministry of John the Baptist, which is, strictly speaking, "the beginning" of the gospel (cf. Ac 1:22).

B. John the Baptist (1:2 – 8)

Mark begins his account of the ministry of John the Baptist with a quotation that combines three OT passages: Ex 23:20; Mal 3:1; Isa 40:3. These passages identify John the Baptist as the fulfillment of the promise of a "messenger" who was to prepare for the Messiah. According to Mal 4:5, the messenger was to be the prophet Elijah. Mark presumably means the "messenger" would be a prophet "like Elijah," in the same way that the Messiah was to be a prophet "like Moses" (cf. Dt 18:15; 34:10).

Central to John is his emphasis on the forgiveness of sins (v.4). Already Mark is preparing the way for presenting Jesus as the servant of the Lord who would take away the sin of the world. John's words about baptism (v.8) should be understood in light of the OT view of the messianic kingdom. When the Messiah came, God would gather the people of Israel, sprinkle them clean with water, and put his Spirit within them (Eze 36:24–28).

C. The Baptism and Temptation of Jesus (1:9–13)

Mark introduces Jesus with an account of his baptism and the descent of the Spirit on him. Jesus, identifying with his sinful nation, was baptized by John. As he came up out of the water, the heavens were "torn open," the Spirit descended upon him as a dove, and a voice said, "You are my Son, whom I love; with you I am well pleased" (v.11). Jesus is here identified as the Spirit-filled messianic prophet of Isa 61:1, the messianic Davidic King in Ps. 2:7, and the Servant of the Lord in Isa 42:1.

II. The Beginnings of the Galilean Ministry (1:14–3:6)

A. Summary Statement (1:14–15)

Verses 14–15 establish the framework of Jesus' Galilean ministry. Mark telescopes this into a short ministry of Jesus that took place before the imprisonment of John the Baptist.

The summary of Jesus' message is: "The time has come. The kingdom of God has come near. Repent and believe the good news." In fulfillment of Isa 9:1, Jesus preached this message first in Galilee. As the concept of the kingdom of God comes into clearer focus throughout Mark, it is shaped by Daniel's vision of the messianic Son of Man who was to receive God's kingdom and rule over all nations in the last days (see comments on Da 7:10–14).

B. The Call of the Disciples (1:16–20)

Jesus called four disciples here: Peter, Andrew, James, and John. All were fishermen, and Jesus promised to send out his disciples to "fish for people." Mark returns to the theme of the call to discipleship elsewhere in his gospel (3:13–19; 6:7–13). Thus, Mark's gospel, like Matthew's, was intended as instruction in discipleship.

C. Jesus in the Synagogue at Capernaum (1:21 – 28)

Jesus' message about the coming of the kingdom of God was backed up by divine authority. The demons recognized his authority, and their words reveal that the age-old battle was coming to a head: "Have you come to destroy us?" (v.24). They were aware that the battle foretold in Ge 3:15 was now moving into its final stage. But though the battle had begun, the victory lay yet in the future. The ultimate defeat of the devil would wait until the final victory over sin and death in Jesus' own death and resurrection.

D. Jesus Heals the Sick (1:29 – 34)

The first healing miracle of Jesus, Peter's mother-in-law (vv.29 – 31), demonstrated Jesus' authority over physical disease. Jesus would not permit the demons to speak "because they knew who he was." Thus, Jesus had the authority to quiet the evil spirits; his victory over them was assured. The coming of the kingdom of God was not to be announced by the powers of evil.

E. Jesus' Prayer and Departure (1:35 – 39)

Though the news of Jesus' miracles had attracted large crowds, Jesus went out alone to pray. Already his mission was beginning to baffle his disciples. Jesus, who knew well what his mission was, calmly explained that he had come to preach in the synagogues throughout Galilee, and that was what he intended to do. Jesus was not looking for large crowds to be awed by his miracle-working power. Rather, God had sent him to proclaim his message throughout the land (v.38). Thus Jesus traveled throughout Galilee "preaching and driving out demons" (v.39).

F. The Healing of the Leper (1:40 – 45)

Jesus was approached by a leper and he healed him — further evidence of his divine authority. His warning to the leper to keep silent about this deed, go to the priest, and offer the necessary gift for cleansing shows that Jesus followed the requirements of the Mosaic law. Jesus did not offer a new way of approaching God. Rather, he saw himself as the fulfillment of the old.

G. Conflicts Begin (2:1 – 3:6)

In chs. 2 – 3 Mark brings together a series of incidents, each of which involves Jesus in a conflict with the Jewish leaders. As a background to this conflict, we see the growing popularity of Jesus with the common people. But as it grew, so did the opposition. Mark concludes these accounts with the ultimate confrontation between Jesus and the Jewish leaders—their accusation that Jesus was in collusion with Beelzebub (3:20–30).

III. Later Stages of the Galilean Ministry (3:7 – 6:6a)

A. Summary Statement (3:7 – 12)

The latter part of Jesus' Galilean ministry is described in summary fashion. Jesus had withdrawn from Capernaum to the Sea of Galilee. Large crowds followed him there. Also large crowds came to him from all parts of Galilee and Judea. Mark reiterates Jesus' authority over the unclean spirits and his preventing them from revealing his identity.

B. Appointment of the Twelve (3:13 – 19)

The twelve disciples were appointed by name and, according to some manuscripts of this gospel, were called "apostles" (see note on v.14). An apostle is someone sent from the beginning to preach with authority (cf. comment on Ac 1:22).

C. Opposition from Jerusalem (3:20 – 35)

This account gives an assessment of the judgments being formed about Jesus—by his kinsmen and by the religious leaders in Jerusalem. The teachers of the law from Jerusalem charged him with being "possessed by Beelzebul! By the prince of demons he is driving out demons" (v.22). Jesus demonstrates that such a charge was gravely dangerous and false (vv.23–27). The parable concludes with a stern warning about blasphemy against the Holy Spirit (v.29).

D. The Parables of the Kingdom (4:1 – 34)

Jesus had come teaching that "the kingdom of God has come near" (1:15). His message, however, had not been widely received by the people to whom the kingdom had been promised in the OT. In fact, the leaders of the people had rejected the kingdom Jesus offered. But this rejection did not take him by surprise. A time would come when the bridegroom would be taken away from his own (2:20). Nevertheless, the idea that the kingdom could come and yet be rejected by God's people was a new idea in the Bible's eschatology. Mark thus gives his readers a sampling of Jesus' parables to help explain the nature of this new idea.

The parable of the sower (vv.3–20) shows that only a few of those who hear the word of Christ will accept it. The parable of the lamp set on a stand (vv.21–25) teaches that even though the message of Christ is a mystery to some, it should be proclaimed to all. The parable of the growing seed (vv.26–29) teaches that God alone is responsible for the growth of Christ's kingdom. The parable of the mustard seed (vv.30–32) shows that the ultimate success of Christ's kingdom is assured precisely because God will give it its growth.

Verse 11 introduces two important terms: "secret" (Gk *mysterion*, "mystery") and "the kingdom of God." A "mystery" is a truth previously unknown that now has been revealed. Jesus distinguishes between those who know the "mystery" of the kingdom of God and those who only receive the parable. In other words, the parable is a way of both revealing and concealing the truth about God's kingdom (see v.12).

E. Jesus' Power over the Enemies of Humankind (4:35 – 5:43)

In each of the next four accounts Jesus is portrayed as one who has authority over our great enemies: storms, spirits, disease, and death.

1. The calming of the storm (4:35 – 41)

The significance of Jesus' calming the raging sea lies in the role that the sea played in the OT. God divided the sea to allow the dry lands to appear on behalf of humankind (Ge 1). When human beings forsook God's way, God was grieved and sent the sea back over the whole earth and all living beings (Ge 6–9). When God wanted to make known his power to save his people, he brought them to the Red Sea, rebuked it, and dried it up (Ps 106:9). Thus, when Jesus stilled the raging sea here, he was demonstrating his authority over humanity's age-old enemy, the sea (cf. Ps 89:9; 69:2, 15; 18:16).

The most prominent feature is the question of the disciples: "Who is this? Even the wind and the waves obey him!" (4:41). Mark leaves the question unanswered, but the answer is clear in light of the OT emphasis on God's power over the sea (cf. Job 38:8–11). There is no clearer demonstration of the deity of Jesus in the NT. He has the power of the Creator who can rebuke the sea and wind and bring calm.

2. The healing of the demoniac from Gerasenes (5:1 – 20)

The demoniac, like the sea, raged out of control, posing a threat to all who walked by. When Jesus confronted him, the man became calm (v.15). When the people of the region saw the work of Jesus, they, like the disciples earlier in the boat, "were afraid" and pleaded with Jesus "to leave their region." Those who heard the news from the demoniac himself "were amazed" (v.20). Jesus had begun to do the mighty works of God among the people of Israel and the nations. He thus gave clear evidence that the kingdom of God was at hand.

3. The healing of the woman and the raising of the dead girl (5:21 – 43)

Jairus, the lay leader of a synagogue, asked Jesus to heal his daughter. On his way Jesus was met by a woman with a bleeding problem, a condition that had lasted twelve years. She secretly touched Jesus in the crowd, hoping to be made well (v.28). Mark has already shown that many had come to Jesus to be healed just by touching him (3:10; cf. 6:56). Jesus perceived that the power for healing went forth from him (v.30).

While Jesus was speaking to the woman, the servants of the synagogue ruler's household came to tell him that his daughter was dead and Jesus did not need to come (v.35). When Jesus told them that the child was not dead but only sleeping, they laughed at him. But Jesus, knowing he had authority even over death, knew he had power to raise her. The people were "completely astonished" at this demonstration of power.

F. Rejection of Jesus at Nazareth (6:1 – 6a)

Mark concludes his narrative of the ministry of Jesus in Galilee by an account of his rejection in his own city, Nazareth. The words of the close friends of Jesus' family ("Isn't this Mary's son?") provide a striking contrast to Mark's overall presentation of Jesus as "the Son of God" (e.g., 1:1, 11). Their question receives a resounding reply in the words of the centurion standing at the cross when Jesus died: "Surely this man was the Son of God!" (15:39).

Jesus used a proverb to explain his rejection: "A prophet is not without honor except in his own town, among his relatives and in his own home" (v.4). Through this proverb, Mark gives further proof that Jesus' claims were true. His rejection in his own city proves he was a true prophet!

IV. Jesus Goes outside Galilee (6:6b – 8:26)

A. Sending of the Twelve (6:7 – 13)

In 3:14 – 15 Jesus chose his disciples "that he might send them out to preach and to have authority to drive out demons." Jesus now began to use them for this purpose, to prepare the way for his coming. This sending immediately began to draw fire from Jerusalem (cf. 3:22). Thus Mark turns our attention to Herod and gives us a glimpse of the spread of God's kingdom from within the enemy camp.

B. Opposition from Jerusalem (6:14–29)

The account of the death of John the Baptist is inserted here within that of the sending of the Twelve (which concludes in 6:30), even though that death happened much earlier. The opposition Jesus was facing from Herod is the same as that which John the Baptist had faced. Just as Herod and those in Jerusalem had opposed John, a true prophet sent from God, so also they were now plotting against Jesus. The conclusion is transparent: Jesus also is a true prophet. Curiously, Herod himself acknowledged John as a true prophet in that he believed that John had "been raised from the dead" (6:16).

C. Feeding of the Five Thousand (6:30–44)

When the Twelve returned to Jesus, they reported all they had accomplished and taught. Together, Jesus and the Twelve withdrew into the desert to rest, but a large crowd gathered to hear Jesus teach. Mark describes them as "sheep without a shepherd" — a link to Israel in the desert (Nu 27:17); thus it provides a further link between the manna that the Israelites received in the desert and this account of the feeding of the five thousand.

After everyone had eaten their fill, twelve basketfuls of bread and fish remained (v.43), which shows that Jesus' miracle even surpassed that in the days of Moses. In Moses' day no one could keep any until morning (Ex 16:19).

D. Walking on the Sea (6:45–52)

Jesus' power over the sea is reminiscent of the Lord's use of Moses to conquer the Red Sea (Ex 14:21). Note again a contrast between Moses' dividing the sea and walking through it on dry ground and Jesus "walking on the lake" (6:49). Just as Moses shouted to the people, "Do not be afraid. Stand firm and you will see the deliverance the LORD will bring you today" (Ex 14:13), so Jesus told his terrified disciples, "Take courage! It is I. Don't be afraid" (6:50). Mark's conclusion highlights the unbelief and hardness of heart of the disciples, similar to Israel: "They had not understood about the loaves; their hearts were hardened" (6:52).

E. Summary of Healings (6:53–56)

As an introduction to the growing opposition of the Jewish leaders from Jerusalem, Mark summarizes what the crowds were asking Jesus to do. From within these large crowds Jesus met opposition from "the Pharisees and some of the teachers of the law who had come from Jerusalem" (7:1).

F. Teaching against the Rules of the Pharisees (7:1 – 23)

A question about "washings" provides an occasion for a discourse on religious rites and rules. The Pharisees asked a question about the validity of the "tradition of the elders" (i.e., a Jewish custom about washing of hands, vv.3 – 4). Such a clarification is important because Jesus' answer undermined the basic premise of the Pharisees' question by rejecting the validity of their tradition: "Thus you nullify the word of God by your tradition" (v.13).

G. A Syrophoenician Woman (7:24 – 30)

Here a Gentile woman found acceptance with God through her faith, apart from any dependence on the Jewish purity laws. Moreover, her request was for Jesus to cast an "impure spirit" out of her daughter. The narrative thus graphically illustrates the need to purify the heart. This is precisely the theme of the preceding passage, where Jesus said, "All these evils come from inside and defile a person" (7:23).

H. Deaf Man Healed (7:31 – 37)

According to the prophet Isaiah, when the promised Messiah comes, "then will the eyes of the blind be opened and the ears of the deaf unstopped" (Isa 35:5). Mark provides specific examples of the fulfillment of this prophecy in the ministry of Jesus. The deaf man can hear (vv.31 – 37) and the blind man can see (8:22 – 26). The people, both Jews and Gentiles, recognized this "with amazement."

I. Blindness Removed (8:1 – 26)

Mark has arranged several scenes to show the gradual process of Jesus' removing the blindness of those around him. First he recounts Jesus' feeding the four thousand (vv.1 – 9; cf. 6:30 – 44); Mark's emphasis falls on the similarity between Jesus' miracle and God's gift of manna to the Israelites in the desert (Ex 16). Moreover, the bread provided by Jesus can be "left over" for continual provision. This is the very point Jesus stressed to his disciples in the next section when they were again worried that they had no bread to eat. Jesus provided continuously but the disciples still did not understand (vv.14 – 21).

To show that such an understanding comes as a gradual process, Mark recounts the story of the healing of the blind man at Bethsaida (vv.22 – 26). When this man was healed, he could see, but only partially (v.24). This man's sight provides the perfect picture of Mark's view of the disciples' faith. Only when Jesus touched the man again could he see perfectly (v.25).

V. The Way to Jerusalem (8:27 – 10:52)

Here is the turning point of the book. Up to now Jesus has been silent about his full intentions to suffer for the sins of the human race. There have been allusions and hints that he is the Servant of the Lord, but his disciples have not fully grasped the significance of his mission. We must assume Mark's readers do not yet understand either. From here on, the mission of Jesus becomes clearer: He must be delivered up to die and to be raised again as the Messiah.

A. Peter's Confession — the Turning Point (8:27 – 30)

While traveling outside Galilee, in Caesarea Philippi, Jesus asked the disciples what the people were saying about his ministry. Clearly the people had little understanding of who Jesus was. Jesus then asked the disciples: "But who do you say I am?" It was Peter who answered, "You are the Messiah" (v.29; cf. 1:1). Mark leaves this confession as the climax of the account.

Following Peter's confession, Jesus began to teach the disciples, and Mark's readers, the full significance of what the title Messiah meant.

B. Jesus' Teaching on the Messiah (8:31 – 38)

The chief element in Jesus' teaching is the emphasis on the suffering and death of the Messiah: "The Son of Man must suffer many things and ... be killed" (v.31). The primary OT passage underlying Jesus' teaching is Isa 53, where the messianic figure of the "servant of the LORD" pours out his soul in death for the sins of the people. The upcoming sacrificial death of Jesus is the means whereby he would give his life as a ransom for many.

C. Events on the Way to Jerusalem (9:1 – 10:52)

1. The Transfiguration (9:1 – 13)

In the transfiguration of Christ, Peter, James, and John "see ... the kingdom of God ... come with power." This brief glimpse of Jesus' future glory was only a foretaste of the kingdom, but it clearly demonstrated the nature of that kingdom and its power. Like Moses at Mount Sinai (Ex 34:29 – 35), Jesus "was transfigured" and became "dazzling white" (vv.2 – 3). Moses and Elijah, two great prophets of the OT (cf. Dt 18:15; 34:10; Mal 4:4 – 5), appeared along with Jesus. When the transfiguration ended, the disciples realized that the time of the establishment of the kingdom had not yet come. In fact, it would not come until after the resurrection (vv.9 – 10).

2. The healing of the possessed boy (9:14 – 32)

The story of the healing of the possessed boy turns on two different but related points. (1) Faith is the key to God's work and power. When the disciples were unable to drive out the impure spirit, Jesus stressed the centrality of faith by replying, "Everything is possible for one who believes." The father confessed, "I do believe."

(2) The father then requested, "Help me overcome my unbelief!" About this siutation Jesus told his disciples, "This kind [of demon] can come out only by prayer." Behind the call to faith is a further call for a stronger faith. Faith must grow to maturity. Mark is challenging his readers to go beyond an initial recognition of Jesus as the Son of God; they must strengthen their faith through prayer.

The need for more faith is reinforced in vv.30 – 32. Jesus again reminded the disciples of his impending betrayal and death. The disciples, however, "did not understand what he meant." The readiness of the boy's father to ask Jesus for more faith is thus contrasted with the disciples' reticence to ask Jesus for more understanding.

3. Questions (9:33 – 10:12)

Mark has grouped a series of questions that the disciples and followers of Christ will face in the future as well as several warnings regarding Jesus' impending death in Jerusalem. Jesus had an immediate mission but also knew that the consequences of that mission extend far into the future.

4. Discourses on the Kingdom of God (10:13 – 52)

Here are five narratives on the nature of the kingdom of God. The kingdom is to be received as a little child (vv.13 – 16). The rich will enter the kingdom only with great difficulty (vv.17 – 27). Discipleship will have its reward in the kingdom (vv.28 – 31). Greatness in the kingdom will be characterized by service, not by privilege (vv.32 – 45). The King of the kingdom is the promised Son of David (vv.46 – 52), and salvation comes to those who have faith in this King (10:52; cf. Ps 2:12).

VI. Ministry in Jerusalem (11:1 – 13:37)

A. The Entry into Jerusalem (11:1 – 11)

When Jesus entered Jerusalem on a donkey, the Messiah promised in the prophets was officially presented to the Jews. This event fulfilled Zec 9:9, where the Messiah is depicted as a victorious King, bringing salvation and peace to a rejoicing nation. Zechariah's king was "lowly and riding on a donkey," but his dominion "will extend from sea to sea" (cf. Zec 9:9 – 10; Ge 49:8 – 12).

In 11:10 the crowd shouted, "Blessed is the coming kingdom of our father David," but by v.11 the crowd was gone as quickly as it came. With only his disciples, Jesus left the city and returned to Bethany. The King left Jerusalem without his people. Thus Mark has turned our attention to the rejection of Jesus. The next narratives will provide more details about what happened to the people's hope. Like the fig tree, they had withered from the root by the next day (11:12 – 14, 20 – 21).

B. The Barren Fig Tree and the Cleansing of the Temple (11:12 – 25)

The fig tree was cursed for not producing fruit. Mark adds the explanation that the figs were not in season — thus Jesus was cursing the tree, not simply because it had not produced fruit, but because it was a symbol of the unfaithfulness of God's people.

Like the fig tree, the worship of the people at the temple was not pleasing to God. There was no faith there. Jesus drove out those who focused on the external aspects of Israel's worship. His actions warned of impending judgment on this people.

C. Controversy at the Temple (11:27 – 12:34)

Mark includes five brief narratives that show the nature of the controversy that arose between Jesus and the Jewish leaders. Most of the discussion took place within the temple courts. The section ends with the brief and curious interchange between Jesus and "one of the teachers of the law" who approached him individually after the others. Unlike the others, Jesus said to this one, "You are not far from the kingdom of God" (12:34). Thus there were two main groups represented in these controversies: the religious leaders who sought only to find fault in Jesus' teaching and the one who truly sought wisdom.

1. Question of Jesus' authority (11:27 – 33)

The chief priests, the teachers of the law, and the elders asked Jesus, "By what authority are you doing these things?" Jesus related the question of his authority to the larger question of the ministry of John the Baptist, but the Jerusalem leaders were unwilling to commit themselves on this subject before the crowds. Mark thus exposes the hypocrisy of the religious leaders, but he also draws a connection again between John the Baptist and Jesus, a recurrent theme in this gospel since the beginning (1:2–8). A new aspect here is that even the leaders in Jerusalem, by their silence, were willing to concede the connection.

2. The wicked tenants (12:1 – 12)

Jesus' parable of the wicked tenants was addressed to these same leaders (v.1). The parable is about Israel's treatment of the prophets (including John the Baptist) throughout their long history; "some of them they beat, others they killed" (v.5). In this parable Jesus again anticipated his own death at their hands (see vv.7–8). The parable thus exposed the plans of the chief priests and teachers of the law who were "looking for a way to kill him" (11:18).

3. Question of taxes to Caesar (12:13 – 17)

Did Jesus' controversy with the leaders in Jerusalem also pit him against the Roman authorities? No, for this attempt of the Pharisees and Herodians to catch Jesus in his words only showed that Jesus bore no malice against Rome. He was not a rebel; he was a revivalist. Jesus answered his accusers with a proverb: "Give back to Caesar what is Caesar's and to God what is God's" (v.17).

4. Question of the resurrection (12:18 – 27)

The question raised by the Sadducees was intended as an argument against the notion of a resurrection (cf. v.18). Jesus assailed their apparent lack of understanding, for the Scriptures speak of a future that is altogether different than the past or the present. The resurrection will be a totally different life from present human existence; people "will be like the angels in heaven" (v.25). Jesus obviously read the OT Scriptures differently than the Jewish leaders. The resurrection will mean a new order of life.

5. The great commandment (12:28 – 34)

One of the teachers of the law posed a question to Jesus, apparently out of sincere interest: What is the essence of the law? When Jesus replied that it is to love God and your neighbor, the scribe agreed and confirmed it by adding a central teaching from the OT, "to love [God] ... and to love your neighbor ... is more important than all burnt offerings and sacrifices" (cf. Hos 6:6; Mic 6:8). Seeing that he answered "wisely," Jesus said, "You are not far from the kingdom of God." Jesus affirmed the importance of love over burnt offerings.

D. Teaching at the Temple (12:35 – 44)

Jesus' discourses at the temple ended with three examples of his teaching. In the first (vv.35 – 37), he raised the issue of the Messiah as the Son of God. Referring to Ps 110, he asked: How can the scribes say that the Messiah is only an earthly king if David himself calls him Lord? The kingdom of God he proclaimed was not an earthly kingdom but the heavenly kingdom, the reign of the Son of Man that will be established on earth in the last days.

A further lesson about the nature of the kingdom of God came next in the form of a warning: Beware of teachers of the law who seek their own power and glory (vv.38 – 40). When the kingdom comes, "these men will be punished most severely."

Finally, Jesus gave the object lesson of the widow's penny (vv.41 – 44). The wealthy gave only a portion of themselves to God's work, whereas the widow gave "all she had to live on." Such is the nature of the kingdom of God.

E. The End of the Age (13:1 – 37)

Jesus and the disciples left the temple, and Jesus was now speaking only with his followers. In v.2 he predicted the destruction of the temple, which happened in AD 70.

Later, on the Mount of Olives, four of his disciples asked him, "When will these things happen? And what will be the sign that they are all about to be fulfilled?" The disciples' question related not to the time of the destruction of the temple but rather to the time of the appearance of the Son of Man (v.26). In response to these questions, Jesus immediately called for discernment. The disciples will have to distinguish between false claims that the times have arrived and true signs that the times are near. When they see the world around them going from bad to worse, they should take heed that this is not yet the end (v.7); it is only "the beginning" of the end (v.8). That is, there will be a time of great distress before "the end" comes. When it does, only "the one who stands firm to the end will be saved" (v.13).

Jesus then described what the "beginning" of the end would be like (vv.9 – 13). Some of these things happened to the disciples in the book of Acts, but much of it goes far beyond those events, such as the event Jesus described in v.14, " 'the abomination that causes desolation' standing where it does not belong." This event will signal the final moments before the end, a time of "distress [tribulation] unequaled from the beginning" (vv.19 – 25). The Lord will mercifully cut this time period short (v.20), and then the Son of Man will come in the clouds, gather the elect, and establish his kingdom (vv.26 – 27).

What is the "abomination that causes desolation"? Mark himself inserts a comment to the reader to take special note. Why? Because the "abomination that causes desolation" is specifically developed elsewhere in Scripture (Da 9:25 – 27), and Jesus wants his readers to draw on that passage for understanding this one.

VII. The Death of Jesus (14:1 – 15:47)

A. Events Leading Up to His Death (14:1 – 52)

The chief priests and teachers of the law were plotting to kill Jesus (vv.1 – 2). Jesus was in Bethany at the home of Simon the leper (vv.3 – 9) when a woman came to him with a vial of costly perfume and poured it over his head. Jesus interpreted her action as a prophetic act announcing his coming death. At this same time, Judas was with the Jewish leaders giving them Jesus' whereabouts (vv.10 – 11).

In vv.12 – 26, Mark stresses that the Last Supper was the Passover meal. His account of the meal serves two purposes. (1) It demonstrated that the salvation of the Lord, commemorated in the Passover meal, was about to be realized in the death of Jesus, and that it was also to be commemorated by God's people.

(2) Mark's account demonstrated that Jesus' death was not a catastrophe that overtook Jesus, but rather something for which he had long prepared. Moreover, the scattering of the disciples after his death was also known beforehand (v.27; Zec 13:7). Jesus also prepared them for his resurrection by promising to go before them to Galilee after he was raised (v.28).

In the account of Jesus' prayer in the garden (vv.33 – 42), the disciples again failed to understand his mission. This was the time prepared by God, before the foundation of the world, when the ultimate sacrifice of his Son would be offered, but the disciples fell asleep three times. After the third time, Jesus said, "Are you still sleeping and resting? Enough! The hour has come" (v.41). Mark was offering some explanation why the disciples abandoned Jesus during the crucifixion (v.50). Soon after, Peter publicly denied Jesus three times (vv.66 – 72). There is a lesson here for Mark's readers: "Watch and pray so that you will not fall into temptation" (v.38).

In his portrayal of Jesus' betrayal, Mark demonstrates that, as the Servant of the Lord (Isa 53), Jesus voluntarily gave himself as an offering. Though the guards came out for him armed with swords and weapons, Jesus reminded them that he was not a criminal to be taken by force (cf. v.49). Rather, he was being taken since "the Scriptures must be fulfilled" (e.g., Isa 53:7 – 8).

B. The Trial of Jesus (14:53 – 15:15)

After his arrest, Jesus was taken to the home of the high priest, where the chief priests, elders, and teachers of the law had gathered. The council was the Sanhedrin, the official ruling body of the Jews in Palestine. The first stage of the trial consisted of testimonies against Jesus, but his enemies were unable to find the necessary agreement among the witnesses to condemn Jesus to death (14:55). Mark adds, "Many testified falsely against him." Jesus was not guilty of any charge. Like the Servant of the Lord (Isa 53), Jesus did not die for his own guilt but was delivered up on our behalf.

Seeing that the witnesses could not convict Jesus, the high priest (Caiaphas) stepped forward to question him. Jesus remained silent, and Caiaphas asked: "Are you the Messiah, the Son of the Blessed One?" (v.61). Jesus gave the simple answer, "I am," and he continued with quotations from Da 7:13 and Ps 110:1, both of which contain prophecies about the Messiah. This was deemed sufficient to condemn Jesus.

Following the verdict, some began to mock Jesus for his messianic claim. At this same time, Peter was below in the courtyard, denying Jesus. He serves as a stern reminder of the need to remain faithful to Jesus in spite of the severest adversity.

Early the next morning the Sanhedrin presented their case against Jesus to Pilate (15:1 – 15). Jesus was charged with being the "king of the Jews." In effect, Jesus remained silent throughout the ordeal (v.5). Behind Mark's emphasis on the silence of Jesus before his accusers lies the picture of the silent Suffering Servant of Isa 53:7. Before Pilate condemned Jesus to death, he did all he could to free Jesus because he could find no fault with him. He even offered to release him as part of the festival custom, but the crowd asked for Barabbas instead. For Mark this was unmistakable testimony to the innocence of Jesus. In the end, however, because of the insistence of the crowd, Pilate felt he had no choice but to deliver Jesus over to be crucified.

C. The Crucifixion (15:16 – 41)

Roman law mandated that a conviction of capital punishment be carried out immediately. Jesus was forced to carry his cross to the site of his death, Golgotha. He was offered a mixture of wine and myrrh, but he refused. Mark stresses the personal shame and sorrow of the crucifixion rather than physical pain. It thus lays great stress on the theological aspects of Christ's death, not the physical.

From noon ("the sixth hour") until midafternoon ("the ninth hour") darkness fell over the whole land. At the end of that time, Jesus cried out,

"My God, my God, why have you forsaken me?" These words come from Ps 22:1 and express the cry of the righteous Messiah for God's help as he bore the sin of the world. After his final cry and death, a Roman centurion standing near said: "Surely this man was the Son of God!" (v.39). By these words, Mark sees the summation of his gospel: Jesus is the Son of God (cf. 1:1, 11).

D. The Burial (15:42 – 47)

A wealthy Jewish leader, Joseph of Arimathea, "who was himself waiting for the kingdom of God," courageously asked permission to bury Jesus. When Pilate learned that Jesus had died, he gave the body to Joseph (15:45). Mark may have had Isa 53:9 in mind: "He was assigned a grave with the wicked, and with the rich in his death."

VIII. The Resurrection of Jesus (16:1 – 8)

These verses record the resurrection of Jesus. Mark focuses only on the empty tomb and the angel who announced to the women that Jesus had risen from the dead. The angel told the women to tell the disciples and Peter that they would see Jesus in Galilee, as he had told them (14:28). The women fled from the tomb "trembling and bewildered" and, out of great fear, told no one what they had seen and heard (16:8).

The ending of Mark found in the NIV (vv.9 – 20) is not attested by the earliest manuscripts. Most believe it was attached to the end of the gospel of Mark at a much later date. Most of the material can be found in Matthew, Luke, and Acts.

LUKE

Introduction

This gospel has the same author as the book of Acts. Both contain a prologue addressed to the same man—Theophilus. In Ac 1:1–2 the writer refers to "my former book" concerning "all that Jesus began to do and teach until the day he was taken up to heaven." This description fits the gospel of Luke. Neither book, however, names Luke as the author.

I. Early History of the Forerunner and of the Messiah (1:1 – 2:52)

The author clearly states his purpose in 1:1–4. There had been other works written about Jesus, some by eyewitnesses and others that relied on accounts handed down from eyewitnesses. Luke himself intends to go beyond them to give a more strictly chronological account. In this way he intends his gospel to provide a firm basis for Christian teaching.

Luke begins with John the Baptist, the first key figure in the series of events in the unfolding of the message of the gospel of Christ. But before recording John's birth, Luke announces the impending birth of Jesus to Mary, his mother (1:26–56). The announcement and birth of both key figures are closely intertwined in this gospel.

Mary's song (1:46–55), like Hannah's (1Sa 2:1–10), sees her promise of a son as a sign that God was fulfilling his blessing to Abraham (v.55; 1Sa 2:10). Zechariah's song (vv.67–79) also sees John's birth as a sign that God was fulfilling his blessing to Abraham (v.73) and to David (v.69).

In line with Luke's intent to tell the story of Jesus chronologically (see 1:3), he places Jesus' birth within the context of Roman history. Jesus was born in the days of Caesar Augustus, the first Roman emperor, when "Quirinius was governor of Syria" (2:1–2). Being from the line of David, Joseph had to register in a census at his ancestral birthplace, Bethlehem. Jesus was born there, as it had been foretold by the prophet Micah (Mic 5:2). After Jesus' birth, Mary wrapped him in cloths and placed him "in a manger," and his birth was announced to shepherds who lived out in the fields (2:1–20). What could be more lowly and unassuming? As with John the Baptist (1:65–66), the news of his birth spread throughout the countryside (2:17–18).

As the Mosaic law stipulated (Lev 12:3), on the eighth day Jesus was circumcised (Lk 2:21). Later he was taken to the temple to be presented as the firstborn (Ex 13:2, 12; cf. 1Sa 1:21–28), and his mother fulfilled the necessary rites for purification (Lev 12).

In a rare glimpse of Jesus' childhood, Luke shows that Jesus was well aware of his identity and calling from the Father. At twelve years old, he was found among the teachers at the temple, "listening to them and asking them questions" (2:46). Moreover, "everyone who heard him was amazed at his understanding and his answers" (v.47). When his parents scolded him, Jesus replied, "Didn't you know I had to be in my Father's house?" (v.49). Apparently the Messiah was to have a central role in the worship of God at the temple.

In spite of Jesus' self-awareness as the Son of God, he "was obedient" to his earthly parents. Luke closes his brief view of this time in Jesus' life with the summary statement: "Jesus grew in wisdom and stature, and in favor with God and men" (2:52).

II. The Beginning (3:1 – 4:13)

Luke again offers dates (cf. 2:1–2), now for the beginning of the ministry of John the Baptist in the "fifteenth year of the reign of Tiberius Caesar" (3:1). On the basis of the Roman calendar, this date would be AD 29.

A. John the Baptist, Forerunner of the Messiah (3:1 – 23)

Many saw in John's ministry the possibility that he might be the Messiah (v.15). But John quickly dispelled such ideas. As Luke stresses by quoting Isa 40 (see vv.4–6), John was the forerunner of the Messiah. Jesus' baptism was to be the occasion for the announcement of the Messiah. There a voice from heaven declared Jesus to be the Son of God (v.22).

B. The Genealogy of Jesus (3:23 – 38)

As in the narratives of the OT, the central character of Luke's gospel, Jesus, is introduced by means of a genealogy (cf. Ge 5:28 – 29). Note how Luke uses this genealogy. Jesus has just been identified as the Son of God in 3:22. Moreover, in the next chapter, his own townsfolk will ask themselves, "Isn't this Joseph's son?" (4:22). Thus, Luke strategically places his genealogy here to show that Jesus' lineage does, indeed, trace back to God; it was only supposed that he was the son of Joseph (3:23).

C. The Preparation of the Messiah (4:1 – 13)

Luke stresses the role of the Holy Spirit in the work of Jesus. He was "led by the Spirit into the wilderness" (v.1), where he was tested by the devil forty days. The first test came when Jesus had not eaten and was hungry. The devil said to him, "If you are the Son of God, tell this stone to become bread" (v.3). When God sent Israel manna in the desert, it was to "test them and see whether they will follow [his] instructions" (Ex 16:4). Jesus answered the devil's temptation with the lesson Moses himself drew from Israel's test of manna (as reflected in Dt 8:3).

Jesus, unlike Israel in the past, did not succumb to the temptations. By means of God's Word, he successfully deflected Satan's attacks. Though defeated this time, the devil only made a strategic withdrawal "until an opportune time" (v.13). The remainder of Jesus' ministry can be characterized as an ongoing battle with the devil.

III. Jesus in Galilee (4:14 – 9:50)

The Spirit led Jesus back to Galilee (4:14). There he taught in the Jewish synagogues and was highly acclaimed. At Nazareth (4:16 – 30), his hometown, Jesus went to his own synagogue and participated in the regular Sabbath reading. Turning to a well-known messianic text (Isa 61), Jesus openly and unambiguously declared that the passage was fulfilled in him (v.21). The hearers responded with predictable amazement, even raising the same question with which Luke himself was concerned in writing Jesus' genealogy: "Isn't this Joseph's son?" (v.22). But Jesus was not the son of Joseph; he was the Son of God. Moreover, their failure to see this had numerous antecedents in the OT prophets, such as Elijah and Elisha. The people's anger was aroused by Jesus' inference that their rejection of him "in his hometown" had its roots in OT times when God sent his prophets to Gentiles rather than to the rebellious Israelites (vv.25 – 27).

The amazement of the people continued in Capernaum (4:31–44). There Jesus quieted a man possessed by a demon and demonstrated his authority over "impure spirit[s]" by casting the demon out. At the home of Simon's (i.e., Peter's) mother-in-law, Jesus healed many people and cast out many demons. He continued preaching "the good news of the kingdom of God" in the synagogues of the region.

Jesus' call of his disciples began with Simon Peter, James, and John by the Lake of Gennesaret (5:1–11). When they obeyed Jesus' instructions to cast their nets on the other side of the boat, "they caught such a large number of fish that their nets began to break" (v.6). While they were astonished at the number of fish, Peter, falling on his knees, saw the broader implication: "Go away from me, Lord; I am a sinful man!" (v.8). Pulling their boats on shore, "they ... left everything and followed him" (v.11).

In spite of Jesus' own efforts to carry on a quiet ministry of healing and preaching the good news in the synagogues of Galilee, news of such healings as the leper (vv.12–14) and the paralytic (vv.17–26) quickly spread through the region, and Jesus began to attract large crowds.

Increasing opposition from the leaders of the people also came (vv.17, 21). Jesus was careful to pay respect to and obey the Mosaic law (v.14), but he drew sharp attacks from the Pharisees and the teachers of the law. When the Pharisees asked, "Who can forgive sins but God alone?" (v.21), Jesus responded with the explanation that it was for precisely this reason that he healed the sick — "I want you to know that the Son of Man has authority on earth to forgive sins" (v.24). His miracles were signs of his identity as the Son of God.

When the Pharisees asked why he ate and drank with tax collectors and sinners, Jesus responded that it was to sinners such as these, not to "the righteous," that he had been sent (5:32). When they asked why his disciples did not fast, Jesus explained his relationship with the religious rites and duties of the past: "New wine must be poured into new wineskins" (v.38).

Jesus, having called twelve disciples and designated them as apostles (6:12–16), taught them the central ideas of the kingdom of God (vv.20–49). He first defined the nature of God's blessing (vv.20–26), then stressed the central importance of love (vv.27–36), forgiveness (vv.37–42), sincerity (vv.43–45), and obedience (vv.46–49).

Jesus then returned to Capernaum (7:1), where Luke records two miracles: healing the centurion's servant (vv.1–10) and raising the widow's son in Nain (vv.11–15). The centurion, a Gentile, came to Jesus in faith, believing that Jesus could heal his servant. As such he became an object lesson in the faith of the nations around Israel and thus a contrast to the kind of faith that Jesus found in Israel (v.9). The result of Jesus' healing the widow's son was a heightened sense in Israel that God had sent a great prophet (vv.16–17). The similarities between these two stories and that of Elisha (2Ki 4–5) are intended by Luke to strengthen the people's conclusion.

The miracles Jesus performed were the decisive proof to John the Baptist that Jesus was the chosen one promised in the OT Scriptures (7:18–23). John was the last of the line of OT prophets and the first fulfillment of the promises of the OT prophets (vv.24–28). His word carried much weight with the people (v.29), though not with the Pharisees and experts in the law, who rejected John's baptism (v.30). The treatment John received at their hand was a sign that the kingdom he announced was rejected. Judgment, rather than blessing, awaited the present generation (vv.31–35).

Jesus' own explanation for his rejection by the religious leaders is disclosed in the act of the sinful woman who washed his feet with her tears, "wiped them with her hair, kissed them and poured perfume on them" (7:36–50). The Pharisee who had invited Jesus to his house was unable to understand such devotion to Jesus because, unlike this woman, he had not experienced the depth of forgiveness that this woman had.

Besides the twelve apostles, several women followed Jesus (8:1–3). These, like the woman who washed Jesus' feet, had been forgiven much and had been "cured of evil spirits and diseases" (v.2). Some also were wealthy (v.3). These followers were like the seed that landed on the good soil who heard Jesus' word, retained it, and persevered in producing a crop (vv.4–15). They would be richly rewarded (vv.16–18) and were considered closer than Jesus' own family (vv.19–21).

The disciples continually learned something new about Jesus that left them "in fear and amazement" (8:25). When he calmed the storm (vv.22–25), for example, they asked, "Who is this? He commands even the winds and the water, and they obey him." Luke's readers know the answer: Jesus is "the Messiah, the Lord" (cf. 2:11). Moreover, Jesus showed authority over a legion of demons, who begged Jesus not to send them "into the Abyss." In a graphic demonstration of his power, Jesus sent them into a herd of swine, who then rushed over a steep cliff into a lake and drowned (8:26–39). Jesus healed a woman sick for twelve years whom no one could heal, and he raised a twelve-year-old girl who lay dead in her father's house (vv.40–56).

This same authority of Jesus was given over to the disciples, and they went from village to village preaching the gospel and healing sick (9:1–6). When the news of Jesus' deeds reached Jerusalem, the leaders were dismayed (vv.8–9). Herod was left with only the question, "Who, then, is this I hear such things about?"

Even after their return from preaching and healing in the villages throughout the region, the disciples were still dependent on Jesus for their daily bread (vv.10-17). When they obeyed his word, however, their needs were met, and there were twelve basketfuls left over.

The last great lesson the disciples had to learn was that Jesus had come to give his life in preparation for the kingdom of God. Unlike many in the crowds, Peter understood that Jesus was the Messiah of God (vv.18-20). But Jesus also had to tell Peter that as the Christ, he had to be rejected, killed, and raised to life before the establishment of the kingdom of God (vv.21-27).

As a foretaste of that kingdom, Jesus took Peter, John, and James to the Mount of Transfiguration. These disciples saw a glimpse of the "glorious splendor" of the future kingdom, with Moses and Elijah talking to Jesus "about his departure, which he was about to bring to fulfillment at Jerusalem" (v.31). They also heard a voice from heaven that proclaimed Jesus as the Son of God. At this crucial turning point in Luke, Jesus "resolutely set out for Jerusalem" (v.51), and there is no doubt in the mind of the readers as to what would happen to him there.

IV. Jesus' Journey to Jerusalem (9:51 – 19:27)

In ch. 9 Jesus resolutely began his journey to Jerusalem. His purpose was clear, and he made it known to his disciples: "The Son of Man is going to be delivered into the hands of men" (9:44). He "must suffer many things and be rejected ... killed and ... raised to life" (9:22). In Luke's gospel, Jesus arrived in Jerusalem in 19:28. There are thus ten chapters devoted to his journey. Much in these chapters recounts his teaching to his disciples as well as his deeds.

Luke first recounts that Jesus passed through Samaria (9:51-56). Luke perhaps mentions this because of the similar pattern to the spread of the gospel in the early church. In Acts, Jesus told the disciples to preach the Gospel "in Jerusalem, and in all Judea and Samaria, and to the ends of the earth" (Ac 1:8). Jesus' ministry had already prepared the way for the gospel by starting in Judea and Galilee and then moving to Samaria.

The focus of Jesus' teaching turned to the kingdom of God. In the OT, Jerusalem was to be the center of the kingdom (cf. Isa 2:2-4). There was a price to pay for those who would enjoy the blessings of God's kingdom. The disciples had to count the cost (9:57-62). Moreover, those who were sent out to proclaim the gospel of the kingdom had to go as representatives of the King. Jesus thus gave his disciples strict instructions on how to carry out his work (10:1 – 24). Representatives of God's kingdom must be like lambs amid wolves (v.3). They were not to seek personal gain, but were to rely on the Lord's provision and accept the help and support of those who served him (vv.4 – 16). Their message was simple: "The kingdom of God has come near you" (v.9).

Prayer is central to the members of God's kingdom (11:1 – 13). Jesus gave his disciples a simple pattern by which to pray (vv.1 – 4). He then taught them about the importance of persistent and expectant prayer (vv.5 – 13).

With the ever-growing crowd pressing in on him, Jesus began to warn his disciples about the importance of sincerity and honesty before God (12:1 – 12). Greed and possessions can keep one from the kingdom of God (vv.13 – 21). One must trust in God, not wealth (vv.22 – 34), and must live in constant expectation of the coming Son of Man (vv.35 – 40). Such exhortations surface also in the concerns and needs of the early church.

Luke's perspective of Jesus is highlighted by Peter's question, "Lord, are you telling this parable to us, or to everyone?" (v.41). Jesus' answer further directed his message to those in the early church awaiting the second coming of the Son of Man. The faithful and wise servant, Jesus says, is one whom the master finds doing his will when he returns (vv.42 – 48).

Jesus had "a baptism to undergo" that would "bring fire on the earth." He had not come to bring peace, but division (12:49 – 53). The disciples, and Luke's readers, must learn to "interpret this present time" (vv.54 – 56). It must be remembered that when Luke wrote his gospel and its sequel, the early church knew of the things of which Jesus was here speaking.

Jesus called on the crowd to repent (13:1 – 5). Those in Jerusalem were under the same divine judgment as those in Galilee. If they had been spared thus far, it was only because they were being given another opportunity to repent (vv.6 – 9). The prospect of Jerusalem being given a second chance to repent suggests that Luke had in mind the preaching of Peter and the early church in Ac 2, when they called Jerusalem to repent. But when the people refused this second offer, God turned to the nations and offered his kingdom to them (Ac 28:28).

In the meantime, the Pharisees continued to cling to their own understanding of the law and the Sabbath and thus failed to understand the nature of the kingdom Jesus preached (14:1 – 6). As Jesus understood it, the kingdom was not for the proud but for the humble (vv.7 – 11); not for the rich and exclusive but for the poor, the crippled, the lame, and the blind (vv.12 – 14). While the kingdom would not intentionally exclude the proud and the rich, they would refuse the invitation to come (vv.15 – 24). Those who do come must count the cost, forsake all, and follow Jesus as his disciples (vv.25 – 35).

The chief stumbling block among those who considered themselves righteous and thus already members of the kingdom of God was Jesus' offer of the kingdom to those whom they had excluded. The Pharisees said, "This man welcomes sinners and eats with them" (15:2). Jesus, however, warned them that the purpose of the kingdom was to provide redemption for the lost, not a mere haven for the righteous. He illustrated this with three parables: the lost sheep (vv.3-7), the lost coin (vv.8-10), and the lost son (vv.11-32). In each of these Jesus focused on the salvation of the lost and the joy their acceptance into the kingdom should engender.

Rather than seeking to exclude such new members from the kingdom, Jesus admonished his disciples to court friendly ties with those on the outside in order to win their acceptance (16:1-15). Luke likely intended Jesus' words, "Use worldly wealth to gain friends for yourselves, so that when it is gone, you will be welcomed into eternal dwellings" (v.9), to address the situation in the early church reflected in Acts, where the early believers shared their worldly goods (Ac 2:44-45).

Forgiveness and faith must characterize the life of a disciple (17:1-6); this is the duty of a servant (vv.7-10) and arises out of a grateful heart (vv.11-19). Though the Pharisees were expecting to see the coming of the kingdom of God in their own day, Jesus warned them that it was already in their midst and they had rejected it (vv.20-21).

Jesus' disciples did not understand his teaching regarding his death and resurrection in Jerusalem (18:31-33). The blind beggar whom Jesus passed on his way to Jerusalem, however, knew that Jesus was the "Son of David" (vv.38-39). Even when rebuked, he persistently called out all the more to Jesus for mercy (v.39). Jesus answered his call, and he was healed because of his faith (vv.40-43). In the same way the chief tax collector, Zacchaeus, persistently pursued Jesus and promised to give half of his possessions to the poor and to right those he had wronged. Such a man, Jesus said, was a "son of Abraham," whom the Son of Man came to save (19:1-10).

As Jesus neared Jerusalem, the expectation arose that the kingdom of God would soon be established. Jesus warned, however, that the time had not yet come. There was to be a delay, and those who would enter the kingdom had to wait faithfully until the return of the King (vv.11-27).

V. Jesus in Jerusalem (19:28-21:38)

The King came to Jerusalem, but the kingdom was rejected (19:28-37, 41). Only his disciples recognized him as "the king who comes in the name of the Lord" (v.38). To the rest "it [was] hidden" (v.42). Jesus wept, knowing what great blessings there could have been for Israel and what great judgment lay ahead (vv.41–45). As Jesus taught in the temple, events turned quickly and decisively against him (vv.45–48).

The first question raised by the Jewish leaders was "by what authority" Jesus preached (20:1–8). Jesus related the question of his authority to the larger question of the ministry of John the Baptist. The leaders were willing to concede the connection between John and Jesus, and by their silence, they left unchallenged Jesus' implicit claim to the same authority as John.

In 20:9–19, Jesus continued to link his ministry to that of John the Baptist. The parable of the tenants is about Israel's treatment of the prophets, God's servants, throughout their long history. John was the last of these. Finally the landlord's son was sent, and "they threw him out of the vineyard and killed him" (v.15). Jesus was again anticipating his own death at their hands. Moreover, the parable exposed the plans of the chief priests and teachers of the law who "looked for a way to arrest him immediately" (v.19).

With the resurrection of Jesus only days away, the Sadducees unwittingly raised a central question (vv.27–40). Jesus assailed the apparent lack of understanding that lay behind their lack of belief in the resurrection. What they failed to see was that the Scriptures speak of a future that will be altogether different from the past or the present. To understand God's work in Scripture, one cannot merely project the present order into the future. The resurrection will be a totally different life from present human existence. The resurrection will not mean a return to the status quo; rather, it will mean a new order of life. Jesus' own resurrection would mark the beginning of that new order.

The Christ foretold in the OT as the Son of David was not a mere descendant of David. He was David's Lord (vv.41–44), and David humbly submitted to him. The Jewish teachers of the law, however, were proud and loved to hear the praises that they received from the people (vv.45–47). By contrast, the poor widow depicted here, who gave all she had, exemplifies the kind of worship that pleases God (21:1–4).

Though the present temple had great physical beauty, a time was coming when it would be destroyed and be left abandoned (21:5–6). No one knew when this would happen, but many signs would precede it. There would be wars, Jerusalem would be destroyed and "trampled on by the Gentiles," and her people would be "taken as prisoners to all the nations" (v.24). This would extend "until the times of the Gentiles are fulfilled" (v.24). After all this, the Son of Man will return, as foretold by Daniel, "in a cloud with power and great glory" (v.27). At that time, "the kingdom of God is near" (v.31).

VI. Crucifixion and Resurrection (22:1 – 24:53)

Jesus was betrayed during the time of the Passover (22:1–6). That night Jesus gathered with his disciples for a last supper before his death (vv.7–38). During the meal, he spoke of his impending death and his future return to establish his kingdom. His death meant the sacrifice of his own body for his disciples, both present and future (v.19), and the shedding of his blood was the beginning of the "new covenant" (v.20), promised by the OT prophets (Jer 31:31; Eze 36:26). Its coming signaled the end of the old covenant between God and Israel at Sinai (Jer 31:32).

Jesus explained to his disciples that his death was to be understood in terms of the "servant" prophecy of Isa 53, which "must be fulfilled" in him (22:37). The disciples were to follow his example of service and not seek to lord over others, as Gentile kings do (vv.24–28). Their time to rule would come when Jesus returned to establish his kingdom (vv.29–30).

Though the disciples said they were willing even to go to death for Jesus (22:31–38), in the hour of temptation they slept (vv.39–46), and later Peter disowned Jesus (vv.54–62). Jesus, however, knew that he would be alone in this hour (v.34). His concern was for the disciples' ongoing ministry after his resurrection and return to the Father: "I have prayed for you, Simon, that your faith may not fail. And when you have turned back, strengthen your brothers" (v.32). The perspective is clearly that of Acts, in Peter's central role in building the church.

Jesus now commissioned the disciples for the much larger task of waiting for his return: "But now if you have a purse, take it, and also a bag" (22:36). They were even told to purchase a sword, though not for taking the kingdom by storm (see vv.49–50); apparently, the swords were only to be used for protection (cf. Ne 4:17). In stressing the ongoing nature of the disciples' commission and the idea of self-support and protection entailed in Jesus' instructions, Luke perhaps has in mind the example of the apostle Paul, who in his travels and work of evangelism supported himself by making tents (Ac 18:3).

Jesus was arrested and taken by the chief priests and temple guards into the house of the high priest (vv.52–54). Peter, waiting in the courtyard, denied any association with Jesus (vv.55–60). At the high priest's house, the guards mocked and beat Jesus (vv.63–65). At daybreak Jesus stood before the council to face the charges they brought against him.

Jesus refused an outright claim to be the Messiah, saying, "If I tell you, you will not believe me, and if I asked you, you would not answer" (vv.67–68), adding, "But from now on, the Son of Man will be seated at the right hand of the mighty God" (v.69). Luke's readers can see that Jesus' words refer to the establishment of the church in Ac 2:33 and thus are a positive answer to the council's question.

When they asked further, "Are you then the Son of God?" (22:70), his answer at first glance seems even more evasive ("You say that I am"), but his enemies used it as enough evidence to hang an indictment on (v.71). The Jewish leaders then took Jesus to Pilate, the Roman governor, and offered this charge, "He … claims to be Messiah" (23:1–2). When Pilate asked for confirmation, Jesus again replied with an ambiguous answer, "You have said so" (v.3). Thus Pilate could find "no basis for a charge against" Jesus (v.4).

When Pilate discovered that Jesus was a Galilean and hence under the jurisdiction of Herod, he sent Jesus to him. Herod, having heard much about Jesus, wanted to see him perform a miracle (vv.5–8). Jesus, however, refused to answer any of Herod's questions (v.9).

Luke stresses that Pilate found Jesus to be innocent of the charges brought against him (vv.10–25). Instead, it was the crowd who wanted Jesus crucified (vv.18–23). In the end, Pilate gave in to their wishes (vv.24–25).

Even as they led Jesus off to be crucified, Jesus spoke of the impending destruction of Jerusalem (vv.26–31). On the cross, however, Jesus said, "Father, forgive them, for they do not know what they are doing" (v.34). Luke has in mind a link between these words of Jesus on the cross and Peter's appeal to the people of Jerusalem after the resurrection: "God has made this Jesus, whom you crucified, both Lord and Christ.... Repent and be baptized, every one of you, in the name of Jesus Christ for the forgiveness of your sins" (Ac 2:36–38).

On the cross, Jesus was surrounded by scoffers. There were three notable exceptions. (1) One of the criminals crucified with Jesus said, "Jesus, remember me when you come into your kingdom" (23:40–43) and thus became the first to enjoy the new covenant. (2) The centurion guarding Jesus said, "Surely this was a righteous man" (v.47). (3) A member of the council that had turned Jesus over to Pilate, Joseph of Arimathea, took the body of Jesus and laid it in his own tomb (vv.50–54). Each one of these openly confessed allegiance to him. The rest of the crowd "beat their breasts and went away" (v.48). Only the women who had been with Jesus followed to see where the body of Jesus was being laid (v.55).

When the women returned two days later to prepare the body of Jesus for burial, they found the tomb empty. Two angels announced that Jesus had risen (24:1-8). When the women reported to the disciples what they had seen, no one believed them. Luke gives a revealing picture of the state of mind of Jesus' followers on the day of the resurrection. Peter ran to the tomb and found it empty. He left the tomb "wondering to himself what had happened" (vv.9-12).

Two of Jesus' disciples, en route to Emmaus, confessed to their unknown inquisitor, "We had hoped that [Jesus] was the one who was going to redeem Israel" (v.21). Moreover, they said, it had been three days since the crucifixion, and all they had heard was the report of the women's vision at the empty tomb that Jesus was alive (vv.22-24). It was not until Jesus explained the OT Scriptures to the disciples and broke bread with them that "their eyes were opened and they recognized him" as the risen Lord (vv.25-32). These two features are likewise stressed in Acts: proof from Scripture (Ac 2:14-28) and fellowship around the breaking of the bread (Ac 2:42).

The two men returned to Jerusalem with the news of Jesus' resurrection, only to be told that Jesus had appeared to Simon Peter as well (vv.33-35). Suddenly Jesus himself appeared in their midst. They were still slow to believe (v.38), at first because they thought they saw a ghost (v.37) and then because of their joy and amazement (v.41). The disciples looked on as Jesus ate a piece of broiled fish in their presence (vv.42-43). As with the two men on the road to Emmaus, however, they understood these events only when Jesus explained to them the Scriptures.

Jesus went on to say that because of his sacrificial death as the Messiah and because of his resurrection (24:46), "repentance for the forgiveness of sins will be preached in his name to all nations" (v.47). The disciples themselves were to wait in Jerusalem until Jesus sent the Holy Spirit whom the Father had promised (v.49). After that, they were to be powerful witnesses of what God had done in Christ Jesus (v.48).

In obedience to Jesus' command, the disciples remained in Jerusalem and worshiped regularly at the temple (vv.50-53). Luke continues with the account of the witness of this early group of disciples in the book of Acts.

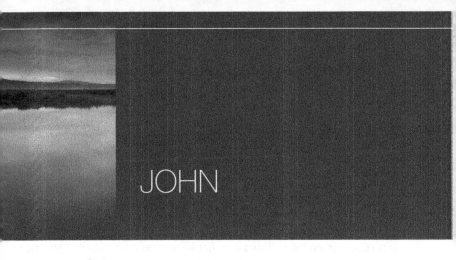

JOHN

Introduction

The author of this gospel is described as "the disciple whom Jesus loved" (21:20–24). The most likely date of writing is the last decade of the first century. The basis of this date is primarily the lack of the mention of the destruction of Jerusalem in John. It must have been written much later than AD 70, after the memory of this event had faded (though some use this argument to propose a date prior to 70).

John states clearly his intention: "that you may believe that Jesus is the Messiah, the Son of God, and that by believing you may have life in his name" (20:31). John's concept of "believe" is a central factor in the gospel—to believe is to have eternal life (3:16). This gospel was written to present the early church with a collection of signs Jesus performed to be used in evangelism.

I. Prologue (1:1 – 14)

This gospel's introduction to Jesus goes far beyond the other gospels. Jesus is the Word who was with God before creation. As the Word of God, Jesus became flesh and lived among God's people Israel. Those who believed in him were given the right to be God's children. Israel had received a revelation of God's will in the law of Moses, but they had not seen God. He lived in the tabernacle Moses built, but his glory was concealed within the Most Holy Place. Jesus revealed God's grace and truth by living among his people. In him they saw God's glory (v.14).

II. The Revelation of Jesus to the World (1:15 – 12:50)

A. The Witness of John the Baptist (1:15 – 3:36)

John the Baptist plays a key role in linking the old with the new, for he was the prophet sent from God to announce the coming of the Messiah. John the Baptist also introduces Jesus as the OT Passover Lamb, seen as a sacrifice who "takes away the sin of the world" (1:29).

The author identifies those among God's people Israel who received the light—the first disciples (1:35 – 51). When they heard John the Baptist identify Jesus as the Lamb of God, they turned and followed him (vv.36 – 37). Jesus said, "Come," and "they went" (v.39). The simplicity of this first call is no doubt intended to illustrate what Jesus would later teach: "My sheep listen to my voice; I know them, and they follow me" (10:27).

When Andrew brought his brother Simon to Jesus, Jesus already knew him: "You are Simon son of John" (1:42). When Jesus said to Philip, "Follow me" (v.43), Philip heard his voice and knew him: "We have found the one Moses wrote about in the Law, and about whom the prophets also wrote" (v.45). When Philip brought Nathanael to Jesus, Jesus already knew him as "an Israelite in whom there is no deceit" (v.47). He in turn knew Jesus as "the Son of God" and "the king of Israel" (v.49).

At the marriage at Cana (2:1 – 12), Jesus "revealed his glory" (v.11), but only "his disciples believed in him" (v.11). The master of the banquet knew that the new wine was "the best," but "he did not realize where it had come from" (vv.9 – 10). Since John often allows his characters' words to say more than they intended (cf. 11:49 – 53), these words may be characterizing the blindness of those who rejected Jesus (cf. 9:35 – 41).

Jesus' cleansing the temple (2:13 – 25) presents a more dramatic picture of those in Jerusalem. A central feature of the OT's picture of the Messiah is the building of God's temple (2Sa 7:13; Zec 6:12 – 13). In John's gospel this is extended to include the resurrection. Even the disciples did not understand Jesus' words until "after he was raised from the dead" (v.22a); then "they believed the scripture and the words that Jesus had spoken" (v.22b). Thus the words of Jesus must often be understood in light of later events that uncover their real intent.

John moves to an extended discussion between Jesus and Nicodemus, "a member of the Jewish ruling council" (3:1), which centers on "heavenly things" (v.12). To see the kingdom of God one must be "born again," or "born from above" (v.3, cf. NIV note), i.e., be "born of water and the Spirit" (v.5). This discussion clarifies Jesus' spiritual understanding of God's people, which was already foretold in Eze 36:24 – 27; a leader in Israel such as Nicodemus "should not be surprised" to hear of it (3:7; cf.

v.10). Membership in God's spiritual kingdom will not be limited to the OT people of God. Physical birth is neither a requirement nor a guarantee. God sent his Son to die for the whole world. The only requirement is faith (vv.16, 18).

In John the Baptist's final witness to Jesus (vv.22 – 36), the author shows that John was in full accord with Jesus' teaching about the kingdom. John, who continued to baptize, saw his own ministry fading out as Jesus' ministry increased. That's as it should be. Jesus was the Son of God, the bridegroom to whom the bride belonged. In him there is eternal life.

B. Jesus and the Samaritans (4:1 – 54)

In ch. 4 John continues his explication of Jesus' teaching on the Spirit. The central theme is the "living water" (v.10) that gives eternal life (v.14). The Samaritan woman could only understand Jesus in the context of the well of water from which Jacob drank. But Jesus reminded her that "everyone who drinks this water will be thirsty again" (v.13). If she wanted the water Jesus offered, she must set straight her deeds before God (cf. v.18). Jesus raised the issue of eternal life to the level of the woman's behavior. The author no doubt intended this to illustrate Jesus' words in the previous chapter: "Whoever lives by the truth comes into the light" and "their deeds will be exposed" (3:20–21). When the woman came to Jesus, her deeds were exposed. Only then could she receive the living water.

The woman's question on the dispute between the Jews and the Samaritans concerning the place of worship (4:19–20) provided a context for raising again the idea of spiritual worship: "the true worshipers will worship the Father in the Spirit and in truth" (v.23). Just as Jacob's well could not quench thirst forever, a physical temple could not provide lasting worship.

When the disciples raised a similar question about Jesus' need for physical food, Jesus told them, "I have food to eat that you know nothing about" (v.32). His disciples were perplexed. " 'My food,' said Jesus, 'is to do the will of him who sent me and to finish his work' " (v.34). The readers know Jesus was referring to his death (19:30) and resurrection, the work he did finish.

John concludes this section with an account of many Samaritans coming to faith in Jesus (4:39–42). Thus Jesus was recognized as more than the Redeemer of Israel; he was "the Savior of the world" (v.42). This is further demonstrated in vv.43–54, where Jesus, a prophet without honor "in his own country," healed the son of a Gentile official.

C. Miracles and Signs; Jesus and the Old Testament (5:1 – 6:71)

Back again in Jerusalem, Jesus went to the Pool of Bethesda and healed a man who had been crippled thirty-eight years. Since it was the Sabbath day and the man walked away carrying his mat, the Jews who saw him were scandalized that he was doing work on the Sabbath. Jesus justified doing work on the Sabbath by appealing to the fact that God, his Father, did not cease work on the Sabbath and "is always at his work to this very day" (v.17). This answer served only to heighten the anger of these devout Jews against Jesus: "not only was he breaking the Sabbath, but he was even calling God his own Father, making himself equal with God" (v.18).

Jesus discussed with them what it means to be the Son of God (vv.19–47). The context of this discourse is the Son of Man passage in Da 7:10–14, where the Son of Man carries out the task of judgment given him by the "Ancient of Days": "The Father judges no one, but has entrusted all judgment to the Son" (5:22). As the Daniel passage shows, all nations are to honor the Son with the same honor as given to the Father (v.23). Having identified himself as the Son of Man in Daniel (see Da 7:13), it was natural for Jesus to turn to the idea of the resurrection from the dead (Jn 5:25), for the coming of the Son of Man in Daniel is signaled by the resurrection from the dead (Da 12:2).

Thus, Jesus' defense against the accusation that he made himself equal to the Father was his appeal to the Scriptures, for they "testify" that the Son of Man is equal with the Father (5:39). When he completes the work the Father has given him, i.e., his death on the cross (19:30), that work will testify "that the Father has sent" him (5:36) and that he is in fact the promised Son of Man. The only question that remains is whether his accusers will accept the authority of the OT. Jesus says, "If you believed Moses, you would believe me, for he wrote about me" (5:46).

After Jesus appealed to the OT Scriptures as the foundation of his messianic claim, John now adds the account of Jesus' feeding the five thousand (6:1–15) and his walking on the sea (vv.16–24), the two miracles that most closely represent the work of Moses in the OT (cf. comments on Mk 6:30–52).

In light of these allusions to Moses, those following him raise the question of the manna in the desert and the work of Moses (6:25–71). In response, Jesus reminded them that it was not Moses who gave Israel the manna, but rather the Father who gave true bread (v.32). Moreover, Jesus added, the true bread from heaven is not what Israel ate and was hungry again the next day, "for the bread of God is the bread that comes down from heaven and gives life to the world" (v.33). In other words, the OT narratives of Israel receiving the manna pictured God the Father giving life to his people through the Son. He said, "I am the bread of life" (v.35; cf. v.38).

When the crowd questioned how Jesus, "the son of Joseph, whose father and mother we know" (v.42), could be the one who came down from heaven, Jesus explained that he came from the heavenly Father (v.46). Though his hearers remain perplexed, the readers of John's gospel know what he is saying because in 1:1–14, John has already introduced Jesus as the Word who was with God and who was God (1:1).

Jesus now explained his allusion to the OT manna narratives (see 6:49–51). Just as Jesus would give the world the "living water" that was eternal life (4:14), so in his own death for their sins, Jesus would give his body and flesh as the manna that would be eternal life for the world.

Once again, those listening to Jesus did not understand (vv.52, 60). John's readers will understand what Jesus meant; he was speaking of his death on the cross by which he would give life to the world. Only those who were called by the Father could receive that life (v.65). Hence many turned away "and no longer followed him" (v.66). By contrast, Peter, speaking for the rest of the Twelve, said, "You have the words of eternal life. We have come to believe and to know that you are the Holy One of God" (vv.68–69).

D. Jesus at the Temple (7:1–8:59)

John now gives an extended summary of various discourses of Jesus at the temple. We see a wide range of responses among the people and the Jewish leaders to the claims of Jesus. John begins with an inside look at Jesus from the point of view of his own brothers, who "did not believe in him" (7:1–9). There is a mocking tone to their remarks. Before he began to speak publicly at the temple, the crowds had already formed opinions about Jesus. Some said he was a good man, others said he "deceives the people" (v.12). In the midst of the celebration of the Feast of Tabernacles, Jesus began to speak and the diverse responses multiplied.

On repeated occasions Jesus addressed the question of the source of his teaching, stressing each time that his message came from God and that he himself had come from God (7:16–19, 28–29; 8:12–20, 48–59). It is on these themes that the discourses concluded, at which time the people "picked up stones to stone him" (8:59). Jesus also defended healing on the Sabbath (7:21–24), in which he called for the use of right judgment in making such decisions (v.24).

Another topic in these summaries is Jesus' departure to be with the Father (7:33–36; 8:21–30). This is coupled with the notion that the "time" for his departure had been definitively set but had not yet come (7:6–8, 30). It is not surprising that those who heard him were continually perplexed by this, though we, the readers, have little difficulty understanding him. The prologue (1:1–18) has told us that Jesus was with the Father in eternity, and the rest of the book points us to the resurrection.

Throughout Jesus' discourses, the opinions remained divided about his identity (7:40–52). Jesus turned the tables on his opponents and questioned their identity. They claimed to be the children of Abraham, but that would be true only if they did the works that Abraham did (8:31–41). But if they did the works of the devil, they ran the risk of becoming children of the devil (vv.42–47).

During this time, the teachers of the law attempted to trap Jesus in a matter of legal interpretation. They brought to him a woman caught in adultery (7:53–8:11). Their question was whether the stringent requirements of the Mosaic Law should be applied in their day. Jesus' answer was straightforward. Although the law should be carried out, it could not justly be applied. Its administration required a kind of righteousness that did not exist in Israel at that time: "Let any one of you who is without sin be the first to throw a stone at her" (8:7).

E. Healing of the Man Born Blind (9:1 – 10:42)

The failure of his opponents to understand is dramatically portrayed in Jesus' healing of the man blind from birth. The meaning of this story occurs in Jesus' last words to the Pharisees: "If you were blind, you would not be guilty of sin; but now that you claim you can see, your guilt remains" (9:41). Because the blind man knew he was blind, he also knew when he received sight (v.25). Those who could see, however, were in danger of confusing their sight with understanding. The blind man could easily draw the conclusion from his healing that Jesus was sent from God (v.33). The Pharisees saw with their eyes but refused to believe (v.34).

Jesus is the good shepherd (10:1–21). Like the blind man, his sheep hear his voice and follow him; they do not follow the thief who comes only to steal and destroy. When they hear Jesus and follow him, he gives them life. Though the Pharisees and those listening to these parables did not understand them (v.6), the reader has the whole book of John. Again, the prologue provides the key. Jesus is the one sent from God who came to his own people but who was rejected by them (1:11–12). He was the light of the world that "shines in the darkness, and the darkness has not overcome it" (v.5); hence, he gives sight to the blind (cf. v.4). Though his own rejected him (v.11), there were many who would accept him (v.12); hence, Jesus has other sheep that will listen to his voice (10:16).

It is not hard to see why those who heard Jesus speak "were again divided" over his meaning (10:19). They had to judge by the signs they had: "Can a demon open the eyes of the blind?" (v.21). John's readers have much more to go on. Seen from the perspective of God's eternal plan, Jesus' words not only make sense but place Jesus himself at the center of God's eternal decrees for the salvation of people.

At the Feast of Dedication, Jesus continued these themes among those who did not believe. His miracles were to demonstrate that he was sent from God; in spite of them, not all believed (10:25), but only those whom the Father had given to Jesus (v.29). They were the sheep who heard the voice of the shepherd (vv.26–27). The crowd that picked up stones to kill Jesus showed by their actions that they understood his claims: "You, a mere man, claim to be God" (v.33); but they did not believe him or his message (vv.38–39). They found themselves fighting against what was written in their own law (v.34).

F. The Raising of Lazarus (11:1 – 12:11)

The key to John's understanding of Jesus' raising Lazarus lies in the mourners' response to his death: "Could not he who opened the eyes of the blind man have kept this man from dying?" (11:37). Jesus saw the death of Lazarus as an occasion to demonstrate that he was "the resurrection and the life" (v.25). Though some who were present believed that Lazarus would "rise again in the resurrection at the last day" (v.24), John shows that those "last days" had arrived in the person of Jesus, the Son of God. Jesus said to them, "The one who believes in me will live, even though they die; and whoever lives by believing in me will never die" (vv.25–26).

As a result of this miracle, many believed in Jesus (v.45). Ironically, the resurrection of Lazarus also became the turning point for the Jewish leaders. Henceforth, they made plans to kill Jesus (vv.47–57). In their plans, however, the will of God would be accomplished. Caiaphas, the high priest, "prophesied" unwittingly that Jesus would give his life "for the Jewish nation" (v.51) as well as for "the scattered children of God" (v.52).

John gives a brief account of Jesus at Bethany having dinner with Lazarus and his family (12:1–11). On this occasion, Mary poured expensive perfume on Jesus' feet and wiped them with her hair. Over Judas' objection, Jesus praised Mary and said her action prepared him for his own burial, when he would be taken away from them.

G. Entry into Jerusalem (12:12–50)

There were great crowds in Jerusalem for the Passover (11:55). They had been looking for Jesus to come (v.56) and had been alerted by their leaders to report it to them (v.57). When Jesus came, however, the crowds rushed into the street, gathering palm branches and shouting, "Hosanna!... Blessed is the king of Israel" (12:13). Even his own disciples did not understand the significance of Jesus' entry into Jerusalem. Only after his death and resurrection did they understand, for they then saw the whole of his ministry in light of the OT (v.16).

John, however, keeps the reader fully informed as the events happen by supplying the relevant OT texts (Zec 9:9, quoted in Jn 12:15). Jesus was the King foretold by the OT prophets. He was the son of David, promised in 2Sa 7, and he was the Son of Man, promised in Da 7:9–14. The fact that Jesus entered Jerusalem at the time of the Passover (11:55; 12:12, 20) shows that Jesus fulfilled the OT; he was the Passover Lamb. The words of John the Baptist in 1:29, who was the last of Israel's prophets, were also being fulfilled.

When Gentile Greeks came to Jesus during the time of the Feast (12:20–23), Jesus saw this as a sign that the Son of Man was to be glorified. John probably has in mind the fact that in Da 7, the glorification of the Son of Man is marked by "all nations and peoples of every language" coming to worship him (Da 7:14; see also Jn 12:32).

In 12:37–50, John gives a final summary of the response to Jesus' self-revelation (1:15–12:50). The Jews' rejection of Jesus is explained from the Jewish Scriptures. The greatest of the OT prophets, Isaiah, had long ago seen "Jesus' glory and spoke about him" (12:41). John explains Jesus' rejection, first as a fulfillment of Isaiah's prophecy (v.38, quoting Isa 53:1). Second, John shows that the reason for the people's unbelief lay in God's blinding their eyes (v.40). But John was not content to let this be the last word; he immediately added the fact that "many even among the leaders believed in him" (v.42). That is, the unbelief of the people lay rather in the heart of those who had rejected Jesus (v.43).

III. The Revelation of Jesus before His Own (13:1 – 20:29)

A. The Last Supper (13:1 – 17:26)

John understood Jesus' death as the death of Isaiah's Servant of the Lord (Isa 52:13–53:12). Thus it was important for him to show that Jesus carried out the role of the Lord's Servant in all respects. This is the central theme of Jesus' washing the feet of his disciples (13:1–20). The Servant, who gives himself for God's chosen ones, cleanses them thoroughly by his sacrificial death: "Unless I wash you, you have no part with me" (v.8). The disciples, having already put their faith in Jesus, are clean. Presumably the Servant's coming death has already cleansed them. They have need only that their feet be washed (v.10).

Judas plays an important role here. He was the exception to all that Jesus spoke of in this text. He was the one who was not clean (vv.10–11). As Jesus washed his disciples' feet, Judas was the one who "turned against [him]" (v.18). But the presence of the betrayer among his disciples also demonstrates the truthfulness of Jesus' claims. As the quotation from the OT shows, Judas' betrayal of Jesus was also a sign of fulfilled prophecy (v.18).

John records Jesus' farewell discourse at length (14:1–16:33) and concludes with Jesus' prayer for his disciples (17:1–26). In both the discourse and the prayer, Jesus' words look far beyond the specific needs and concerns of his disciples on the night of his death. They look to the whole of the subsequent history of the church. The background to his words is the teaching of Jesus found throughout this gospel. Jesus is the Son of God and the Son of Man. As the Son of God, he had come to fulfill the command of the Father to redeem his chosen people. As the Son of Man, he had come to establish God's kingdom.

The specific issue that the lengthy discourse addresses is the fact that Jesus is about to return to the Father and will no longer be physically present with his disciples. They will continue to follow him, however, and wait for his return. It is this time of waiting and watching that Jesus specifically has in mind throughout the discourse. Jesus' departure means a further step in the progress of God's purpose. He will prepare a place for his people in the heavenly temple ("my Father's house," 14:2).

The key to the meaning of the discourse is given at its conclusion. Jesus said, "I came from the Father and entered the world; now I am leaving the world and going back to the Father" (16:28). This discourse explains what will happen to the disciples and the early church in the time between Jesus' death and his return to establish his kingdom. He will send the Holy Spirit to guide them and comfort them. They will continue to have fellowship with Jesus through the Spirit. They will have the life he promised them through the work of the Spirit. The Spirit will take his place, convicting the world of sin, righteousness, and judgment. The Spirit will guide the believing community "into all the truth" (v.13).

The one rule of faith that will define the disciples as a believing community will be their love for each other. This love will be the fruit of the Spirit who lives in them. The kind of community Jesus here envisions is the one that unfolds in Acts. This gospel presupposes and anticipates the establishment of the church.

Thus, Jesus defines more clearly the nature of his community during the time he will be with the Father. It will be the spiritual community. Each individual will be indwelt with the Spirit of God and will have life and bear fruit as a branch on a vine (15:1–7). It is this form of spiritual life that Jesus had spoken about to the Samaritan woman: "The true worshipers will worship the Father in the Spirit and in truth" (4:23). By giving believers the Spirit, "rivers of living water will flow from within them" (7:38).

In Jesus' final prayer (ch. 17), the whole of his ministry and purpose is summarized and explained to the reader. Jesus was returning to the Father who had sent him (v.2). He had found his disciples and revealed to them the knowledge of the only true God (v.3). All that Jesus had done fulfilled God's will for him (v.4). Now he was returning to his original glory with the Father (v.5). This theme is identical to that of the prologue (1:1–14).

As Jesus was now about to leave his disciples, he prayed for their protection (17:6–12) and for their continued joy and sanctification (vv.13–19). Jesus looked beyond these disciples to their disciples and prayed on their behalf (vv.20–22). His central concern was that these future generations of disciples would continue in unity and love for one another (v.23). Finally, Jesus looked to the time of his return to gather his community to himself (v.24).

B. Death and Resurrection (18:1 – 20:29)

1. Jesus' arrest, trial, death, and burial (18:1 – 19:42)

The narrative picks up from 13:30 with the betrayal of Jesus by Judas (18:1–11). Jesus was taken both to Annas and to the high priest Caiaphas and questioned "about his disciples and his teaching." During this time Peter denied Jesus three times (vv.12–27). John stresses that Jesus had predicted Peter's denial in 13:38 (cf. 18:9, 32). Everything was happening as it had been planned. God was at work in every detail.

Jesus was then taken before Pilate (18:28–19:16a). Here John stresses the time of Jesus' death and correlates it with the Jewish Passover. John had introduced Jesus with the words of John the Baptist, "Look, the Lamb of God" (1:29); now he returns to that imagery in his account of Jesus' death. Moreover, in Jesus' reply to Pilate, the earthly ruler representing Rome, Jesus stressed the spiritual aspects of his kingdom: "My kingdom is not of this world.... [It] is from another place" (18:36). By now the readers of John's gospel have a good understanding of what Jesus meant.

John is particularly concerned to show that Pilate only reluctantly had Jesus crucified. It was only at the Jews' insistence that he finally agreed. Thus even at this point in the book, John still has the theme in mind with which he began: "his own did not receive him" (1:11). Jesus was the Servant of the Lord who was "despised and rejected" (Isa 53:3) by his own people.

John recounts the crucifixion of Jesus (19:16b–37) in such a way that its fulfillment of OT prophecies is highlighted (e.g., vv.23–24). Particularly important to John is the identification of Jesus as the King of the Jews (vv.19–22). In the title given Jesus at his death, he was recognized as the Davidic King, the Messiah, and the Son of Man who received the kingdom (Da 7:9–14). More importantly, it was a Gentile official who called him "king of the Jews," just as in Daniel the Gentile nations acknowledge the Son of Man as king of the Jews (Da 7:14, 27).

In keeping with John's emphasis on the work that Jesus was sent into the world to do, the final words of Jesus before his death were simply, "It is finished" (19:30). Jesus had completed the work of the Father. The fact that the Roman guards did not break Jesus' legs (vv.31, 33) but instead pierced his side (vv.34–35) shows that even in the smallest details, OT prophecies were fulfilled (vv.36–37; cf. v.24) and thus gave witness to Jesus as the Messiah (cf. 20:31).

When Jesus was buried, two "secret" Jewish believers, Joseph of Arimathea and Nicodemus, openly acknowledged their faith in Jesus (19:38–42). This fact may suggest that many more such believers were to be found among even the leaders of the people (cf. 12:42).

2. Jesus' resurrection (20:1–29)

John stresses the empty tomb throughout his account of the resurrection. He gives the names of the first witnesses, Mary Magdalene, Simon Peter, and himself (anonymously, as "the other disciple"; vv.4, 8). John shows that the level of the disciples' understanding of Jesus was still incomplete (v.9). In doing so he gives some justification for his own gospel, which has focused on how, in God's eternal plan, it was necessary that the Messiah "rise from the dead."

As an instance of the disciples' failure to understand the resurrection, John records the events of Mary's surprise meeting with Jesus (vv.11–18). In a scene reminiscent of the healing of the blind man (9:1–10:42), Mary did not recognize Jesus when she saw Jesus (20:14), but she knew his voice (v.16; cf. 10:14). As Jesus had promised on the night of his arrest (16:7), he again told the disciples to "receive the Holy Spirit." This anticipates the early chapters of Acts (Ac 2:1–4).

The concern of Thomas to feel and touch the wounds in the body of the risen Lord is an important element in John's gospel. Later, in his first letter, John refers to the events of the Lord's resurrection as that which "we have looked at and our hands have touched" (1Jn 1:1). Jesus fully appreciated Thomas's concern: "Put your finger here; see my hands. Reach out your hand and put it into my side. Stop doubting and believe" (20:27).

IV. Conclusion (20:30 – 21:25)

At the conclusion of this gospel, John summarizes his purpose in writing (20:30 – 31). He has given the reader an account of the signs and miracles that Jesus did, proving that Jesus is the Christ, the Son of God. By believing in Jesus, life is offered in his name (cf. 1:4, 12).

The account of the third and last appearance of Jesus in Galilee (21:1 – 25) presents a picture of the future ministry of the disciples as fishers of people. When the disciples follow the words of Jesus, they will make many disciples (v.6). John clearly intends his gospel to be a guide to the words of Jesus. Jesus had said, "I, when I am lifted up from the earth, will draw all people to myself" (12:32). By means of this book, the message of Jesus will be heard and received by many.

Jesus' final instruction to the disciples was to care for his growing number of disciples: "Feed my sheep" (21:17). Jesus' first word to his disciples was, "Follow me" (1:43); that was also his last (21:19). He again warned them of trouble (cf. 16:33), even anticipating the kind of death (21:18) Peter would die. Peter's own death would also be in God's plan.

Attached to the end of John's gospel is a verification of the truthfulness of the author and the reliability of his work (21:24 – 25).

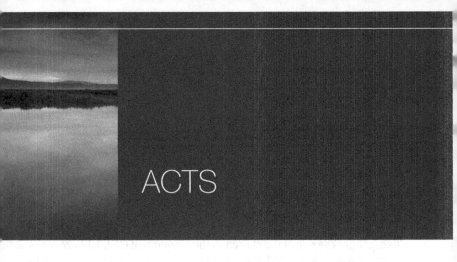

ACTS

Introduction

Both the gospel of Luke and Acts contain a prologue addressed to "Theophilus." In Ac 1:1–2 the writer refers to "my former book," which concerned "all that Jesus began to do and teach until the day he was taken up to heaven." This description fits Luke precisely. A close study of the language and style of Luke and Acts shows that they were written by the same author. While both books are anonymous, Luke is a plausible author for both (see introduction to Luke).

Acts concludes with Paul being imprisoned in Rome for two years under relatively good conditions (28:30). Presumably the author concludes at that point because he was with Paul. There are no indications in the book of the persecutions under Nero or of the destruction of Jerusalem. Hence, a date prior to AD 64 seems most likely.

I. Prologue (1:1 – 11)

Acts begins with an explicit reference to the gospel of Luke, which the author calls "my former book." The present book is a continuation of that gospel. In the gospel, events in the life of Jesus are recounted up to the time of his resurrection and ascension. Acts, after a brief introduction, continues with events of the early church after Jesus' ascension. The focus of the book is on the work that Christ carried on in the church by the Holy Spirit.

Jesus spent forty days teaching his disciples about the kingdom of God between his resurrection and ascension (1:3). The disciples raise a central question at this time: "Lord, are you at this time going to restore the kingdom to Israel?" (v.6). Acts as a whole is intended to answer to this question. Note that at the end of the book (28:31), Paul was in Rome proclaiming "the kingdom of God" and teaching about the Lord Jesus Christ. In other words, the establishment of the church and the spread of the gospel is to be understood as the beginning of the reign of the kingdom of God.

II. The Early Church (1:12 – 12:25)

A. The Early Congregation (1:12 – 5:42)

To highlight the role of the church in the kingdom of God, 1:12 – 26 focuses on the replacement of Judas as one of the Twelve — a number that continues to reflect the twelve-tribe unity of the nation of Israel.

The events of Pentecost (2:1 – 47) represent the fulfillment of the OT promises of the Davidic messianic kingdom. In 2:17 – 21, Peter gives an extended quotation from Joel 2:28 – 32. In 2:25 – 28 he links it with another quotation from Ps 16:8 – 11, and in 2:34 – 35 with Ps 110. Luke uses Peter's sermon to establish his main point at the opening of this book: the messianic kingdom of David was now being offered again to Israel. It had been offered to Israel by Jesus before his death (Lk 13:34 – 35; 23:3), and it was now being offered again (Ac 2:36; 3:19 – 26). This offer fulfilled Jesus' last request on the cross: "Father, forgive them, for they do not know what they are doing" (Lk 23:34).

Thus Peter tells those gathered at Pentecost, "This is what was spoken by the prophet Joel" (Ac 2:16). Unfortunately, only a remnant from the house of Israel followed Jesus (2:37 – 41), but this became the seed from which the early church grew. The new believers devoted themselves to "the apostles' teaching and to fellowship, to the breaking of bread and to prayer" (v.42). The apostles performed "many wonders and signs" (v.43), and "all the believers were together and had everything in common" (v.44). Although they met for fellowship in their own homes, they continued to meet in the temple courts (v.46).

Luke then recounts an important miracle performed by the apostles, the healing of the crippled beggar (3:1 – 10). This healing led to Peter's second sermon in Jerusalem (3:11 – 26).

Although Luke does not record the response of the people, he does give a detailed report of the reaction of the leaders of the Jews to Peter and John (4:1 – 22). Unable to deny that Peter and John had worked a miracle (v.16), the "rulers, the elders and the teachers of the law," along with the high priest and others of his family (vv.5 – 6), warned the apostles "to speak no longer to anyone" in the name of Jesus (v.17). Not knowing "how to punish them" (v.21), they released them.

Luke stresses how God was working in this small group of believers. They prayed for boldness to speak the word and for God to "perform signs and wonders" through the name of Jesus (vv.23 – 30). God answered their prayer by filling them with the Holy Spirit so that they "spoke the word of God boldly" (v.31) and did great signs (v.33; 5:12 – 16). But God still examined the hearts of these believers. Some, like Barnabas, selflessly shared all that they owned with the church (4:32 – 37). Others, like Ananias and Sapphira, lied to both the apostles and God and were severely punished (5:1 – 10).

As a result of the growth of the early church, opposition from the leaders in Jerusalem increased. The apostles were arrested (v.18), but an angel released them during the night, and at daybreak they were again proclaiming the gospel in the temple. Taken once again to the Sanhedrin, Peter defended the apostles (vv.29 – 32). The Jewish leaders charged him with inciting the people against them by making them responsible for the death of Jesus (v.28).

Peter and the apostles, however, responded forthrightly, "We must obey God rather than human beings!" (v.29). At the last moment, the cautious words of the Pharisee Gamaliel won the day, which provide the apologetic background to the rest of Acts: if the spread of the early church were to fail, it was only a human work. Luke is intent on showing that, far from failing, the early church grew, in Jerusalem, in Judea and Samaria, and to the ends of the earth (cf. 1:8).

B. The Early Spread of the Church (6:1 – 12:25)

1. The Hellenists, Stephen, and Persecution (6:1 – 8:3)

The focus of Acts turns now to key individuals instrumental in spreading the gospel: Stephen (6:1 – 8:3), Philip (8:4 – 40), Saul (i.e., Paul; 9:1 – 31), and Peter (9:32 – 11:18). The first two men, Stephen and Philip, were not of the Twelve. They were numbered with the seven deacons appointed to help administer the daily needs of the growing church (6:1 – 7).

Opposition to Stephen's teaching broke out among Jews from the Greek-speaking world. When argumentation failed, Jewish agitators stirred up widespread resentment against Stephen, based on false witnesses. Their charge was that Stephen was speaking against the temple and the law of Moses (6:13 – 14). Stephen received an opportunity to speak to the defend his message.

Stephen's speech before the Sanhedrin appealed to the whole of the OT in defense of the gospel. He stressed the promised blessings of God and their continual delay because of the people's unfaithfulness. Unwittingly mimicking the words of judgment against Israel spoken by Isaiah (Isa 6:10), the people "covered their ears" and stoned him (7:57–58a).

Standing at their side was the young man Saul (later to become the apostle Paul), who himself later said of Israel's rejection of Jesus, "they hardly hear with their ears.... Otherwise they might ... hear with their ears, understand with their hearts and turn" (28:25–27). From the time of Stephen on, a great persecution arose against the church; Saul was at the forefront in trying to "destroy" it (8:1–3). But as in the time of the Exodus, "the more they were oppressed, the more they multiplied and spread" (Ex 1:12).

2. The mission of Philip (8:4 – 40)

Philip spread the gospel during a time of oppression. Forced to flee from Jerusalem to Samaria, he preached the gospel there and performed miraculous signs (vv.4–8). The gospel had now been offered to and accepted by the Samaritans. When Peter and John prayed for them, these Samaritan believers received the Holy Spirit (cf. Ac 2), confirming that they had been accepted by the Lord into the church.

Luke records the incident of Simon the sorcerer's attempt to purchase the ability to impart the Holy Spirit (8:18–24) in order to drive the point home: the work of God *cannot* be purchased with money. One whose heart is set on gaining wealth from ministry can have no share in it (v.21). Though Peter's words are a stern warning to the readers of this book, his call for repentance and forgiveness is also meant as a source of great comfort (vv.22–23).

The gospel now spread to Ethiopia (vv.26–40). Just as the angel of the Lord had led Israel through the desert (Ex 23:20), so here Philip was led in "the desert road—that goes down ... to Gaza" (Ac 8:26) to tell the story about Jesus to an Ethiopian eunuch.

3. The conversion of Paul (9:1 – 31)

This is the first of four times Luke recounts Paul's conversion (9:3–6, 27; 22:3–21; 26:12–18). This was a decisive stage in the spread and development of the early church. It meant a new direction for the spread of the gospel, for Paul became the apostle to the Gentiles (9:15).

Following his conversion, Paul began to preach the gospel in the synagogues (9:20), proving that "Jesus is the Messiah" (v.22). As was often the case throughout the rest of Acts, Paul had to flee because of the opposition he faced from his teaching.

4. The mission of Peter (9:32 – 11:18)

With Paul safely in Tarsus and the church in Judea, Galilee, and Samaria growing in numbers and strength (9:31), Luke turns to the ministry of Peter. He records the details of two miracles Peter performed: the healing of the paralytic Aeneas (vv.32 – 35) and the raising of the disciple Dorcas (vv.36 – 43).

Later, an angel appeared to Cornelius, a Roman centurion in Caesarea, and directed him to find Peter in Joppa and return him to Caesarea. As they were arriving in Joppa, Peter also received a corresponding vision, which puzzled him.

When Cornelius asked Peter what the Lord had commanded him to say, Peter told the story of the gospel. He began with the life and ministry of John the Baptist, then spoke about Jesus' ministry, death, and resurrection, and concluded with the spread of the gospel in the early church (vv.36 – 42). He ended up baptizing Cornelius and his family.

Peter had much explaining to do on his return to the Jerusalem church (11:1 – 18). When criticized for eating with Gentiles, Peter merely offered a description of what had transpired (vv.4 – 15). He then recalled the earlier words of Jesus (v.16) and the witness of the Holy Spirit, which was the same as that which they themselves had received on Pentecost (v.17). His conclusion was, "Who was I to think that I could oppose God?" Thus the offer of the gospel to Gentiles as well as to Jews was not a planned strategy of outreach. Rather, "even to the Gentiles God has granted repentance that leads to life," and the early church could only praise God and offer "no further objections" (v.18).

5. The congregation at Antioch (11:19 – 30)

In 11:19 – 26, Luke adds an explanation that Peter's experience was not isolated. Even though, for the most part, Christians were spreading the gospel "only among Jews" (v.19), some were also evangelizing the Greeks in Antioch (v.20), and believers were being added. The Jerusalem church decided to investigate and sent Barnabas to Antioch; they were content with the evidence of "the grace of God" as seen there (vv.22 – 24). At this time, Paul (Saul) came to Antioch, and both he and Barnabas remained there for a full year, teaching "great numbers of people" (vv.25 – 26). Here believers were first called "Christians" (v.26b). Barnabas and Saul went to Judea (i.e., Jerusalem) with a gift of provisions for the churches there (vv.27 – 30).

6. Persecution of the early community by Agrippa (12:1 – 25)

Barnabas and Saul returned to Antioch when they "had finished their mission ... taking with them John, also called Mark" (v.25). During this time Peter was imprisoned and miraculously rescued (vv.1–19). Luke has carefully woven the two narratives together to emphasize the dual leadership of Peter and Paul in the church at Jerusalem.

As his last word on the situation in Jerusalem, Luke includes a brief account of the death of Herod (12:19b–25), one in a long line of kings who opposed Jesus and the church (cf. Lk 9:9; 13:31–33; 23:7–12). Luke perhaps intends this narrative as a commentary on the fate of the Jewish leaders who, in response to the growing church, "did not give praise to God" (Ac 12:23).

III. The Mission of the Early Church (13:1 – 28:31)

A. Paul's First Missionary Journey (13:1 – 14:28)

PAUL'S FIRST MISSIONARY JOURNEY

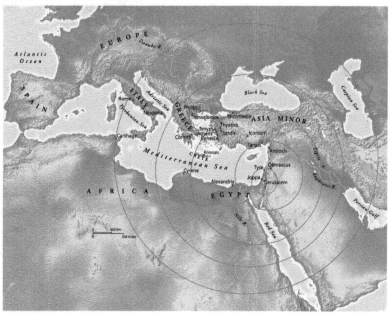

The leaders of the church at Antioch, having been led by the Holy Spirit, sent Barnabas and Saul on a missionary journey to Cyprus (13:4–12), Pisidian Antioch (13:13–52), Iconium (14:1–5), and Lystra and Derbe (14:6–20).

They then returned to Antioch (14:21–28). They took John Mark with them (13:5b; cf. 12:25), but he returned to Jerusalem after a short time into the journey (13:13). According to 15:38, Paul saw this as a desertion of their work (cf. 15:36–41).

In recounting this journey, Luke focuses on the work of Saul, whom he begins to call Paul in 13:9. Paul and those with him "proclaimed the word of God" in the Jewish synagogues (13:5, 14–44; 14:1), but they were nearly always forced to go outside Judaism to gain a hearing (13:6–12, 45–52; 14:2, 19). The result was that both Jews and Gentiles came to faith in Jesus as the Messiah. The opposition of the Jewish sorcerer and false prophet Bar-Jesus, for example, resulted in the conversion of the Roman proconsul, Sergius Paulus (13:6–12).

Luke includes a lengthy summary of one of Paul's synagogue sermons (13:16–41), addressed to those of Israel and to "Gentiles who worship God" (v.16). "Many of the Jews and devout converts to Judaism" accepted Paul's words about Jesus and were encouraged by Paul and Barnabas to "continue in the grace of God" (v.43). The next week, however, Paul and Barnabas met with stiff opposition, and as a result they turned to the Gentiles (vv.44–48).

As their journey progressed, Paul and Barnabas came to Iconium and there "spoke so effectively that a great number of Jews and Gentiles believed" (14:1). There was also much opposition (vv.2–5), but it only served to further the spread of the gospel (vv.6–7).

Paul and Barnabas returned to Antioch of Syria by retracing their journey and encouraged the new Christians "to remain true to the faith" (14:21–22). They also appointed elders in each of the new churches (v.23). On their arrival in Antioch they reported all that had happened to them, stressing especially that God "had opened the door of faith to the Gentiles" (v.27). It was this fact that erupted into the Jerusalem Council (ch. 15).

B. The Jerusalem Council (15:1–35)

Among the Christians in Antioch were some from Jerusalem teaching that a believer had to be circumcised and obey to the law of Moses to be saved (15:1). Paul and Barnabas, at Antioch at that time, opposed their teaching vehemently. The church in Antioch sent Paul and Barnabas to Jerusalem to seek the advice of the apostles and elders there (vv.2–4).

The early church was careful and thoughtful of the central issues at work in the development of the early church (vv.5–20). They did not tolerate unauthorized preaching, as had originally stirred up the problem in Antioch, and they discussed the questions openly. They based their decision on the Scriptures, the teaching of Jesus, and the work of the Holy Spirit.

C. Paul's Second Missionary Journey (15:36 – 18:22)

PAUL'S SECOND MISSIONARY JOURNEY

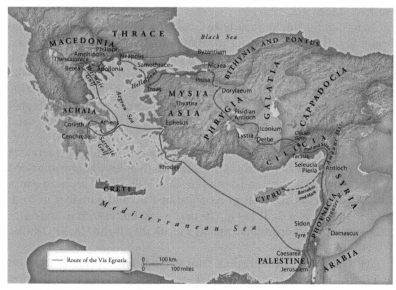

Paul and Barnabas decided to return to the churches they had founded in Asia Minor. Because of a "sharp disagreement" over including John Mark on the journey, Paul and Barnabas parted company (15:36 – 39). Barnabas, with John Mark, went by sea to the churches in Cyprus, while Paul, with Silas, went by land through Syria and Cilicia. Even in adversity and struggle, God's work was carried out.

Paul and Silas, continuing through Asia Minor, met Timothy at Lystra. The three of them traveled to Troas (15:40 – 16:10). They did not preach on the way (16:6), and, though intending to head north and west to Mysia and Bithynia, by the Spirit's direction they set sail for Macedonia.

At Philippi they met Lydia, a tradeswoman who heard Paul preach the gospel and believed in Jesus. Ironically, the people of the city charged Paul and Silas with being "Jews" and "advocating customs unlawful for us Romans to accept or practice" (vv.20 – 21). Behind their charge lay the simple fact that Paul had cast a "spirit" out of a slave girl who had earned her owners a great deal of money by fortune-telling.

At Thessalonica the disciples were back in a synagogue, preaching and reasoning "with them from the Scriptures, explaining and proving that the Messiah had to suffer and rise from the dead" (17:1-9). Some were persuaded, including many Gentiles and prominent women.

Arriving at Berea, Paul again went to a Jewish synagogue where, this time, his message was well received. In Athens (vv.16-34), Paul not only "reasoned in the synagogue with both Jews and God-fearing Greeks," but he also went to the marketplace "day by day" to speak with those who gathered there. His presence aroused the curiosity of the philosophers of the city, and they sought from him an explanation of his teaching in the Areopagus (vv.22-31), a place where they customarily gathered to discuss "the latest ideas."

On the next leg of the journey, Paul was in Corinth and back in the synagogue, "trying to persuade Jews and Greeks" (18:1-17). Paul's focus was "testifying to the Jews that Jesus was the Messiah" (v.5). Again, meeting stiff opposition from the Jews, Paul left the synagogue and moved to the house next door to continue his teaching (v.7). Having received encouragement from the Lord in a vision, Paul remained teaching in Corinth for a year and a half (vv.9-11).

Luke gives only a summary of Paul's return to Antioch (vv.18-22). He stresses, however, that Paul's primary focus remained the synagogue, where he "reasoned with the Jews" (v.19).

D. Paul's Third Missionary Journey (18:23-21:16)

PAUL'S THIRD MISSIONARY JOURNEY

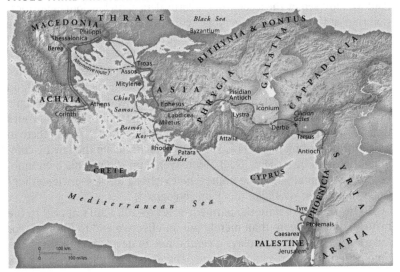

Having spent some time in Antioch, Paul decided to travel throughout the regions of Galatia and Phrygia (18:23) before moving on to Ephesus. There he met some disciples of John the Baptist (19:1–7). They may have been those who had followed Apollos, an Alexandrian Jew (18:24–28) with a thorough knowledge of the OT Scriptures. They were Christians, but they had not yet been baptized by the Spirit into the church.

In Ephesus, Paul also taught in the synagogue (19:8). When opposition arose, Paul left the synagogue and held daily discussions in "the lecture hall of Tyrannus" (v.9). He continued there for two years and enjoyed a widespread audience (v.10). Luke stresses the "extraordinary miracles" that God did through Paul here (v.11). With great success, however, came great opposition. Luke gives a vivid account of such opposition that faced Paul in Ephesus (vv.23–41).

Paul journeyed from Ephesus to Macedonia to Greece and back to Troas (20:1–6). After a brief stay in Troas (vv.7–12), he went to Miletus (vv.13–16). Calling the elders of the church at Ephesus, Paul bid them farewell (vv.17–38) and continued on to Jerusalem (21:1–16).

E. Paul's Arrest (21:17–23:10)

Paul faced controversy with fellow Christians in the Jerusalem church immediately on his return there (21:17–26). The newly converted Jewish Christians, who were zealous for the law, were concerned with reports they had heard that Paul taught Jewish Christians outside Jerusalem "not to circumcise their children or live according to [Jewish] customs" (v.21). Paul was advised by the leaders of the Jerusalem church to join in purification rites at the temple so "everyone will know there is no truth in these reports about you, but that you yourself are living in obedience to the law" (v.24). Paul conceded to their wishes and avoided conflict.

Nevertheless, Paul was arrested on the false charge of teaching against Israel and the law (vv.27–40). Once again the Romans intervened and saved his life (vv.31–32). Amid all the talk of the law of Moses, it was only by appealing to Roman law that he could get a fair trial (22:29–30). Paul's response to the high priest reinforced such an intention: "You sit there to judge me according to the law, yet you yourself violate the law by commanding that I be struck!" (23:3). Moreover, Paul showed his own innocence in recognizing that he himself had violated the law in "insult[ing] God's high priest" (v.4). For that Paul apologized.

In his defense before the Sanhedrin (vv.6–10), Paul's appeal to the resurrection did more than merely put an effective end to his trial. For Luke's account in Acts, it plays a central role in developing the explanation for Jerusalem's rejection of Jesus. The division of the Jewish leaders over the question of the resurrection pointed to the real issue at stake in the message of the gospel. The Sadducees, who did not believe in the resurrection, were not prepared to accept the gospel that the early church preached. Peter's first sermon in Acts had set the tone of the book's overall theme. David had foreseen the resurrection of the Messiah (2:25–31), and "God has raised this Jesus to life, and we are all witnesses of it" (2:32). The basis of the gospel was God's exaltation of Jesus in the resurrection, whereby God fulfilled his promises to David to establish an eternal kingdom (2:34–36).

F. Paul's Journey to Rome (23:11 – 28:31)

PAUL'S JOURNEY TO ROME

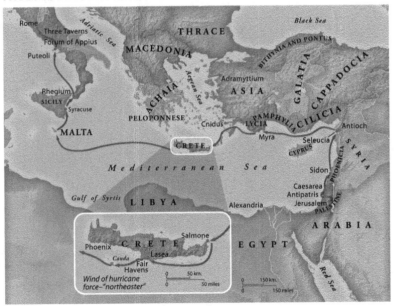

The course of events now took a final turn, signaled by a word from Jesus: "As you have testified about me in Jerusalem, so you must also testify in Rome" (23:11). These events follow a determined purpose. The Lord is behind all that happens, and it is for his purpose (cf. Ro 8:28).

Paul remained in prison in Caesarea for two years, until Felix was replaced by Festus (24:27). Again, the Roman government protected to Paul (25:1–6) and gave him a fair trial (vv.6–12). In the end it was his appeal to Caesar that provided his rescue (vv.12, 21; 26:32) and ultimately his journey to Rome (25:25; 27:1–28:14). On the negative side, the central point stressed in Luke's various summaries of the proceedings is that Paul had broken no laws and that the charges against him were trivial matters dealing with the Jewish law (25:8, 19, 25–27; 26:31). The positive point in Paul's own defense was the centrality of Jesus' resurrection: "Why should any of you consider it incredible that God raises the dead?" (26:8, 23).

Once in Rome (28:17–31), Paul continued his practice of meeting with "the local Jewish leaders" (v.17), and "he witnessed to them from morning till evening, explaining about the kingdom of God, and from the Law of Moses and from the Prophets he tried to persuade them about Jesus" (v.23). Some believed, but others disputed. As Luke concludes the book, the verdict of Paul is allowed to remain as the verdict of the book itself: "God's salvation has been sent to the Gentiles, and they will listen!" (28:28).

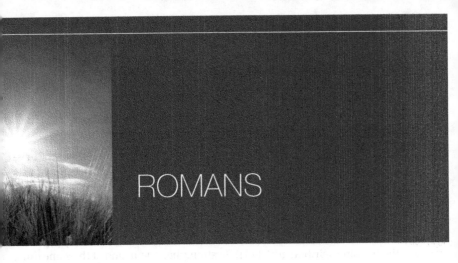

ROMANS

Introduction

The title "to the Romans" is found in the earliest complete NT manuscripts. This letter was written by Paul. At the end of his third missionary journey (Ac 20:1–5), he was in Macedonia and Achaia, taking up a collection for the poor among the saints in Jerusalem (Ro 15:25–32). He likely wrote the letter in Corinth, where he stayed three months (Ac 20:3). This dates the book at about AD 58.

I. Opening Greeting (1:1–7)

Paul's opening greeting, which constitutes a single sentence, introduces four primary subjects: (1) Paul, the writer; (2) the gospel of God; (3) the Son of God; and (4) the Christians in Rome. Paul is writing about "the gospel"—the good news about Jesus Christ. In vv.1–4 he summarizes the contents of his message.

Paul had never visited the believers in Rome. But since he had received the apostleship to the Gentiles, the church in Rome was a reasonable audience to address, for it was still within the sphere of his apostolic commission.

II. Personal Notes Regarding Paul and the Church at Rome (1:8 – 15)

A. Paul's Thanksgiving to God for the Faith of the Roman Christians (1:8)

Paul begins with a personal note regarding the faith of the Roman Christians. This church was known throughout the world as a church that was obedient to the faith.

B. Paul's Desire to Visit the Church at Rome (1:9 – 15)

Paul stresses his desire to visit the church at Rome in order to impart to them "some spiritual gift" (v.11), to strengthen them, and at the same time, to be strengthened by them (v.12). In vv.14 – 15, Paul adds that he is under obligation to preach the gospel to them as he has been to preach it to all people — the wise and unwise, Greeks and barbarians. But thus far he has been hindered from coming (v.13).

III. Paul's Statement of the Theme of the Book (1:16 – 17)

Paul now presents the theme of his letter — a capsule view of the relationship of salvation and faith. He begins with the term "the gospel" (1:16), which has its source in the power of God. This power is a power to save those who believe, both Jews and Gentiles. Paul's use of both the verb "to believe" and the noun "faith" shows that he understands the word to be one of action. The idea of faith always has with it the idea of a message one believes.

Paul then enters the main topic of his discussion: the righteousness of God (v.17). In God's gracious act of sending his Son to die for the human race, God has revealed a way of getting right with him, namely, by faith alone. Those who are righteous will not fall under God's wrath but will be saved. As support, Paul quotes Hab 2:4, "The righteous will live by faith."

We must understand what Paul means by "righteousness." The Greek notion of righteousness in general described one's ethical conduct — living a correct manner. The corresponding Hebrew word, however, denoted "righteousness" as a legal term, used primarily within the context of the OT system of law and judgment. "Righteousness" was something one had in relationship to a system of law, a standard. It meant "conformity to a norm." In the OT that standard was Torah, the revelation of the will of God.

IV. The Revelation of the Righteousness from God Alone (1:18–4:25)

The central section of Paul's argument is stated in 3:21–26, namely, that the righteousness that makes one acceptable before God has been made available to all who believe. This section is preceded by two longer sections (1:18–32 and 2:1–3:20), in which Paul shows not simply that all people are sinners and thus under God's wrath, but, more specifically, emphasizes that the Jew, who trusts in human works, is under God's wrath in the same way as the idolatrous Gentile. Paul's argument is not simply "justification by faith" but also the denial of its opposite, "justification by works."

A. The Portrait of the Pagan Gentile (1:18–32)

God has made himself known to the human race in nature (v.19). His "invisible qualities—his eternal power and divine nature" are clearly evident (v.20). Nevertheless, the human race fell into idolatry (v.21); people "exchanged the glory of the immortal God for images" (v.23). Accordingly, God abandoned the human race to gross sins and perversion (vv.28–32). Paul thus concludes that the Gentile pagan is without excuse (v.20).

B. The Failure of Judaism (2:1–3:20)

Paul next takes a sober look at himself as a Jew with respect to the law of God. Does he himself keep this law? The answer Paul expects is no. Thus, in reality the Jew is in the same position as the pagan Gentile. Both have a law but neither has truly kept it (see esp. 2:26–27).

Paul's conclusion leads naturally to the question of 3:1: "What advantage, then, is there in being a Jew?" Paul goes on to deal with several important objections to what he has been saying. The first one is the value of being a Jew in light of Paul's statements about Judaism and circumcision in 2:25–29. What value is the covenant that is signaled by circumcision? Paul's answer is cut short after discussing only one "advantage"—namely, that the Jews were entrusted with "the very words [oracles] of God" (a reference to the OT in general). In other words, the chief advantage of being a Jew was the gift of the Torah, the revelation of God's will.

Paul's second objection is: "What if some were unfaithful? Will their unfaithfulness nullify God's faithfulness?" Paul's response to this question is "Not at all! (3:4). Israel's unbelief cannot cancel God's plan that is working through this people.

Then comes the next obvious question: What if the Jews did not carry out their responsibility? Would the plan fail? Paul's answer is "No!" Israel's unbelief cannot cancel God's plan. "Let God be true, and every man a liar" (3:4).

Paul then raises another objection (3:5): If our unrighteousness demonstrates so clearly God's righteousness, is God then unrighteous when he judges and inflicts wrath? Paul's answer again is an emphatic "No!" The explanation he gives is in the form of another question: "How could God judge the world?" Paul assumes that God will judge the world for its unrighteousness, and he is certainly just in doing so.

At this point (3:7–8), Paul asks why God judges him as a sinner if God's truth is made more abundant by his lie. Is it fair for a person to be blamed for his falsehood, when it has actually resulted in God's glory? Otherwise put, why is not sin a good thing since it shows forth God's righteousness (v.8)? Paul does not think this question is worth answering. He simply says, "Their condemnation is deserved."

If there is still any doubt that the Jews have no special status of merit before God and they all stand equally in need of God's grace, Paul finalizes it all with a series of OT passages that describe all people as guilty before God (3:9–18). He then summarizes and draws the conclusion in 3:19–20: We are accountable before God, and through the law we become conscious of ourselves as sinners.

C. The Righteousness That Is from God (3:21–26)

In vv.22–24 Paul describes the righteousness that comes to us through faith apart from anything we do. Conversely, those who do not believe do not have this gift of righteousness from God. To "fall short of the glory of God" means to fail to receive the glory God bestows. In v.24, the word "redemption" means "to ransom by the payment of a price." Its usage is primarily from the slave market in the ancient world. Slaves could be bought out of slavery by the payment of a price by an individual or a country. This is what God did through the sacrifice of Christ.

D. The Exclusion of Boasting (3:27–31)

Having said that one can be made righteous only by faith, Paul concludes that no one can claim any merit before God on the basis of his or her works. Boasting is excluded by the law of faith. Paul then turns to the one individual who might conceivably claim a right to boast, the patriarch Abraham; he too cannot claim righteousness before God by what he did.

E. The Case of Abraham (4:1–25)

Abraham cannot claim any merit before God because the Scriptures clearly teach that he was justified by faith, not by works (vv.1-5). Abraham became righteous by faith (Ge 15:6) before he entered into the covenant with God that was marked by circumcision (Ge 17). The promises to him were given while he was yet uncircumcised; thus the things God promised Abraham were also based on faith (vv.13-14) and given by grace (v.16). The nature of Abraham's faith was such that he believed God was able to give life to himself and Sarah, in spite of the obvious physical impossibility of their age (vv.17-22). Thus Abraham's faith is a model for our own faith and demonstrates that we too cannot lay claim to any boasting before the finished work of God's grace (vv.23-25).

V. Implications of Righteousness in the Life of the Believer (5:1 – 8:39)

A. Reconciliation (5:1 – 21)

The ideas presented in this section center around the NT conception of reconciliation. Reconciliation is the doing away of enmity, the bridging over of a quarrel.

This section speaks of *justification* and *reconciliation* as two distinct elements in the work of the death of Christ. Christ's death for believers removed their sin; on this basis God can declare that believers are righteous. That is justification. On the basis of Christ's death God's wrath was satisfied, i.e., the cause of the enmity between God and humanity, sin, was removed, which thus made peace. This is reconciliation. Paul describes "peace" with God in terms that call to mind the sacrificial terms of the OT.

In vv. 12-21, following a discussion of the consequences of Adam's sin as the head of the human race, Paul addresses the nature question of how sin is transmitted to all people. The answer lies in a comparison of Adam and Christ. The sin of Adam, as the representative head of the human race, was passed to all; but in a similar manner, Christ's righteousness is passed on to all those declared righteous by faith. The method of transaction is the same.

In other words, Adam was a "pattern of the one to come" (v.14). The second person of the Trinity, the Son of God, became the representative of all humanity and thus through him, God's righteousness passed to all. The basis of Christ's work, then, is the incarnation. Because there is a real link between all humanity and Christ, a real imputation of righteousness can occur. Adam's sin results in a common relationship of sin among all humanity; Christ's incarnation results in a common relationship of righteousness with all humanity.

B. Sanctification (6:1 – 8:39)

1. Dying to sin (6:1 – 14)

Having dealt with the relationship of the believer to the matter of *guilt* before the law, Paul now turns to the question of the believer's relationship to the *power* of sin (6:1 – 23). He begins with the concept of dying to sin (vv.1 – 14). This question arises naturally from Paul's argument in 5:20, where Paul said that "where sin increased, grace increased all the more."

What does Paul mean by saying believers have "died to sin" and therefore will not "live in it any longer"? Does it mean that believers no longer *can* sin? no longer *will* sin? or no longer *should* sin? To say believers no longer *can* sin contradicts what Paul says about himself in 7:15, "What I want to do I do not do," and in 7:21, "Although I want to do good, evil is right there with me." Moreover, to say that believers *will* no longer sin contradicts Paul's continuous exhortations not to let sin have dominion over them (6:12 – 13). The last possibility alone, that believers *should* no longer sin, is consistent with both the idea that believers still experience a warfare with sin and are called upon to continue to wage war against sin's dominion. Moreover, God has provided believers with the necessary power to wage that war, the Holy Spirit (8:4).

2. Slaves to righteousness (6:15 – 23)

In vv.15 – 23 Paul draws a comparison between two kinds of lifestyles: slaves to sin and slaves to righteousness. Paul's point is that one is a slave to what one submits oneself, whether to sin or to righteousness. Formerly, Paul's readers were slaves of sin, and their obedience to sin involved all of their lives. In the same way, Paul argues, they ought now to submit fully to righteousness (v.19). Paul postpones any explanation of how this is to be done (see ch. 8).

3. The believer's relationship to the power of God's law (7:1 – 6)

In 6:14 Paul had stated: "You are not under the law, but under grace." He now turns to demonstrate why this is true in the life of the believer. His argument is that the law of God applies to one who is alive. Death, in other words, cancels the authority of that law. To illustrate the point, Paul appeals to the marriage law that bound a husband and wife together for life. If the husband died, the wife was free to remarry (vv.2 – 3). Thus, Paul concludes, the believer who died in Christ to the law (as a law of works) is free from the law and can belong to another, namely, to Christ (v.4). Thus the believer is now freed to serve God apart from the law.

4. The nature and function of God's law in relationship to the believer (7:7 – 25)

From all that Paul has said regarding the law thus far, an important question arises, "Is the law sinful?" (v.7). Paul emphatically denies this. Far from being a sinful instrument, he states that the law has, in fact, a positive role in the life of the believer. First of all, it is the means whereby sin can clearly be revealed: "I would not have known what sin was had it not been for the law" (v.7b). That is, one's sins are not clearly shown to be rebellion against God's will except where that will has been revealed.

5. The leading of God's Spirit (8:1 – 39)

Having discussed the nature of the law and the believer's relationship to it, Paul now continues the argument from 7:6 by discussing the implications of the believer's death in Christ. Since believers have died to sin, now, by the power of the Spirit of God, they can live in fulfillment of the requirements of the law. Grace, in other words, makes it possible for one to live according to God's will. In sum, the law is not the means of justification or sanctification; rather, it is the goal of both salvation and sanctification. This is the teaching of the new covenant found in the OT prophets (cf. Jer 31:31 – 34; Eze 36:27).

VI. The Question of Israel (9:1 – 11:36)

A. Introduction of the Problem (9:1 – 6a)

Paul begins this unit with a description of his personal attitude toward Israel (vv.1 – 3). He is grieved by the fact that the nation of Israel has rejected the new covenant and does not now experience what he has been describing in ch. 8. In v.6a Paul raises the question indirectly: "It is not as though God's word had failed." He feels the tension in the mind of his readers as to how to explain Israel's rejection of the new covenant in light of the sovereignty of God and the power of his eternal promises. Why have God's promises not fallen? For two reasons: the Gentiles owe their salvation to the rejection of Israel; and, in the long term, God's purposes will embrace his own people. Before probing these two points, Paul lays the groundwork for his answer by clarifying some of the basic concepts involved in the solution.

B. The Clarification of the True Israel (9:6b – 13)

Paul states: "For not all who are descended from Israel are Israel" (v.6b), and "nor because they are his descendants are they all Abraham's children" (v.7).

Having said this, Paul describes the concept of a "true Israel" that is formed by the sovereign election of God: "It is through Isaac that your offspring will be reckoned" (v.7b). Israel's existence, at least as a theological entity, is not determined by mere natural lineage. Rather, it is based on the promise given by a sovereign God (vv.8–13).

Note that Paul uses "Israel" as opposed to the term "Jew" throughout this section. Strictly speaking, he is not discussing what happened to Jews in God's program, but rather, what happened to "Israel." Thus, he is not merely speaking of the Jews of his day who had rejected the gospel. He is talking about the chosen people of Israel, through whom God promised to fulfill his sovereign plan of redemption. Paul's categories are theological and biblical, not national and political.

C. Divine Sovereignty and Israel's Election (9:14–29)

Having introduced the concept of God's sovereign will in his definition of the term "Israel," Paul is compelled to discuss divine sovereignty and Israel's election (vv.14–29). "Is God unjust?"—or better: "God certainly is not unjust, is he?" It is important to see how Paul answers this question. He does not present a logical argument intended to "prove" the justice of God in light of his sovereignty. Rather, he simply quotes a Scripture passage that states that God is merciful in his sovereign election. The argument is simply that since the Scriptures state God is merciful, he cannot possibly be unjust.

Paul anticipates another question in v.19: "Why then does God still blame us?" That is, "Why does God hold humanity responsible when, in light of his sovereignty, no one can oppose his will?" Paul again appeals to Scripture, that no creature of God has the right to question the justice of the Creator. Human beings are in no position to question the propriety of God's will (vv.20–22). Thus, in v.23 Paul again raises the question of God's election of his chosen people—not just Jews but Gentiles also. That this was God's plan all along is demonstrated from the OT passages he quotes in vv.25–29.

D. Israel's Unbelief (9:30–10:21)

At the close of ch. 9, Paul summarizes the question that he has raised: the Gentiles were made righteous by faith, but the Israelites could not attain to righteousness because they sought it through works rather than faith (vv.30–33). Paul devotes all of ch. 10 to a discussion of Israel's failure to respond to the gospel in faith. True Israel is distinguished on the basis of faith (9:30–33); historical Israel failed in faith (10:1–21). Yet God's plan for Israel did not fail; rather, it was enlarged to include the Gentiles (11:1).

E. Israel's Present and Future Status in God's Plan (11:1 – 36)

Having laid the groundwork in chs. 9 – 10, Paul is ready to discuss the primary question of Israel's present and future status in God's plan.

1. The concept of a remnant in Israel (11:1 – 7b)

Paul begins with a question: "Did God reject his people?" (v.1) that is really meant as a statement of fact: "God has not rejected his people, has he?" His answer is emphatic: "By no means!" His first line of evidence for this is the fact that Paul himself, an Israelite, has not been cast off by God (v.1b). Therefore, "God did not reject his people, whom he foreknew" (v.2a). But Paul does not stop here. He goes on to show that the idea of a few being chosen out of the whole (i.e., a remnant) is not new. It is seen already in the OT, such as in the account of Elijah at Mount Horeb (vv.2b – 4). In v.5 Paul draws the conclusion, "So too, at the present time there is a remnant chosen by grace."

2. The hardening of the rest (11:7c – 10)

Paul, still speaking of the present Israel, groups the entire nation into a second category — the nonelect. These, he argues, have been hardened or made insensitive (v.7c). Paul quotes the OT again to demonstrate the nature of this hardening of the nonremnant, using the passive voice. Thus Paul has avoided attributing this hardness to God. Nevertheless, the Scriptures Paul quotes (Dt 29:4) state explicitly that it was God who gave Israel a "spirit of stupor" (v.8). Israel was in the desert, and in spite of God's miraculous provision, they proved unfaithful, and God responded by refusing to give them further understanding. A second passage quoted by Paul is Isa 29:10, "The Lord has brought over you a deep sleep." Here again the context speaks of Israel's unbelief followed by God's punishment — the spirit of "a deep sleep" (cf. Isa 29:11 – 14).

3. The result of Israel's hardening (11:11 – 24)

The result of the hardening of Israel, Paul makes clear, was salvation for the Gentiles. He begins with a question to which he will return in v.25: "Did they [the Jews] stumble so as to fall beyond recovery?" His answer is clear: "Not at all!" But their fall, he argues, did have a good outcome in God's program, for it resulted in the salvation of the Gentiles. That fact is to make Israel jealous (v.11c). Moreover, their fall was not a total fall, and thus we await "their full inclusion," which will bring even greater riches to the nations (vv.12 – 16).

In vv.17 – 24, Paul discusses the Gentiles' position as part of God's elect over against the position of the Israelites who have fallen out of this position.

The image he uses is that of the grafted wild olive branch and the natural olive branch that has been cut off. The Israelite is the natural olive branch that grows out of the "nourishing sap from the olive root" (v.17). This root is the Abrahamic covenant promise, which, from the beginning, has been the basis of God's dealing with Israel and which also forms the basis of God's dealings with Gentiles (Ge 12:1–3). The wild olive branch is the Gentile now grafted into the root—namely, the promised blessings of Abraham. The basis of Israel's being cut off and the Gentiles' being grafted in is faith (v.20).

The result of the hardening of Israel to salvation by faith is, then, a worldwide body of elect from every nation who are the spiritual heirs of the covenant promises to Abraham. The notion that the Gentiles could be "grafted" into the covenant promises of Abraham, however, opens the question about the efficacy of the promises yet to Israel. It is, then, to this question that Paul turns in v.25.

4. The future of Israel (11:25 – 36)

In v.25 Paul speaks of a "mystery," namely, that a partial hardening has come on the Israelites "until the full number of the Gentiles has come in." That temporary hardening to allow for the inclusion of the Gentiles into God's plan was unknown in the OT, but it is now revealed in the NT. The expression "full number [lit., fullness] of the Gentiles" apparently refers to the total number of Gentiles who will be included in God's plan during the time of Israel's hardening. After this "fullness" has come in, then "all Israel will be saved."

It is generally agreed that this refers to Israel as a national entity; they will yet be saved at some time in the future. Moreover, Israel as a national unit will be saved by believing in Christ as Savior. There is, however, a difference of opinion about the status of this believing nation of Israel in God's overall program. Some hold that upon believing, the nation of Israel becomes a part of the true Israel, the church. Others hold that the belief of the national Israel will mark the fulfillment of the OT promises to physical Israel (Isa 2:2–4; 60:1ff.; 62:2; Zec 9:16–17).

VII. Exhortations (12:1 – 15:13)

A. Introduction (12:1 – 2)

Paul now describes the Christian life by using an analogy to the OT sacrificial system: "Offer your bodies as a living sacrifice" to God (v.1). The motive for such obedience is "God's mercy." In a similar fashion (see Ex

20:2; Dt 6:12), the basis of Israel's obedience was the gracious act of God in delivering them from slavery in Egypt.

God is interested in the whole of a person's life, both body and soul. For Paul, the body was the battleground of spirituality, to the extent that he could even summarize the spiritual life as putting to death the deeds of the body by means of the Spirit (8:13). Paul does not merely say to present one's body to God for service. He says, in addition, "offer your bodies as a living sacrifice" to God—sacrifices that are "pleasing" to him. Christians should be free from living according to the sinful nature (cf. 6:13). Paul calls this "your true and proper worship."

In v.2 Paul continues to admonish his readers to "renew" their minds so that they can please God in their daily lives. The world should not determine what is "pleasing to God." Rather, our minds must be "transformed" by the will of God.

B. A List of Admonitions (12:3 – 21)

1. A realistic look at oneself within the body of Christ (12:3 – 8)

The danger Paul anticipates in the church at Rome is a growing polarity within the body of Christ—some members usurping more than their share in the work, and consequently others within the same body doing less than their share. To Paul, each member has been given a measure of faith (cf. Eph 4:7), a specific sphere where one's faith is exercised. Paul illustrates this by using the physical body (vv.4 – 5; cf. 1Co 12:14 – 27). Whatever your gift, use it as the exercise of the faith given you by God.

2. General principles (12:9 – 27)

Here Paul lists a series of general principles that should govern the Christian's life.

C. Obedience to Authorities (13:1 – 7)

Christians are also to submit to the government authorities because they are commissioned by God to provide peace and stability within society. Paul qualifies the kind of government he is speaking of by focusing on government in the ideal sense, whose high calling is to maintain the "good" (v.4). When a government does this, it is fulfilling its God-ordained role, and Christians are to submit to it. If a government fails to do this, it loses its God-ordained status as government, and the Christian is not obligated to submit to it. Christians should be continually evaluating the role of their government in providing and protecting "the good."

D. The Centrality of Love in the Life of Christians (13:8 – 10)

Christians are also to pay all they owe. In this context the reference is to taxes, revenue, respect, and honor (v.7). In a modern society built on a credit economy, Paul's statement would be difficult to follow. Thus the NIV has translated this verse as, "Let no debt remain outstanding." Christians must not refuse to pay their obligations. The second idea Paul raises is the obligation of Christians to love others. This debt can never be fully paid.

E. The Christian's Perspective on Time (13:11 – 14)

The Christian's eyes should ultimately be on the expectation of the coming of Christ; "the day is almost here" (v.12). All of this life should be viewed in the light of the next life, the one lived with Christ. Paul does not argue that the return of Christ is near. Nevertheless, lying behind his instructions is the idea that each day brings us closer to Christ's return (v.11). In light of his return, Paul admonishes his readers to live as those who are soon to be with him.

F. The Question of Doubtful Things (14:1 – 15:13)

Though Paul is here discussing questionable areas of conduct, they are not explicitly defined by him. He lists only three examples: (a) eating meat or vegetables; (b) observing special days; (c) drinking wine (14:21). These areas are religious in nature in that they are considered to be done "to the Lord" (v.6). The background of these matters is perhaps the pattern of clean and unclean instructions known from the OT and Judaism. They relate to the worship of God, not to one's personal salvation.

Paul also raises the question of the "weaker" Christian here. He describes such a one as holding to a particular kind of religious observance as a means of expressing devotion to God. Weaker Christians do not believe that their observance of this act holds any salvific merit with God. Paul would not allow that to remain questionable. But we should honor such devotion.

A third line of thought is the discussion of one who has faith or one who is strong enough "to bear with the failings of the weak." Paul includes himself in the latter group. Such a person sees beyond specific acts to the acts of one's whole life as a devotion to God. For example, a strong person "considers every day alike" (14:5), for "if we live, we live for the Lord; and if we die, we die for the Lord. So, whether we live or die, we belong to the Lord" (v.8).

In light of such issues, Paul formulates the principle that Christians must not judge one another in questionable areas of conduct because God himself will judge each one according to one's own standard of devotion (14:10–12). More important than judging others, Paul says, is the rule of loving others and bearing their weaknesses. The goal of this kind of love is the strengthening of the weaker believer (15:2) and unity in the church (v.6).

In 15:7 Paul generalizes this principle of acceptance within the church: all whom Christ has received should be accepted. Paul then applies the principle to the situation he has been concerned with throughout the letter, the Jew and the Gentile together in one body (vv.8–12).

VIII. Closing Words (15:14–16:27)

Paul again reminds the Romans that he had long intended to come to their city but had been hindered (15:22–23). He had been in Macedonia and Achaia, where he was taking a collection for the poverty-stricken saints in Jerusalem (15:25–33). He closes the letter with numerous greetings.

1 CORINTHIANS

Introduction

Although this letter is called 1 Corinthians, in actual fact Paul had already written an earlier letter to the church in Corinth (see 5:9), but that letter is not preserved in the NT. Paul apparently wrote four letters to the church at Corinth: (1) 1Co 5:9; (2) 1 Corinthians; (3) 2Co 2:3; (4) 2 Corinthians.

The apostle Paul, as indicated within this letter itself (1:1), was the author of this letter. He wrote it while ministering and teaching in Ephesus on his third missionary journey (16:8). He had been in Corinth for a year and a half on his second journey (Ac 18:1 – 18). If it was written at the end of Paul's time in Ephesus (16:7), the date of the letter would be around AD 55 – 56.

I. Introduction (1:1 – 9)

Paul begins the letter with a strong assertion of the steadfast faithfulness of the church at Corinth. They "do not lack any spiritual gift" (v.7a), and they "eagerly wait for our Lord Jesus Christ to be revealed" (v.7b). Paul's confidence lies in the Lord's faithfulness in keeping the Corinthian church strong.

II. Divisions within the Church (1:10 – 4:21)

Paul turns quickly to the problem issues and questions within the Corinthian church, the very questions that had given rise to his letter. The first of these was the growing quarrels and divisions among its members. Each group had its own leaders, who were apparently arrogantly asserting their own learned views on the nature and implications of Paul's gospel.

Paul's response is complex, but underlying all of his remarks is the fact that, for him, the message of the gospel is simple and can be understood in the ordinary language of common people. Though the wisdom of God displayed in the gospel is sublime, God's wisdom is easily distorted when forced into categories of human wisdom. The gospel, in fact, becomes foolishness when seen within that context.

Paul himself, in presenting the gospel at Corinth, had not attempted to dress it in "eloquence or human wisdom" (2:1). The simple fact of Jesus' death on the cross was sufficient to demonstrate the life-giving power of God. It is the Spirit of God who enlightens the hearts of believers and enables them to "understand what God has freely given" (v.12). Without the Spirit, such simple truths would not be acceptable to the average person, for he or she simply would not understand them.

If the leaders of the Corinthian church want to assume a role of importance, then they should follow the example of Paul himself and of the other apostles and church leaders (such as Apollos, whom Paul considers a coworker, not a rival). God's leaders are, in fact, servants. They do not receive great acclaim for their work and their faithfulness. They are not seeking great wealth and power. For the sake of the gospel, these leaders of the church have given all and are content with serving the Lord.

III. Moral Scandals in the Church (5:1 – 6:20)

In ch. 5 Paul turns to the question of sexual immorality within the Corinthian church, i.e., the problem of incest. Not only was such behavior expressly forbidden in the OT (Lev 18:6), but it was even abhorrent to pagans. To make matters worse, the Corinthians were proud of such behavior in their midst (5:2)! Perhaps they were proud because they regarded such behavior as a sign of their liberty in Christ. Or perhaps the Corinthian church had been so blinded by the stellar qualities of some among them that they overlooked obvious instances of immorality in these people. In any event, Paul argues that such a situation should have been dealt with summarily. Such offenders should be put out of the church where, presumably, they would learn their lesson, repent, and be "saved on the day of the Lord" (v.5).

From this example, Paul draws a larger principle. Christians are not to associate with one who claims to be a Christian and yet is "sexually immoral or greedy, an idolater or slanderer, a drunkard or swindler" (v.11). In this way, Christians should exercise judgment among themselves (v.12). Paul leaves to God the judgment of those outside the church (v.13).

The fact that Christians are to judge one another within the church leads Paul to the second moral problem at Corinth: Christians were taking other Christians to court. Paul emphasizes that "they" (i.e., Christians) will one day judge the world with Christ. Why, then, do they not now judge one another? For Paul, a Christian should strive to live out the principles of God's kingdom in the present age. That may mean being mistreated and cheated, but that is far better than violating God's will. The ultimate question for Paul was the future inheritance of the kingdom of God.

For Paul, as in the OT (cf. Da 12:2), the coming of God's future kingdom will be initiated by the physical resurrection of the body from the dead (6:14). Thus, sexual immorality, a sin of the body, is particularly damaging to the Christian's life in Christ. God prizes the body so much, Paul argues, that those who have died will rise again to receive their bodies back, just as Jesus did in his resurrection. The body belongs to God as one of the "members of Christ" (v.15). The body is a temple of the Holy Spirit, so that sexual immorality desecrates the Lord's temple. Paul's imagery here is in keeping with the OT prophets' view of idolatry and apostasy as prostitution (cf. Dt 31:16).

IV. Questions Regarding Marriage (7:1 – 40)

Paul now moves to the topic of sexuality and marriage, responding to questions the Corinthian church had asked him (7:1). Paul's advice is both practical and realistic. Although he wishes that Christian men and women would not marry (vv.1, 7), he knows that in real life — this side of the resurrection — men and women have God-given physical desires. Moreover, the Scriptures teach that marriage is a part of this world (Ge 2:24) and that God himself had said, "It is not good for the man to be alone" (Ge 2:18). Paul, however, knows that Jesus could return at any moment: "The time is short.... For this world in its present form is passing away" (7:29 – 31). For those whose sights are set that high, there is little time for everyday concerns that marriage entails: "To the unmarried and the widows I say: It is good for them to stay unmarried" (v.8).

Paul, however, is not an ascetic. He knows that not all have the same focus; many are consumed with other desires. Thus, "if they cannot control themselves, they should marry, for it is better to marry than to burn with passion" (v.9). That Paul has a much larger question in mind is evident from the fact that he extends his principle on marriage to include virtually every aspect of the Christian's life (vv.17–40).

V. Questionable Issues in the Church (8:1 – 11:1)

To the question of eating meat offered to idols, Paul applies two key biblical principles: " 'I have the right to do anything,' you say—but not everything is beneficial" (10:23); and, "No one should seek their own good, but the good of others" (v.24). Paul applies these two principles in the context of evangelism and to Christian maturity (i.e., the issue of the weaker believer).

Whether Christians should eat meat offered to idols was apparently a pressing question in the church at Corinth. For Paul, however, the more important question was how such issues were dealt with. It had become a matter of pride on both sides of the question, so Paul begins at that point (8:1–3). As the OT teaches (e.g., Isa 44:9), Paul affirms that idols are "nothing at all" (8:4) and hence not a serious threat in themselves. (This is not to say that idolatry cannot be an occasion for the worship of demons, as Paul later suggests in 10:20.) If, however, a Christian brother should think otherwise, it would be wrong for him to eat meat offered to an idol.

Moreover, if that person were to see another Christian eat meat that in his mind was "defiled," it would surely send the wrong signal. It could easily be interpreted as a license to do something one feels is wrong, and this would disturb the conscience of the weaker brother (8:12) and affect his behavior. For the sake of such persons, one should not eat meat offered to idols or do anything else that may be wrongly interpreted.

Paul gives his own situation as an example of putting aside individual rights out of concern for others. As an apostle, he had all the rights and privileges of an apostle. For the sake of the gospel, however, he relinquished those rights. Everything Paul did was for a higher purpose, i.e., "for the sake of the gospel" (9:23). His mind was set on the prize at the end of the race—the coming of the kingdom of God that he looked for at any moment. Paul did not want to be found "disqualified" when he faced the risen Lord (v.27).

Was it possible that someone like Paul could be disqualified? To answer that question, he gives the example of the Israelites in the desert. They "were all under the cloud" and "passed through the sea" (10:1); moreover, "they were all baptized into Moses in the cloud and in the sea" (v.2). If anyone could have claimed to have made it, it would have been those Israelites—they even "drank from the spiritual rock that accompanied them, and that rock was Christ" (v.4).

Most of them, however, were disqualified; "their bodies were scattered in the wilderness" (v.5), and they did not enter the Promised Land. As with the OT prophets (Nu 20:9–12; Am 5:25–26), Paul looks at Israel's sojourn in the desert as a time of failure. Only Joshua and Caleb were found faithful (Nu 14). Thus, these OT narratives are lessons for us (10:11), lest we too test the Lord's forbearance and fall, as it were, in the desert. Paul, apparently sensing the stringency of his warning, quickly adds the comforting promise that God is faithful and will not allow anyone to be tempted beyond what one is able to bear (v.13).

The warning, nevertheless, remains, that Christians are not to presume upon their rights and privileges, but are to act responsibly toward the mutual good of all (10:33). Their freedom in Christ should not be turned against the weaker members of the church.

VI. Questions of Public Worship (11:2 – 34)

Paul addresses two procedural problems in the public worship services of the Corinthian church: (1) the proper procedure for covering one's head in prayer (vv.2–16), and (2) the proper procedure for commemorating the Lord's Supper (vv.17–34). Like the earlier sections of this letter, Paul appeals to general principles, but here he also cites custom and precedent.

In the case of head coverings, Paul appeals to the general principle of headship: "the head of every man is Christ, and the head of the woman is man, and the head of Christ is God" (v.3). This principle, based on the pattern of the creation of the man and woman Ge 2:7–24, had been used to support a well-known custom in the early church (v.16). When men prayed in public, they uncovered their heads, whereas women prayed with their heads covered. To do otherwise was considered dishonorable (vv.4–7). This was ultimately a question of authority (v.10), and, as Paul maintained in 1Ti. 2:12, women should not have authority over men in the church.

The situation with the Lord's Supper was different. Paul censures the Corinthians' practice of commemorating the Lord's Supper (see v.17); their disruptive "divisions" and practice of greedy feasting and drunkenness obscured the purpose of that event. The bread and cup are intended to "proclaim the Lord's death until he comes" (v.26) and thus are symbols of his own body (v.29). The meal was not intended to satisfy hunger but to remember the work of Christ. Failure to do so brings one under God's judgment. As a remedy for their abuse in the practice of the Supper, when they came together to eat, they "should all eat together" (v.33).

VII. Questions of Spiritual Gifts (12:1 – 14:40)

In Paul's discussion of spiritual gifts, he emphasizes that the exercise of such gifts should be for the "common good" (12:7) of the whole church, and it should center on worshiping Christ (v.3). The church, as Christ's body, has many parts. One Spirit has baptized all members into the same body (v.13). God has arranged the parts of the body to fulfill his plan and purposes. Though each part plays a vital role in God's design, some parts (or gifts) are more honorable than others. The honor bestowed on some gifts, such as apostleship, prophecy, and teaching, is for the sake of unity and mutual concern (v.25). Not all, however, are given these gifts, nor is any single individual given all of the gifts; but everyone can eagerly desire to have "the greater gifts" (v.31).

Paul, however, shows his readers "the most excellent way" (12:31), one that transcends the exercise of one's gifts. That is the way of love. Without love, the exercise of even divinely given gifts is "nothing" (13:2). Love is the manner and the goal of exercising spiritual gifts. Gifts are important but temporary. They are provisions that God has given to his church, like the helps that small children need in growing to maturity. Love, by contrast, is like the sound mind of an adult. Such maturity is the result of being properly nourished on the gifts of the Spirit.

Thus, for Paul, the Christian's life should be characterized by a striving for spiritual gifts, practiced in the spirit of love. That will result in harmony and order in the life of the Christian and in the life of the church. In the everyday exercise of a gift, one's concern should be the building up others, not self-satisfaction and fulfillment.

When applied to specific gifts, such a rule suggests that a gift like prophecy, which is speaking to others "for their strengthening, encouraging and comfort" (14:3), has greater value for the church (vv.4 – 5) than tongues, which "do not speak to people but to God" (vv.2, 4). If, however, someone interprets the tongues, the church can thereby profit (v.5b). In the church, one must be conscious of speaking clear "intelligible words" (vv.6 – 9) that "build up the church" (v.12). Thus, the gift of tongues should be accompanied by the gift of interpretation (vv.13 – 19).

The gift of speaking in tongues, as the NT shows, was given to the church as a sign for unbelievers. Paul's description of this purpose of the gift of tongues follows the example of Ac 2, where disciples spoke "in other tongues as the Spirit enabled them" (Ac 2:4). "God-fearing Jews from every nation under heaven" (v.5) "heard their own language being spoken," and they were "utterly amazed" (vv.6 – 7). As a result, three thousand unbelieving Jews became believers that day (2:41).

The worship of the church was to be characterized by singing hymns and using words of instruction, revelations, and tongues with interpretation (1Co 14:26). The focus of the service was "that the church may be built up" (v.26). Only two or three persons were to speak in tongues consecutively, with interpretations, or to prophesy (vv.27–29). The others were to "weigh carefully what is said" (v.29). The women were to "remain silent" (v.34). Paul warns of stringent consequences for those who ignore his teaching (v.38).

An enlightening example of an early worship service such as this is found in Acts. The church at Antioch was "worshiping the Lord" (Ac 13:2) when the Holy Spirit spoke, apparently through one of the prophets (v.1). In this case, the goal was direction for the spread of the gospel into Asia.

VIII. Questions about the Resurrection (15:1 – 58)

Paul's last topic is the resurrection. Paul eagerly awaited the return of Christ and the resurrection of the dead, which, according to OT prophecy (e.g., Da 12:2), would accompany it. It was imperative for him to address the question raised by those who doubted the resurrection. Many in early Judaism (such as the Sadducees, Mt 22:23) taught that there was no resurrection. Paul, like Jesus, believed strongly in the resurrection. For him, the hope of a future bodily resurrection of all Christians was founded on the central facts of the gospel, namely, that Jesus died for our sins, was buried, and rose again (15:1–4, 12–23). Moreover, it was fundamental to the founders of the apostolic church (vv.5–8), of which he was one (vv.9–11). The fact that he had seen the risen Lord on the road to Damascus turned Paul from a persecutor of the church to one of its leading apostles (see Ac 9).

Central to Paul's understanding of the return of Christ and the establishment of God's kingdom is the concept of the resurrection (vv.23–28). Paul follows the OT closely in his explanation of the events of the last days, the return of Christ, and the resurrection. As with Jesus, his basic text is the Son of Man passage in the book of Daniel (chs. 7; 12). When Christ returns (15:23b), those who belong to him will arise from the dead (v.23c). This will mark the coming of the end (v.24a). Christ will return to destroy "all dominion, authority and power" (v.24c), reign until the time he "has put all his enemies under his feet" (v.25), including death itself (v.26), and then hand "over the kingdom to God the Father" (vv.24b, 28).

Paul's next argument for the necessity of the resurrection has been variously interpreted: "Now if there is no resurrection, what will those do who are baptized for the dead?" i.e., "Why are people baptized for them?"

(v.29). Paul's comment in v.30 suggests that "baptism for the dead" refers to the martyrdom that many Christians in Paul's day suffered for the sake of Christ. Jesus himself referred to his own death as a "baptism" (Mk 10:38). In other words, Paul tells the Corinthians that such sacrifices as he and others are making by daily risking and losing their own lives are futile if there is no resurrection (15:32).

A major objection to the notion of a resurrection was the question of the kind of body the dead will have (v.35). The objection, as Paul answers it, centers on the fact that the dead no longer have bodies because their physical bodies have decayed. Paul responds by showing that in nature itself, dust and decay precede regeneration: "What you sow does not come to life unless it dies" (v.36). Just as in nature, Paul continues, so also in the resurrection "God gives it a body as he has determined" (v.38). God will give us a body that will never decay again (vv.42–44). The chief characteristic of the new body given to those in the resurrection is its spiritual nature; that is, bearing "the image of the heavenly man" (v.49), it will be an imperishable body that will not have "the sting of death," which is sin (v.56). Because of the resurrection of the body, a Christian's work, done for the Lord, will never be in vain (v.58).

IX. Personal Matters (16:1 – 24)

Paul closes the letter with a reminder of the collection for God's people in Jerusalem, the churches in need of assistance. He signs off with some final admonitions and greetings.

2 CORINTHIANS

Introduction

This letter is really the fourth letter Paul wrote to the Christians in Corinth (see introduction to 1 Corinthians), though the letter mentioned in 2Co 2:3 may be our 1 Corinthians.

The apostle Paul was the author of the letter (1:1), which he wrote during his travels in Macedonia (2:13; 7:5; 9:2). Its date of composition is dependent on that of 1 Corinthians, since both letters were written within a short span of time. If 1 Corinthians was written at the end of Paul's time in Ephesus (1Co 16:7, around AD 55 – 56), the present letter was written later in the same year.

I. Introduction (1:1 – 11)

Paul immediately sets the tone of his letter with a reminder of the great suffering he has endured for the sake of the Christians at Ephesus (vv.3 – 11). All the essential elements of the remainder of the letter are found in this opening volley. The hope that sustained Paul in the midst of "great pressure" was that of the resurrection (cf. comments on 1Co 8 – 10; 15). God was faithful and answered the prayers of many on Paul's behalf, and now Paul has been spared to write this letter of comfort to the church at Corinth. For Paul, behind all the misfortune he has endured lies the all-encompassing divine compassion: "If we are distressed, it is for your comfort and salvation" (v.6). There is a purpose for all that has happened.

II. Change of Plans and Delay (1:12 – 2:13)

The first matter Paul turns to is his change of plans in visiting the Corinthian church. He had planned to visit Corinth, but sent a letter instead — a letter that had caused them sorrow (7:8). That letter was either what we now call 1 Corinthians or, more likely, a letter that has not been preserved in the NT. In any event, it is to the Corinthians' painful response to that letter that Paul now addresses himself. First on his agenda is the restoration of one of their members who had been disciplined (2:5 – 11). Paul instructs that he should now be restored and comforted "so that he will not be overwhelmed by excessive sorrow" (v.7).

III. Paul's Apostolic Ministry (2:14 – 7:16)

Paul digresses at this point in the letter to put his personal situation in a larger context for his readers. That larger context is the apostolic ministry to which he has been called within the new covenant. The concept of the new covenant, promised in the OT (Jer 31:31 – 34; Eze 36:22 – 32), becomes a particularly apt way for Paul to address the problems in the Corinthian church. In the new covenant, the external law of God, written on tablets of stone, was replaced by God's law written on the hearts of his people (Jer 31:33). Thus, as Jesus taught in the gospels and as Paul repeatedly stresses, Christians are those who love God and serve him with their whole heart.

Since the Spirit of God dwells in them (Eze 36:27), they are God's temple, the "aroma of Christ among those who are being saved" (2:15). They themselves are a testimony, a letter of recommendation, of Paul's apostleship, "written not with ink but with the Spirit of the living God, not on tablets of stone but on tablets of human hearts" (3:3). Thus, the very lives of the Christians at Corinth testify to Paul's new covenant apostleship.

To reassure his readers of the real difference the new covenant has made in their lives, Paul contrasts their experience of God's glory in the new covenant with the fading and fearful response of Israel at Mount Sinai, i.e., in the old covenant. His main point is the great superiority of the glory of the new covenant (vv.9 – 11).

Paul assumes that the old covenant at Sinai had failed to produce a righteous people of God. Paul is not referring to the entire OT Scriptures here. Rather, he is referring to the Mosaic covenant that God made with Israel at Mount Sinai, which is described in the OT. As Paul shows in his reference to the veil of Moses in Ex 34, the OT itself shares his view of the fading glory of the old covenant. After being with God on the mountain,

Moses had to wear a veil over his face to shield God's glory from those who looked at him (3:7).

Paul, however, sees a second aspect to the veil that Moses wore. It not only shielded the Israelites from facing God's glory, but it also hid from them the fact that the glory on Moses' face was fading (v.13). To this very day, he argues, "the same veil remains when the old covenant is read" (v.14); that is, "when Moses is read, a veil covers their hearts" (v.15). For Paul, the veil on the face of Moses now lies over the face of the OT Scriptures and hides their meaning from anyone who reads them without turning to the Lord. With believers who have the Spirit of God in the new covenant, however, the veil is taken away. They both see God's glory revealed and reflect that glory "with unveiled faces" (vv.17–18).

Paul is not endorsing a "spiritual" or "allegorical" reading of the Scriptures as a way of seeing Jesus in the OT. He is, in fact, saying just the opposite. He is arguing that the truth of the new covenant is already there in the OT, so much so that those who do not see it are blinded by a veil. The truth is there, but they cannot see it. For Paul, we should read the OT with "spiritual eyes."

What kind of glory do Christians reflect? Lest his readers begin to look around themselves for shining faces, Paul immediately points to the ways in which God's glory radiates from the faces of new covenant believers. It is, first of all, by renouncing "secret and shameful ways" (4:2a), not using deception (v.2b), not distorting God's Word (v.2c); it is by living a life with a clear conscience before God (v.2d). The light that "shine[s] out of darkness" is the work of Christ seen in the actions of Christians (vv.3–6); the glory does not radiate from Christians in themselves. They "have this treasure in jars of clay" (v.7). The glory shines from these jars of clay so that all may see that "this all-surpassing power is from God and not from us" (v.7).

Paul, looking at his own inglorious circumstances, concludes that it is in just these kinds of circumstances that Christ's "life may … be revealed in our mortal body" (4:11). It is the truth of the new covenant gospel that keeps Paul from losing heart when he looks at all the things happening around him (vv.16–18). It also gives him hope for the eternal dwelling that awaits him when his temporary, earthly clay jar has passed away (5:1–5). We can learn to be content in our present state, but our lasting hope is for that time when we are "away from the body and at home with the Lord" (vv.6–10).

The importance of Paul's concentration on the new covenant concept of a new heart can be seen in his description of those at Corinth who were turning the church against his apostolic leadership. They were "those who take pride in what is seen rather than in what is in the heart" (v.12). This was not merely an attack on Paul's authority; it was a distortion of the very gospel Paul had preached to them. Thus what lies behind Paul's assertions of his apostolic authority is the love of Christ and the truth of the gospel (5:13 – 6:2). In the gospel God is "reconciling the world to himself in Christ, not counting people's sins against them" (5:19). It is the gospel of grace (5:21 – 6:1). Such a gospel should be kept clear at all times (6:3 – 13) and never be linked with unbelief of any kind (vv.14 – 18). It demands purity of life (7:1) and open acceptance of one another (vv.2 – 4).

IV. The Collection (8:1 – 9:15)

In this section, Paul revisits the collection that he had talked about in 1Co 16:1 – 4. Using the example of the Macedonians' giving as well as Christ's own self-sacrifice for us, Paul seeks generosity on the part of the Corinthians for the needy believers in Jerusalem.

V. Defense of Paul's Apostolic Ministry (10:1 – 12:21)

Paul turns now to a passionate defense of his apostolic ministry. Paul is concerned that the Corinthians do not confuse his defense of his apostolic authority with boasting, though he readily admits that much of what he has to say could be construed as boasting (10:1 – 18). Thus he vows, "We will not boast beyond proper limits, but will confine our boasting to the sphere of service God himself has assigned to us, a sphere that also includes you" (v.13).

Paul's major concern with what he has heard of the church at Corinth is the presence there of false apostles (11:13) and their attempt to undermine his own authority as an apostle in order to gain that authority in Corinth. The threat to the church is that someone may present them with a "Jesus other than the Jesus [Paul] preached" (v.4) and that their "minds may somehow be led astray from your sincere and pure devotion to Christ" (v.3).

In defending himself before the church at Corinth, Paul is determined not to adopt the methods of these "super-apostles" (cf. 12:11), and yet he is not going to let them outboast him in matters that clearly demonstrate the sincerity of his ministry (11:6 – 12:10). Lest anyone mistake his motives, Paul reminds his readers that his boasting has been entirely limited "to things that show [his] weakness" (11:30).

VI. Paul's Apostolic Ministry Exercised (13:1 – 10)

Paul brings the letter to a close with a stern warning lest his intentions and plans be misunderstood. His desire to be weak in Christ must not be interpreted as weakness. The matter was one that required serious reflection: "Examine yourselves to see whether you are in the faith; test yourselves" (v.5). Paul was no longer under examination, his readers were. For him, this letter was proof that he had not failed the test (cf. v.5); it was now time for the church at Corinth to see if they had (v.5). The question was not "Who is right?" but whether they would "do what is right" (v.7). In the end, Paul is confident that truth will prevail because the apostolic authority that the Lord gave him was "for building you up, not for tearing you down" (v.10).

VII. Conclusion (13:11 – 14)

As a conclusion Paul summarizes the underlying exhortation of his letter: "Strive for full restoration, encourage one another, be of one mind, live in peace" (v.11). He closes with one of the most beautiful benedictions in the NT, reflecting the qualities of the triune God.

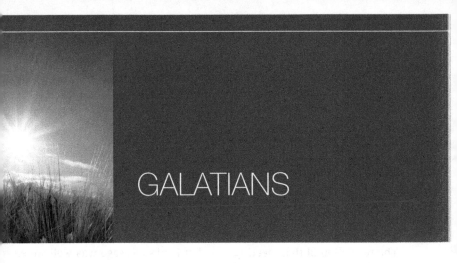

GALATIANS

Introduction

In the early NT manuscripts this letter, written by the apostle Paul (1:1), is entitled "To the Galatians." The date this letter was written cannot be determined with precision. For one thing, the destination, Galatia, is not a precise geographical term and could be located in more than one of Paul's missionary journeys. But it seems likely that it was written during Paul's active ministry in Asia Minor and that it deals with a central question in the early church, the role of the Mosaic law in the life of the Gentile Christian.

I. Introduction (1:1 – 10)

Paul establishes the main line of argument in the book in his introduction. His apostleship was "not from men nor by a man, but by Jesus Christ and God the Father, who raised him from the dead" (v.1). It is important for Paul to demonstrate that he was directly and divinely appointed as an apostle. The gospel he preached is the only gospel (vv.6 – 10). Some in the churches in Galatia, however, were preaching another gospel, which was "really no gospel at all" (v.7). It meant "deserting the one who called [them] to live in the grace of Christ" (v.6).

II. The Divine Origin of Paul's Gospel (1:11 – 2:10)

Paul sets out to demonstrate that the gospel he preached was the one and only true gospel. He received it "by revelation from Jesus Christ" (1:12), and it was confirmed by the early church leaders. This revelation was his vision of Jesus that he saw on his way to Damascus (Ac 9). Afterwards, Paul did not consult with the other apostles in Jerusalem for three years. Only after three years in Arabia and Damascus did he go to Jerusalem to meet with Peter and James for fifteen days. But these were the only apostles he met with.

After fourteen years of continuous ministry, Paul later returned to Jerusalem and, at that time, was privately examined by the leaders of the church there. The issue centered on the place of the Mosaic law in the preaching of the gospel and, specifically, the question of whether Gentile Christians should be circumcised. Paul held stringently to the view that Gentiles were not to be made subject to the stipulations of the Mosaic law. The resolution of that meeting was that Paul's message was well suited for his commission as an apostle to the Gentiles and that Peter's message was suited for his ministry to the Jews. On that basis, the leaders of the Jerusalem church—James, Peter, and John—agreed and gave Paul "the right hand of fellowship" (2:9).

III. The Statement of the Problem (2:11 – 16)

The flashpoint came with Peter's actions in Antioch. Although initially content to live free of the law, Peter later "began to ... separate himself from the Gentiles because he was afraid of those who belonged to the circumcision group" (v.12). In other words, Peter, who knew better, disregarded the gospel and buckled under pressure from "the circumcision group." Others, including Barnabas, followed his example (v.13). Paul confronted Peter with the charge of hypocrisy. While in Antioch, he had been willing to live like a Gentile, free from the restrictions of the Mosaic law, but when representatives from Jerusalem came, he gave in to pressure and began insisting that Gentiles follow the Mosaic law (v.14). Something was wrong!

IV. Statement of the Gospel (2:17 – 21)

Peter's actions were contrary to the basic gospel. Even Jewish Christians knew that "a person is not justified by the works of the law, but by faith in Jesus Christ" (v.16). The question, as Paul puts it, is clearly centered on salvation. According to his gospel, salvation is not dependent on keeping the Mosaic law (v.16). Ultimately, it boils down to the meaning of what

Christ did on the cross: "If righteousness could be gained through the law, Christ died for nothing!" (v.21).

V. Sanctification by Faith and Freedom from Law (3:1 – 5:12)

Paul now turns to the question of the Christian's way of life. Having begun by faith and not by obedience to the law, should one now return to the law? Is it the Spirit or human effort that empowers the Christian's life (3:3)? That question, says Paul, is answered for us in a number of ways. Does God give Christians his Spirit and work miracles by the law or by faith? The answer is either too obvious for Paul to give or it is rolled over into the next example, Abraham. Paul quotes directly from Ge 15:6, that Abraham "believed God, and it was credited to him as righteousness" (3:6). In this example, Paul argues, the Scriptures themselves are looking to a time when the Gentiles, apart from the law, would receive the gift of righteousness through faith (vv.7 – 9).

Having given two examples to prove the point that righteousness comes by faith, not by law, Paul now turns to the reverse side of the question. What is life like under the law? Here again Paul relies on a direct quote from the OT: "Cursed is everyone who does not continue to do everything written in the Book of the Law" (v.10; cf. Dt 27:26). That is, no one is righteous before God by the law (v.11). Moreover, Paul states, "the law is not based on faith" (v.12). It is just the opposite: "The person who does these things will live by them" (v.12, a quotation from Lev 18:5). Thus it is by faith that Gentiles were given Abraham's blessing, and it is by faith that we receive the promise of the Spirit (v.14).

God made a covenant promise to Abraham that the Gentiles would be blessed in the Messiah, who would come from his descendants (vv.15 – 16). That promise was made four centuries before the law was given (v.17), and hence the law cannot nullify it. If, once the law was given, the blessing of Abraham was based on that law, it would mean that the promise had been done away with. But even within human society, promises cannot be nullified. They must be kept. Thus the law cannot replace or add to the original promise made to Abraham.

The law did have a definite purpose. Israel needed the law for their own survival. Their numerous transgressions in the desert proved their need for special measures. It was not given to impart life and fulfill the promises of blessing. Rather, it was used to hold them, as it were, as prisoners until the time when "the faith that was to come would be revealed" (v.23). Now that faith in Christ has come, Paul says, "we are no longer under a guardian" (v.25).

Thus in Christ we have all been made children of God (v.26). No longer are there to be distinctions such as Jews and Gentiles, slave and free, male and female. In Christ all are Abraham's descendants. Before the coming of Christ, God's people were heirs of the promises to Abraham, but they were "subject to guardians and trustees," i.e., the law (4:1–2). In the divine plan of the ages, God sent Jesus to redeem his people from the law and to give them their full rights as his children (vv.3–7). The Gentiles were in no better position before the coming of Christ. They were enslaved to false gods in ignorance (v.8). Now that Christ has come to set all of us free, why would anyone want to go back to this former state of slavery (vv.9–20)?

For Paul the issue comes down to the biblical example of Hagar and Sarah and the two covenants they represent, the Sinai covenant and the new covenant. Hagar, the slave, represents the covenant at Sinai (vv.24–25), and, in Paul's day, the Jews in Jerusalem. They were under the guardianship of the law. Sarah, however, the wife of Abraham, represents a different Jerusalem, one from above. She is the mother of those who enjoy the blessings of Abraham in Christ (vv.26–28). Then, as now, the son of the slave persecuted "the son born by the power of the Spirit" (v.29). Then, as now, Paul continues, Christians should not forfeit their freedom in Christ by going back into the state of bondage to the law (4:30–5:12).

VI. Living by the Spirit (5:13 – 6:10)

The fact that Christians are not under the Mosaic law should not be taken to mean they are free to live as they please. There is a higher law, "the law of Christ" (6:2): "Love your neighbor as yourself" (5:14). Those who live by the Spirit will not "gratify the desires of the flesh" (5:16–21; 6:8a); rather, they will exhibit the "fruit of the Spirit" (5:22–6:6, 8b–10).

VII. Conclusion (6:11 – 18)

Paul concludes with a brief summary of the letter, saying that the real motive of those attempting to push obedience to the law upon Gentile Christians was fear of persecution (v.12). Paul's parting thought is that believers enjoy God's peace and mercy, not by circumcision or uncircumcision, but rather by being a "new creation" in Christ (vv.14–15).

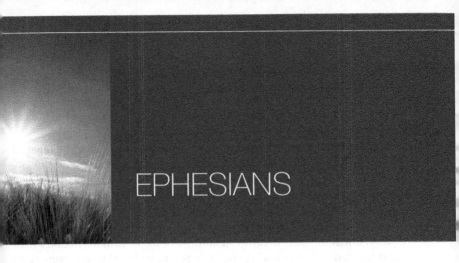

EPHESIANS

Introduction

In early NT manuscripts this letter is entitled "To the Ephesians," but since some early manuscripts do not have "in Ephesus" in 1:1, the title may be a later addition. The apostle Paul is identified as the author. Because he calls himself a "prisoner" in this letter (3:1; 4:1), it is assumed to have been written around AD 60, the time of Paul's imprisonment in Rome.

I. Introduction (1:1 – 2)

Paul gives little personal introduction, either of himself or his readers. Moreover, the phrase "in Ephesus" is not found in some of the earliest and best NT manuscripts. The letter may have been written as a circular letter to be read by many churches throughout the early church.

The crucial bit of information given about the readers is simply that they are "God's holy people," i.e., Christians, and that they have faith in Christ Jesus (v.1). It is written to Christians to explain and expound their status as Christians within the larger context of God's plan for the ages.

II. The Gentile Church in God's Plan (1:3 – 3:21)

A. God's Accomplishment of the Plan (1:3 – 14)

Paul begins the body of his letter with a sweeping panoramic view of God's plan for humanity, beginning in eternity past before creation. He first looks at a Christian's divine blessings "in the heavenly realms" (v.3). Paul presents the Christian's life in Christ as one that draws on a treasure of inherited wealth stored in heaven under God's safekeeping. The Christian has this inheritance solely because of God's eternal plan for the human race and for creation.

Before he created the world, God chose each individual believer to be adopted as his own child, to be redeemed, and to inherit the heavenly wealth of his only Son. Why? Because he loved them. God's plan involved the death of his Son, Jesus. God also determined to reveal his plan to humanity and to set a specific time when that plan would be carried out. The ultimate goal of his plan was to bring praise to himself. As each individual Christian turns to Christ in faith, he or she is included in God's plan and marked with the seal of the Holy Spirit, which thus guarantees an inheritance when the time comes.

B. Implication of the Plan for Gentiles (1:15 – 23)

Paul's immediate concern for his readers is that they properly understand and appreciate what their inheritance is and what it means for their daily living. Much of what they need to know comes from a deeper knowledge of the spiritual things that must be given the Christian by God himself. The "eyes of [their] heart" need to be enlightened for them to know "the riches of his [God's] glorious inheritance" (v.18). Thus Paul knows all he can do is pray that God will give his readers an understanding of these things as he himself sets out to explain them.

He begins by explaining Jesus' resurrection (vv.19–23), by which God exalted Christ to his right hand and gave him dominion over all things. Paul assumes his readers will recognize the imagery from the Son of Man passages in Da 7:9–14. Thus, Paul's revelation of this great mystery comes from his own eyes having been enlightened as he read and poured over the OT. For him, Daniel's vision of the promise of a messianic King ruling over all the world (Da 7:9–14) has been realized "in the heavenly realms" in Christ's resurrection and ascension; it has also meant Christ's becoming the head of the church.

C. Description of the Plan (2:1 – 22)

Central to Daniel's vision of the kingdom of the Son of Man is the fact that those who belong to that kingdom include not only the OT "holy people of the Most High" (Da 7:27) but also the Gentiles, i.e., "all nations and peoples of every language" who will worship the Son (Da 7:14). With an eye on the Gentiles, Paul describes the mutual condition of all humanity before the coming of Christ (2:1–10). The Gentiles "were dead in transgressions and sins" because they "followed the ways of this world" (vv.1–2). But so also were the Jews: "All of us also lived among them at one time, gratifying the cravings of our flesh" (v.3). Thus, in Paul's view, both Jews and Gentiles were "deserving of [divine] wrath" and in need of God's grace (v.8). When God raised Jesus from the dead, he also made believers "alive with Christ," even while they were still "dead in transgressions" (v.5). All this came by grace (vv.6–7).

Paul then turns specifically to the divine inheritance of the Gentiles (vv.11–12). Before Christ, they were not a part of God's people. They were "without hope and without God" (v.12). In the death of Christ, the shedding of his blood, Gentiles are brought into the people of God (v.13). Christ's death did this by abolishing the Mosaic law "with its commandments and regulations," thus destroying "the barrier, the dividing wall of hostility" (vv.14–15). In Christ both Jews and Gentiles are one, with one sacrifice giving them all access to God. Thus in the church, Gentiles are now "fellow citizens with God's people and also members of his household" (v.19).

D. The Revelation of the Mystery (3:1–13)

Earlier generations of God's people did not understand God's plan for the Gentiles as Paul now did. They were unaware that Jews and Gentiles were to be united as one people of God in Christ (v.6). Now, says Paul, this "mystery" has been revealed "to God's holy apostles and prophets" (v.5). It was Paul's specific calling to make this mystery clear, since it had been "for ages past ... kept hidden in God" (v.9). But now God's work with the nations through the church has been revealed to Paul and to others. Earlier generations knew from the OT that God's kingdom would include the Gentiles (e.g., Isa 2:2–5; Da 7:9–14), but in those texts, the plan of God was portrayed in terms of the kingdom of Israel (e.g., Da 7:27). The concept of the church as the body of Christ remained hidden with God until the coming of Jesus.

E. Riches and Power (3:14–21)

Paul returns to the theme of the riches stored up for those who are in Christ (cf. 1:3–14), though now he views the riches as spiritual power in living the Christian life (3:16). The resources of the Christian's inheritance in Christ is "his power that is at work within us" (v.20). Thus, Paul now turns to his instruction on how Christ's power is to be lived out in the everyday life of the Christian and the church.

III. The Way of Life for the Church (4:1 – 6:20)

A. The Unity of the Church as the Basis and Goal of Life (4:1 – 16)

Paul describes the general goal of the Christian life: to exhibit the love of Christ with one another, thereby arriving at "unity in the faith" (v.13a) and "attaining to the whole measure of the fullness of Christ" (v.13b). This is accomplished in the church by a proper application of the gifts each member of the body has received (vv.11 – 12) and by achieving maturity in the knowledge of the truth (vv.14 – 16).

B. Warning against Worldly Practice (4:17 – 24)

An understanding of what God has done in Christ should lead to a transformed life. Former ways of thinking should be consciously put aside and replaced by the practice of "true righteousness and holiness" (v.24). Paul goes on to list specific examples of true righteousness.

C. Examples of True Righteousness (4:25 – 6:9)

Paul begins with a general summary of the nature of true righteousness. This includes speaking the truth; controlling anger; not stealing; doing hard work; sharing with others; using clean talk; mutually building up others; honoring the Spirit; ridding oneself of bitterness, rage, anger, brawling, and slander; being kind; and forgiving one another (4:25 – 32). He stresses further the importance of avoiding sexual immorality, obscenity, foolish talk, coarse joking, and greediness. Such acts and attitudes are not a part of God's purpose for the Christian's life but are, rather, habits of his or her former way of life (5:1 – 20).

Paul then applies these principles to key areas of life, beginning with the family. Wives are to submit to their husbands as they submit to Christ (vv.22 – 24). Husbands are to love their wives as Christ loves the church (vv.25 – 33). Children are to obey their parents, and parents are to be kind to their children (6:1 – 4). Slaves are to obey their masters sincerely, and masters will be held accountable before the Lord for how they treat their slaves (vv.5 – 9).

D. Divine Equipping for Spiritual Warfare (6:10 – 20)

Paul concludes with a reminder of the spiritual warfare that exists in a Christian's life. The kind of equipment needed for daily struggles with the old way of life are precisely those gifts that the Spirit gives to the church.

IV. Conclusion (6:21 – 24)

Paul, in asking for prayer at the conclusion, reminds his readers that he is now in prison for proclaiming the mystery that he has just explained to them in this letter. It is a vivid reminder for them that the world was not ready to receive the message of the kingdom.

PHILIPPIANS

Introduction

In the early NT manuscripts this book is entitled "To the Philippians" and was written by the apostle Paul (1:1). Because he was "in chains" when he wrote this letter (1:12–14), many think it was written around AD 60, the time of Paul's imprisonment in Rome.

I. Introduction (1:1–11)

Paul addresses "God's holy people," i.e., the Christians, at Philippi and their leaders. Judging from his tone and the points he stresses in his opening remarks, Paul is concerned with the direction the church is about to take. He is confident that their walk with the Lord has been exemplary up to this point, but there are forces at work in the church that could alter or even reverse that direction. Thus Paul's primary interest is in encouraging them to continue in the direction they have been going. For this they will also need discernment.

II. Encouragement of the Community (1:12–3:1)

A. Report of Imprisonment (1:12–26)

One of the factors at work within the church at Philippi was their concern for Paul's imprisonment and what it meant for the gospel. Paul assures them that, however perilous his troubles have been, they have resulted in the effective spread of the gospel and thus are a cause for joy. He casts his own situation in terms that reflect those of the church at Philippi. He has weathered much and has seen the progress of the gospel in his struggles. Like the Philippians, the crucial moment for Paul is what lies ahead. For that he needs discernment. Thinking aloud, he asks, "What shall I choose? I do not know!" (v.22). He wants to continue on faithfully as he has in the past (vv.23–30). They also should follow his example, he tells them, "since you are going through the same struggle you saw I had, and now hear that I still have" (v.30).

B. Continue in Humility (1:27–3:1)

Another factor at work within the Philippian church was an impending and menacing factionalism. Paul turns to the example of Jesus himself to stress the importance of humility, "do[ing] nothing out of selfish ambition or vain conceit" (2:3). Jesus, "being in very nature God," did not hesitate to make "himself nothing, by taking the very nature of a servant" (vv.6–7). It was only through such deep humility that "God exalted him to the highest place" (v.9).

Having presented Christ, the highest example of humility and concern for others, Paul presents two additional examples from their own midst, Timothy and Epaphroditus (2:19–30). These two men embodied the kind of humility and love for the church that Paul wishes the Philippians themselves had.

III. Warning against False Teaching (3:2–4:1)

In his warning against the false leaders among them—those threatening to turn the church in the wrong direction—we can see why Paul focuses on humility. These would-be leaders were beginning to stress "confidence in the flesh" (3:3), i.e., elevating the importance of personal achievement and status over dependence on the work of Christ. Paul's argument against such claims stems from his own experience. Although he has more to boast about than any of them in matters relating to personal achievement, he considers it all as "loss for the sake of Christ" (v.7). Paul wants only a righteousness "that comes from God on the basis of faith" (v.9).

As with his other letters, Paul's ultimate goal is "to know Christ and ... to know the power of his resurrection" (v.10). Again casting his own experience in terms that relate to the Philippians, Paul acknowledges that he has not yet obtained this goal. It will, however, continue to be the focus of his Christian walk in the days that lie ahead (vv.13–14).

This attitude, Paul states, is the mark of Christian maturity (v.15). Rather than follow those "enemies of the cross of Christ" among them who stress personal achievement and self-gratification (vv.18 – 19), Paul exhorts his readers to follow his example and to seek leaders who also "live as we do" (v.17). The key difference between the two kinds of leaders is their ultimate goal. The would-be leaders set their minds "on earthly things" (v.19), but Paul eagerly awaits the coming of Christ and the resurrection (3:20 – 4:1).

IV. Exhortations (4:2 – 20)

Paul speaks specifically to a problem of dissension between two faithful Christian women, Euodia and Syntyche (vv.2 – 3). He then broadens out his appeal in the most general terms: rejoice, be gentle, do not be anxious, give thanks in everything, and think on that which is true, noble, lovely, admirable, excellent, and praiseworthy (vv.3 – 8). Paul appeals to his own example and teaching as their guide in Christian living (v.9), as well as to the example of the Philippians themselves in the help they had given him (vv.10 – 20).

V. Conclusion (4:21 – 23)

Paul closes by greeting all "God's people" at Philippi, given from the "brothers and sisters" who are with him.

COLOSSIANS

Introduction

In the early NT manuscripts this book is entitled "To the Colossians." The apostle Paul is identified as the author (1:1). When he wrote this letter is uncertain. Most date it at the same time as Ephesians, i.e., around AD 60, while Paul was in prison in Rome.

I. Introduction (1:1 – 14)

Paul acknowledges the strong faith and love of "God's people" in the church at Colossae. It is a faith and love rooted in hope (v.5). He then speaks of their need for further "knowledge of [God's] will through all the wisdom and understanding that the Spirit gives" (v.9); the sense is that this letter will direct itself to that end. To Paul, quality Christian living is engendered by a proper understanding of the gospel (vv.10 – 11). Christians are members of and share an inheritance in "the kingdom of the Son" (vv.12 – 14). As such, they have redemption and the forgiveness of sins, and they shine as lights in a dark world.

II. The Lordship of Christ over the World (1:15 – 2:23)

A. Christ, Creator and Savior of the World (1:15 – 23)

For Christians to have a proper understanding of their inheritance in "the kingdom of the Son," Paul knows they must understand who Jesus, the Son of God, is. Thus he rehearses for them a short Christian hymn (vv.15–18a). Scholars today are virtually unanimous in holding that Paul quotes an early Christian hymn already in use in the early church.

According to this hymn, Jesus is the "image of the invisible God" (cf. Ge 1:26), the "firstborn over all creation." Paul then adds, "He is the head of the body, the church," alluding to the fact that the Hebrew word for "beginning" can also be rendered "head" and was, in fact, also translated that way by early Greek translators. Finally, the same Hebrew word also has the sense of "supremacy"; thus Paul adds, "that in everything he might have the supremacy" (1:18).

Paul continues to speak about Christ, turning to his work of redemption on the cross (vv.19–20). For Paul, the practical implication of Christ's shed blood is that through it, Christians, who were once "alienated from God" (v.21), have now been reconciled to God and made "holy in his sight, without blemish and free from accusation" (v.22) — clearly an allusion to the sacrificial lamb of the Passover Feast (cf. Ex 12:5).

B. The Apostle as Minister of the Gospel and Church (1:24–2:5)

Concerned about the spread of false doctrine at Colossae, Paul briefly recounts his calling as an apostle and gives a summary description of the nature of the church. The church is the community of saints, both Jews and Gentiles, in whom Christ dwells (1:27). This "mystery" was not made known "for ages" (v.26), i.e., it was not revealed in the OT Scriptures. Paul's commission as an apostle to the Gentiles was, in part, intended to make this mystery known (see the book of Ephesians). The importance that he attached to that commission is shown by the many afflictions he had suffered for the sake of the gospel (1:28–2:5).

C. Warning of False Doctrine (2:6–23)

Part of Paul's responsibility as an apostle, sent to reveal the "full riches of complete understanding" of the gospel (2:2), involved confronting all forms of false doctrine. Those who had "received Christ Jesus as Lord" (v.6) needed to be exhorted to "continue to live ... in him, rooted and built up in him, strengthened in the faith" (vv.6–7). Paul wants a firm foundation in the faith, with no slippage into areas of false doctrine or false practice.

He therefore warns the Christians at Colossae of the dangers of "hollow and deceptive philosophy, which depends on human tradition and the elemental spiritual forces of this world rather than on Christ" (v.8). He contrasts these things with the "fullness of the Deity" that is found in Christ. For the Christian, knowing Christ is all-sufficient. In him is the power of

God to save sinners and give them a new heart. Such power can never be found in human wisdom, no matter how subtle or high-minded it may be.

The central focus of the Christian's life is not an elaborate philosophy (v.8), traditions, a list of rules (v.14), or religious festivals (v.16); the center is the simple message of the crucified Christ (vv.13 – 15). The religious celebrations of the past, found throughout the OT, all point to the death of Christ and the new life found in him (v.17); but they are shadows and should never be allowed to eclipse the central importance of Christ's death in the gospel (vv.16 – 23).

III. Instructions (3:1 – 4:6)

Paul now elaborates on what it means to live a new life in Christ. In the first place, it means looking forward with eager expectation to the return of Christ (3:4). Second, it means no longer living according to the standards and patterns of one's former life (vv.5 – 11). Finally, it means practicing godly virtues in the church (vv.12 – 17), in the home (vv.18 – 21), and at work (3:22 – 4:1) — always aware and ready to proclaim the gospel to others (4:2 – 6).

IV. Conclusion (4:7 – 18)

Paul closes the letter with a somewhat lengthy series of greetings. Curiously, he mentions both Mark (v.10) and Luke (v.14), two individuals who, according to early tradition, were writers of the second and third gospels. He also gives instructions that this letter to the Colossians be circulated to the church at Laodicea (v.16), and for them, in turn, to read the letter that he had sent to Laodicea. It is sometimes thought that the letter sent to Laodicea was the letter Paul wrote to the Ephesian church.

1 THESSALONIANS

Introduction

The apostle Paul is identified as the author in the first verse (1:1). The letter is usually dated at AD 51 and thus was the first of Paul's letters in the NT. It is written to the church in Thessalonica, one of the churches Paul began on his second missionary journey (see Ac 17:1 – 7). Paul was writing to a church that had suffered much for the sake of the gospel. He knew they had weathered the persecution well, but he wanted to encourage them further. The central focus of the book is the eager expectation of churches everywhere for the return of the Lord.

I. Introduction (1:1)

Although three men are listed in the opening verse of this letter, the apostle Paul is usually considered to be the one who wrote it. He greets the Christians in Thessalonica with the simplest of Christian greetings: "Grace and peace."

II. Praise Section (1:2 – 3:13)

A. The Return of the Son and the Coming Wrath (1:2 – 10)

Paul begins with a glowing report of the faith and endurance of the Thessalonian Christians. They have begun well and have demonstrated their faith throughout the whole region. Moreover, they are awaiting the return of Jesus, the Son of God, "from heaven," who will rescue them "from the coming wrath" (v.10). Paul will return to this topic again.

B. Previous Persecutions for Christ (2:1 – 3:13)

Grateful for the faithfulness of the Thessalonian Christians, Paul reminds them of both his and their past persecutions. In his earlier visit, he had delivered the gospel to them under great persecution (2:1 – 12). These afflictions, in fact, demonstrated his commitment to Christ and his love for the Thessalonians — the love of a "nursing mother car[ing] for her children" (v.7). Moreover, the Thessalonians "suffered from [their] own people" when they received the gospel (2:13 – 16). Paul aptly draws a comparison between their suffering and that of the early Christians, Jesus, and the prophets of the OT (vv.14 – 15). Persecution can, in fact, be expected by all true followers of Christ (3:3 – 5).

But having heard the recent report from Timothy that the Thessalonians' faith was strong in spite of their tribulation, Paul was overjoyed: "For now we really live, since you are standing firm in the Lord" (v.8). Throughout this section, Paul returns to his expectation of the Lord's return (e.g., 2:19; 3:13).

III. Waiting for the Lord's Return (4:1 – 5:22)

A. Ethical Exhortations (4:1 – 12)

In light of the return of the Lord and the hope of his appearing, Paul stresses the importance of godly living. It is God's will that the Christians in Thessalonica be holy and abstain from sexual immorality (v.3). No one should wrong or take advantage of a fellow believer (v.6); rather, each one should practice brotherly love (vv.9 – 10), attempting to live a quiet life by working with one's own hands (v.11). Such a life will not only win the respect of those outside the church, but will also enable one "not [to] be dependent on anybody" (v.12).

B. The Coming of the Lord (4:13 – 5:11)

Apparently some in Thessalonica had become discouraged at the deaths of several of their members. They wondered whether the hope of these believers for being raised from the dead ceased. As an answer to their concern and as an encouragement for their faithfulness and patience, Paul summarizes the events that will surround the return of Christ. Jesus, who himself died and rose again, will return with those who have died (4:13 – 14).

First, Jesus will come down out of heaven, with a shout and the sound of a trumpet, and the "dead in Christ" will rise from their graves to meet him (vv.15 – 16). After that, those Christians still alive at the time of his coming will be gathered up into the air to meet him as well (v.17).

When will Christ return? No one knows. His coming will take most by surprise, but his true followers will be ready. They are those who are watching and waiting for his return. They are those who will not lose faith in waiting (5:1 – 11).

C. Instructions for Community Life (5:12 – 22)

Paul closes the body of this letter with several instructions for maintaining unity in the church: respect your leaders (vv.12 – 13), work hard, be patient, be kind to one another, always be joyful, pray continually, and give thanks in all circumstances (vv.14 – 18).

IV. Conclusion (5:23 – 28)

Paul ends by stressing the importance of holy living in view of Christ's return (v.23).

2 THESSALONIANS

Introduction

Like 1 Thessalonians, the apostle Paul wrote this letter to the church that he had begun in Thessalonica. It was written shortly after the first one and thus was also one of the first NT letters Paul wrote (about AD 51).

I. Introduction (1:1 – 12)

As with 1 Thessalonians, Paul begins with a glowing report of the faith and endurance of the Thessalonian Christians. They have demonstrated their faith throughout the whole region by persevering in the midst of persecution (vv.3–4). Paul's focus, however, shifts to the return of the Lord. The suffering of the Thessalonians shows that they were "counted worthy of the kingdom of God" for which they were suffering (v.5). God is just, and their sufferings would be redressed when the Lord is revealed from heaven with his powerful angels (vv.6–7).

II. Instruction Regarding the Return of Christ (2:1 – 12)

Apparently letters purporting to be from Paul had circulated among the churches, announcing that Jesus had already returned to establish the kingdom and that the Thessalonian Christians had been bypassed. Paul disclaims any authenticity to those letters and argues strenuously against the truthfulness of what they reported. His argument against the Lord's having already come is simply that "the man of lawlessness" and his rebellion have not yet occurred (v.3). This is an argument based on the proper sequence of events.

His defense for the proper sequence is strictly biblical. He had already taught them about these events and the return of the Lord when he was with them in person (v.5). Though we do not have record of that teaching, Paul's text was probably Daniel. Throughout Daniel, the coming of the kingdom of God is preceded by an individual or a powerful nation that exalts "himself over everything that is called God" (v.4). In Daniel he was called the "fourth kingdom, strong as iron" (Da 2:40); the "fourth beast—terrifying and frightening and very powerful" (7:7); "a little horn" that came out of the fourth beast (7:8); "the ruler who will come [and] destroy the city" (9:26); or the king who "will exalt and magnify himself above every god" (11:36). In these visions, this ruler rebels against God and his people for a little while, but after that the Son of Man will come from heaven to destroy him and establish an eternal kingdom (7:23–28).

Paul's "man of lawlessness" will set himself up in the temple and proclaim himself to be God (v.4; cf. Da 9:27, "And at the temple he will set up an abomination that causes desolation"). This will continue "until the end that is decreed is poured out on him" (9:27b). Paul's point is clear. Though "the secret power of lawlessness is already at work" (2:7), this individual has not yet been revealed. Therefore, the Lord cannot yet have returned.

Paul continues by stressing that when this "lawless one" does come, he will do such "displays of power through signs and wonders that serve the lie" that all who are not true followers of Christ will be deceived by him and perish with him (vv.9–12).

III. Paul's Confidence in Their Steadfastness (2:13–3:5)

Paul is confident that the Thessalonian Christians will not be deceived by "the man of lawlessness." God has chosen them, and they will stand firm in that day by holding on to the teaching they have received from him.

IV. Instructions (3:6–15)

Paul warns the church to keep away from those teachers who do not, like him, work with their own hands for a living.

V. Conclusion (3:16–18)

In light of the fact that there were letters in circulation falsely purporting to be from him (2:2), Paul is careful to mark this letter with his own "distinguishing mark" (3:17).

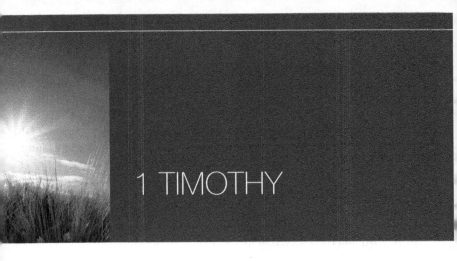

1 TIMOTHY

Introduction

This is the first letter that Paul wrote to his dear friend and coworker Timothy. Together with 2 Timothy and Titus, these letters are called "The Pastoral Letters," for they deal with instructions Paul gave to two young men in pastoral situations. There is no clear indication when Paul wrote 1 Timothy. It is usually dated late in his life, sometime after his imprisonment in Rome in AD 60–62 (Ac 28:30).

I. Introduction (1:1–2)

Rather than addressing a church or group of churches (cf. Paul's earlier letters), Paul addresses Timothy personally. Thus this is a pastoral letter, i.e., a letter addressed specifically to pastors or leaders of churches. This is reflected throughout the letter. Paul greets Timothy as his "true son in the faith," meaning that he was the "father" who had led Timothy to faith in Christ (cf. 1Co 4:15–17).

II. False Teachers (1:3–20)

Timothy was in Ephesus (v.3) and was representing Paul in that church. But there were also teachers of false doctrine there. Thus, Paul's first instructions to Timothy concern what he should do and say to these teachers. Paul approaches the problem by principle and example. The principle he gives Timothy is the "goal of this instruction" (v.5, NIV, "this command").

Timothy must examine his teaching and that of others by the criterion of the life produced by the instruction. Correct teaching will result in godly living, i.e., "love, which comes from a pure heart and a good conscience and a sincere faith" (v.5).

The first example Paul gives Timothy is the negative result of the false teachers who "departed [from sincere faith] ... and ... turned to meaningless talk" (v.6). They do not understand the things they are teaching. The positive example comes from Paul himself. The grace of God that Paul learned in the gospel resulted in "faith and love that are in Christ Jesus" (v.14). As a result of the instruction he received, his former wicked way of life was transformed "as an example for those who would believe in [Jesus Christ] and receive eternal life" (v.16).

III. Church Order (2:1 – 3:16)

A. Prayer in the Church (2:1 – 15)

Paul turns to the matter of prayer in the church. As is typical of his concerns throughout his letters, he admonishes Timothy to ensure that the life of the church be maintained and sustained through prayer. They must pray for everyone, even for kings and those in authority. Prayer for kings and authorities will enable Christians to live "peaceful and quiet lives in all godliness and holiness" (v.2) and will result in the wider spread of the gospel (vv.3 – 4).

The men of the church were to pray "without anger or disputing" (v.8). The women were to attend the worship services dressed modestly (v.9). They were to clothe themselves with good deeds (v.10). What this should entail, Paul explains, was "learn[ing] in quietness and full submission" (v.11). Women were not "to teach or to assume authority over a man" but were to "be quiet" in the worship service (v.12).

Paul gave warrant for his instruction regarding the primacy of the husband's role in public worship from the creation narratives in Genesis. Adam was created first, and then his wife, Eve; hence, the Scriptures assign to the husband a primary responsibility for his family's well-being (v.13). Paul's rationale is based on the role of the firstborn in Genesis. If Adam was created first, that makes him the firstborn, and thus he bore the responsibility for the family.

Paul also derives his warrant for the importance of the wife's modest dress and demeanor from Genesis. In Ge 3:15, God promised that a son would be born of the woman, who would crush the head of the serpent and restore God's blessing. Thus, Paul asserts, salvation for all humankind was promised "through childbirth [NIV, childbearing] — if they continue in faith, love and holiness with propriety" (2:14 – 15). Paul seems to derive the importance of modest clothing from the fact that in Genesis, God provided Adam and Eve with clothing to cover their nakedness (Ge 3:21). Hence, for Paul, modesty was a sign of dependence on God's provision.

B. Qualification for Leadership in the Church (3:1 – 16)

1. Elders (3:1 – 7)

Paul lists, in summary fashion, the requirements of an "overseer" or elder in the church. He must be a sober-minded, amiable family man who knows Scripture and how to apply it to the life of the church. Paul does not explain what the elders were to do in the church, though undoubtedly he assumes that they, like Timothy, were to provide the leadership. Hence, the instruction Paul gives to Timothy can be taken as a guide to elders. An important part of their responsibility lay in teaching sound doctrine and combating false teachers. They were to devote themselves "to the public reading of Scripture, to preaching and to teaching" (4:13).

2. Deacons (3:8 – 16)

Since elders are distinguished from deacons here, the analogy of Ac 6:1 – 6 seems appropriate. Just as the elders were to provide the teaching and general oversight, the deacons were to attend to the everyday business of the church. Their requirements are essentially the same as those for the elders, though with a different emphasis. For deacons, Paul highlights characteristics of trustworthiness and a proven track record, both important in light of the day-to-day concerns entrusted to them. Their wives must also be trustworthy and worthy of respect.

IV. Combating False Teachers (4:1 – 16)

A. The Importance of Sound Doctrine (4:1 – 11)

Realistically, Paul argues, church leaders can expect that "some will abandon the faith and follow deceiving spirits" (v.1). Characteristic of such teaching is that it was a perversion of God's good gifts. Paul alludes to Ge 1 to show that "everything God created is good" (v.4; cf. Ge 1:31). Just as the serpent had wrongly suggested that God had said, "You must not eat from any tree in the garden" (Ge 3:1), so these false teachers were perverting God's good gifts and forbidding one's enjoyment of them (vv.3 – 5). The task of Timothy and other pastors, who have been "nourished on the truths of the faith and of the good teaching" (v.6), is to "point these things out to the brothers and sisters" (v.6) and to live them out in their own lives (4:7).

B. The Importance of Timothy's Example (4:12 – 16)

Paul wants a living example of his teaching among the churches. Timothy is to be that example, just as all pastors should be. What is thus required is diligence and devotion in both sound doctrine and godly living. This is what will "save both yourself and your hearers" (v.16).

V. Instructions for Church Life (5:1 – 6:2)

Paul goes on to give Timothy sound, practical advice on how to treat various members of the church (5:1 – 2). The treatment of widows requires special attention (vv.3 – 16). Judgment is necessary to determine those with genuine needs and those for whom help is available elsewhere.

The basic principle for supporting teaching elders is that they should be given double honor (vv.17 – 19). This entails both financial support and clear investigation in cases where their honor has been challenged. They must receive twice as much support for their work in teaching, and twice as many witnesses are required to convict them of any wrongdoing. If any elders are found to be in the wrong, they must be publicly rebuked.

Servants must give their masters respect and honor (6:1 – 2). The servants Paul has in mind are the household servants supported by their masters as part of their employment. That Paul is not here endorsing involuntary slavery is clear from 1:10, where he has condemned "slave traders" in the harshest of terms. Paul does not deal with the other side of the question here, such as how masters should treat their servants. Paul's letter to Philemon, however, addresses precisely that point (cf. also Eph 6:9; Col 4:1).

VI. Warnings and Admonitions (6:3 – 21)

Paul concludes his letter with a renewed warning against false teachers who seek to make a profit from their teaching (vv.3 – 10). Such men are "conceited and understand nothing" (v.4). Teachers should pursue godliness and sound doctrine, being content with the support given them from the church (5:17 – 18). In that way they will "fight the good fight of the faith" (6:12) and be found faithful when the Lord returns.

If the wealthy want lasting treasures, they should generously share their riches with those less fortunate (vv.17–19). Wealth is uncertain, but God is a lasting source of hope.

In his final word to Timothy, Paul charges him to guard what has been entrusted to him. To go beyond that to seek "what is falsely called knowledge" (v.20) is to risk departing from the faith. Though it is difficult to determine precisely what "knowledge" Paul is referring to, the general sense of this letter suggests it was knowledge gained apart from the Scriptures (cf. 4:13). Paul s second letter to Timothy has more to say about this.

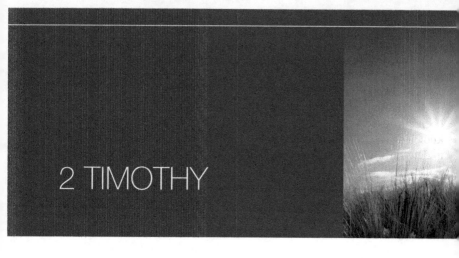

2 TIMOTHY

Introduction

This is the second letter that Paul wrote to his dear friend and coworker Timothy. There is no clear indication of the date of this letter. Undoubtedly, from the content of the letter itself (cf. 4:6), it was written late in Paul's life. This was probably his last letter.

I. Introduction (1:1 – 14)

Conditions in the churches were becoming more urgent. On the one hand, godly leaders such as Timothy were coming close to losing heart. On the other hand, false teachers were becoming more impudent in their teaching and actions. Thus, Paul begins his letter with an impassioned appeal to Timothy to "fan into flame the gift of God" and not to be timid, but to exercise "the power, love and self-discipline" the Spirit gives (vv.6–7). Paul admonishes him to not be ashamed to testify about the Lord (v.8).

Paul's solution to Timothy's need for encouragement is to stress the dimensions of the grace of God given him in the gospel. The gospel was not a new idea. It was a grace planned and given by God "before the beginning of time" (v.9) and has now been revealed through Jesus (v.10).

Thus, the scope of the gospel Paul preached was the same as that of the OT. It extended back beyond the beginning (Ge 1:1). Jesus' death, which destroyed death (Ge 3:15), has brought about life and immortality (1:10; cf. Ge 3:23–24). Such a message inevitably stirs up opposition and invites distortion (v.12). All the more important, then, is it to remain faithful to the teaching Timothy received from Paul (vv.13–14).

II. Warnings to Timothy (1:15 – 4:8)

In warning Timothy of the perils of remaining faithful to God's Word, Paul reminds him that throughout Asia even he himself had been deserted (1:15–18). But Paul remained faithful, and so now he pleads with Timothy to remain faithful and strong in Paul's teaching (2:1–2). Like a good soldier, a successful athlete, or a hardworking farmer, Timothy must focus on the work of the Lord rather than on worldly affairs (vv.3–7).

In times of trouble, Paul warns, one must focus on the essentials of the gospel (vv.8–13). One needs to know precisely why and for what one is suffering. In this case it centers on the resurrection of Jesus and on his claim to be the Davidic Messiah (v.8). Moreover, Paul's confidence in God's election enables him to "endure everything" (v.10).

Timothy's task is to keep reminding those in the church of the teaching of God's Word (vv.14–26). He should study it well, focus on the central points, and know how to answer when serious questions arise. He must gently instruct those who oppose his instruction, leaving the task of changing their minds to God (v.25).

Some groups, however, are impossible to teach. They are the godless who will arise in increasing numbers as the return of the Lord approaches (3:1–9). Timothy should have nothing to do with them; their motives are impure (v.6), they are unteachable (vv.7–8), and "their folly will be clear to everyone" (v.9).

Paul's teaching, by contrast, has been thoroughly tested and proven by his way of life and the troubles he endured (vv.10–13). Therefore, Timothy should continue in the teaching that he learned from Paul, knowing that it is grounded in the OT (vv.14–17). For Paul, the Scriptures are a central witness to the truth of the gospel because they are inspired (i.e., "God-breathed," v.16); they teach salvation that comes through faith in Christ.

Therefore, Timothy must "preach the word" at all times, exercising great patience and careful instruction (4:1–2). He must continue in God's Word even if and when the time comes that those who hear his teaching will not be able to endure it (vv.3–5). They will leave him and instead follow teachers who say what they want to hear. That experience, Paul suggests, has already begun to happen to him (vv.6–8; cf. 1:15; 4:16).

III. Personal Notes (4:9 – 22)

In his final personal instructions, Paul appropriately asks for his "scrolls [and] … parchments" (v.13), i.e., his copy of the Scriptures. Paul, a rabbi by training, would have had much of the Scripture committed to memory, but, true to his instructions to Timothy, he wants to search the God-breathed Scriptures.

TITUS

Introduction

The apostle Paul wrote this letter to his dear friend and coworker Titus. Together with 1 and 2 Timothy, these letters are called "The Pastoral Letters." There is no clear indication when this letter was written, but it was likely after Paul's imprisonment in Rome (i.e., after AD 62).

I. Introduction (1:1 – 4)

Paul considerably expands the introduction of this letter, not so much in length as in depth. He writes of the hope of eternal life, "which God, who does not lie, promised before the beginning of time" (v.2), and which at the appointed time was entrusted to him "by the command of God" (v.3). A Christian's life should be lived in light of this hope. Paul emphasizes the Christian's hope at the beginning because in the course of his argument, it is the "hope of eternal life" that motivates the Christian to live a godly life (cf. 2:13).

II. Task of Titus at Crete (1:5 – 16)

Paul begins the body of his letter with instructions for Titus, who is serving as pastor on the island of Crete. Titus must complete work that has been left undone. He must appoint elders in every town; hence, Paul reviews for him the qualifications for those elders (vv.6 – 9). Numerous false teachers are ruining the churches and seeking dishonest gain by their teaching.

These teachers must be dealt with decisively before they can do any further damage (vv.10 – 16).

III. Order of Community (2:1 – 3:11)

What must Titus do to combat the false teachers? Paul's answer is simple: "You must teach what is appropriate to sound doctrine" (2:1). Older men are to be taught to act worthy of respect (v.2). Older women are to live in reverence, not slandering others but teaching what is good (v.3). The younger women are to "love their husbands and children" and provide a good home for them (vv.4 – 5). The young men are to be self-controlled (vv.6 – 8). Household servants are to carry out their duties faithfully and honestly (vv.9 – 10).

In every relationship, Christians must reject ungodliness and live "self-controlled, upright and godly lives," eagerly awaiting the return of Christ (vv.11 – 15). Meanwhile, Christians are to live in subjection to the "rulers and authorities" and always be ready to do what is good (3:1 – 3). Paul grounds his call to godliness in the nature of the gospel itself. God saved sinners, not because of their righteousness but in order to produce good works in their lives. In Christ, Christians have been washed and renewed by the Holy Spirit and made fit "to devote themselves to doing what is good" (vv.4 – 8).

IV. Conclusion (3:12 – 15)

Along with personal greetings, Paul concludes with an explanation of the practical importance of sound doctrine: "Our people must learn to devote themselves to doing what is good, in order to provide for urgent needs and not live unproductive lives" (3:14).

PHILEMON

Introduction

This letter to Philemon was written by Paul during one of his imprisonments — presumably the one in Rome in AD 60 – 62 (i.e., the same time that he wrote Ephesians and Colossians). Paul appeals to the Christian leader Philemon to receive back Onesimus, his former servant who had run away.

I. Introduction (1 – 7)

After a brief greeting, Paul begins his appeal to Philemon by acknowledging the work of God in Philemon's life and ministry (he was a resident of Colossae; see Col 4:9). Based on his "love for all [God's] holy people" (v.5), Paul appeals to him for a gracious reception of Onesimus, his former servant, whom Paul is sending back to him.

II. Request for Reception of Onesimus (8 – 20)

The main point of the letter is Paul's appeal to Philemon on behalf of Onesimus. From the letter we gather that Onesimus was a former household servant of Philemon (v.16). He had apparently escaped from or deserted Philemon, but he had subsequently met Paul and heard the gospel. Thus both Philemon and Onesimus were in Paul's eternal debt.

Paul urges Philemon pastorally to accept Onesimus back as a brother (v.16) — that is, either to treat him as a brother in Christ or perhaps to release Onesimus as a slave. In either case, it would be a great display of the power of the gospel in the ancient world. Paul, with apostolic authority, says he could order Philemon to accept Onesimus, but that would not have the effect of a voluntary act of brotherly love. Paul wants Philemon's actions to "not seem forced but ... be voluntary" (v.14). He is fully confident that Philemon will accept Onesimus with open arms (v.16); nevertheless, he offers to pay any outstanding debts or penalties Onesimus might owe.

This short book clearly owes its acceptance within the NT canon in that it speaks directly to an issue that lies not too far beneath the surface throughout the NT—i.e., the effect of the gospel on the existing social structures of the ancient world. The Bible clearly opposes involuntary slavery. In 1Ti 1:10, for example, Paul reckons "slave traders" along with "the sexually immoral ... those practicing homosexuality ... liars and perjurers." But what was the impact of the gospel on those economic structures that included servants who were bound to their masters under full force of the law? In 1Ti 6:1–2 Paul writes that servants should treat their masters with respect, including believing masters. But what about believing masters' treatment of believing servants? Paul urges that just as Christian servants must respect their masters, so Christian masters must accept their Christian servants as brothers, even if they have wronged them.

III. Conclusion (21 – 25)

We do not have Philemon's response, but Paul's confidence expressed here makes its absence immaterial. The very existence of this letter suggests Philemon heeded Paul's request.

HEBREWS

Introduction

The title "To the Hebrews" is found in the earliest complete manuscripts of the NT. This probably does not describe the particular community to which the book was addressed, but rather its content. The term "Hebrews" was a name for Jews in contrast to Gentiles. Thus this is a book dealing with matters that relate to the Jews, or more specifically, probably Jewish Christians.

The author is unknown. The fact that he refers to the temple worship as still being practiced strongly suggests it was written before the destruction of the temple in AD 70. The central theme of the book is the work of Jesus Christ as the mediator of the new covenant.

I. Introduction (1:1 – 6:20)

A. The Work of the Son of God (1:1 – 2:4)

The book begins with an exposition of the work of Jesus Christ, the Son of God. The revelation of the salvation of God, promised in the OT, has now been made known in Jesus, the Son of God. He was with God at creation and is the "exact representation of his being" (1:3). He "provided purification for sins" and has been exalted to "the right hand of the Majesty in heaven."

In making these points, the writer has summarized the work of Christ in terms of the OT's messianic hope. The Messiah is the Son of God who reigns with God in his eternal kingdom (Ps 2; Da 7), as well as the sacrificial lamb of God who gave his life for the sins of humanity (Isa 53). Thus, he is the only mediator between human beings and God. As a mediator, he is far superior to angels, who are "ministering spirits sent to serve those who will inherit salvation" (v.14).

With such a momentous event unfolding before one's eyes, confirmed by signs and miracles, neglect or failure to appreciate it constitutes the worst kind of rejection. Thus the writer urges his readers not to "ignore so great a salvation" (2:1–4).

B. The Incarnation and Exaltation of Christ as Prerequisite to His Role as a Merciful High Priest (2:5–4:16)

The author quotes Ps 8:4–6 from the Greek Old Testament and draws out two central ideas. (1) God made the Son lower than the angels "for a little while" (2:7, NIV note). (2) God "crowned [mankind] with glory and honor and put everything under their feet." The "little while" in Ps 8:5 is interpreted here as the time of the incarnation of Christ, i.e., the time of Jesus' earthly ministry. Thus, after his death and resurrection, Jesus was "crowned with glory and honor," and through his death, he has brought "many sons and daughters to glory" (2:9–10). In other words, God made Jesus suffer with humanity before making him a "merciful and faithful high priest" (v.17), one who "is able to help those who are being tempted" because "he himself suffered when he was tempted" (v.18).

Moses established the high priesthood of the house of Aaron; but Jesus, by his incarnation and resurrection to the right hand of God, became a high priest "of the same family" (v.11) as all humanity. He is a high priest who can claim to be a brother to everyone, not merely those of the house of Aaron. In this respect, the priesthood of Jesus is superior to that of Aaron (3:1–6).

In the same way, those who trust in Jesus as their high priest should take heed to the warnings and lessons of God's people in the desert (3:7–4:13). Using Ps 95:7–11, the author emphasizes how Israel's heart grew hard during that time. They rebelled against (3:8) and tested God; thus God "was angry with that generation" (v.10), and they did not inherit "[God's] rest" in the land promised to them (v.11). For the Christian, the warning is to guard against "a sinful, unbelieving heart that turns away from the living God" (v.12). The writer also uses Nu 20:12 to point out that Israel's failure to enjoy God's rest was because of their unbelief. This example of the Israelites shows that no one is exempt from the warning against sin and unbelief. Thus, as in the Pentateuch, only those "who have believed enter that rest" (4:3).

Though many Israelites in Moses' day did not find the divine rest promised them, Ps 95 implies that a rest still remained for them in the future (vv.3–9). The rest given the new generation under Joshua was not the

promised rest (v.8), for David, long after the time of Joshua, was still looking for a rest for God's people. It is that rest that the writer of Hebrews sets
before his readers: "Let us, therefore, make every effort to enter that rest"
(4:11). This is the message of the "word of God" (v.12).

C. Jesus as High Priest (5:1 – 6:20)

The writer outlines the central duties of a high priest. He was selected
before God to offer sacrifices and gifts (5:1). It was necessary for him to be
human in order to represent human beings adequately before God. Jesus
met this requirement in his incarnation and earthly life.

Moreover, the high priest must be called by God (v.4). Jesus was also
called by God, as Ps 2 demonstrates. By quoting this messianic psalm, the
writer of Hebrews links the role of Jesus as high priest to that of Davidic
Messiah. In Ps 110, which he quotes next, these two features of the OT's
theology, the Messiah and the priesthood, are linked (5:6). In Ps 110, however, it is not the Aaronic priesthood that was in view, but that of Melchizedek. Melchizedek was both a king and a priest (Ge 14:18); hence he was a
particularly apt image of Christ's priesthood. Melchizedek was also a king
of Jerusalem and thus a perfect picture of the Davidic king through which
the promise of a Messiah had come (5:6 – 10; 6:20).

The writer interrupts his train of thought in 5:11 – 6:20 in order to clarify
for his readers the direction he is about to take. He plans to present an
in-depth exposition of the nature of Christ's high priesthood (7:1 – 10:18).
He is aware, however, that not all of his readers are prepared to follow his
arguments and thus derive benefit from his exposition. He warns them not
only of his intention to delve deeper into the "solid food" for the spiritually
mature, but also, pastorally, of their need for someone to teach them "the
elementary truths of God's word all over again" (5:12). If we look at topics of
the "elementary teachings" given in 6:1 – 3, the writer has in mind the kind
of teaching found in the NT letters, especially those of the apostle Paul.

The author offers two main reasons why he intends to move beyond
these elementary truths. (1) He is confident that his readers are ready to
move on in their understanding, even though they are still in need of prod-
ding (vv.9 – 12). (2) It is impossible for those who "have fallen away, to be
brought back to repentance" (v.6).

The exact sense of v.6 is uncertain when viewed in the context of all
Scripture. Some say this passage teaches that Christians can lose their salvation if they fall away, but this view stands in stark contrast with God's
choosing of his people in Christ "before the creation of the world" (Eph 1:4;
cf. Ro 8:31 – 39). Consequently, others argue that the writer of Hebrews must
be speaking hypothetically; that is, if it ever were possible for Christians

to fall away, it would be impossible to renew them to repentance. A third option is that the writer is speaking hyperbolically, taking "impossible" to mean "very difficult." Finally, some interpret this reference to mean that if professing Christians fall away from the faith, it only serves to prove that their faith was not genuine in the first place (cf. 1Jn 2:19). In any case, on the pattern of Mk 10:27, we should always acknowledge that "all things are possible with God."

Having given his readers one of the sternest warnings in the NT (6:4 – 8), the writer concludes with an emphasis on God's faithfulness (vv.9 – 19). Inheritance of the promises is based both on the sure word of God who made the promise (vv.13 – 19) and on the faith and patient obedience of his people (vv.9 – 12).

II. The High Priesthood of the Son (7:1 – 10:18)

A. The Priesthood of Melchizedek (7:1 – 28)

The priesthood of Jesus, the Son of God, was not that of the house of Aaron established in the Mosaic covenant. It was, rather, a priesthood offered as one of the functions of the messianic descendant of David promised in Ps 110. The writer of Hebrews demonstrates from the OT, first, that the messianic priesthood, exemplified in biblical Melchizedek, was superior to the priesthood of the house of Aaron, and second, that Aaron's priesthood was always a temporary priesthood and, as such, had to be superseded. The main argument is the eternal nature of the Messiah-Priest promised to David (Ps 110:4), which far exceeded the priesthood of Aaron established by Moses. Much of his argument hinges on the simple fact that the priesthood noted in Ps 110 implies that already the OT recognized the temporary nature of Aaron's priesthood.

Here is the writer's main argument. Melchizedek and Aaron each represented a different type of priesthood. According to Ge 14, Abraham paid tithes to Melchizedek (Heb 7:2), and Melchizedek bore special names, such as "king of righteousness" and "king of peace" (v.2) — names that apply to Christ. Moreover, Melchizedek's priesthood was not limited to specific genealogical factors (v.3), for he is introduced without a list of his ancestors; the author of Hebrews understands this to mean that his priesthood was not dependent on a family line (as Aaron's was); thus his role as high priest did not pass from one member of the family to another. He remained "a [high] priest continually" (v.3; NIV, "forever"), i.e., for as long as he lived.

Having established this essential characteristic of Melchizedek's priesthood, the writer turns to Ps 110 to show that David was promised an eternal descendant to occupy the office of Melchizedek's priesthood. If the priesthood he represented was unlimited, then an eternal priest such as that promised to the house of David could serve eternally. This priest is Jesus, the eternal Son of God who lives forever.

B. The High Priestly Service (8:1 – 10:18)

1. The service of the new covenant (8:1 – 13)

Christ, the Son of God, being an eternal high priest, does not offer sacrifices in a sanctuary made "by man" but in "the true tabernacle set up by the Lord" in heaven (vv.1 – 2). The earthly temple, with its priesthood, is only a copy of this heavenly sanctuary, made according to the pattern shown to Moses on Mount Sinai (v.5). The true temple, then, exists in heaven, where the Son of God lives. The contrast between the earthly temple and its priests, and the heavenly temple and its eternal high priest, is that which the prophet Jeremiah spoke of in contrasting the old covenant and the new (vv.6 – 12). The new covenant, promised in the OT, has made the old covenant obsolete (v.13).

The long quotation from Jer 31:31 – 34 in 8:8 – 12, the longest OT quotation in the NT, plays an important role in the writer's overall message. Not only does it show the temporal nature of the old covenant and the superiority of the new covenant, but it also shows that the chief characteristic of the new covenant is its renewal of the heart and the mind: "I will put my laws in their minds and write them on their hearts" (v.10). Hence, in the following section, when the external regulations of the old covenant are contrasted with the internal renewal of the heart in the new covenant, these elements have been anticipated in the OT (cf. 9:10, 14).

2. Exposition of the new covenant (9:1 – 10:18)

The details of Israel's worship at the tabernacle contained many spiritual lessons. Central to them was the necessity of a yearly atonement of blood sacrifice offered by the high priest. The fact that it had to be repeated yearly and was offered not only for the people, but also for the high priest himself, demonstrates its inadequacy. These were merely "external regulations applying until the time of the new order" (9:10).

Just as in the old covenant the high priest continually offered the blood of sacrificial animals as redemption from sin, in a once-for-all act as high priest of the new covenant, Christ offered his own blood as a sacrifice in the Most Holy Place of the true tabernacle, the heavenly one. Christ thus became the mediator of the new covenant between God and his chosen people, offering eternal salvation through his death (vv.11 – 15).

The Greek word for "covenant" also has the sense of "last will and testament." Thus, in 9:16 – 17, the writer of Hebrews draws on the analogy of a "will" to illustrate the necessity of Christ's death in establishing the new covenant. For a "will" to go into effect, there must be the death of the one who made the will (v.17). Thus by the death of Christ, those entering the "will" have received the inheritance; their sins have been forgiven by the Lord (vv.19 – 22).

What was formerly practiced under the old covenant by way of a "copy," or a foreshadowing of heavenly realities, was accomplished once and for all by Christ in the heavenly temple itself (9:23 – 28). In contrast to the annual Day of Atonement sacrifices, the sacrificial death of the eternal Son of God does not need to be repeated. Being an eternal offering, it is sufficient for every act of sin since the creation of the world; thus, "at the culmination of the ages," it did away with all sin.

Like Paul and the other NT writers, the final hope for the writer of Hebrews lies in the return of Jesus Christ "to bring salvation to those who are waiting for him" (v.28). At that time Jesus will judge the world (v.27). The imagery of the writer is informed by the prophetic vision of Da 7:9 – 14, the coming of the Son of Man to establish the eternal kingdom of God.

The fact that the rituals of the old covenant had to be repeated annually is evidence of their temporality and ultimate inability to cleanse the human heart from sin (10:1 – 2, 11). After all, if the rituals of the old covenant had been effectual, why were they repeated year after year? Their value lay not in their final effect but in the reminder of human sin and guilt that they provided (v.3). The justice of God could not be settled by the offering of animal sacrifice (v.4). Hebrews reveals the divine solution to redemption in the quotation of Ps 40:6: Christ, when he came into the world, said, "A body you prepared for me." Thus, "we have been made holy through the sacrifice of the body of Jesus Christ once for all" (10:10).

Having performed his eternal sacrifice, the Son of God takes his seat "at the right hand of God" (v.12) and awaits the full arrival of his kingdom (10:13). Meanwhile, the work of the new covenant in perfecting the saints and writing the law on their hearts is already at work.

III. The Consequences (10:19 – 13:17)

A. Application of the New Covenant in the Life of the Christian (10:19 – 39)

The writer of Hebrews turns now to practical application. That application consists both of exhorting Christians to live according to the new heart given them in Christ (vv.19–25), and of warning about judgment to come for neglecting Christ's sacrifice (vv.26–31).

The first readers of this letter had fared well in their faith in past times, but they face an uncertain future. Therefore, the writer earnestly calls them to continue in well-doing and not to "shrink back" from receiving the promises. He holds out to them both the hope of the imminent return of Christ (vv.35–39) and the commendable examples of faithfulness in the past (11:1–40).

B. The Nature of Faith (11:1–40)

Hebrews has repeatedly demonstrated the importance of looking to the OT not only for instruction in God's plan of salvation but also as a source of comfort for the Christian life. Hebrews 11 is a paradigm for a Christian reading and meditation on Scripture. The author first defines the nature of biblical faith (v.1) and then illustrates it from the examples of Scripture (vv.2–38). He follows the order of events as depicted in the OT.

Faith means being confident in what is hoped for but not yet seen (v.1). The first example of faith from the OT comes in the creation account (Ge 1). The Bible teaches that "the universe was formed at God's command, so that what is seen was not made out of what was visible" (v.3). For the writer of Hebrews, faith accepts the biblical view of creation as God's word because this is what the Scriptures teach. The list continues with Abel (v.4), Enoch (v.5–6), Noah (v.7), Abraham (vv.8–19), Isaac (v.20), Jacob (v.21), Joseph (v.22), Moses' parents (v.23), Moses (vv.24–28), Israel in the Exodus (v.29), Israel in the Conquest (v.30), Rahab (v.31), Gideon, Barak, Samson, Jephthah, David, Samuel, and the prophets (vv.32–38).

The list is an interesting one, both for what it says and what it does not say. For the most part, it does not assume that the reader will merely acknowledge a particular person as a valid demonstration of faith. Rather, it provides a running commentary on the lives of several individuals and thereby explains the life of faith they lived. In the case of Enoch, for example, the writer reasons that since the biblical text in Genesis states that Enoch "was commended as one who pleased God" (v.5b), he must have had faith because "without faith it is impossible to please God" (v.6a). Genesis, however, does not explicitly state that Enoch "pleased God"; rather, its says that Enoch "walked faithfully with God" (Ge 5:22, 24). But since Genesis also states that Noah "walked faithfully with God" (Ge 6:9b) and that "Noah found favor in the eyes of the Lord" (Ge 6:8), the writer of Hebrews concludes that walking faithfully with God means to find favor with God.

In other words, the list in ch. 11 is evidence of a great deal of thoughtful meditation on Scripture, in which the author links words and ideas in one passage to those of another. It is precisely this kind of reading that the authors of the OT anticipated when they composed their writings. Moreover, it was the importance of "faith" that many, if not all, of the OT writers wanted most to elucidate.

There are some names on the list that are identified within the OT text itself as having faith: for example, Abraham (Ge 15:6) and Israel in the Exodus (Ex 4:31a; 14:31b). It is significant that the writer of Hebrews omits from his list of the faithful any mention of the time of Israel's desert wandering. He has already portrayed that period in Israel's history (cf. Nu 14:11; 20:12) as a time of unbelief (Heb 3:7–19).

C. Exhortation to Holiness (12:1–29)

The writer returns to the central theme of the book: perseverance in the face of adversity. In his exhortation to put away "the sin that so easily entangles," he appeals both to the example of Jesus (vv.1–4) and to the implication of Christians being children of God (vv.5–13) — cf. "the Lord disciplines the one he loves" (v.6). Finally, he shows how the believer's relationship with God in the new covenant has changed (vv.14–29). God himself has not changed. He is still the same "consuming fire" (vv.18, 29) that Israel experienced at Mount Sinai (12:18–21). What has changed, however, is that Mount Zion, the heavenly Jerusalem, the "joyful assembly," has replaced Mount Sinai, the place where even Moses was "trembling with fear" (v.21).

D. Instructions in Practical Holiness (13:1–17)

The implications of Christ's work as mediator of the new covenant are spelled out here by means of concrete examples: brotherly love (v.1), hospitality (v.2), visiting the imprisoned and mistreated (v.3), faithfulness in marriage (v.4), contentment (v.5), trust in God (v.6), teachability (v.7), doctrinal stability (v.9), bearing disgrace for Christ's sake (vv.11–13), hope (v.14), offering praise (v.15), sharing with others (v.16), and obedience and submission to authority (v.17).

IV. Conclusion (13:18–25)

After a benediction (vv.20–21), the writer makes a final appeal to hear the difficult matters he has raised in this letter (v.22). The concluding greetings are reminiscent of the letters of Paul.

JAMES

Introduction

The author of this book—"James, a servant of God and of the Lord Jesus Christ" (1:1)—is most likely the son of Mary and Joseph, the half brother of Jesus (cf. Mk 6:3). After Peter left Jerusalem in Ac 12:17, James took over the leadership of the church in Jerusalem (see Ac 15:13). No certain date can be ascribed to this book. Most scholars date it among the earliest NT books.

I. Introduction (1:1)

This book begins simply with the introduction of its author, James, and a brief description of its audience, "the twelve tribes scattered among the nations." The general "wisdom" nature of the letter, however, suggests that the addressees are not limited to Jewish Christians but to God's people (i.e., symbolized as "the twelve tribes") everywhere. The wisdom in this book is not generic wisdom but biblical wisdom.

II. Divine Wisdom (1:2–27)

James gives an exposition of divine wisdom dealing with two specific areas of the Christian's life: trials (1:2–18) and obedience to Scripture (1:19–27).

A. On Trials (1:2–18)

The book of James begins with exhortation to perseverance in a time of trials (cf. the theme of Hebrews, esp. 12:1). James stresses that God will use testing and trials as a way of perfecting faith (v.4; cf. Heb 12:5–6). In the midst of trials one should see the "wisdom" that God intends to teach. Unlike worldly wisdom, divine wisdom does not come from mere observation. It comes from much prayer and divine illumination (v.5), as well as from an unwavering faith (vv.6–8).

Like biblical wisdom in general, James' wisdom shows signs of reflection on OT Scripture. The exaltation of the humble and the decline of the proud (vv.9–10), for example, is a common theme in the OT (cf. 1Sa 2:7–8), as is the passing glory of wealth in the face of divine judgment (cf. Ps 37:1–2; Isa 40:6–8). The blessed person is the one who remains faithful through trials (cf. Ps 37:5–7).

Moreover, James's discourse on the origin of trials and sin is taken directly from the fall of Adam and Eve (Ge 3:1–13). God did not tempt our first parents; it was their own desire that enticed them (vv.13–14; cf. Ge 3:6), led them astray, and ultimately resulted in their death (vv.12–15; cf. Ge 3:19). "Don't be deceived" (v.16; cf. Ge 3:13b), God, "the Father of the heavenly lights" (v.17; cf. Ge 1:3), gives only that which is good (v.17; cf. Ge 1:31). He "does not change like shifting shadows" (v.17; cf. Ge 1:2).

B. On Obedience to Scripture (1:19–27)

As James has just demonstrated, divine wisdom comes from reflective listening to God's Word, implanted in a godly life (vv.19–21). Not merely listening, but doing what God's Word teaches leads to blessing. Again James comes close to the central themes of Hebrews in stressing the new covenant ideal of the law written on the heart (cf. Heb 8:10).

III. Application of Divine Wisdom (2:1 – 3:12)

James now gives three applications of the divine wisdom described in ch. 1. It is the divine wisdom that comes from having the law written on the heart.

A. Humility (2:1 – 13)

In 1:9–11, James wrote that according to divine wisdom, the humble, not the rich and prideful, can expect to enjoy God's blessing. He offers a concrete example of the application of this truth in the life of the church: relations between the rich and the poor in the church. Giving preferential treatment to the wealthy and mistreating the poor violate the central message of the law: "Love your neighbor as yourself" (v.8).

B. Faith and Works (2:14 – 26)

In 1:22 James warned against merely listening to the Word of God and not doing it. He now applies this truth to the concrete situation of a living faith. The faith by which one claims to be saved (v.14) is a living faith that produces action (v.17). Thus works of love serve as evidence of saving faith. Abraham's offering of Isaac (Ge 22) is an example of the faith by which he was declared righteous in Ge 15:6. God called him to a specific action (Ge 22:1 – 2), and when he obeyed (22:3 – 10), Abraham showed evidence of his faith — "his faith was made complete by what he did" (Jas 2:22).

C. On the Tongue (3:1 – 12)

In 1:19 James admonished the reader to be "slow to speak." He now turns to the concrete example of the power of the tongue. Teachers have to talk; they cannot merely listen. Thus they risk a stricter judgment and should be doubly careful of what they say (cf. 2:12), knowing, however, that they are not perfect and "stumble in many ways" (3:2). The real problem of the tongue lies in a lack of control (vv.3 – 8). It is an instrument that can be used for both praise and cursing (vv.9 – 12); Christians should use it to bless God and other people.

IV. Further Lessons in Wisdom (3:13 – 5:11)

A. Divine Wisdom (3:13 – 18)

The test of divine wisdom lies in the results it produces in life situations. Earthly wisdom stems from envy and selfish ambition and produces disorder (3:14 – 16). Divine wisdom stems from a pure heart and produces peace and righteousness (vv.17 – 18).

B. Admonition to Follow Divine Wisdom (4:1 – 5:11)

Behind biblical wisdom lies the overwhelming confidence in divine justice. It is God and God alone who metes out reward and retribution for human action: "God opposes the proud but shows favor to the humble" (4:6); therefore, "Humble yourselves before the Lord, and he will lift you up" (v.10). There is nothing the wise Christian can do that will facilitate God's righteous judgment. All one can do is rest in the all-encompassing will of God (vv.11 – 16) and do what is good (v.17).

Where, then, does the hope of the Christian lie? Like all biblical wisdom (cf. Ecc 12:13 – 14), our hope lies in the fulfillment of God's eternal plan: "Be patient, then, brothers and sisters, until the Lord's coming" (5:7).

The rich and the proud, though they prosper now, are only storing up divine judgment for themselves when Christ returns (vv.1–6). The book of Job is a paradigm of God's ultimate vindication of the righteous wise man (v.11).

V. Concluding Examples of Wisdom (5:12–20)

The wise person is one who trusts God in all things and waits for him to fulfill his promises. Nevertheless, there is still much room for prayer (vv.13–15) and confession of sin (v.16). Elijah (1Ki 17–18) is an example of the effective prayer of a righteous man (vv.16–18). Moreover, there is also room for admonishing one another to walk in God's wisdom (5:19–20).

Introduction

The apostle Peter wrote this letter, though we have no idea when. He wrote it to give hope and encouragement to Christians suffering for the sake of Christ. Their hope lies in the joy that awaits them at the return of Christ. The encouragement Peter offers comes from the fact that they share in the sufferings of Christ.

I. Introduction (1:1 – 2)

Peter introduces his central theme. He writes to "God's elect," who are "exiles scattered throughout the provinces of Pontus, Galatia, Cappadocia, Asia and Bithynia" (v.1). With Peter, they eagerly await the return of the Lord to establish his kingdom (cf. 1:17; 4:7). In this world they are suffering a "fiery ordeal" (4:12), but they have a better hope when Christ's "glory is revealed" (4:13). Moreover, they are "God's elect"; they "have been chosen according to the foreknowledge of God … to be obedient to Jesus Christ" (1:2). All that is happening to these Christians is part of God's "sanctifying work" for them.

II. The New People of God (1:3 – 4:11)

A. Election and Sanctification (1:3 – 2:10)

1. The return of Christ (1:3 – 12)

Peter's starting point for hope in the midst of the Christian's suffering is Christ's resurrection (v.3), but the focus of his hope is set on his second coming (v.5). Our present sufferings have their place in God's plan. They are intended, in God's wisdom, to prove our faith to be true (v.7). The OT prophets searched intently their own writings to know the time and circumstances of Christ's coming, though they were well aware that what they wrote about would not happen in their own day but in the future (vv.10–12).

2. The Christian's holy life (1:13–21)

Peter's emphasis on Christ's imminent return shapes his appeal for holy living. They should not live according to the standards of this world, for they are strangers here (v.17), where values are measured in terms of silver and gold (v.18). Rather, they are at home in the presence of a holy God who has purchased them "with the precious blood of Christ" (v.19).

Throughout this book, Peter returns to the imagery of the OT to describe the Christian's relationship to Christ. Here he uses the imagery of the first Passover celebration in the Exodus, when a sacrificial lamb without blemish or defect was set apart four days before the feast to be offered as a substitute for the death of the firstborn (Ex 12:2–6). In the same way, Christ was set apart "before the creation of the world" to be "revealed in these last times for your sake" (v.20).

3. A holy people (1:22–2:10)

God's intent in his covenant with Israel given on Mount Sinai was that they would be a "kingdom of priests and a holy nation" (see Ex 19:6). Thus he revealed his word to them through Moses (19:6b), written on tablets of stone (24:12). Drawing on these images, Peter views the church as those who have been born of the Word of God; they are a "spiritual house to be a holy priesthood" (1Pe 2:5). They have been born again "through the living and enduring word of God" (1:23). They are "living stones" (2:5), offering "spiritual sacrifices" (v.5b); they are a "chosen people, a royal priesthood, a holy nation" (v.9).

B. Instructions (2:11–4:11)

In light of their standing as a new "people of God" (2:10), Peter instructs believers to "live such good lives among the pagans" so that many will turn to the Lord in faith and thus "glorify God" at the coming of Christ (v.12). To live good lives means abstaining from worldly desires (vv.11–12), submitting to authority (vv.13–17), submitting to one's master and thus following the example of Christ (vv.18–25), submitting to husbands (3:1–6) and thus following the example of Sarah, respecting wives (v.7), and living in harmony with one another (vv.8–12).

If Christians live in this manner, they will call attention to themselves in a wicked world. They should be ready, then, at all times "to give an answer to everyone who asks" the reason for their hope (vv.13 – 15), and they should be ready, if need be, to suffer for doing good (vv.16 – 17).

In a similar way, Christ himself preached salvation to a wicked world when he "went and made proclamation to ... those who were disobedient long ago when God waited patiently in the days of Noah" (vv.19 – 20). Noah and those with him in the ark were saved from their own wicked generation by the flood, which symbolizes how the water of baptism saves Christians from the world and, in the resurrection, makes them alive to Christ (vv.21 – 22). Through the resurrection, Christians become members of Christ's kingdom, over which he reigns at the right hand of God (v.22).

As members of that kingdom they must live according to God's will and not in the ways of their former lives (4:1 – 6). Their only hope should be fixed on Christ's return (vv.7 – 11).

III. Suffering for Christ (4:12 – 5:11)

Christians should not be surprised if they suffer for Christ, for Christ himself suffered. Christians can rejoice because they "participate in the sufferings of Christ" (4:12 – 19).

Just as Jesus' last words to Peter were "Feed my sheep" (Jn 21:17b), so Peter's last words to the elders were, "Be shepherds of God's flock.... And when the Chief Shepherd appears, you will receive the crown of glory" (5:2 – 4). Elders are to oversee the church not by lording over them or being greedy for earthly gain, but being "examples to the flock" (v.3). Young men are to serve in submission to older men. All are to be humble and self-controlled (vv.6 – 9), trusting God for strength and power (vv.10 – 11).

IV. Conclusion (5:12 – 14)

Peter concludes with a cryptic reference to "she who is in Babylon, chosen together with you" (v.13). This refers to the Christian community in the city from which he is writing, but it is not clear which city. In the Bible, Babylon is often a code word for any city or nation united against God, i.e., the Antichrist (cf. Rev 18). Peter probably uses the term to identify himself with the saints of all ages who live in a world united against God and his Christ.

2 PETER

Introduction

The author of this letter is identified as the apostle Peter (1:1). We cannot assign a definite date to its writing, but it is undoubtedly one of the later NT books (see 3:15–16). Peter writes this second letter to the churches scattered throughout Asia Minor (cf. 1Pe 1:1) in order to address the problem of false teachers. Some in the churches had lapsed back into their former ungodly ways and were teaching that God's lack of judgment on them was a sign of his approval. To Peter, such thinking is counter to all that the Scriptures teach about God's righteous judgment of sin.

I. Introduction (1:1 – 2)

In this opening greeting, no specific churches, cities, or individuals are mentioned. The book appears to be consciously addressed to virtually every Christian reader, though presumably its target audience is the same as 1 Peter (cf. 2Pe 3:1). The central theme is established in the greeting. "Grace and peace" are to be found in abundance "through the knowledge of God and of Jesus our Lord" (v.2). Peter intends to strengthen the reader's knowledge of God and Jesus through an emphasis on the importance of sound doctrine.

II. Defense of Christian Eschatology (1:3 – 3:13)

A. Effective Knowledge of Jesus (1:3 – 11)

Peter begins by describing the importance of a well-balanced knowledge. Knowledge of Jesus is an important link in the Christian's possession of divine power (v.3). The starting point is faith (v.5) and the goal is love (v.7), but to these must be added goodness, knowledge, self-control, perseverance, godliness, and brotherly kindness (vv.5–8). Such qualities keep Christians "from being ineffective and unproductive in [their] knowledge" of the Lord Jesus Christ (v.8).

B. Witnesses of Christ's Divine Power (1:12–21)

Christians must be continually reminded of the knowledge of Christ's power in their lives (vv.12–15). The apostle, who is about to give his life as a martyr for the Lord (cf. Jn 21:18–19), reminds his readers that he was an eyewitness to the honor and glory Christ received from his Father at his transfiguration (1:18; cf. Mt 17:5; Mk 9:7; Lk 9:35). Peter's uses similar words to John: "That ... which we have heard, which we have seen with our eyes ... this we proclaim" (1Jn 1:1).

Not only can Peter claim his own eyewitness account of Christ's glory, but there is also "the [OT] prophetic message," which has proved even more certain (v.19). God's prophetic word is like "a light shining in a dark place" (v.19b; cf. Ps 119:105). That is, reading and meditating on Scripture dispel the darkness of the mind just as the sunrise brings the clear light of day. The prophets themselves did not devise these OT prophecies about Jesus; they were "carried along by the Holy Spirit" (vv.20–21). Peter himself shows the importance of this statement in his many allusions to the OT.

C. Warnings of False Doctrine (2:1–22)

Just as there were true and false prophets in OT times, so also there are false teachers in the church who deny the sovereign Lord and bring swift destruction by their teaching (vv.1–4). The motivation for these false teachers is greed (v.3). The fact that they are not receiving divine judgment does not mean that God does not judge such people. Drawing on lessons from the OT, Peter argues that, though there may be delay, God's judgment always falls on the ungodly.

The OT pages that Peter turns to concern the fallen angels in the garden of Eden (v.4; cf. Eze 28:11–19), the flood in Noah's day (v.5; cf. Ge 6–9), the destruction of Sodom and Gomorrah (vv.6–14), the story of Balaam (vv.15–16), and certain proverbs (v.22; cf. Pr 26:11).

In his account of the destruction of Sodom and Gomorrah, for example, Peter expands on the treatment of Lot and his angelic visitors (vv.8–14) because it provides a particularly graphic example of Christians living within an ungodly world. In v.8, Peter describes Lot among the wicked at Sodom; then in vv.9–10a, Peter turns to the unrighteous in his own day. But in v.10b, he returns to the story of Sodom where the men of Sodom were "not afraid to heap abuse on celestial beings" (cf. Ge 19:5); all the while Peter has his eye on the wicked of his own day (vv.12–14).

Peter concludes with a stern warning to have nothing to do with these false teachers. They have turned away from Christ and, because they have perverted the gospel message, they are worse off now than before they had any knowledge of it (vv.17–22).

D. The Return of the Lord (3:1–13)

In his first letter, Peter had urged his readers to look forward to Christ's return and to live in eager expectation of it. Lest he leave the impression that Christ's return will happen in the immediate future, he now turns to explain the necessity of God's delay in sending his Son.

Peter is here addressing the view that God will not intervene in judgment in the affairs of human beings and creation because he has never done so in the past (vv.3–4). Obviously God did intervene by bringing judgment in the days of the flood. God made the earth from the waters, and he destroyed it from the same waters (vv.5–6). The same divine word that brought the world into existence has promised to judge this world with fire and destroy the ungodly (v.7).

In the delay of his coming, God is not slow about keeping his promise. He is patient, wanting to give everyone, even the ungodly, time to repent and turn to him. God reckons time differently from what we do. With God "a day is like a thousand years, and a thousand years are like a day" (v.8). The end will indeed come; when it does, the ungodly and all God's creation will be destroyed by fire (vv.10–12). At the same time, there will be a new heaven and a new earth (cf. Isa 65:17), which, unlike the old fallen one, will be "where righteousness dwells" (v.13).

III. Concluding Warnings (3:14–18)

The Christian's hope is the return of Christ to establish his kingdom. It is in light of this hope that God's people should strive to live godly and pure lives. The apostle Paul has already written about these same things (e.g., 1Co 15; 2Th 1–2). Nevertheless, some were distorting his writings, along with the rest of the Scriptures; thus, our constant attention to these doctrines are the only defense against error.

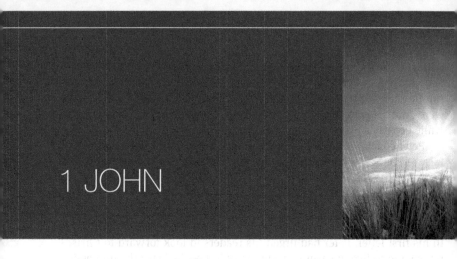

1 JOHN

Introduction

The author of the letter is not identified in the text. Its close association with the fourth gospel has led to the identification of its author as John. It is best to keep in mind, however, that the book is anonymous. No definite date can be assigned to this book.

I. Introduction (1:1 – 4)

John begins by claiming to be an eyewitness to "the Word of life" (1:1 – 2). With clear allusions to the prologue to the gospel of John, he says the Word was "from the beginning" (v.1; cf. Jn 1:1) and "with the Father" (v.2; cf. Jn 1:2), but also he saw and touched the Word and now testifies to it. What is the Word? It is that which the author now proclaims in this book. The goal of his writing is that he might have fellowship in the Word with his readers (1:3).

II. Fellowship with God (1:5 – 2:17)

The way of life pictured here reflects the life of God's people as seen through the new provisions of Christ's death and the new covenant. The Christian, like the Israelite, comes into God's presence only on the basis of the shed blood of a sacrifice. For John, Jesus, God's Son, is that "atoning sacrifice" (2:2; cf. the theology of Heb 9). Through his blood, those who walk in God's light are purified from all sin (1:7). Moreover, the Christian, like the Israelite, must maintain an upright relationship with God through confession and repentance (1:9).

By drawing on these analogies, John does not identify the Mosaic covenant with the new covenant; rather, like the writer of Hebrews, he is showing the superiority of the new covenant by virtue of its eternal sacrifice and priesthood. In the new covenant, Jesus is not only "our advocate with the Father" (2:1), but also "he is the atoning sacrifice" (v.2).

Under the Mosaic covenant, the Israelites exhibited their fellowship in their obedience to the Mosaic law; so, John says, Christians must obey Christ's commands and "live as Jesus did" (2:6). For John, walking as Jesus walked is not "a new commandment but an old one" (v.7), which they "have had since the beginning" (v.7b), i.e., the command to love one another (cf. Lev 19:18; Dt 30:6b). The fact, however, that this commandment was revealed in Jesus and can be realized through the light that shines in him makes this a "new command" (v.8). Therefore, those who live in the light will "love their brother and sister" (vv.9–11). John closes this section with a poetic summary of the believer's position in Christ (vv.12–17).

III. The Apostasy of Those Who Turned Away from Christ (2:18–27)

John is concerned about those who had fallen away from the gospel and were attempting to lead others astray with them. The fact that they have fallen away is evidence that they never truly belonged to Christ (v.19). Those who have a genuine "anointing from the Holy One" will not fall away, though they are always in need of a warning (v.26). The only safeguard against falling away is to hold firm to the teaching of Jesus (v.27).

The central question for anyone's teaching about Jesus is whether one believes him to be the Christ, i.e., the Messiah (v.22). John's conception of the Christ is clearly that expressed in the OT as well as throughout the NT books, namely, Jesus is the heavenly Son of Man who, in his death and resurrection, has received the kingdom and the people promised him before the foundation of the earth (cf. Da 7:9–14; Jn 17:1–5). Thus to deny Jesus as the Christ is to deny "the Father and the Son" (v.22); to accept Jesus as the Christ is to accept the Trinitarian confession of Jesus as Lord.

IV. The Test of True Faith (2:28–4:21)

Having described the marks of the false teachers, John turns to the distinguishing characteristics of the true children of God. Their primary characteristics are righteousness (2:29 – 3:10), love (3:11 – 20), and faith (3:21 – 24).

Christians are to test the spirits of prophets who profess to speak in God's name (4:1 – 6). The main test is whether they acknowledge that "Jesus Christ [Messiah] has come in the flesh" (v.2). Every spirit that "does not [thus] acknowledge Jesus is not from God" but is "the spirit of the antichrist" (v.3). According to 2:22, the one who is an antichrist "denies that Jesus is the Christ," whereas here the antichrist denies "Jesus [as] Christ has come in the flesh." In 4:15, however, the one who is of God "acknowledges that Jesus is the Son of God"; and in 5:1 "everyone who believes that Jesus is the Christ is born of God."

In 4:4 – 6 John himself moves beyond this confessional test to give a more general criterion for distinguishing the Spirit truth from the spirit of falsehood: "whoever knows God listens to us; but whoever is not from God does not listen to us" (v.6). To this John adds the test of love in 4:7 – 5:4: "Whoever does not love does not know God, because God is love" (4:8).

V. The Witness of the Spirit (5:5 – 13)

At this point, John's line of thought regarding Christ reaches its highest point in the confession that "Jesus is the Son of God" (v.5). As the Son of God, Jesus "is the one who came by water and blood" (v.6), i.e., he came in the flesh (cf. 4:2). Moreover, it is the Spirit who bears witness to him (v.6b) by means of an internal testimony: "Whoever believes in the Son of God accepts this testimony" (v.10). What is the testimony? It is the eternal life given in the Son (v.11); "he who has the Son has life" (v.12).

VI. Conclusion (5:14 – 21)

John has written this letter to those who believe in Jesus as the Son of God. His purpose was to give them assurance that their faith in him was true (v.13). In such an assurance there is also confidence that God hears and answers the Christian's prayer (vv.14 – 15).

In light of all that John has written about Jesus, the Son of God, it follows that at the close he would identify him as "the true God and eternal life." He then concludes with a warning against idolatry, which is the worship of false god(s).

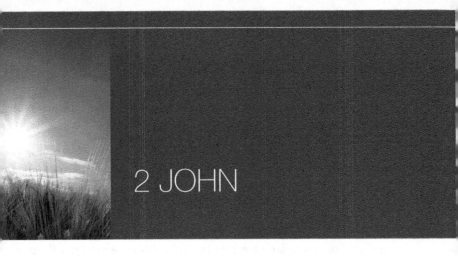

2 JOHN

Introduction

The author is identified only as "the elder" (v.1). The close association of this letter with the fourth gospel and 1 John has led to identifying John as its author. We should remember, however, that the book is anonymous. No definite date can be assigned to it.

This letter seems clearly intended as a summary of 1 John. It succinctly focuses on the main points of that letter (walking in Christ, brotherly love, and false doctrine), and adds the warning against inadvertently sharing in the work of the antichrists (vv.10 – 11). Note that 3 John takes these same themes and applies them to a specific church situation.

I. Introduction (1 – 3)

The book is addressed to "the lady chosen by God and ... her children" (v.1). This is usually taken to refer to a local church, though some think it refers to a specific house church in the home of a prominent woman. The letter's closing greeting from "the children of your chosen sister" suggests that these are titles given to various church bodies, not specific individuals.

John opens the letter with a greeting that focuses on the central themes of his first letter (1 John), i.e., the Trinitarian notion of Jesus Christ as God's Son and the twin themes of truth and love (v.3). The rest of the letter summarizes the major points of 1 John.

II. Summary Themes (4 – 11)

As in 1Jn 1:5–2:2, the writer emphasizes the importance of maintaining a consistent walk with Christ (v.4). The importance of this walk includes the command to love one another (v.5; cf. 1Jn 2:7). Walking in the light also means walking in love (v.6; cf. 1Jn 5:3).

Love involves trust, and thus John warns his readers to "watch out" for the "many deceivers, who do not acknowledge Jesus Christ as coming in the flesh" (v.7; cf. 1Jn 4:2–3), and who would cause them to lose their reward (v.8). The test of true discipleship is whether one continues in the teaching about Jesus as the Son of God who has come in bodily form to give himself as an "atoning sacrifice" (1Jn 2:2, 22). John heightens his warning about these false teachers by urging his readers to give them no support whatever. To welcome them is to participate in their work (v.11).

III. Conclusion (12 – 13)

The letter's closing anticipates John's third letter, for the author still has "much to write." More is to come, though his immediate intention is to visit them "and talk ... face to face" (v.12). Moreover, this final note acknowlededges the incontestable brevity of this letter.

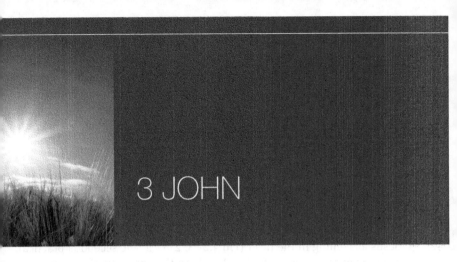

3 JOHN

Introduction

Like 2 John, the author of this letter is "the elder" (v.1). Its close association with 1 and 2 John has led to the identification of its author as John. We should remember, however, that the book is anonymous. No definite date can be assigned to it.

I. Introduction (1)

The letter is addressed to Gaius, apparently a leader in a local church. Though brief, the introduction establishes the fact that the writer and Gaius are in fundamental agreement in the teaching of Christ. John says of him, "whom I love in the truth." Love and truth are the central themes of all three of John's letters.

II. Walking in the Truth (2 – 4)

In both 1Jn 1:5 – 2:2 and 2Jn 4, the writer began by emphasizing the importance of a consistent walk with Christ. Here he commends Gaius for continuing to walk in the truth (v.3). Thus Gaius is a concrete example of John's teaching in the other letters.

III. Brotherly Love (5 – 8)

In 1 and 2 John, one's personal walk with Christ includes the command to love one another (1Jn 2:7; 2Jn 5). Walking in the light also means walking in love (1Jn 5:3; 2Jn 6). Thus, again, Gaius is a concrete example of brotherly love that roots itself in walking in the truth.

IV. The Test of False Teachers (9 – 12)

In his previous letters, John repeatedly warned his readers of false teachers. There are two kinds of tests. The first is doctrinal: Do they acknowledge Jesus as coming in the flesh (1Jn 4:2 – 3; 2Jn 7)? The second is practical: Do they exercise love (1Jn 4:7 – 12)? John thus presents Gaius with two opposing examples of professing teachers in the church, Diotrephes and Demetrius. He must apply John's tests to distinguish between the two.

John describes Diotrephes as one "who loves to be first" and "will not welcome us" (v.9). He "spread[s] malicious nonsense" and "refuses to welcome other believers" (v.10). Demetrius, however, "is well spoken of by everyone — and even by the truth" (v.12). In other words, Demetrius's life is consistent with the teachings of Christ. The choice between these two teachers, then, is clear. Diotrephes is rejected; the example of Demetrius is to be imitated (v.11).

V. Conclusion (1:13 – 14)

Within the present canonical order, the writer's concluding statement that he has "much to write" (cf: 2Jn 12) perhaps anticipates Revelation. But it probably means by this remark only that he desires to talk to his readers "face to face" rather than write any more (v.14).

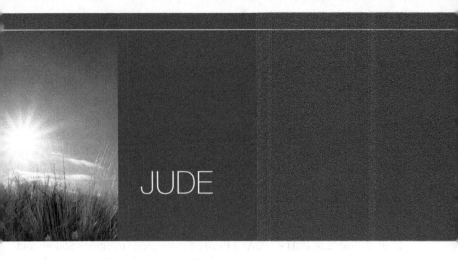

JUDE

Introduction

The author is identified as Jude, a brother of James (v.1) — most likely
the half brother of Jesus (see Mk 6:3, where "Judas" means "Jude"; see
introduction to James). No definite date can be assigned to this letter. The
author warns his readers against the clever devices of the false teachers
among them. Their false teaching may be new, but their error, manifested
by an ungodly manner of life, is as old as time.

I. Introduction (1 – 2)

Jude does not address his letter to a specific audience. Rather, he writes "to
those who have been called" (v.1). In v.18 he quotes from 2Pe 3:3; thus we
may assume he had the same general audience in mind as Peter did (cf.
1Pe 1:1). In any event, this letter is remarkable for its "strictly business"
approach, concluding only with a formal doxology (vv.24 – 25).

II. False Doctrine (3 – 23)

A. Contend for the Faith (3 – 4)

Jude begins cordially enough ("Dear friends"), with a plea to "contend for
the faith that was once for all entrusted to God's holy people" (v.3). But he
moves quickly into a scathing denunciation of false teachers (v.4). What

was at stake was nothing less than a perversion of God's grace into "license for immorality" (v.4b) and a denial of Jesus (v.4c).

B. Beware of False Teachers (5 – 16)

The threat to the church posed by these false teachers was the same as the apostasy of Israel in the desert. Those whom God delivered from Egypt, he later destroyed because they did not believe (v.5; cf. Nu 14:11; 20:12). Likewise the angels, who were created to be with God, "did not keep their positions of authority" and were subsequently "bound with everlasting chains for judgment" (v.6). Jude, like Peter (2Pe 2:4), probably has in mind here the fall of Satan and his angels alluded to in Ezekiel's prophecy against the king of Tyre (Eze 28:11 – 19). As a third example, Jude mentions Sodom and Gomorrah, whom God once delivered through Abraham (Ge 14:11 – 24), but who "gave themselves up to sexual immorality and perversion" (v.7; cf. Ge 19:5) and God destroyed them (Ge 19:24).

Jude warns that the false teachers among the churches "pollute their own bodies, reject authority and heap abuse on celestial beings" in the same way as the people of Sodom (v.8; cf. Ge 19:5 – 9). In Jude's mind, these men assumed more authority than Michael the archangel. According to a popular story about the death of Moses, known to Jude and his readers but no longer extant, Michael refused to condemn Satan in his dispute about the body of Moses, being content to call upon God to rebuke him (v.9). Such respect for divine authority was not to be found with these false teachers (v.10). They were like Cain, who refused to pay heed to God's warning (Ge 4:6 – 12), and like Balaam and Korah, who sought gain from destroying the work of God (v.11).

Jude then describes the modus operandi of these false teachers. They blatantly seek their own profit among God's people (v.12 – 17). Jude, quoting a first-century work about Enoch (1 Enoch 1:9), reassures his readers that divine judgment is awaiting these ungodly men (vv.14 – 16). Jude perhaps appeals to the book of Enoch rather than an OT book because "ungodly" occurs repeatedly in this quote and forcefully drives home his main point in the letter: "they are godless men" (v.4). The word "ungodly" also occurs in Jude's quotation of the apostle Peter (v.18).

C. Importance of Sound Doctrine (17 – 23)

Jude's final appeal is to the authority of Jesus and the apostles — in this case, Peter's reference to Jesus' words reflected in 2Pe 3:2 – 3: "In the last times there will be scoffers who will follow their own ungodly desires" (vv.18 – 19). Jude describes them as those who divide the people, follow their own "natural instincts," and "do not have the Spirit" (v.19). In opposition to such men, Jude says, his readers should build themselves up by paying attention to doctrine ("faith"), prayer, love, and mercy (vv.20–23).

III. Conclusion (24–25)

Jude closes the letter with a formal doxology that stresses God's power to preserve believers until Christ's return.

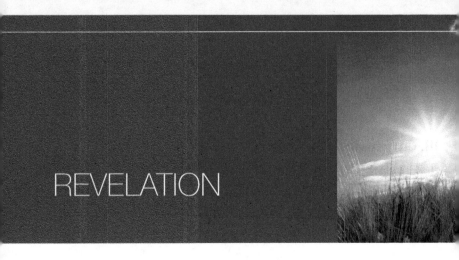

REVELATION

Introduction

Though some dispute this, the book of Revelation was likely written by the apostle John, the same one who wrote the gospel of John and the three letters of John. It was written toward the end of the first century AD, when John was exiled on the island of Patmos because of his Christian faith and witness.

I. Introduction to the Book (1:1 – 3)

The book describes itself as a "revelation from Jesus Christ," given to John by God. It describes "what must soon take place" (v.1). God the Father is the ultimate source of the revelation, while Jesus Christ, the Son of God, is the mediator of that revelation. Through him it passes on to an angel and then to his servant John.

II. Summary of the Contents of the Book (1:4 – 8)

John introduces himself and identifies his readers — seven churches in Asia Minor. These churches are representative of all churches, for the book surely is intended to have a wider circulation.

John gives Jesus Christ a threefold title that stresses his death, resurrection, and exaltation as well as his ultimate victory and exaltation over the nations. Before recounting the vision he received, John announces the nature of his letter: to announce that Jesus Christ is returning (v.7).

III. Eight Visions for the Churches (1:9 – 22:5)

A. The First Vision: One like the Son of Man Who Comes to Judge the Saints (1:9 – 3:22)

1. John's call vision (1:9 – 20)

As is common in prophetic books, John recounts the call he received and the means whereby God gave him his revelation of things to come. He had been exiled to the island of Patmos, southwest off the coast of Asia Minor. John states that he was "in the Spirit" on "the Lord's Day" (v.10). "In the Spirit" suggests that John had been overcome by the Spirit so that he was ready to receive the divine visions that follow.

John heard a voice behind him, telling him to write in a book the things he was about to see and to send it to the seven churches. These things constitute the entire book of Revelation. When John turned to see who was speaking, he saw a vision of Christ. The appearance of Christ is the same as that of the Ancient of Days in Da 7:9 – 10, yet John identifies him as one "like a son of man" (v.13; cf. Da 7:13 – 14).

John received the meaning of only two features of this vision. The first is the mystery of the seven stars; they are the angels of the seven churches (v.20). It is apparently to these angels that John was instructed to write in chs. 2 – 3. Who are these "angels"? The term itself can refer to heavenly beings or earthly officials. Thus they can be identified either as heavenly beings who represented each local church in the heavenly courts or as actual church officials within each church. Many consider them as analogous to the leaders in the early Jewish synagogues. Second, John received an explanation of the mystery of the seven lampstands. These represented the seven churches (v.20).

The other features of the vision are left unexplained, perhaps because their meaning is self-evident or can be determined from other passages where they reoccur within the book. What appears certain from the vision itself, however, is that the images were all intended to portray the majesty and lordship of the Savior.

John was then told to write down "what you have seen, what is now and what will take place later" (v.19). This verse is often taken as the key to the structure of Revelation. "What you have seen" is the vision of Christ that has just been described (vv.9 – 20). "What is now" refers to the words of Christ to the seven churches (2:1 – 3:22). "What will take place later," then, refers to the things that will happen in the future, after the church age.

2. The seven letters (2:1 – 3:22)

Many believe that the seven churches in chs. 2 – 3 represent the "spiritual history" of the church during the last nearly two thousand years. The church at Ephesus (2:1 – 7) represents the church of the first century; Smyrna (vv.8 – 11), the church under persecution (AD 100 – 316); Pergamum (vv.12 – 17), the church mixing with the world in the Middle Ages; Thyatira (vv.18 – 29), the time of decline in the pre-Reformation period; Sardis (3:1 – 6), the time of the Reformation; Philadelphia (vv.7 – 13), period of revivalism in the church; and Laodicea (vv.14 – 22), final state of apostasy in the visible church. There are a number of variations of this view.

Another common interpretation is that these letters are, in fact, historical churches to whom the book of Revelation was written. The fact that there are seven churches is taken as an indication that these churches were chosen to represent all the churches at that time and thus Revelation was intended for a much larger audience.

The phrase "he who overcomes," which occurs in each of the messages to the seven churches, needs clarification. Some suggest that these "overcomers" are those who endure the tribulation faithfully. They thus indicate that the church will be present on earth during the time of the tribulation. In 15:2 the overcomers seem to be victims of persecution during the tribulation because of their faithfulness to Christ. Others, however, argue that the word "overcoming" is John's expression for "faith" (see esp. 1Jn 5:4). The "overcomer," then, in the language of John's writings, generally refers to anyone who is victorious in faith. Overcomers are true members of God's people. Such an understanding fits well the description of the overcomers in 21:7, where they are those who will drink of the water of life forever, in contrast to "the cowardly" and "the unbelieving" (21:8).

B. The Second Vision: The Throne, the Lamb, and the Book with Seven Seals (4:1 – 8:1)

John now receives a vision of the "throne in heaven," with various creatures around it (on "after this" in 4:1, see comments on 1:19). Then John sees a "scroll with writing on both sides and sealed with seven seals" (5:1). This is a two-part document that has an initial summary written on one side with seven seals (6:1 – 8:1). When the seals are opened, the full description is given on the inside of the scroll (8:2 – 22:5).

1. Theophany: The throne scene (4:1 – 11)

Before John sees the vision of the tribulation wrath, he sees a scene from heaven. Some features of the heavenly vision are identified. The seven lamps of fire are the "seven spirits of God" (v.5). The seven eyes of the Lamb are also the seven spirits of God (5:6). Several features are obvious and are thus not interpreted. The one sitting on the throne (vv.2–3), for example, is clearly God. The throne (4:2) represents God's sovereignty and kingship.

Other features of the vision leave us on our own for an explanation. The identity of the twenty-four elders, for example, is not given and is not immediately obvious. Most likely they represent the church in that they are distinct from the angels in 5:11 and are shown offering up the prayers of the saints (5:8). Their white garments and crowns of gold are presumably symbols of their purity and rewards.

Finally, some elements of the vision cannot be identified at all. These include the rainbow (v.3), the flashes of lightning and peals of thunder (v.5), the sea of glass (v.6), and the four living creatures (v.7).

2. The Lamb and the book with seven seals: (5:1 – 14)

The Lamb is identified as "the Lion of the tribe of Judah, the Root of David" (v.5). The "Lion of the tribe of Judah" refers to Ge 49:9–10, "the Root of David" to Isa 11:1. The golden bowls of the twenty-four elders are identified as "the prayers of God's people" (v.8), and the scroll in v.1 is identified as a scroll of judgment in ch. 6.

3. The vision of the seven seals (6:1 – 8:1)

There are definite features of the first four seals that suggest these belong together as a distinct unit within the seven seals. Each one is introduced by one of the four living creatures (6:1, 3, 5, 7). Each is preceded by the call to "come" and contains the image of a horse and rider (vv.2, 4, 5, 8). There is, moreover, a progression of the meaning given for each seal: conquering (v.2), making war (v.4), famine (vv.5–6), and death (v.8).

The four living creatures are known from 4:6–7. (1) One is like a lion, (2) another like an ox, (3) another like a man, and (4) the last like a flying eagle. Each creature is "covered with eyes," has six wings, and speaks endlessly the words, "Holy, holy, holy is the Lord God Almighty, who was, and is, and is to come." Many have tried to explain the significance of these living creatures. They are similar to the "four living creatures" in the vision of Eze 1. If there is a connection, then Ezekiel's identification of them as cherubim is a help (Eze 10:1). They may also be identified with the seraphim in Isa 6:1–3.

The most plausible interpretation of these creatures is that they represent all the living creatures God created in the creation account (Ge 1): the lion represents the wild animals; the calf, the domesticated animals; man, humanity; and the eagle, the fowl of the air. Certainly in these points there is a close agreement between the two biblical passages. The fact that these creatures were appointed to praise God continuously suggests that the theme of Ps 19 is also present in the imagery of the four seals.

The four horsemen present a picture of divine judgment poured out on the earth. It anticipates the final judgment of the sixth seal and the trumpets (8:1ff.). The identity of the rider on the white horse is not given here. Regardless of who the rider is, his task is clear: "He rode out as a conqueror bent on conquest" (6:2). Within the larger structure of Revelation, it seems likely that this vision of the rider on a white horse and that of Jesus on a white horse in 19:11ff. are intended to offset each other.

In these first four seals John sees a time of increasing warfare, famine, pestilence, and death by wild beasts. He hears the groans of the four living creatures, symbolizing creation itself as it cries out to God for its redemption (cf. Ro 8:22–23). The cry of the four living creatures is amplified in the cries of the martyrs of the fifth seal (6:9–11).

The scene introduced by the fifth seal raises the question of the relationship between the events it records and the first four seals. The martyred souls are likely those who have suffered and died for the gospel during the time of the first four seals. We thus receive a brief glimpse of what was happening on earth during these days of wrath. The powers of earth were under God's wrath, but they continued to slay his saints and reject his gospel message.

Who are the martyred saints (v.9)? They are likely a specific group of believers martyred during the time of the tribulation. They are, however, only the first group to be martyred; more will join their ranks (v.11). A more precise identification is not possible from the text, though we can link them to the martyrs who have come out of the great tribulation in 7:9ff. and to those who do not accept the mark of the Beast in 13:15ff.

The content of the sixth seal is different from that of the first five. There was a great earthquake (6:12), accompanied by four cosmic phenomena. The sun became black and the moon red as blood, the stars fell from heaven (v.13), and the sky was split open as a scroll rolled up (v.14). John then records the response of people on the earth. He lists seven groups of human beings, covering all classes of society. These people hide from the one who sits on the throne and from the Lamb, for the great day of wrath has come.

Some hold that the events of this seal are too cosmic to be taken literally. The earthquakes, for example, may refer to the shaking of all political and ecclesiastical institutions. Others, however, take these images literally. Just as the sun was darkened before the day of the exodus from Egypt (Ex 10:22), for example, so the sun will actually lose its light.

Finally, some hold that the language used to describe these events is, in fact, symbolic, but the events themselves are real cosmic events. There is similarity, for example, between the events of the sixth seal and the description of the end times in the OT (Isa 34:4; Joel 2:31; 3:15; Hag 2:6) and in Mt 24:29. The language used here is poetic or symbolic, though real cosmic catastrophes are described, not mere spiritual realities.

What method or procedure should we use to determine the best interpretation of these visions? The major drawback to a symbolic interpretation is that it leaves us with no controls over the meaning of the passage. Interpretations of symbols easily become arbitrary. Nevertheless, a strictly literal interpretation overlooks the obviously symbolic nature of John's vision, as John himself has stated. The first four seals, for example, are manifestly symbolic. It seems reasonable that if there are clear symbolic features in the visions of the first five seals, then there would be symbolic features in the sixth. John himself uses symbolic terminology in the description of the vision. He says, for example, "the heavens receded like a scroll" (6:14).

In 7:1–8, we meet two groups of people. The first group consists of 144,000 "servants of our God" who have been sealed by him—12,000 from each of the twelve tribes of Israel (named). There is no universal agreement on the identity of this group; some identify them with the physical descendants of these early Israelite tribes, while others understand them as a symbolic reference to the church, the new Israel.

John's list of the twelve tribes varies somewhat from the usual listing in the OT. Dan and Ephraim are omitted, and Joseph has been added. But there is no "normative" list of the tribes of Israel in the OT. There are, in fact, some twenty different orders and lists of Israel's tribes. The most important element is the stress on the number twelve, which reflects an interest in the identification of this group with OT Israel.

The pretribulation view of Revelation identifies this group as representing the godly remnant of Israel on earth during the great tribulation. These are Jews who will be saved and who will be physically protected during the tribulation. This large group will proclaim the message of the gospel, and their preaching will result a great multitude of Jewish and Gentile believers.

Posttribulationalists identify the 144,000 as "spiritual Israel," i.e., the church, though some suggest that they form a Jewish remnant. They are orthodox but unconverted Jews who will resist the seductions of the Antichrist.

Apart from the fact that the 144,000 are identified as coming from the twelve tribes of Israel, the strongest argument that they are to be understood as physical Israel lies in the distinction John makes between this group and the great multitude that follows (7:9–14). The "great multitude" comes "from every nation, tribe, people and language" (v.9). They are thus non-Israelites who have "come out of the great tribulation" (v.14). It seems clear that many will turn to Christ during the tribulation and will suffer martyrdom for the sake of the gospel. The scene that John sees here appears to occur after the end of the tribulation. It finds its parallel in the scene at ch. 21, the new Jerusalem.

The seventh seal has no content (8:1): "When he opened the seventh seal, there was silence in heaven for about half an hour." The apparent purpose of the seal and the silence provides a link to the next set of seven events, the seven trumpets.

C. The Third Vision: Seven Trumpets (8:2 – 11:19)

1. The first four trumpets (8:2 – 13)

This vision opens with a depiction of seven angels being given seven trumpets and another angel burning incense on the altar before the throne of God (8:2–5). Each angel prepares to blast his trumpet (v.6). The first four trumpets signal four great catastrophes on the earth: hail and fire mixed with blood (v.7), something like a huge mountain being hurled blazing into the sea (vv.8–9), a great star falling from the sky (vv.10–11), and the sun and moon being stricken and unable to give a third of their light (v.12). The last three trumpet blasts are preceded by a special warning about their severity (v.13).

2. The fifth trumpet (9:1 – 12)

The fifth trumpet signals the onset of several simultaneous catastrophes. When it sounds, a star falls from heaven and is given the key to the Abyss. Smoke arises from the Abyss and darkens the sky. Locusts come out of the smoke and torment all those who do not have the seal of God on their foreheads.

3. The sixth trumpet (9:13 – 21)

At the sound of the sixth trumpet (9:13–21) the command is given to release the four angels who are bound at the great river Euphrates. At this, 200 million horses and riders are released to slay a third of the human race. Those not slain by these horsemen do not repent but remain in their idolatry and immorality.

4. Interlude before the seventh trumpet (10:1 – 11:14)

Before the sounding of the seventh trumpet, three additional scenes are recounted: the angel with a scroll (10:1–11), the temple (11:1–2), and the two witnesses (vv.3–14). The apparent purpose of the angel with the scroll is to show that there is a limit to the apocalyptic visions given to John. There could have been more, but God calls it to a halt. The book with the seven thunders is not to be recorded by John. He is, instead, to eat the book and thus keep its contents entirely to himself.

The account of the measurement of the temple and the story of the two witnesses are related by referring to a three-and-one-half year time period in each. The temple will be trampled by the Gentiles for 42 months (11:2), and the two witnesses will prophesy for 1,260 days (v.3). Each period represents half of the final seven-year tribulation prophesied in Da 9:24–27. The Beast (11:7; 13:1) and the death of the two witnesses are thus correlated with the "abomination that causes desolation" (see Da 9:27; Mt 24:15).

Though the text does not identify the two witnesses, they have often been associated with Moses and Elijah. As with these two witnesses, Elijah was given power to shut up the sky (1Ki 17:1), and Moses turned the waters of Egypt into blood (Ex 7:17).

5. The seventh trumpet (11:15 – 19)

The seventh trumpet signals a time of great praise and celebration in heaven. It marks the beginning of the reign of God's kingdom.

D. The Fourth Vision: The Battle with the Wicked Powers (12:1 – 14:20)

1. The vision of the dragon and the woman with child (12:1 – 17)

John sees a woman about to give birth to a male child and an enormous red dragon with seven heads and ten horns standing ready to devour the child at birth. When the child is born, he is snatched up to God, and the woman is protected for 1,260 days. This is followed by a war in heaven, in which Michael and his angels defeat the dragon and cast him out upon the earth. In heaven there is great celebration in that with the defeat of the dragon, "that ancient serpent called the devil, or Satan," God's kingdom has finally been established. Only on earth is there still cause for concern, for the dragon makes war with the woman and "the rest of her offspring" (v.17).

2. The two beasts (13:1 – 18)

As his vision continues, John sees two beasts. The first one arises out of the sea; it represents the Antichrist (vv.1 – 10). To it is given the authority, power, and kingship of the dragon. It is thus able to make war with the saints and to conquer them. All nations worship the Beast, except those whose names have been written in the book of life belonging to the Lamb. This beast is the fourth beast of Da 7.

The second beast in this chapter (the third one in John's visions) arises out of the earth; it represents the False Prophet (vv.11 – 18). It has two horns like a lamb, but it speaks like a dragon. It has all the authority of the first beast and performs great, miraculous signs, deceiving all the earth. It sets up an image of the first beast and kills all who refuse to worship it — clearly an allusion to the story of Nebuchadnezzar's image in Da 3. The number of the Beast is 666.

3. The coming of the Son of Man (14:1 – 20)

John first sees the Lamb standing on Mount Zion with the 144,000. This is followed by the vision of an angel flying in midair, proclaiming the eternal gospel to every nation on earth. A second angel proclaims the fall of Babylon. A third angel warns people not to receive the mark of the Beast. Then John sees a vision of one like the Son of Man seated on a white cloud (cf. Da 7:9 – 14). A sickle is put into his hands to harvest the earth. The harvested grapes from the earth's vineyards are then put into the great winepress of God's wrath, where they are trampled outside the city (cf. Isa 63:2 – 6).

E. The Fifth Vision: The Seven Plagues (15:1 – 16:21)

In 15:1 – 16:1 John recounts the preparation for the last of the series of seven judgments. He first sees a heavenly scene of those who have not served the Beast and who are now worshiping and praising God before his throne. His attention then turns to the heavenly temple, where he watches one of the four living creatures fill seven bowls with the wrath of God and give them to the seven angels.

These seven angels pour out the seven bowls of God's wrath (16:2 – 21). Those who suffer these judgments refuse to turn to God in repentance (vv.9, 11, 21). When the first bowl is poured out, ugly and painful sores occur on those who have taken the mark of the Beast (v.2). With the second bowl, the sea turns to blood and every living creature dies.

The third bowl causes the rivers and springs to turn to blood (vv.4 – 7). A vindication of this judgment is given, similar to the vindication of God's turning the Nile waters into blood in Ex 7:14 – 24. The bloodshed of the nations against God's saints and prophets is vindicated by giving the nations "blood to drink" (v.6). The conclusion is expressly stated, "Yes, Lord God Almighty, true and just are your judgments" (v.7).

During the fourth bowl, the sun becomes hot and sears the inhabitants of the earth with its intense heat. With the fifth bowl, the kingdom of the Beast is plunged into darkness. When the sixth bowl is poured out, the Euphrates River dries up and the kings from the East come across it to gather for battle at Armageddon (vv.12 – 16). The seventh bowl marks the final stage of God's judgment. There is a great earthquake, thunder and lightning, and huge hailstones. The city of Babylon and the cities of the nations are destroyed (vv.17–21).

F. The Sixth Vision: The Fall of Babylon (17:1 – 19:10)

John is now given a closer look at the judgment and fall of the city of Babylon. The city is depicted as a prostitute sitting on many waters. Then John sees another vision of the woman—in the desert sitting on a red beast. She is called "Babylon the Great" and is described as being "drunk with the blood of God's holy people" who bore testimony to Jesus (17:1–6).

John receives an interpretation of this vision, beginning with the Beast on which the woman was riding. The Beast has seven heads and ten horns. He "once was, now is not, and yet will come up out of the Abyss and go to its destruction" (v.8; cf. Da 7). The angel who gave John the interpretation acknowledges that understanding it "calls for a mind with wisdom" (v.9). This perhaps refers to the fact that much imagery here comes from OT passages such as Da 7 and thus requires an understanding of those texts.

The seven heads are "seven hills on which the woman sits," and they are "seven kings" (vv.9–10). Five of these kings have now passed away. The sixth king "is," and the seventh "has not yet come" (v.10). The Beast itself represents "an eighth king" (v.11). The Beast thus represents the last king of a kingdom that has ruled in the past and in John's own day and will rule again in the future. Its ten horns are ten kings who have yet to rule along with the Beast, i.e., the eighth king. These kings and the Beast will make war against the Lamb, who will be accompanied by his "faithful followers" (v.14; cf. Da 7:21). The waters that John has seen are the peoples of the earth (v.15). The woman who sat on the beast represents Babylon, "the great city that rules over the kings of the earth" (v.18). The Beast and the ten kings will destroy her as God's instruments of judgment.

The sudden ruin of the city of Babylon is victoriously described by the angels (18:1–24), and the saints, apostles, and prophets are called on to rejoice over it (v.20).

In response to the angels' call, the saints in heaven lift up their voices in praise and thanksgiving for the defeat of the great prostitute and for avenging their own shed blood (19:1–10).

G. The Seventh Vision: The Destruction of the Godless Forces (19:11 – 20:15)

1. The victorious Messiah (19:11 – 21)

The fall of Babylon is accompanied by a battle of the armies of heaven, led by the one mounted on a white horse whose name is "the Word of God" (vv.11–16). This is clearly a picture of Christ (cf. 20:4), "KING OF KINGS AND LORD OF LORDS" (19:16). At his appearance he mounts an attack on the Antichrist, the False Prophet, and the kings (vv.17–21). The Antichrist and the False Prophet are captured and thrown into "the fiery lake of burning sulfur" (v.20). The kings who follow them into battle are slain by the sword of the one mounted on the white horse.

2. The defeat of the dragon (20:1–10)

An angel from heaven is sent to seize the dragon, bind him in chains, and cast him into the Abyss for one thousand years (vv.1–3). Then follows a resurrection of those martyred by the Beast. They reign with Christ for one thousand years (v.4). Another resurrection is announced at the end of the one thousand years (v.5). At that time Satan (the dragon) is released. He gathers all the nations (Gog and Magog) together and mounts an attack against Jerusalem. He is defeated by fire from heaven and cast into the same burning lake as the Beast and the False Prophet (vv.7–10).

3. The Great White Throne Judgment (20:11–15)

The last act of judgment that John sees in this vision is a great court session in which all of the dead are gathered and the deeds of each are read off from the books kept in the court (cf. Da 7:10). Death itself is thrown into the lake of fire, along with Hades. Then another book is opened in the court, "the book of life." Anyone whose name has not been written in this book is also cast into that lake (see 21:8 for who these individuals are).

H. The Eighth Vision: The New Heaven and the Hew Earth (21:1–22:5)

John's vision takes up again the theme of Ge 1: God creates a new heaven and a new earth (21:1–8). In the midst of this vision, John sees a new Jerusalem (21:9–27) in which God will again dwell with humanity, as in the garden of Eden (Ge 2). A river flows through the city and waters the tree of life (22:1–2). The curse of Ge 3 is removed (v.3), and God again dwells with his people in an eternal kingdom (vv.4–5).

IV. Conclusion (22:6–21)

John concludes his book with two further sayings of Jesus that stress his imminent return (vv.6–17). John then warns against adding anything further to the visions or sayings he has recorded (vv.18–20). He concludes with a salutation to his readers (v.21).